TOOLS AND PROCESSES IN MATHEMATICS TEACHER EDUCATION

The International Handbook of Mathematics Teacher Education

Series Editor:

Terry Wood
Purdue University
West Lafayette
USA

This *Handbook of Mathematics Teacher Education*, the first of its kind, addresses the learning of mathematics teachers at all levels of schooling to teach mathematics, and the provision of activity and programmes in which this learning can take place. It consists of four volumes.

VOLUME 1:
Knowledge and Beliefs in Mathematics Teaching and Teaching Development
Peter Sullivan, *Monash University, Clayton, Australia* and Terry Wood, *Purdue University, West Lafayette, USA* (eds.)
This volume addresses the "what" of mathematics teacher education, meaning knowledge for mathematics teaching and teaching development and consideration of associated beliefs. As well as synthesizing research and practice over various dimensions of these issues, it offers advice on best practice for teacher educators, university decision makers, and those involved in systemic policy development on teacher education.
paperback: 978-90-8790-541-5, hardback: 978-90-8790-542-2, ebook: 978-90-8790-543-9

VOLUME 2:
Tools and Processes in Mathematics Teacher Education
Dina Tirosh, *Tel Aviv University, Israel* and Terry Wood, *Purdue University, West Lafayette, USA* (eds.)
This volume focuses on the "how" of mathematics teacher education. Authors share with the readers their invaluable experience in employing different tools in mathematics teacher education. This accumulated experience will assist teacher educators, researchers in mathematics education and those involved in policy decisions on teacher education in making decisions about both the tools and the processes to be used for various purposes in mathematics teacher education.
paperback: 978-90-8790-544-6, hardback: 978-90-8790-545-3, ebook: 978-90-8790-546-0

VOLUME 3:
Participants in Mathematics Teacher Education: *Individuals, Teams, Communities and Networks*
Konrad Krainer, *University of Klagenfurt, Austria* and Terry Wood, *Purdue University, West Lafayette, USA* (eds.)
This volume addresses the "who" question of mathematics teacher education. The authors focus on the various kinds of participants in mathematics teacher education, professional development and reform initiatives. The chapters deal with prospective and practising teachers as well as with teacher educators as learners, and with schools, districts and nations as learning systems.
paperback: 978-90-8790-547-7, hardback: 978-90-8790-548-4, ebook: 978-90-8790-549-1

VOLUME 4:
The Mathematics Teacher Educator as a Developing Professional
Barbara Jaworski, *Loughborough University, UK* and Terry Wood, *Purdue University, West Lafayette, USA* (eds.)
This volume focuses on knowledge and roles of teacher educators working with teachers in teacher education processes and practices. In this respect it is unique. Chapter authors represent a community of teacher educators world wide who can speak from practical, professional and theoretical viewpoints about what it means to promote teacher education practice.
paperback: 978-90-8790-550-7, hardback: 978-90-8790-551-4, ebook: 978-90-8790-552-1

Tools and Processes in Mathematics Teacher Education

Edited by

Dina Tirosh
Tel Aviv University, Israel

and

Terry Wood
Purdue University, West Lafayette, USA

SENSE PUBLISHERS
ROTTERDAM / TAIPEI

A C.I.P. record for this book is available from the Library of Congress.

ISBN 978-90-8790-544-6 (paperback)
ISBN 978-90-8790-545-3 (hardback)
ISBN 978-90-8790-546-0 (e-book)

Published by: Sense Publishers,
P.O. Box 21858, 3001 AW Rotterdam, The Netherlands
http://www.sensepublishers.com

Cover picture:

The rich flowers could be seen as the profusion of rich tasks, attracting students to engage, and which belong in a highly complex space of intertwining branches. Only when students engage in several related tasks is there a chance of pollination, for the transformation of activity into understanding.

Tasks that seem similar may be 'far apart' mathematically, tasks which seem far apart may be 'close' mathematically. The real effect of engagement in tasks is the ongoing life of the tree, and the production of 'seeds' which require the transformational effects of photosynthesis and sap (reflection and integration) in order to mature.

The tree can be seen as the teacher's knowledge, firmly planted in the soil of mathematics, and flowering profusely, a reminder of the variety of teacher proficiency required to teach effectively and indicating the mathematical connections and structures of which they are aware. The intertwining vine is a reminder of the necessity of depth as well as breadth of connections in order to constitute understanding.

John Mason 2008

Printed on acid-free paper

This book is dedicated to the memory of
my dear father
who always believed in me
and encouraged me

TABLE OF CONTENTS

Section 3: Research in Mathematics Education
as Tools in Mathematics Teacher Education

General Perspectives and Critical Response to Chapters

PREFACE

It is my honor to introduce the first *International Handbook of Mathematics Teacher Education* to the mathematics education community and to the field of teacher education in general. For those of us who over the years have worked to establish mathematics teacher education as an important and legitimate area of research and scholarship, the publication of this handbook provides a sense of success and a source of pride. Historically, this process began in 1987 when Barbara Jaworski initiated and maintained the first Working Group on mathematics teacher education at PME. After the Working Group meeting in 1994, Barbara, Sandy Dawson and I initiated the book, *Mathematics Teacher Education: Critical International Perspectives,* which was a compilation of the work accomplished by this Working Group. Following this, Peter de Liefde who, while at Kluwer Academic Publishers, proposed and advocated for the *Journal of Mathematics Teacher Education* and in 1998 the first issue of the journal was printed with Thomas Cooney as editor of the journal who set the tone for quality of manuscripts published. From these events, mathematics teacher education flourished and evolved as an important area for investigation as evidenced by the extension of JMTE from four to six issues per year in 2005 and the recent 15th ICMI Study, *The professional education and development of teachers of mathematics.* In preparing this handbook it was a great pleasure to work with the four volume editors, Peter Sullivan, Dina Tirosh, Konrad Krainer and Barbara Jaworski and all of the authors of the various chapters found throughout the handbook.

In Volume 2, *Tools and Processes in Mathematics Teacher Education*, edited by Dina Tirosh, various promising tools and processes that are aimed at facilitating the mathematics teacher development are described and critically analyzed. This volume provides a look at how mathematics teacher educators think about and approach their work with teachers. This is the second volume in the handbook.

Terry Wood
West Lafayette, IN
USA

REFERENCES

Jaworski, B., Wood, T., & Dawson, S. (Eds.). (1999). *Mathematics teacher education: Critical international perspectives.* London: Falmer Press.

Tirosh, D., & Wood, T. (Eds.). (2008). *International handbook of mathematics teacher education: Vol. 2 Tools and processes in mathematics teacher education.* Rotterdam, the Netherlands: Sense Publishers.

Wood, T. (Series Ed.), Jaworski, B., Krainer, K., Sullivan, P., & Tirosh, D. (Vol. Eds.). (2008). *International handbook of mathematics teacher education.* Rotterdam, the Netherlands: Sense Publishers.

DINA TIROSH

TOOLS AND PROCESSES IN MATHEMATICS TEACHER EDUCATION

An Introduction

The title of this volume includes five concepts that carry many definitions and interpretations: *tools, processes, mathematics, teacher, education.* Of these, two are mainly addressed in this (second) volume of the International Handbook of Mathematics Teacher Education. The first is "tool" and the second is "process".

The use of tools is viewed as an important step in the evolution of mankind. The production and usage of the first tools, that were probably made of stone, started at the Stone Age (and possibly even before), and provided our ancestors with a mechanical advantage that was not naturally available to them. The nature and spectrum of tools have vastly expended during the years to include physical, conceptual and symbolic tools (language, for instance, is often viewed as the most important symbolic tool provided by society). Nowadays, we live in a world that is increasingly dependent on tools.

In this volume, a range of tools that are often used in mathematics teacher education, all aimed at facilitating various proficiencies needed for teaching mathematics, are described and critically analysed. Obviously the choice of a tool to be used for a certain aim is a major decision taken by a mathematics teacher educator. Yet, the process (the particular manner in which the tool is used) is not less important. The effectiveness of a tool is largely determined by the specific manner in which it is implemented (e.g., the role of the mathematics teacher educator, the roles of the prospective and/or practising teachers, and the nature of the tasks). Awareness of the scope of a tool and its limitations is essential for wisely using it.

Getting to know the tools and the processes is a demanding, time-consuming endeavour. The authors of the chapters share with us their invaluable experience in employing the tools in mathematics teacher education. This accumulated experience could assist us in making decisions about both the tool(s) and the process(es) to be used for various purposes in mathematics teacher education.

In this introduction I first briefly summarize the major themes of each chapter according to their order of appearance in the volume. Then, I suggest some central questions to consider while reading the chapters.

D. Tirosh and T. Wood (eds.), Tools and Processes in Mathematics Teacher Education, 1–11.

SECTION 1: CASES IN MATHEMATICS TEACHER EDUCATION

Cases in mathematics teacher education vary in many aspects, including the intended audience (e.g., prospective elementary school teachers, prospective secondary school teachers, practising elementary school teachers, practising secondary school teachers), the mathematical content (e.g., specific mathematical ideas, general mathematics structures), the pedagogical content (e.g., students' reasoning and ways of thinking, socio-mathematical norms of explanations and justifications), the type of media (e.g., narrative, video), authorship (e.g., teachers' own experiences and practices, written by a third party) and authenticity (e.g., a depiction of real events, "invented" situations). In this volume, four types of cases that are often used in mathematics teacher education are described and discussed. These are narratives, mathematics case discussions, video-recordings, and lesson studies.

In the first chapter, Olive Chapmann describes and discusses the use of narratives in mathematics teacher education. For Chapmann, narrative is a key form through which individuals come to know themselves, construct their lives, and make sense of their experiences. In her chapter, narratives refer to self-authored, written or oral stories, which allow teachers to present their teaching or learning experiences from their perspectives and to weave descriptions of their thinking, feelings, attitudes, and other personal attributes relevant to these experiences into the stories. Her review of the literature indicates that, beginning in the mid-1990s, there was a small but growing body of work involving the use of narrative in mathematics teacher education.

Chapmann describes the use of narrative as a research tool for studying teacher knowledge and teaching, and as a pedagogical tool for teacher professional development and education in prospective and practising mathematics teacher education, and then focuses mainly on the use of narratives as a pedagogical tool with prospective teachers in mathematics education. She organises her description of her ways of using narratives in two themes: writing the narratives and narrative reflection/analysis/inquiry. The section on writing the narratives provides practical suggestions of types of guidelines that are likely to elicit stories that address mathematics pedagogy as opposed to generic pedagogy, along with useful examples of guidelines and of stories written by prospective teachers. The section on narrative reflection/analysis/inquiry presents eight ways in which prospective secondary teachers can be engaged in learning through narratives (e.g., narrative inquiry through peers, comparing imagined versus actual actions, and comparing personal versus theoretical knowledge). At the end of the chapter, Chapmann raises two, broad issues for future research: What is the role of narrative in the construction of mathematics teachers' knowledge? What is the meaning and usefulness of narrative to teachers learning to teach, as well as to experienced teachers? She concludes by stating that there is still a lot that could be done with narrative as a pedagogical tool and even more to understand about it as a process and product of research.

While Chapman's chapter (Chapter 1) addresses self-authored stories, Zvia Markovitz and Margaret Smith (Chapter 2) focus on cases that are written by a third party. They describe two broad classes of cases: exemplars and problem situations. Exemplars are lengthy narratives that portray an instructional episode in its entirety, highlighting the actions and interactions of a teacher and her students. Problem situations are short scenarios that focus on specific problems or dilemmas encountered by teachers as they listen to and interact with students. The main body of the chapter provides in-depth examples for each of these two classes of cases. The example of an exemplar is based on the work of Smith and her colleagues in the United States, and the examples of problem situations on the work of Markovitz and her colleagues in Israel. The chapter clearly specifies the characteristics of each of these types of cases and provides valuable suggestions for engaging prospective and practising teachers in meaningful activities related to a case (e.g., encourage the teachers to solve and discuss the mathematical task on which the case is based and to generalise beyond the case). Markovitz and Smith, much like Chapmann, conclude the chapter with several, central issues in need of further study: What do teachers learn from different types of cases? How do they learn it? How what teachers learn impacts their teaching performance?

Carolyn Maher (Chapter 3) opens a window on using videos as pedagogical tools in mathematics teacher education. Maher demonstrates that (and how) videos can provide prospective and practising teachers with opportunities to closely observe students' emerging processes of learning, analyse teaching episodes in a variety of classroom conditions for learning and teaching, and study their own teaching. She argues that in comparison with other evidence of students' learning, such as verbal statements and explanations, written work, and other forms of evaluation, video recordings can capture the moves that are made and thus offer the opportunity for studying subtle details of students' evolving learning.

Maher reviews various projects that use video collections as tools in mathematics teacher education, including video cases (e.g., the STELLAR system, University of Michigan 'Library Collection' and the Private Universe project in mathematics) and video recordings that were initially developed for research processes beyond teacher self-study (e.g., TIMSS and the Longitudinal Study of Student learning at Rutgers University). She then provides detailed examples of how video collections have been used as pedagogical tools for the study of learning and teaching and for mathematics teacher education. The example of the use of the longitudinal study of student learning at Rutgers university, initially developed for tracing the mathematical thinking and reasoning of students from a low Socio-economic (SES) community, can serve as a model for a potential, fruitful interplay between using videos as a research tool and as a pedagogical tool.

The first three chapters in this section presented three types of cases that are described as relatively new tools in mathematics teacher education. Makoto Yoshida (Chapter 4) introduces the *lesson study*, a professional learning process that originated and has a long history in Japan, and is gaining increased attention in the United States and in a growing number of countries in Asia and Europe. Lesson study is a process of professional learning that practising Japanese teachers engage in continuously throughout their teaching careers to examine systematically their instructional methods, teaching content and curriculum, as well as their students' processes of learning and understanding. Yoshida discusses, in his chapter, three main forms of lesson study that are used for various purposes in Japan: school-based lesson study, district-wide lesson study, and cross-district lesson study.

Yoshida describes the major, three activities that constitute the lesson study: establishing a lesson study goal; engaging in a lesson study cycle to develop, implement, observe, and reflect on research lessons; and reflecting on the whole lesson study process by producing a written report. He then examines, in detail, one of the important parts of the lesson study process, *kyozaikenkyu* (instructional material investigation) and illustrates, in a vivid manner, the various features of this inquiry, using an example of a research plan on the area of triangles. Towards the end of the chapter, Yoshida raises and provides in-depth answers to two major questions: Why lesson study? What does it provide? The chapter concludes with valuable ideas for conducting effective lesson studies.

The four chapters in this section provide a glimpse into various types of cases that are used in mathematics teacher education. Readers are advised to continue thinking about the similarities and differences between these and other types of cases that are commonly used in mathematics teacher education and about the relevance of each of these types of cases for different aims in prospective and practising mathematics education.

SECTION 2: TASKS IN MATHEMATICS TEACHER EDUCATION

This section presents several, predominant tools that are used in mathematics teacher education. Two chapters (Chapter 5 and Chapter 6) describe textual tools (written tasks and examples). The other two chapters (Chapter 7 and Chapter 8) focus on physical tools (manipulatives and machines). The major issue that is addressed in each of these four chapters is: Which tasks have been significant for the learning and development of mathematics teachers?

Anne Watson and Peter Sullivan (Chapter 5) clarify that the centre of attention in their chapter are classroom tasks. They suggest several ways in which the study of classroom tasks and mathematics lessons can be used to enhance teacher learning. They note that mathematics teacher educators can use the obvious interest of prospective and practising teachers in planning and teaching lessons to draw their attention to major aspects of student learning. They then identify several purposes for using classroom tasks and mathematics lessons in mathematics teacher education, including highlighting the range and purpose of possible classroom tasks, stimulating teachers' theorising about students' learning, providing opportunities to learn more about mathematics and about the nature of mathematical activity.

The four, major parts in Watson and Sullivan's chapter are devoted to describing and discussing four types of tasks, each of which aimed at fostering one of four of the major strands of mathematical proficiently (as suggested by

Kilpatrick, Swafford and Findell, 2001, with some adaptations): conceptual understanding, mathematical fluency; strategic competence, and adaptive reasoning. In each of these parts they elaborate on the nature of the learning associated with the strand, offer illustrating tasks that mathematics teacher educators can use with the teachers and propose a template of a lesson structure to which tasks within that strand can be adapted.

Rina Zazkis (Chapter 6), much like Watson and Sullivan, starts by identifying the two major goals at which the specific types of examples that she describes and discusses in her chapter are aimed, namely, enhancing teachers' personal understanding of mathematics, and introducing the variety of students' possible understandings or misunderstandings of mathematics. She focuses on teachers as learners and suggests instructional examples that are effective in increasing teachers' awareness of basic assumptions that are parts of information used in mathematical activity, but not mentioned explicitly in the tasks. Zazkis shows how examples that are aimed at challenging basic assumptions related to mathematical content can be used as effective tools to increase teachers' mathematical understanding and to invite them to re-examine their very basic assumptions related to the teaching and learning of mathematics.

Zazkis distinguishes between three kinds of basic assumptions: mathematical conventions, shared understandings, and assumptions that present unintended constraints to problem solving. She then provides several, illustrative examples that she often uses for challenging each of these three kinds of basic assumptions and discusses their effectiveness in increasing teachers' mathematical understanding and pedagogical sensitivity. Zazkis concludes by arguing that the presented examples not only extend the teachers' example spaces, but also act, through creating dis-equilibrium, as significant catalysts for the construction of richer cognitive schemas that are relevant to the learning and teaching of mathematics.

Marcus Nührenbörger and Heinz Steinbring (Chapter 7) propose, in their chapter, that manipulatives have a dual role in mathematics teacher education. On the one hand, they serve as learning objects for prospective teachers, in the sense that various manipulativies can be used to promote their own learning and understanding of mathematics. On the other hand, prospective teachers need to gain practical knowledge on the use of manipulatives in mathematics instruction. For example, they should learn which manipulatives are often used in various grade levels, how to appropriately employ them, and how to analyse and diagnose the students' learning processes when using manipulatives.

Nührenbörger and Steinbring introduce a theoretical perspective on the role of manipuatives in mathematics teacher education and provide several examples to illustrate the various aspects of this perspective. A major argument is that manipulatives and mathematics are initially separated from each other and a relation between them can only be productively constructed by the learner's own interpretations of these relationships. Thus, the value of a specific manipulative in both mathematics education and mathematics teacher education depends on the relationship between this object and the mathematical relations and structures it represents. Nührenbörger and Steinbring observe that prospective teachers have their own, often naive views of the nature, role and effects of manipulatives on mathematics learning. They argue that it is necessary to confront prospective teachers, in their education, with essential theoretical aspects related to the use of manipulatives, as well as with concrete material. Such a confrontation is apt to cause cognitive conflict and thus to encourage changes in existing subjective conceptions and to stimulate further developments. In their concluding remarks, Nührenbörger and Steinbring suggest several guidelines for evaluating manipulatives (e.g., in what way do the manipulatives embody basic, structured, mathematical ideas? Is it possible to continue with the manipulatives using the same structure in different school years? Are the manipulatives well structured and manageable for students?). They clarify that knowledge about interpretations and use of manipulatives evolves through interactive learning and not in a procedural manner.

Maria Bussi and Michela Maschietto (Chapter 8), in the last chapter in this section, invite the readers to "pay a visit" to the Laboratory of Mathematical Machines of the University of Modena and Reggio Emilia, a well known research centre for the teaching and learning of mathematics by means of instruments. This laboratory holds a collection containing more than 200 working reconstructions (based on the original sources) of many mathematical instruments taken from the history of geometry. The laboratory also contains arithmetical machines and Information and Communication Technologies (ICT). In this chapter Bussi and Maschietto focus on the use of concretely handled machines that require motor abilities. They argue that it is a true challenge for teachers to effectively use such artefacts in their mathematics classrooms – it requires specific professional competences, which cannot be taken for granted.

In the two major parts of this chapter, Bussi and Maschietto describe and discuss two examples, the first addresses the use of arithmetical machines related to place value in primary school and the second focuses on using geometrical machines related to symmetry in secondary school. In each of these two parts, Bussi and Maschietto first define the mathematical object that is mediated and describe the related network of artefacts (counting sticks, spike abacus and pascaline in the first part, geodreieck and symmetry linkage in the second). They then describe, in brief, the mathematical meanings that could potentially be attached to these artefacts, analyse the related *instrumentalisation* (the emergence and the evolution of the different components of the artifact, drawing on the progressive recognition of its potentialities and constraints) and *instrumentation* (the emergence and development of the utilization schemes) processes, and offer carefully chosen, related tasks to be use in teacher education. Bussi and Maschietto conclude by noting that the use of physical manipulations is becoming less frequent in mathematics education and that they are too often substituted by ICT. They argue that the features of these two systems (physical manipulations, ICT) differ and that each system should have its own place both in mathematics classroom and in teacher education.

Before ending the brief description of this section, I would like to emphasize the obvious: Only four main types of tasks are described and discussed here. There are, however, many other types of tasks that are used in mathematics teacher education. An issue deserving attention is: What other tasks in mathematics teacher education have been significant for the learning and development of mathematics teachers?

SECTION 3: RESEARCH AS TOOLS IN MATHEMATICS TEACHER EDUCATION

The third section suggests several ways in which research in mathematics teacher education contributes to the development of tools and processes in mathematics teacher education. The chapters in this section focus, in various ways, on the accumulated research on common students' conceptions and habits of thinking and offer ways of using this knowledge as tools in mathematics teacher education.

Pessia Tsamir (Chapter 9) raises, in her chapter, three major questions: What theories should be presented in mathematics teacher education programs? In what ways and at what stages (e.g., prospective teachers or practicing teachers) should theories be presented? How to assess the impact of teachers' familiarity with theories on their professionalism? She clarifies that the purpose of her chapter is to examine whether theories can serve as tools to promote prospective teachers' and practicing teachers' (1) mathematical knowledge (an SMK component), (2) knowledge about students' mathematical reasoning (a PCK component), and (3) knowledge about the formulation and sequencing of tasks (a PCK component).

Tasmir focuses on two theoretical models that she discusses with secondary school prospective and practising teachers in her courses: The three knowledge components (intuitive, algorithmic, formal) theory and the intuitive rules theory. She then presents three research segments to illustrate that familiarity with these theories can promote prospective and practising teachers' knowledge (mathematical and pedagogical) and teaching practices. She concludes by noting that the ultimate aim of mathematics teacher education is to provide teachers of mathematics with the professional learning opportunities they need to lead their students to succeed in learning mathematics. Thus, she argues, an evaluation of the impact of teachers' familiarity with specific mathematics education theories should not be restricted to evaluating changes in their SMK, PCK and teaching practices. Tsamir urges the mathematics teacher education community to devote more efforts to study the outcomes of teachers' familiarity with theories on students' knowledge and mathematical confidence.

The body of knowledge on young children conceptions, preconceptions, alternative conceptions and misconceptions of number, measurement and geometry is notably wide. In view of this volume of knowledge, theoretical frameworks covering categorization, general sources, and appropriate educational approaches seem to be in order. Such frameworks, if presented in a teacher-friendly manner, have a potential of being a viable tool in mathematics education. Barbara Clarke outlines, in her chapter (Chapter 10) how she and her colleagues developed frameworks of research-based growth points in number, measurement and geometry. She then described how these frameworks, together with a closely-related one-to-one, task-based assessment interview, were used in a professional development program for grade K-2 practising teachers in the Early Numeracy

Research Project (ENRP) in Australia. A main aim of the project was that the practising teachers would, in time, carry the frameworks in their heads, using it as a kind of "lens" through which they could view interactions with children individually, in small group or whole class interactions, as well as during lesson planning.

Clarke focuses, in her chapter, on the impact of the growth points on practising teachers. In several questionnaires, teachers were invited to identify the aspects of their teaching practice that had changed as a result of their involvement in the ENRP. The most common theme emerging was summarised as "growth points inform planning," indicating the value that teachers saw in acquiring systematic knowledge of how children learn mathematics and how mathematical understanding develops. Some emotional, significant aspects were: having more confidence in teaching mathematics and enjoying mathematics more. These expressions of both professional and emotional changes should be viewed in light of the impressive impact of the project on the mathematical learning of the practising teachers' students: Students in trial schools outperformed significantly children in reference schools, at every grade level and in every mathematical domain.

The first two chapters in this section mainly address the body of knowledge on children's conceptions. Susan Empson and Victoria Jacobs (Chapter 11) focus on another aspect of teachers' knowledge of students ways of thinking, that is, on knowing to listen, in a responsive manner, to the mathematical thinking that children use to solve problems, create representations, and make arguments. They cite research indicating that responsive listening to children's thinking during instruction have multiple benefits including (a) improving children's understandings, (b) providing a means of formative assessment, (c) increasing teachers' mathematical knowledge, and (d) supporting teachers' engagement in generative learning.

Empson and Jacobs provide an example of a teacher listening to a young child, highlighting four features of the interaction that are characteristic of responsive listening, including supporting the girl's making sense of the problem without telling her how to solve it, asking her to articulate how she had arrived at her answer after she solved the problem, and maintaining a conversational interaction pattern instead of the traditional initiation-response-evaluation pattern. They then characterise three types of teachers' listening: Directive, Observational, and Responsive, and detail three types of learning experiences that are instrumental for developing responsive listening: (a) discussions of children's written work, (b) discussions of videotaped interactions with children, and (c) opportunities for teachers to interact with children and then to reflect on those experiences with other teachers.

The last chapter in this section largely departs from the other three. Koeno Gravemeijer (Chapter 12) focuses on *one* theory, the domain-specific instruction theory for Realistic Mathematics Education (RME). In this chapter he outlines the complexities of enacting instruction in tune with RME, describes three major, related competencies, and concludes by suggesting several principles for preparing prospective teachers for mathematics education that is in line with RME.

Gravemeijer exemplifies, in the first parts of the chapter, the complexity of designing instructional sequences in line with the RME theory. In view of that complexity he argues that there is no expectation from teachers to design such instructional sequences themselves, and notes that such instructional sequences are developed at the Freudenthal Institute and in other centres. Next, he specifies three major categories of roles and competencies needed for teaching in line with the RME theory, the first concerns planning and designing instructional activities and hypothetical learning trajectories, the second addresses the classroom culture, and the third focuses on the orchestration of the collective reinvention process. The golden rule for fostering RME teacher competencies in mathematics teacher education is to teach what you preach, a rule that evidently applies to this theory and to many other principles and theories.

The four chapters in this section address only few of the theories that are currently used in mathematics education. I encourage the reader to think about the potential contribution of theories that are not mentioned here to the development of tools and processes in mathematics teacher education.

SECTION 4: GENERAL PERSPECTIVES AND CRITICAL RESPONSE

Each of the preceding 12 chapters in this volume presents some tools and processes that are aimed at enhancing the knowledge-base and the skills needed to teach mathematics. The two chapters in this section take a different stance. Shlomo Vinner (Chapter 13) raises a very substantial, general issue: How to use the teaching of mathematics as a tool to promote general educational values? Vinner claims that some dimensions relating to this direction are missing from teacher education practice, including specifying the goals of teaching mathematics, defining the goals of education in general, identifying ways in which the goals of teaching mathematics can be used to achieve the general goals of education, and determining the meaning of the teacher's work.

Vinner demonstrates how some of the characteristics of mathematics can be used to promote general, educational values including the importance of procedures in society and in everyday life, analytical thinking, reflection and rational thinking. He then clarifies that both students and teachers feel better if they realize that they are involved in meaningful activities and points out at three contexts in which this notion of meaning is used: the meaning of notions, the context of values, and the meaning of life. Vinner claims that the latter context in which meaning is used is absolutely missing from school practices. He suggests that issues such as what is the meaning of our life and what are we supposed to do with our life, bother all adolescents, and therefore they should be discussed in mathematics teacher education. He clarifies that mathematics teachers are educators and as such they should be prepared to relate to all problems of their students and not only to the mathematical problems.

In the concluding chapter (Chapter 14), Alan Schoenfeld and Jeremy Kilpatrick pose several major questions: What principles should guide the selection and use of the various tools and processes that are presented in the individual chapters? Where do these tools fit in a "tool space" – the entire collection of tools that mathematics teacher educators might bring to bear in their work? And, more generally, what are the dimensions of proficient teaching? They argue that there is a need for a theory of proficiency in teaching mathematics that could be used to guide the selection and use of tools for mathematics teacher education.

Schoenfeld and Kilpatrick offer, in their chapter, a provisional framework consisting of a set of seven dimensions of proficiency for teaching mathematics: Knowing school mathematics in depth and breadth; knowing students as thinkers; knowing students as learners; crafting and managing learning environments; developing classroom norms and supporting classroom discourse as part of "teaching for understanding"; building relationships that support learning and reflecting on one's practice. They then elaborate on these dimensions and examine the various chapters in this volume with regard to how the tools they offer can contribute to the framework. This innovative contribution to the domain of mathematics teacher education is viewed, by both authors, as the first steps toward a theory of proficiency in teaching, a theory that provides an orientation to a domain and specifies the skills that people need to develop if they are to become proficient.

CENTRAL ISSUES

The 14 chapters in this volume differ in many aspects: They are written by authors from different cultures, draw on various, theoretical frameworks and describe diverse tools and processes. Still, there are some central issues that most chapters struggle with.

In my own reading of each of the chapters, I found it useful to attempt to formulate responses to the following ten questions:

1. What are the definitions of the tools that are described in this chapter?
2. What are the unique and the general characteristic of these tools?
3. Are these tools valuable for prospective teacher education? For what purposes?
4. Are these tools valuable for practising teacher education? For what purposes?
5. What are the limitations of these tools?
6. What are the suggested ways of utilising these tools in prospective teacher education?
7. What are the suggested ways of utilising these tools in practising teacher education?
8. What is the role of the mathematics teacher educator, when implementing these tools?
9. Are these tools similar to other tools that I know? In what ways? What are the pros and cons of using each of these tools?

10.   How relevant and significant are these tools to my own work?

Each of you will probably formulate different questions and different responses while reading the chapters. Please do not hesitate to share these and other issues related to the chapters with me and with the other authors of the chapters.

AN EPILOGUE

The introduction attempts to provide the reader with a preliminary flavour of the book. Many issues and themes are embedded in each chapter. At this point I will let the authors of the chapters tell their own story, so that the reader may explore the variety of tools and processes that interweave to form the fabric of this volume.

SECTION 1

CASES AS TOOLS IN MATHEMATICS TEACHER EDUCATION

OLIVE CHAPMAN

1. NARRATIVES IN MATHEMATICS
TEACHER EDUCATION

This chapter deals with the use of narrative, considered from a literary and a humanistic perspective, as a research and pedagogical tool in mathematics teacher education. It presents the methods of obtaining and analyzing stories used in studies of mathematics teacher education. However, the main focus of the chapter is on narrative as a pedagogical tool with prospective teachers in mathematics education. In presenting this use, eight ways in which prospective secondary teachers can be engaged in learning through narrative are given along with example stories.

NARRATIVE AND TEACHER KNOWLEDGE

Interest in narrative, based on the perspective discussed in this chapter, has grown within the field of education beginning in the early 1990s, mostly because of the link advocated between narrative or story and teacher knowledge. For example, Clandinin and Connelly (2000) claimed that teachers' knowledge can only be thought of in narrative terms, as "something lifelike, something storied" (p. 316). Earlier, Elbaz (1990) explained, "Story is something implicit in teachers' knowledge, that is, teachers' knowledge in its own terms is ordered by and as story and can best be understood in this way" (p. 34). Carter (1993) added; "Through story, then, teachers transform knowledge of content into a form that plays itself out in the time and space of classrooms" (p. 7). In addition to this storied nature of teacher knowledge, the link to narrative is also associated with teachers' knowing in action (Schön, 1983). As Doyle and Carter (2003) explained, "Much of the practical knowledge teachers acquire from teaching arises from actions in situations – the essential ingredients of story" (pp. 130–131). Thus,

> The action feature of story would seem to make it especially appropriate to the study of teaching and teacher education. Teaching is intentional action in situations, and the core knowledge teachers have of teaching comes from their practice, i.e., from taking action as teachers in classrooms. (Carter, 1993, p. 7)

Story, then, is a relevant form for expressing teachers' practical understandings because teachers' knowledge is event structured and stories would provide special access to that knowledge. Finally, narrative is also linked to the complex nature of teaching in that it "represents a way of knowing and thinking that is particularly suited to explicating the issues with which we deal" (Carter, 1993, p. 6). In

D. Tirosh and T. Wood (eds.), Tools and Processes in Mathematics Teacher Education, 15–38.
© *2008 Sense Publishers. All rights reserved.*

particular, a narrative approach is considered to be able to cope with the many ambiguities and dilemmas that emerge from action. Thus, it is useful to capture teachers' perspectives and the situated complexities of their work and classroom practice, which is often messy, uncertain, and unpredictable (Schön, 1983).

These connections between narrative and teacher knowledge suggest that teachers understand their own teaching through a process of storying their teaching lives and that researchers and teachers themselves can benefit from the process and an analysis of such storying. Narrative can provide a basis for studying teacher knowledge and teaching and a basis for teacher professional development and education. This is reflected in the many studies on teacher thinking or knowledge, teacher learning and teaching in the broader field of education. In mathematics education, based on my review of the literature for this chapter, beginning in the mid-1990s, there was a small but growing body of work involving the use of narrative. In this chapter, I briefly discuss the use of narrative in these studies, focusing on those that deal specifically with mathematics teachers. In particular, I consider the perspectives of narrative used in these studies and how narrative was used. I distinguish between studies that use narrative as a research tool and those as a pedagogical tool. Then, I present my work on the use of narrative as a pedagogical tool with prospective secondary mathematics teachers. In doing so, I describe eight ways in which teachers can be engaged in learning through narrative.

PERSPECTIVES OF NARRATIVE

The concept of narrative has been defined in many ways in the research literature depending on the perspective in which it is framed. In this chapter, the focus is on the literary and humanistic perspectives as a basis of tools in mathematics teacher education. From a literary perspective, a narrative is a story that tells a sequence of events that are significant for the author and his or her audience (Denzin, 1989). It has an internal logic that makes sense to the author. It has a plot, a beginning, middle, and an end, where the plot brings together goals, causes and chance within the temporal unity of a whole action (Ricoeur, 1983). It is a "symbolic presentation of a sequence of events connected by subject matter and related by time" (Scholes, 1981, p. 205). While this perspective of narrative focuses on its structure, it is the humanistic perspective that shapes its use in teacher education.

From a humanistic perspective, narrative is a way of specifying experience, a mode of thought, a way of making sense of human actions or a way of knowing (Bruner, 1986; Crites, 1975; Polkinghorne, 1995, 1988; Sarbin, 1986). It is a "symbolized account of actions of human beings that has a temporal dimension" (Sarbin, 1986, p. 3), "a mode of knowledge emerging from action" (Mitchell, 1981, p. x), a reproduction of the "temporal tensions of experience, a moving present tensed between and every moment embracing a memory of what has gone before and an activity projected, underway" (Crites, 1975, p. 26). According to Bruner (1986), narrative is concerned with the explication of human intentions in the context of action. He also describes it as a way of knowing, a way of constructing reality, a mode of thought centred on the meaning of experience, and the primary form by which human experience is made meaningful. In addition, based on Polkinghorne (1988), narrative is a cognitive scheme; a scheme by means of which human beings give meaning to their experience of temporality and personal actions, a framework for understanding the past events of one's life and for planning future actions, the primary scheme by means of which human existence is rendered meaningful, and a meaning structure that organizes events and human actions into a whole, thereby attributing significance to individual actions and events according to their effect on the whole.

Thus, in the context of this chapter, narrative is viewed as a key form through which individuals come to know themselves, construct their lives, and make sense of their experiences. Since the stories we tell reflect who we are and what we may become, they can provide a basis for meaning recovery and meaning construction or reconstruction of our experiences. They can facilitate interpretation and understanding of our experiences and offer a way of recovering, articulating, and understanding the meanings and intentions embodied in our behaviours. In relation to teacher education, then, such stories provide a humanistic basis for understanding teaching, the teacher and teacher learning.

Based on the preceding literary and humanistic perspectives, narrative has been used in some particular ways in education generally. It has been used as:
- A research method in which the process and product involve stories of teachers and researchers' experiences;
- A tool for collecting data on, for example, teachers' knowledge, beliefs, attitude, life story, and practice;
- An object for analysis in studying teaching;
- A basis for, or tool in, teacher professional development or teacher education;
- A basis for reflective thinking.

In relation to teacher learning, narrative practices are intentional, reflective actions in which teachers write and/or tell stories and work with others (peers, colleagues, other educators, and researchers) to interrogate their past, present and future experiences with teaching as a means of learning through these stories (Connelly & Clandinin, 1988; Johnson & Golombek 2002; Lyons & LaBoskey, 2002). Thus, narrative practices not only provide opportunities for practicing or prospective teachers to share what they know; they can also furnish the means for changing and developing knowledge and help teachers to construct and reconstruct their practical knowledge. Narratives can provide opportunities to help teachers come to know what they do not know and need to know about teaching and learning. They can be used to foster reflective thinking, an important skill for both learning and teaching.

These views of narrative have provided a basis for an increased use in mathematics teacher education. A review of the research literature for this chapter suggests that, beginning in the mid-1990s, narrative was becoming a valuable method for studying and making sense of mathematics teacher knowledge, growth and practice. The different uses of narrative noted above have been adopted in these studies to some degree; however, most of the work involves the use of narrative as a research tool, and a few treat it as a pedagogical tool. The use of narratives as a pedagogical tool, with the exception of my work (e.g., Chapman, 2002), has rarely been explored as a means for enhancing prospective teacher learning. This does not refer to case studies (Chapter 2 of this volume) or video recordings (Chapter 3 of this volume) that could include a different form of narratives. Such narratives usually are not written by, nor do they deal with the perspectives of, the teachers who are using them as a basis of their learning. In this chapter, narratives refer to the self-authored, written or oral stories, which allow teachers to present their teaching or learning experiences from their perspectives and to weave descriptions of their thinking, feelings, attitudes, and other personal attributes relevant to these experiences into the stories. In the remainder of this chapter, I discuss studies that deal with this form of stories in order to highlight the state of the art of narrative as a tool in mathematics teacher education. This discussion is organized in themes based on the two broad uses of narrative identified in these studies: narrative as research tool and narrative as a pedagogical tool. The former considers studies of mathematics teachers' thinking, knowledge, and practice that have implications for mathematics teacher education, while the latter considers studies of mathematics teachers' learning.

NARRATIVE AS RESEARCH TOOL

Studies dealing with the mathematics teacher used narrative as a research tool for investigating several topics (Table 1) in order to produce information on teacher knowledge, thinking, and practice that informs teacher education. Although there are similarities in the use of narrative in these studies, there are differences, not only in relation to the purpose, but also the methods of obtaining and analyzing the stories. A brief description of these methods for each of these studies is given to highlight the uses of narrative as a research tool in mathematics teacher education.

Table 1. Examples of topics studied through narrative methods

Development of prospective teachers' beliefs about, and emotions towards, mathematics	Kaasila, 2007a, 2007b
Why prospective teachers are highly motivated in a social constructivist mathematics course	Harkness, D'Ambrosio, & Morrone 2007
Teachers' interpretations and implementations of a reform-oriented mathematics curriculum	Drake, 2006a, 2006b
Prospective teachers' emerging identities as mathematics teachers and beliefs about their roles as mathematics teacher	Lloyd, 2006, 2005
Challenges to teachers' professional knowledge posed by classroom activities involving mathematical investigations	Ponte, Segurado, & Oliveira, 2003

Teacher change in implementing a project-based curriculum	Ziegler, 2003
Teachers' growth in teaching mathematics	Chapman, 2002; Fijal, 1995
Connecting theory and reflective practice	Smith, 2003
Teachers' perspective of teaching problem solving	Chapman, 1997
Teachers' experiences with implementing reform teaching	Schifter, 1996a, 1996b

Obtaining the Stories

In some of the studies, researchers used an interview approach to obtain the participating teachers' stories and participants were encouraged to tell stories of their teaching or learning experiences. In Kaasila (2007a, 2007b), during the interview, each participant told her or his mathematical autobiography. In Drake (2006a, 2006b), a mathematics story interview protocol was adapted from a more general life story interview protocol developed for use in personality psychology research. In the interview, teachers' narrative descriptions of themselves as learners and teachers of mathematics were collected. The teachers were asked to consider all of their experiences learning, teaching, and using mathematics (both in and out of school) as a story and to identify several key events within that story. These events included the high point, low point, and any turning points in the story. Teachers were also asked to describe significant challenges in their stories and how those challenges were overcome, influential characters in the stories, and possible positive and negative futures, or next chapters, for their stories. In my studies (e.g., Chapman, 2002; 1997), during interviews, participants were prompted to tell stories about their thinking or teaching. Examples of these prompts were:

– Do you consciously try to pass on this view of mathematics to your students? How? Tell a story of a specific situation or event in your teaching that shows this.
– Tell a story of a specific situation or event that involved you as a student in a mathematics classroom when the topic was about ….
– Tell a story of a complete mathematics lesson that involved you teaching (a specific topic) to your students.

While prompts like these were predetermined based on the goal of the study, others emerged during the interviews, in particular, as a basis for teachers to support any theories or generalized claims they offered in telling their stories. The teachers were usually briefed at the beginning of the interviews that stories should describe a specific situation or event as they lived through it. So they should avoid causal explanations, generalizations, or abstract interpretations and, instead, describe the experience as it happened, including feelings/emotions, and thoughts in action, as applicable.

In contrast to collecting the stories during interviews, most of the studies reviewed obtained narratives through writing, i.e., the participants were required to write their stories with various degree of guidance from the researchers. In Harkness, D'Ambrosio, and Morrone (2007), the prospective teachers wrote mathematical autobiographies in a mathematics education course at the beginning of the semester. In Ponte, Segurado, and Oliveira, (2003), the stories were drawn from episodes occurring in classes conducted by the teacher in the project. The teacher wrote stories about situations that occurred in classes where pupils were working on mathematical investigations in order to capture aspects of dilemmas, uncertainties and other elements of her professional knowledge. Ziegler's (2003) participants wrote stories to capture their experiences implementing and teaching a recently mandated applied, project-based high school mathematics curriculum. The stories included feelings and attitudes about the curriculum and descriptions of teaching experiences. Schifter's (1996a) teachers were working with constructivist methods and principles to transform their own mathematics instruction, largely along the lines of the National Council of Teachers of Mathematics (NCTM) Standards. The teachers wrote stories that detailed their successes and failures as they proceeded, with guidance, to reshape the teaching and learning processes in their classrooms. Schifter explained,

> The authors vividly narrate students' words and gestures, bringing readers into their classrooms to "see" and "hear" for themselves. But unlike videotape, this medium presents scenes from the teachers' perspective, complete with their thoughts, doubts, frustrations, and second thoughts. Thus, their audience comes to share the dilemmas they face, the decisions they make, and the satisfactions they experience. (1996a, p. 6)

In Schifter (1996b), the focus of the stories shifted to the teachers' struggle to become a new kind of practitioner as they faced the challenge of new mathematics pedagogy. Finally, Fijal (1995) wrote autobiographical stories of his past and current practice to identify and understand the nature of the changes that occurred over his career as a mathematics teacher. While all of the preceding studies involved telling or writing stories based on actual experiences with mathematics teaching or learning, in Lloyd's (2005, 2006) studies, the teachers wrote fictional stories about mathematics classrooms; in particular, classroom situations and scenarios in the role as the teacher. These stories had as an explicit goal to allow the teachers to create images of the self and others that they may or may not have personally experienced.

Analyzing the Stories

Most of the studies focused on identifying themes within and across stories as a central feature of the data analysis. In order to arrive at the themes, some studies used open coding of the stories as the analysis process, searching for characteristics that related to specific research questions. Ziegler (2003), for example, focused on identifying themes to describe change by first coding key statements in the stories that were indicative of the teachers' practice and philosophies of teaching and learning before and after their implementation of the new applied, project-based curriculum. Fijal (1995), in his autobiographical study, also reflected on his stories to identify patterns of change in his practice and the underlying basis for the change. For Harkness, D'Ambrosio, and Morrone (2007), the focus was on identifying themes in the prospective teachers' autobiography as part of their analysis to examine why these students were highly motivated in a social constructivist mathematics course in which the course instructor emphasized mastery goals. In Drake's (2006a) study, the teachers' stories of their prior and current experiences with mathematics were used to identify and understand patterns in teachers' interpretations and uses of reform-oriented curriculum materials. Drake (2006b) further explained that the process also involved categorizing the teachers' mathematics life stories into six types based on the teachers' descriptions of both their early experiences with mathematics and their current perceptions of themselves as mathematics learners and teachers. The focus of the analysis was on the sense-making practices (noticing, interpreting, implementing) of teachers who provided turning-point stories for the purpose of understanding teachers' specific practices in the context of reform.

For other studies, the analysis process was guided by a predetermined model or specific categories based on theory. Unlike the research previously discussed that focused only on the content of the stories, these studies analyzed both the structure and content of the stories. For example, Kaasila (2007a, 2007b), in analyzing the content of the stories, used emplotment to construct a retrospective explanation of how the participant's experiences at school were reflected in the development of her mathematical identity and in how she taught mathematics during teacher education. In analyzing the form of the story, Kaasila looked at the ways in which the participant told her story, using linguistic features to identify core events in the accounts. Lloyd (2005, 2006) also analyzed the stories structurally and thematically. Rather than attending immediately to the content of the story, the initial analysis of the stories involved using the structural elements to focus on how the prospective teachers represented and interpreted classroom issues and events. In the structural analysis, each story was coded according to a perspective that considered the following narrative elements: abstract (summary of the substance of the narrative), orientation (time, place, situation, participants), complicating action (sequence of events, problems), evaluation (significance and meaning of the action or problem), and resolution (what finally happened). Particular attention was devoted to the structure and meanings of the complicating actions and resolutions in the stories. To help this interpretation, thematic analysis of the content of the stories involved identifying and organizing information about the roles of teachers, students, and mathematics in the plots. Together, these three categories served as a framework for the use of thematic analytic strategies to identify major patterns in the data. Ponte, Segurado, and Oliveira (2003) used the same structural narrative elements as Lloyd (2005) in their first level of analysis of the stories. They tried to identify the main components of a narrative: abstract, orientation, complication, evaluation, resolution, and *coda*. In the second level of analysis, they looked for other issues in the content of the stories that appeared to be significant in the stories.

This section of the chapter highlighted ways narrative was used as a research tool in studies that has implications for mathematics teacher education. This tool allows us to obtain and unpack teaching and learning phenomena in order to understand mathematics teachers and their practice from a humanistic perspective. Studies framed in this perspective focus less on identifying deficiencies in teachers' behaviours and knowledge and more on understanding the nature of, and contexts that shape, and their perceptions of reality. This includes understanding teachers from their own perspective; how particular individual teachers understand their work (e.g., how do teachers make sense of implementing practices of mathematics reform). Thus, a focus of these studies is conceptualizing the experiential knowledge of teachers and providing plausible explanations of teaching behaviours as they are for the teacher. This indicates that using narrative as a research tool can lead to ways of making sense of mathematics teacher education that embody the teachers' perspectives based on their past, present and future experiences. Although narrative is effective as a research tool, it also can be a powerful pedagogical tool in mathematics teacher education. Yet, this use of narrative as a pedagogical tool has been highly overlooked in research in mathematics teacher education.

NARRATIVE AS PEDAGOGICAL TOOL

Narrative can be used as a pedagogical tool in both practising mathematics teacher development and prospective mathematics teacher education. From a theoretical perspective, it can allow both groups of teachers to gain insights into their thinking and actions and deepen their understanding regarding the nature of mathematics and it teaching and learning. It can lead to self-awareness of, for example, what they value, what they would like to do and why they want to do that. It can provide opportunities for them to focus on particular instances of teaching and to examine those instances more deeply than they are able during the busyness of their classroom work. However, while there is a growing interest in using narrative, outside of mathematics education, as a basis of teacher learning (e.g., Blake, Blake, & Tinsley, 2001; Doecke, Brown, & Loughran, 2000; Drake, Spillane, & Hufferd-Ackles, 2001; Goodwin, 2002; Hooley, 2005; Johnson, & Golombek, 2002; Olson, 2000), this is not reflected in mathematics education in terms of published work. Thus, the discussion that follows will be based on my use of narrative as a pedagogical tool.

My work with practising teachers (Chapman, 1999b) provides an example of using narrative inquiry as a basis of their development. The approach includes a focus on telling and reflecting on oral stories involving the teachers' own teaching in order to understand their sense-making of teaching problem solving and to facilitate their extension or reconstruction of this sense-making. Barnett (1998) also reported on a professional development process that used teacher-authored narratives about actual classroom experiences as a stimulus for discussing mathematical, pedagogical and philosophical concepts and issues. The discussion focused on four pivotal areas: development of one's own understanding of mathematics; use of the student perspective as a source of feedback; a recast of the familiar as strange and the simple as complex; and critical examination of alternative views and ideas. On a theoretical basis, Mason's (2002) work on 'noticing' provides several useful guidelines that are applicable to practising teachers' use of narratives as a basis of professional development. In my experience, narrative can be used in similar ways for both practising and prospective teachers. The main difference is obviously the experience of the practising teachers that provides them with a rich repertoire of stories of their own practice. They can thus write stories that include more depth in terms of their thinking, see more possibilities emerging from the stories for discussion and possibilities for the future, and engage in oral story telling more effectively. However, my focus in the remainder of this section will be only on prospective teacher education, where most of my experience lies.

In addition to my work, discussed later, the following studies have indirectly reported on engaging prospective mathematics teachers in narrative. Lloyd (2006) had prospective secondary teachers write fictional accounts about mathematics classrooms. However, her focus was not on discussing or examining this activity from a learning perspective. Smith (2006) asked her prospective mathematics teachers to write stories based on their practicum experiences, but focused more on her self-study of her practice than the stories as a way of knowing for the teachers. Earlier, Smith (2003), in her case study to illustrate connecting theory and reflective practice through personal theories, indicated that she engaged her prospective mathematics teachers in writing reflective narratives for the explicit purpose of thinking about beliefs and actions. She concluded that the use of narrative stories in the form of personal theories can provide an innovative pedagogical tool in mathematics teacher education. In general, while these studies do not provide details on, or directly investigated, the nature and use of narrative in teacher learning, they imply that narrative can play an important role in mathematics teacher education.

In the remainder of this section, I draw on my work with narrative in teacher education to illustrate possible ways in which it has and can be used. In the last decade, I have used stories in a variety of ways as an integral aspect of my mathematics education courses with prospective secondary mathematics teachers (e.g., Chapman, 1999a). I have engaged the prospective teachers with narrative as a reflective process, to foster self-study, and to construct or broaden their pedagogical knowledge. The self-study usually required them to inquire into their thinking about, and to consider, the nature of mathematics and teaching and learning mathematics. In this work, I have used narrative as object and process of inquiry. The following discussion of it is organized under two themes: writing the narratives and narrative reflection/analysis/inquiry.

Writing the Narratives

The narrative process begins by having the prospective teachers engage in intentional storying of past, present and/or future events they have experienced or expect to experience, directly or indirectly. The teachers could tell instead of write their stories. I choose to have them write because it provides focus and attention that simply telling does not. There are several situations that can be used as the bases for these stories. My focus has been on the experiences influencing the development of prospective teachers' beliefs and knowledge about mathematics and its teaching and learning. In particular, I have worked with two categories of experiences: teaching and problem solving. The former produces stories about teaching mathematics, the latter stories about mathematical problem solving.

Stories about Teaching
While this could be open-ended, I have used different situations to provide a focus for the stories about teaching. For example, I had prospective secondary mathematics teachers write stories about:
- the teaching of their own teachers when they were students of mathematics;
- their own teaching during their practicum;
- the teaching of others (i.e., peers, cooperating teachers, other teachers) observed during their practicum; and
- their teaching as imagined. This is a narrative equivalent of a lesson plan that allows them to imagine the lesson as they perceive or desire it to actually unfold.

These situations can be presented to the prospective teachers as open, i.e., they choose what they want to write about, or specific, e.g., a situation that they consider to be "good teaching" of mathematics, a situation they consider to be "bad teaching" of mathematics, or a memorable mathematics lesson they experienced. I have used the specific case because, from experience, the open case often produced stories that ignored the mathematics, as further explained later in this section. The stories can be written on any number of these situations as single activities or as a combination of two or more in ways that build on each other depending on the depth with which the use of narrative is being integrated into a course. For example, at the beginning of a mathematics education course, I had the prospective teachers write three stories they had experienced as a student, a teacher or an observer – one that they considered to be "good teaching" of high school mathematics, one that was "bad teaching" and one that was "memorable." The intent of this activity was to capture their preconceptions of mathematics pedagogy on entering the course.

The assumption underlying having the prospective teachers write such teaching stories is that if they are viewing or thinking about mathematics teaching through their preconceptions, then the way they recall or imagine a mathematics lesson will be influenced by this filter. Thus, they write themselves into the situations they describe, either literally or as the observer/author who defines what matters most. This means that in writing the stories, the focus is not on the accuracy of how a past situation or a mathematics lesson unfolded, but, for example, what mathematics lesson they choose to describe, what they choose to recall about it and how they tell it. As a result, they can fill gaps in their memories in a way that makes sense to them. As Polkinghorne (1988) explained:

> Narrative configuration is not simply a personal projection that has no relation to worldly events ... it is required to attend to the accepted reality of those events. Never the less, narrative meaning consists of more than the events alone; it consists also of the significance these events have for the narrator in relation to a particular theme. (p. 160)

However, as mentioned before, it may be necessary to provide the prospective teachers with specific guidelines and boundaries for the stories depending on their intended purpose.

The instruction given to the prospective teachers can influence the nature of the stories they write and the usefulness of the stories in addressing mathematics pedagogy as opposed to generic pedagogy. For example, I found that simply telling them to "write a story about ..." did not produce the type of stories I expected, i.e., with emphasis on mathematics pedagogy. In my early years of beginning to use narrative, asking the prospective teachers to write a story about their teaching of mathematics during their practicum, with an explanation of what I meant by story, produced stories with little or no attention to mathematics pedagogy. Instead, they wrote about classroom management issues or positive rapport with particular students; two of the traditional concerns to them – controlling the class and being liked by their students. It took a few iterations of modifications by adding details before arriving at a written guideline that produced not only powerful stories of mathematics teaching, but also a process that engaged the prospective teachers in deep self-reflection. The following is an example of this guideline used at the beginning of the course before they are exposed to any theory on mathematics pedagogy.

Write a story of a mathematics lesson you experienced as a student or an observer that you consider to be "good teaching" of high school mathematics. The story should describe at least one complete mathematics lesson from beginning to end and provide as much details as possible on the following: what the teacher did and said; what students did and said; how the mathematics content was dealt with or presented. The lesson should involve engaging the students in a mathematics concept for the first time (i.e., not a review or practice lesson). The story should be written in present tense and include direct speech of teacher and student. Do not analyze anyone or anything in the story. Just describe the situation as you think it actually happened. Do not leave gaps in the story, i.e., if you cannot recall a specific detail in exactly the way it happened, describe it based on what makes sense to you. But it must be plausible.

In general, the first sentence of this guideline can be modified to create variations in the stories and what the teachers are prompted to reflect on. In the case of imagined stories, I replace it with: *select a grade and a mathematics topic/concept you expect to teach and write a story of how you will like to teach it.*

Stories about Problem Solving

Like the preceding category of teaching stories, for this second category of stories I used in my teaching, I also provide different situations as a focus for the stories. In

this case, the situations involve problem-solving experiences. For example, I had the prospective secondary mathematics teachers write stories about:
- their problem-solving experience based on a prescribed problem,
- the problem-solving experience of others, usually secondary students or peers, and
- their experience presenting a problem to others, usually peers.

The goal for this story-writing task is for the prospective teachers to inquire about problem solving and their role as teacher.

Similar to the case of the teaching stories, the guidelines I developed to elicit appropriate stories from the prospective teachers evolved in reaction to what they would produce when asked to solve the problem and write a story describing the experience. They would write about how they thought they solved problems in a theoretical way and ignore the experience of doing the assigned problem. They would focus on describing only the steps to the solution and ignore the affective features of the experience. These behaviours suggested the type of modifications that were necessary to develop written guidelines that produced genuine narratives of the experiences involved. The following example is the guideline for the first of the three situations noted above for generating stories about problem solving:

Write a narrative of your experience solving the problem that is attached. The narrative should include your complete solution, feelings/emotions, thought processes, (in general) all actions associated with doing the problem from the moment you read it, so do not read it until you are ready to work on it!!! A page of "steps" to getting a solution is unacceptable and you will be required to re-do the narrative with a different problem. Correct method or answer is not important, but there should be a serious attempt at getting one for the narrative to be meaningful. Your focus should be on describing your personal experience in doing THIS problem. All of your mathematical work in arriving at a solution should be included or attached.

Non-routine mathematical problems are used for this activity. In particular, problems are selected to allow the prospective teachers to experience being stuck and getting out of being stuck.

The stories usually vary from two to five single-spaced pages depending on the individual prospective teacher's experiences. The process of creating the narratives is rich with opportunities for the prospective teachers to engage in reflection. In the case of the teaching stories, choosing what details to include, remembering the conversations that occurred, thinking back on the feelings that were part of the event, remembering who did and said what, deciding on what is good or bad teaching, and so forth, are all parts of the writing process that spurs the prospective teachers to reflect on their thinking and how teaching is or can be lived in the mathematics classroom. In fact, they usually find writing the initial stories challenging because they never had to articulate their thinking about, and experience with, mathematics pedagogy in this holistic and fine-grain way. In the case of the problem-solving stories, the prospective teachers have to attend to, and notice details of, the experience involved beyond their preconceptions of problem solving. In general, then, writing the story itself becomes a reflective and a learning activity because the prospective teachers are forced to attend to details of practice and problem solving they tend to dismiss. Once the stories are written, they form the basis of further reflection, analysis or inquiry, discussed after the following examples of the stories.

Examples of Stories

These examples of teaching stories were written by prospective secondary teachers as part of their course-work in mathematics education. They provided a basis for exploring both mathematics content and pedagogy. Both stories were based on actual lessons the authors had previously observed.

Example 1

This is one of the shorter stories. It is in response to the prompt to write a story that dealt with the treatment of a mathematics concept that raised issues for the author during a lesson he or she observed. The author also posed questions in regard to these issues for group discussions with peers. The story was written three-quarters into the semester. It is based on a Grade 12 lesson.

A teacher I observed was giving a lesson on Ellipse (conic). After defining ellipse as a conic generated when a plain intersects a cone (or a right cylinder) at a certain angle, he proceeded to develop the concept of ellipse by applying a series of transformations on the unit circle $x^2 + y^2 = 1$.

He explained: "If we do a horizontal stretch, say, by a factor 2, and a vertical stretch by a factor 3, the equation $x^2 + y^2 = 1$ becomes $\dfrac{x^2}{4} + \dfrac{y^2}{9} = 1$. If you recall in our first unit, to indicate a horizontal stretch, you multiply x by the reciprocal of the horizontal stretch factor. That is why we have the 4 under x^2. Since y is implicit – take note, we are not dealing with a function here but a relation, so instead of multiplying y by 3, we also multiply y by the reciprocal of the vertical stretch factor."

I saw some students' heads nod in agreement. Also, there were some students who were sitting at their desks with a stoic expression.

The teacher continued, "Now let's translate the new graph, say, 5 units to the left and 6 units up. As what happens with a circle, the center of the new graph becomes (-5, 6). Therefore, the equation becomes,

$$\frac{(x+5)^2}{4} + \frac{(y-6)^2}{9} = 1$$

In general, if we stretch a unit circle with center at (0, 0) horizontally by a factor a and vertically by a factor b, and at the same time horizontally translate it h units and vertically k units, the equation $x^2 + y^2 = 1$ becomes

$$\frac{(x-h)^2}{a^2} + \frac{(y-k)^2}{b^2} = 1$$

27

The graph of this equation is called an ellipse and this equation is called the standard form of the equation of an ellipse.
Note that as in the circle, (h, k) is the center of the ellipse. The translation moved the center (0, 0) to the point (h, k). Consider the following example:
A unit circle whose center is at the origin has undergone the following transformations:
Vertical stretch by a factor 10
Horizontal stretch by a factor 8
Translated to the right 6 units and down 3 units.
The new graph is called an ellipse and its equation in standard form is:

$$\frac{(x-6)^2}{64} + \frac{(y+3)^2}{100} = 1."$$

The teacher gave two more examples in determining the standard form and then asked the students to try a few exercises such as the following:
Using the standard form, write the equation of an ellipse obtained from $x^2 + y^2 = 1$
by:
Vertical stretch by a factor ½
Horizontal stretch by a factor 7
Translation of 1 unit right, 2 units down.
There were several students who wrote,

$$\frac{(x-1)^2}{49} + (\frac{1}{2})(y-2)^2 = 1$$

A response like this was not uncommon for several days to come, up to the time the lesson on conics was concluded.

The following questions were posed by the author for group discussion:
− *How do you make sense of the students' answer to the indicated exercise above?*
− *Would you agree with how the standard form of equation for ellipse was developed/presented? If not, how would you do it?*
− *The first unit was on the transformation of the function y = f(x). The students were taught that a horizontal stretch of 2 units, vertical stretch of 3 units, translation 1 unit to the right and 3 units up on the graph of y = f(x) would yield a new function:*

$$y = 3f(\frac{x-1}{2}) + 3.$$

Knowing this, would it change the way you were to develop the standard form of the ellipse equation? If so, how? Or, would you change the way the concept of transformation was done in the previous unit? How?

Example 2
This example is based on the guideline, discussed earlier in the chapter, for writing a story of "good teaching". It was written at the beginning of the semester before the author had any exposure to theory on mathematics pedagogy, so it is based

solely on her preconceptions of "good teaching". It is based on a Grade 10 lesson at the beginning of a trigonometry unit.

The sound of music began as the bell ended and the students filed into the classroom. The teacher greeted most of the students as they walked in. The teacher also makes note of a few students' new haircut or new shirt and compliments them. The teacher waited a little bit for the students who trailed in just after the sound of the music stopped. The students quickly settled in their seats. The teacher walks to the front of the class.

Teacher: Okay guys, today we're starting a new unit, Trigonometry. Does anyone remember what Trig is, from last year?

The teacher looks around the room and paused to give the students time to think. A student's hand went up.

Student: Is it that thing with SOH CAH TOA?

Teacher: Yes! SOH CAH TOA is definitely part of trig. Great job. Does anyone else remember doing trig before?

Student: Is this the unit with the triangles and angles and $a^2 + b^2 = c^2$?

Teacher: Yes this is definitely that unit. So most of you guys have seen trig before, so this should be a nice little review to refresh your minds and some of you may have not seen this concept before which is okay. In this unit we're going to learn about triangles and how we can get the measurement of the sides and angles of the triangles. We're also going to look at how we can use those in the real world. Near the end of this unit we have a fun project to do where we are going to use what we learned to measure the distance from the school's floor to the ceiling in the main hallway.

The teacher turned to the white board, marker in hand, and started to write notes for this unit. As she writes, she reads the words out loud. Some students already have their notebooks and pencil ready whereas some other students are just taking them out of their bags.

Teacher (talking and writing): Unit 7 – Trigonometry

Teacher: So the first thing we're going to look at in this unit is right angle triangles. Can anyone tell me what makes a right angle triangle?

A student raises his hand. The teacher calls on him.

Student: One of the angles has to be 90 degrees.

Teacher: Good job, you're completely right. So class, when we're looking at triangles, if one of their angles in 90 degrees then we know that it is a right angle triangle.

The teacher turns to the board.

Teacher (talking and writing): Right angle triangles are triangles that have a 90-degree angle.

The teacher draws a picture of a right angle triangle on the board, indicating a square in the corner which represents the angle that is 90 degrees.

Teacher: Now we're going to look at a theory called Pythagorean Theorem. This was mentioned earlier by Jim.

Teacher (talking and writing): Pythagorean Theorem $a^2 + b^2 = c^2$

Teacher: This theorem can only be used for right angle triangles and we use it when we know two sides of a triangle and we are looking for the remaining unknown side.

She then draws a picture of a right angle triangle and asks the class: Does anyone think it matters what letter I label for each side of this triangle?

A student raises his hand. The teacher calls on him.

Student: Does one of the letters must always be the hypotenuse or something like that?

Teacher: Yes, you are absolutely right. Class, when we're using Pythagorean Theorem it is very, very, very important that we label c as our hypotenuse. This is probably the most important part of using this theorem.

The teacher turns to the white board and starts labelling her triangle. She labels c at the hypotenuse. She then asks the class: Do you think it matters which side I label my a and b?

Student shouts out: No.

Teacher: That's right. It really doesn't matter which side I choose for my a and which side I choose for my b, so long as I always, always label my c as the hypotenuse. Do you guys know how you would know which side is always the hypotenuse?

Student: It's the biggest side out of all the sides.

Teacher: Yes, you're absolutely right Tracy; the hypotenuse is always bigger than the other two sides. You can also know which one is the hypotenuse because this side is always across from the 90-degree angle.

The teacher points at the drawing and points at how the hypotenuse is always the side across from the 90-degree angle. The teacher labels a and b on the triangle. The teacher draws an arrow that points at the c on the hypotenuse and writes: c must be the hypotenuse.

Teacher: Okay, let's do two examples using $a^2 + b^2 = c^2$ and then I'll pass around a worksheet for you guys to practice this.

Teacher (talking and writing): Example 1: Find the missing side.

The teacher draws a picture of a right triangle, labels one side 4 and another side 6, leaving the hypotenuse empty.

Teacher: Okay, so who can tell me what I know in this example?

Student: We know that one side is 4 and the other is 6.

Teacher: Can you tell me which side we are looking for?

Student: The hypotenuse.

Teacher: Great job, Kim. Now who can help me fill in the formula $a^2 + b^2 = c^2$?

Student (as teacher writes): Put $4^2 + 6^2 = c^2$

Teacher: Great job. Now can you guys tell me what $4^2 + 6^2$ is?

Student: $16 + 36 = 52$

Teacher writes on the board: $16 + 36 = c^2$ $52 = c^2$

Teacher: Are we done?

Some students shout out yes and some shout out no.

Teacher: No, we're not quite done yet because right now we have c^2 but we want only c, so we're going to have to square root both sides to get c. Can you guys square root 52 in your calculators and tell me what you get.
Students: 7.2

The teacher writes on the board: $\sqrt{52}$ = c   7.2 = c

Teacher: Okay guys great job! Let's do the last example.
Teacher (talking and writing): Example 2: Find the missing side.
The teacher draws a picture of a right angle triangle, labels one side 5 and the hypotenuse 8, leaving one side empty.
Teacher: Okay, so can someone help me fill in the formula?
Student (as teacher writes): Put $5^2 + b^2 = 8^2$
Teacher: Great job. How did you know to put 8 as c?
Student: Because c must be the side across for the right angle.
Teacher: Great job. So class does everyone see how in this example, we must put 8 as c because 8 is the hypotenuse which is the side across from the 90 degree angle? Okay can someone tell me what 5^2 is?
Student: 25
Teacher writes on the board: 25 + b^2 =
Teacher: And who can tell me what 8^2 is?
Student: 64
Teacher writes on the board: 25 + b^2 = 64
Teacher: Now this question is a little trickier than the first example because we don't have b by itself. So we're going to have to get b by itself. Can anyone tell me what you think I should do to get b by itself?
Student: Subtract 25 on both sides.
Teacher: Yup, that's right.
The teacher writes on the board:

$$25 + b^2 = 64$$
$$-25 \qquad -25$$
$$b^2 = 39$$

Teacher: Are we done?
Some students shout out yes and some shout out no.
Teacher: No we're not done yet because right now we have b^2 but we want only b, so we're going to have to square root both sides to get b. Can you guys square root 39 in you calculators and tell me what you get?
Students: 6.2
Teacher writes: b = 6.2
Teacher: Did everyone get the same answer?
The students agreed.
Teacher: OK! Well that's all the notes we're going to take for today, I'm going to pass around a worksheet for you guys to do for the remainder of the class working on questions using Pythagorean Theorem (their worksheets for the week is always due on Monday of next week). Tomorrow we'll start to look at how to find angles in a triangle.
The teacher passes out the worksheet to the students one by one and goes back to her desk and does attendance in her attendance book, then on the electronic

31

system. The students are now getting into gear and into their worksheet. Some work alone, and some work in groups. When the students have questions, some come up to the teacher's desk and some raise their hands and the teacher comes over to them. They continue to work on their worksheet until the period is over. The teacher walks around the room helping students. Near the end of the period, the students start to pack up and wait around the door until the music in the hallways comes on. Once the music comes on, the students head off to their next class.

Reasons the author gave for this being "good teaching" included: Classroom management was very good. The students listened well and were respectful. The teacher taught the concept in a good manner to the students, the concept was taught correctly, and examples were used to show the concept. Later in the semester, the author used the NCTM (1991) standards on discourse, worthwhile tasks and environment to analyze the story. Her response reflected a self-realization of the limitations in her preconceptions. For example, what she initially considered as good questions she now did not. She explained:

> The teacher in my story did not pose meaningful questions to these students, questions that allowed them to think beyond what is told to them. ... Most questions in the story focused on those that had one right answer.

At the end of the semester, she re-wrote the story to indicate how she would teach the topic. This story now contained features of an inquiry-based, student-oriented approach to teaching. The narrative provided a basis for her to understand the shifts in her thinking and knowledge, which she indicated was reinforcing in terms of the teacher she will like to become. The next section discusses this and other ways in which prospective teachers can use their stories in their learning.

Narrative Reflection/Analysis/Inquiry

Narrative reflection, analysis or inquiry allows the prospective teachers to explore their stories to gain deeper understanding of mathematics pedagogy and problem solving, in my case. The written stories become a basis for inquiring into the meaning of specific themes embodied in them. I summarize eight ways in which I have engaged prospective secondary teachers in this process of narrative reflection/analysis/inquiry. All of them are not mutually exclusive. The intent is to indicate a range of what is possible. Thus, all of the ways do not have to be used in the same course, for example. One can select one or a few or create variations that best fit one's context. For example, I have combined ways (i), (ii), and (iii) in a course on mathematics pedagogy.

(i) Initial self-reflection
In this activity, after writing their teaching stories, the prospective teachers wrote journals on why they chose the stories they wrote, e.g., what made their stories "good teaching". They then read a sample of each other's stories and wrote journals on which of the stories they thought represented good teaching and which stories they liked and did not like in terms of the teaching, giving reasons for their

choices. They then shared, compared and discussed their thinking with each other. This initial self-reflection allowed them to confront their preconceptions and beliefs, e.g., resulting from conflicts among them in terms of their views of the stories as good or not good teaching.

(ii) Restorying

For this task, towards the end of the course, after being exposed to theories and other experiences on mathematics pedagogy, the prospective teachers revisited their teaching stories written at the beginning of the course to restory them. They were asked to discuss if their teaching stories were inquiry-based lessons. Usually most of them indicated that the lessons were not and that their understanding of "good teaching" was now different from the initial story. The others, whose stories did include some aspects of inquiry, indicated that their understanding of good teaching was validated and expanded. After this reflection, they rewrote their stories of "good teaching" in the way they would want to see them unfold as inquiry-oriented lessons. Even if they thought their stories consisted of inquiry-based teaching, they had to provide an alternative inquiry-oriented way of conducting them. In rewriting these stories of teaching, they had to make conscious choices about how to conceptualize themselves and their roles. They had to use their imagination, picture the classroom more finely, and consider possibilities for the mathematics and engaging students in learning it. So their rewriting of the teaching story captured the shifts in their knowledge in how they initially viewed teaching and the mathematics.

(iii) Unpacking teaching stories

This activity treated the stories as cases to unpack during the semester as a basis to interpret theory discussed in the course and as a basis for discussing mathematics content in context. The prospective teachers analyzed their stories individually and in groups. The analysis included making sense of: what mathematics was being taught; worthwhile mathematics tasks; how students were engaged in the content; discourse – teacher-student interactions about the mathematics; teacher's role; students' role; and any issues unique to the story or raised by the class (e.g., assessment). This analysis was guided by readings, such as the NCTM (1991) Standards. For example, the prospective teachers had to decide whether or not the mathematical tasks and discourse in their stories were consistent with the characteristics proposed by the NCTM Standards. This analysis of practice broadened their awareness and understanding of details of mathematics teaching they had taken for granted or not noticed. For example, initially, they saw students as being actively involved if they were responding to the teachers' questions, but did not notice that the questions were mostly factual or memory recall. The analysis of the teaching stories also challenged the teachers' mathematics knowledge for teaching and allowed them to think more deeply about the mathematics. In using these stories as cases, they offered the prospective teachers something unique in comparison to more traditional cases. These stories offered the prospective teachers situations of practice that were real to them as a basis of learning about teaching mathematics. These were their stories. They knew the stories' broader and specific contexts, e.g., the teachers, students, culture and schools. This allowed them to deal with the stories as lived experiences as opposed to what may seem as theoretical cases to them if the stories were provided by others.

(iv) Unpacking problem-solving stories

The activities to unpack the problem-solving stories depended on the experience that framed the stories. For example, in the case of the stories that involved the prospective teachers' experience solving an assigned problem, the prospective teachers examined their stories for what they told about problem solving, when and how emotions occurred in the problem-solving process, where the problem solver was stuck and how he or she tried to get out of being stuck, and implications for teaching. This process provided the prospective teachers with a more realistic view of problem solving and more meaningful ways to teach it than they initially held.

(v) Narrative inquiry through peers

This form of narrative inquiry involved using the written story as a stimulus for sharing oral stories of related personal experiences. It required the prospective teachers to work in small groups, sharing and resonating with each other's stories. For example, one person would select and share an excerpt from her or his story, the rest of the group then resonated with it by listening for what they perceived to be similar or different in their own experiences (within or outside of their own written stories), asking questions about it and sharing points of similarity and difference in experiences. This activity allowed the prospective teachers to gain deeper understanding of themselves and to assist each other to clarify her or his understandings.

(vi) Comparing imagined versus actual actions

This activity allowed the prospective teachers to create a bridge between their course work and field experience by comparing their imagined story of how they intended to teach with their actual teaching. For this activity, in the methods course, instead of a traditional lesson plan, each of the prospective teachers created a story, following the guidelines discussed earlier, of how he or she planned to teach a specific mathematics concept during the practicum. This often occurred at least two weeks before they actually taught the lesson. After teaching the lesson they returned to their stories and compared it to what actually happened, focusing on what was similar and different, reasons for differences, and possibilities for the future.

(vii) Comparing personal versus theoretical knowledge

This activity allowed the prospective teachers to use their stories as a basis to compare their knowledge based on their past experiences with theoretical knowledge they were being exposed to in the mathematics education course. For example, they identified the perspectives of mathematics, learning, and teaching portrayed in their stories, then compared and considered the implications of these perspectives in relation to alternative perspectives provided by theory.

(viii) Identifying narrative themes
This final example of activities in which prospective teachers can learn from their written stories involves having them identify and consider a theme from a set of at least three teaching stories based on different teaching situations. This activity provided a way for the prospective teachers to make explicit the meanings underlying their thinking about mathematics pedagogy, and a way of seeing contradictions in terms of conflicting issues encountered in determining the theme.

This section of the chapter highlighted ways in which narrative can be used as a pedagogical tool. These different ways of engaging teachers in narrative as a mode and object of knowing illustrate a range of activities that focus on mathematics teacher education. Formal and informal studies I have conducted on these narrative approaches suggest that they have the potential to enhance prospective teachers' learning. The approaches are learner-focused in that predetermined knowledge does not dominate the learning process; instead, the personal narrative of each prospective teacher forms the direction of the learning experience. The narratives of others ensure that knowledge external to the learner is available. Narrative interactions with peers help to build connections with others in ways that allow and encourage the joint construction of knowledge and to hear and acknowledge multiple perspectives on an experience or idea. However, like any other tool, the usefulness of narrative is dependent on particular factors, including the people and context involved. For example, the prospective teachers need to feel psychologically safe in order to write and share their stories based on actual experiences. Some teachers who dislike writing as mathematics majors are likely to not provide the details necessary for the stories to be meaningful as a basis to reflect on and analyze important pedagogical issues. My experience is that this can be avoided if the guidelines for writing the stories and the purpose for the activities are clearly discussed with them.

CONCLUSION

Narrative as research method seems to have received much more attention in studies related to mathematics teacher education than narrative as pedagogical tool. But stories could provide opportunities to allow prospective teachers to capture lived experiences of mathematics education, to explore their thinking about teaching mathematics, to construct or refine personal theories of learning and teaching and to get to meanings and alternative perspectives that could influence their behaviours in a positive way in teaching mathematics. Narrative provides a reflective way of knowing, which is widely accepted as a central goal in teacher education. It seems that future work in mathematics teacher education should include considerations of narrative as a pedagogical tool. For example, future research can consider: What is the role of narrative in the construction of mathematics teachers' knowledge? What is the meaning and usefulness of narrative to teachers learning to teach, as well as to experienced teachers? However, it is also important to continue to explore narrative as a research method in mathematics teacher education. While this use of it is growing, it is nevertheless very limited. Thus, there is still a lot that could be done with narrative as a pedagogical tool and even more to understand about it as a process and product of research.

REFERENCES

Barnett, C. S. (1998). Mathematics teaching cases as a catalyst for informed strategic inquiry. *Teaching and Teacher Education, 14*(1), 81–93.

Blake, R. W., Blake, B. E., & Tinsley, J. A. (2001, April). *Using narrative to construct personal theories of teaching science among pre-service teachers: Cross-curricular convergences and implications.* Paper presented at the annual meeting of the American Education Research Association, Seattle, WA.

Bruner, J. (1986). *Actual minds, possible worlds.* Cambridge, MA: Harvard University Press.

Carter, K. (1993). The place of story in research on teaching and teacher education. *Educational Researcher, 22* (1), 5–12.

Chapman, O. (2002). Belief structure and inservice high school mathematics teachers' growth. In G. Leder, E. Pehkonen, and G. Torner (Eds.), *Beliefs: A hidden variable in mathematics education?* (pp. 177–194). Dordrecht, the Netherlands: Kluwer Academic Publishers.

Chapman, O. (1999a) Reflection in mathematics teacher education: The storying approach. In N. Ellerton (Ed.), *Mathematics teacher development: International perspectives* (pp. 32–57). West Perth, Australia: Meridan Press

Chapman, O. (1999b). Inservice teacher development in mathematical problem solving. *Journal of Mathematics Teacher Education, 2,* 121–142.

Chapman, O. (1997). Metaphors in the teaching of mathematical problem solving. *Educational Studies in Mathematics, 32,* 201–208.

Clandinin, D. J., & Connelly, F. M. (2000). *Narrative inquiry: Experience and story in qualitative research.* San Francisco, CA: Jossey-Bass.

Connelly, M. & Clandinin, J. (1988). *Teachers as curriculum planners: Narratives of experience.* New York: Teachers College Press.

Crites, S. (1975). Angels we have heard. In J. Wiggins (Ed.), *Religion as story* (pp. 125–145). New York: University Press of America.

Denzin, N. (1989). Interpretive biography. *Qualitative Research Methods Series: 17.* Newbury Park: Sage.

Doecke, B., Brown, J., & Loughran, J. (2000). Teacher talk: The role of story and anecdote in constructing professional knowledge for beginning teachers. *Teaching and Teacher Education, 16,* 335–348.

Doyle, W., & Carter, K. (2003). Narrative and learning to teach: Implications for teacher education curriculum. *Journal of Curriculum Studies, 35*(2), 129–137.

Drake, C. (2006a) Using teacher narrative to understand teachers' uses of curriculum materials. *Proceedings of the 7th International Conference on Learning Sciences* (pp. 134–139), Bloomington, IN: Indiana University.

Drake, C. (2006b). Turning points: Using teachers' mathematics life stories to understand the implementation of mathematics education reform. *Journal of Mathematics Teacher Education, 9,* 579–608.

Drake, C., Spillane, J. P. & Hufferd-Ackles, K. (2001), Storied identities: Teacher learning and subject-matter context. *Journal of Curriculum Studies, 33*(1), 1–23.

Elbaz. F. (1990). Knowledge and discourse: The evolution of research on teacher thinking. In C. Day, M. Pope, & P. Denicolo (Eds.), *Insight into teachers' thinking and practice* (pp. 15–42). London: The Falmer Press.

Fijal, G. (1995). *Mathematics teacher development: A story of change*. Unpublished Master's thesis, University of Calgary, Calgary.

Goodwin, A. L. (2002). The case of one child: Making the shift from personal knowledge to professionally informed practice. *Teaching Education 13*(2), 137–154.

Harkness, S. S., D'Ambrosio, B., & Morrone, A. S. (2007). Preservice elementary teachers' voices describe how their teacher motivated them to do mathematics. *Educational Studies in Mathematics. 65*, 235–254.

Hooley, N. (2005, November). *Establishing professional identity: Narrative as curriculum for preservice teacher education*. Paper presented at the 28th Annual Conference of the Australian Association for Research in Education, Sydney: Australia.

Johnson, K. E. & Golombek, P. R. (Eds.). (2002). *Teachers' narrative inquiry as professional development*. Cambridge: Cambridge University Press.

Kaasila, R. (2007a). Mathematical biography and key rhetoric. *Educational Studies in Mathematics, 66*, 373–384.

Kaasila, R. (2007b). Using narrative inquiry for investigating the becoming of a mathematics teacher. *ZDM, 39* (3), 205–213.

Lloyd, G. (2006). Preservice teachers' stories of mathematics classrooms: Explorations of practice through fictional accounts. *Educational Studies in Mathematics, 63*(1), 57–87.

Lloyd, G. (2005). Beliefs about the teacher's role in the mathematics classroom: One student teacher's explorations in fiction and in practice. *Journal of Mathematics Teacher Education, 8*, 441–467.

Lyons, N., & LaBoskey, V. K. (Eds.). (2002). *Narrative inquiry in practice: Advancing the knowledge of teaching*. New York: Teachers College Press.

Mason, J. (2002). *Researching your own practice: The discipline of noticing*. New York: Routledge.

Mitchell, W. J.T. (Ed.). (1981). *On narrative*. Chicago, IL: University of Chicago Press.

National Council of Teachers of Mathematics. (1991). *Teaching and assessment standards for school mathematics*. Reston, VA: Author.

Olson, M. R. (2000). Linking personal and professional knowledge of teaching practice through narrative inquiry. *Teacher Educator, 35*(4), 109–127.

Polkinghorne, D. (1995). Narrative configuration in qualitative analysis. In J. Hatch & R. Wisniewski (Eds.), *Life history and narrative* (pp. 5–23). London: Falmer.

Polkinghorne, D. (1988). *Narrative knowing and the human science*. Albany, NY: State University of New York Press.

Ponte, J. P., Segurado, I., & Oliveira, H. (2003). A collaborative project using narratives: What happens when pupils work on mathematical investigations? In A. Peter-Koop, V. Santos-Wagner, C. Breen, & A. Begg (Eds.), *Collaboration in teacher education: Examples from the context of mathematics education* (pp. 85–97). Dordrecht: Kluwer Academic Press.

Ricoeur, P. 1983. *Time and narrative, Vol. 1*. Chicago, IL: University of Chicago Press.

Sarbin, T. (Ed.). (1986). *Narrative psychology: The storied nature of human conduct*. New York: Praeger.

Schifter, D. (Ed.). (1996a). *What's happening in math class? Envisioning new practices through teacher narratives, Volume 1*. New York, NY: Teachers College Press.

Schifter, D. (Ed.). (1996b). *What's happening in math class? Reconstructing professional identities, Volume 2*. New York, NY: Teachers College Press.

Scholes, R. (1981). Language, narrative and anti-narrative. In W. J. T. Mitchell (Ed.), *On narrative* (pp. 200–208). Chicago, IL: University of Chicago Press.

Schön, D. (1983). *The reflective practitioner: How professionals think in action*. New York: Basic Books.

Smith, T. (2006). Self-study through narrative inquiry: Fostering identity in mathematics teacher education. In P. Grootenboer, R. Zevenbergen, & M. Chinnappan (Eds.), *Identities, cultures, and learning spaces. Proceedings of the Twenty-ninth Annual Conference of the Mathematics Education Research Group of Australasia* (pp. 471–478). Canberra: MERGA.

Smith, T. (2003). Connecting theory and reflective practice through the use of personal theories. In N. Pateman, B. Dougherty, & J. Zilliox (Eds.), *Proceedings of the 27th Conference of the International Group for the Psychology of Mathematics Education* (Vol. 4, pp. 215–222). CRDG, College of Education, University of Hawai'i.

Ziegler, D. (2003). *Mathematics teacher change: Teaching the Alberta High School Applied Mathematics program*. Unpublished Masters Thesis, University of Calgary, Calgary.

Olive Chapman
Faculty of Education
University of Calgary
Canada

ZVIA MARKOVITS AND MARGARET SMITH

2. CASES AS TOOLS IN MATHEMATICS TEACHER EDUCATION

This chapter explores the use of cases in mathematics teacher education. In particular, notions of what a case is and what teachers learn from their experience with cases is discussed. Drawing on our work we present examples of two different types of cases – exemplars and problem situations – that are examined and discussed in detail. On the one hand, exemplars are used to exemplify a practice or operationalize a theory. They provide vivid images of teachers in real classrooms that ground abstract ideas related to content and pedagogy. On the other hand, problem situations can be used to examine the complexities of teaching and the problematic aspects of performance. They often provide dilemmas to be analyzed and resolved. We conclude the chapter by discussing additional work that is needed regarding the use of cases in teacher education, including the design of additional types of cases and more research that addresses what teachers learn, how they learn it, and the impact of their learning on their professional practice.

INTRODUCTION

Historically, cases were first used at the Harvard Law School more than one hundred years ago (1871), and were subsequently used at the Harvard Medical School (1910) and the Harvard Business School (1920s). Today, cases are used in many other fields as well, such as geography (e.g., Grant, 1997), physical therapy education (e.g., McGinty, 2000) and teacher education (e.g., Merseth, 1991). Case use in teacher education began in earnest in 1986 when Lee Shulman, proposed "case knowledge" as a component of "teacher knowledge" (Merseth, 1996).[1] Although the fields are quite diverse, there appears to be a general belief that cases can address effectively a common tension in the design of experiences for professional education. A professional education curriculum seeks both to provide codified, theoretically based knowledge and to teach reasoning skills and strategies for analyzing and acting professionally in novel settings. Such a curriculum is grounded in the obligation of professional education to prepare practitioners for a practice that is simultaneously routine and uncertain (Sykes & Bird, 1992).

With the growth in the use of cases in a wide variety of fields, many different kinds and types of 'cases' have emerged, calling into question, what is a case? Herreid's (1997, p. 92) definition of cases captures the core element of what makes

---

[1] Although cases were being used in teacher education as early as the 1920s, these efforts were not as extensive or well organized (Lundeberg, Levin, and Harrington, 1999).

D. Tirosh and T. Wood (eds.), Tools and Processes in Mathematics Teacher Education, 39–64.

something a case: "Cases are stories with a message. They are not simply narratives for entertainment. They are stories to educate." Hence a case in the field of teacher education is defined as "any description of an episode or incident that can be connected to the knowledge base for teaching that can be interpreted ..." (Carter, 1999, p. 174). Merseth (2003, p. xvii) argues "good cases bring a 'chunk of reality' into the teacher education classroom to be examined, explored, and utilized as a window on practice ..."

In this chapter we discuss cases and their use in mathematics teacher education. The chapter is divided into three sections. In the first section, we provide a rationale for the use of cases in mathematics teacher education and report on what teachers can learn from their experiences with cases. In the second section we provide in-depth examples of two different types of cases – exemplars (i.e., lengthy narratives that portray an instructional episode in its entirety, highlighting the actions and interactions of a teacher and her students), and problem situations (i.e., shorter scenarios that focus on specific problems or dilemmas encountered by teachers as they listen to and interact with students). Section three concludes the chapter in which we discuss key aspects of the use of cases and raise questions about the use of cases.

THE USE OF CASES IN MATHEMATICS TEACHER EDUCTION

The first book of cases for mathematics teacher education was published in 1994 (see Barnett, Goldenstein, & Jackson, 1994) and launched a new era in the education of teachers of mathematics. Since the publication of this volume over a decade ago, many additional mathematics casebooks have been published in English (e.g., Merseth, 2003; Schifter, Bastable, & Russell, 1999, 2002, 2007; Seago, Mumme, & Branca, 2004; Stein, Smith, Henningsen, & Silver, 2000) and in other languages (e.g., Markovits, 2003). These casebooks vary greatly in terms of content focus (e.g., specific mathematical ideas, students' thinking about particular pieces of mathematics, the pedagogy used to support student learning of mathematics), grade level (e.g., elementary, middle, high school), type (e.g., narrative or video), authorship (e.g., written by teachers describing their own practice or written by a third party describing some aspects of classroom instruction), and authenticity (e.g., a portrayal of events as they actually occurred, episodes based on real events but embellished, or hypothetical situations based on research on teaching and learning). Despite these differences, cases in mathematics education share a common feature of providing realistic contexts for helping teachers "develop skills of analysis and problem-solving, gain broad repertoires of pedagogical technique, capitalize on the power of reflection, and experience a positive learning community" (Merseth, 1999, pp. xi–xii).

Consider, for example, the case shown in Figure 1. This case, written by a middle-school teacher, describes the actual events that unfolded in her classroom when seventh-grade students were introduced to the concept of ratio. The case provides an opportunity for teachers to explore important mathematical ideas related to rational number understandings, to analyze and critically reflect on the teacher's actions and interactions in the classroom, and to consider different courses of actions open to the teacher. By learning how to analyze "messy and complex situations", such as the one presented in the ratio case, teachers can learn to make well-informed decisions in their own classrooms (Barnett & Ramirez, 1996, p. 11).

The Ratio of Boys to Girls

We often hold discussions in my seventh grade class, and sometimes I find myself totally unprepared for the questions my students ask. It's not that I feel I should be the one with the answers, but I do want to guide the discussion productively.

In a recent lesson introducing ratio concepts, I had written the fraction $\frac{1}{2}$ on the board and reminded my students that it meant "1 divided by 2," and that it also meant "1 out of 2."

"It is a division problem and also a ratio because it shows a comparison of two numbers – 1 and 2," I explained. "Let's compare the number of boys and girls in our class." The class determined that there were 17 girls and 15 boys. "What is the ratio of girls to boys?"

Several students called out, "Seventeen to 15." I wrote the fraction $\frac{17}{15}$ on the board.

Carmen blurted out, "That can't be right. You said a fraction means the top divided by the bottom. That'll be more than one whole class."

Laura interjected, "And you said you could say "out of" – like 17 out of 15. That doesn't sound right – 17 girls out of 15 boys."

I realized that I wasn't very clear myself about how fractions and ratios were related or what part context plays in describing ratios. These were good questions and I wasn't sure how to handle them.

Figure 1. An example of a teaching episode.[2]

Hence cases are one way of providing prospective and practicing mathematics teachers with the opportunity to develop knowledge needed for teaching (e.g., knowledge of content, pedagogy and students as learners) as well as the capacity for knowing when and how to apply such knowledge, a capacity that depends on the ability to connect the specifics of real-time, deeply contextualized teaching

---

[2] Taken from *Fractions, Decimals and Percents* edited by Carne Barnett, Donna Goldenstein, and Babette Jackson.

moments with a broader set of ideas about mathematics, about teaching, and about learning. To develop this capacity, teachers must learn to recognize events in their own classrooms as instances of larger patterns and principles. Then they can formulate ways of acting and interacting that are thoughtful, principled, and effective (Shulman, 1996). As Shulman (1992, p. 28) has noted:

I envision case method as a strategy for overcoming many of the most serious deficiencies in the education of teachers. Because they are contextual, local, and situated – as are all narratives – cases integrate what otherwise remains separated. Content and process, thought and feeling, teaching and learning are not addressed theoretically as distinct constructs. They occur simultaneously as they do in real life, posing problems, issues, and challenges for new teachers that their knowledge and experiences can be used to discern.

Although it is unlikely that cases alone are sufficient as a source of professional learning (Patel & Kaufman, 2001), they can be a critical component of a curriculum for teacher education, providing a focus for sustained teacher inquiry and investigation (Ball & Cohen, 1999), an opportunity to make connections to experiences (vicarious or lived), and to theoretical classifications and general principles (Shulman, 1996). By deprivatizing teaching, cases can help teachers deal with the uncertainties presented and begin to think like teachers. According to Richardson (1996, p. ix), one challenge of teacher education is to help teachers "begin to develop practical knowledge that will allow them to survive the reality of the classroom." Cases appear to be one way of facilitating teachers' development of this practical knowledge.

While there is considerable enthusiasm for using cases in teacher education, and many claims regarding the efficacy of this approach (e.g., Merseth, 1991; Sykes & Bird, 1992), establishing an empirical basis for these claims has been a slow process. In 1999 Merseth noted "the conversations about case-based instruction over the last two decades has been full of heat, but with very little light" (p. xiv). Although much more work is needed, research on the use of cases does provide evidence that they can be used to enhance teachers' pedagogical thinking and reasoning skills (e.g., Barnett, 1991); help teachers reason through dilemmas of practice (e.g., Harrington, 1995, Markovits & Even, 1999b); support inquiry into classroom practices (e.g., Broudy, 1990); help teachers learn key pedagogical practices that support student learning (e.g., Stein, Engle, Hughes, & Smith, 2003; Hillen & Hughes, in press); and facilitate the development of content knowledge (e.g., Merseth & Lacey, 1993).

One coherent attempt to define an empirical basis for the use of cases in teacher education is the book entitled, *Who Learns What From Cases and How?: The Research Base for Teaching and Learning with Cases* edited by Mary Lundeberg, Barbara Levin, and Helen Harrrington (1999). The chapters in this book report the findings of a series of studies, mostly descriptive or naturalistic, conducted by the authors in an effort to determine what students enrolled in their teacher education courses learned. The studies, drawing on a variety of data sources (e.g., interviews with teachers, videotapes of sessions, written reflections) and methodologies (e.g., discourse analysis), highlight ways in which cases develop teachers knowledge base and decision making skills but leave many unanswered questions regarding the extent to which cases influence teacher or student performance in the classroom. In general, the studies reported in this book lack objectivity (i.e., the researcher is generally the teacher educator implementing the case instruction that is being studied) and rarely use traditional research designs.

THE 'WHAT AND HOW' OF CASES: A FOCUS ON TWO SPECIFIC TYPES

Cases can be divided into two broad categories, *exemplars* and *problem situations* (Carter, 1999). On the one hand, exemplars can be used to exemplify a practice or operationalize a theory. They provide vivid images of teachers in real classrooms that ground abstract ideas related to content and pedagogy. Problem situations, on the other hand, can be used to examine the complexities of teaching and the problematic aspects of performance. They often provide dilemmas (either mathematical or pedagogical) to be analyzed and resolved. In this section we provide examples of each of these two types of cases. The *exemplars* discussed herein are based on the work of Smith and her colleagues in the United States (Stein, Smith, Henningsen, & Silver, 2000; Smith, Silver, & Stein, 2005a, 2005b, 2005c) and the *problem situations* are based on the work of Markovits and her colleague in Israel (Markovits & Even, 1999a; Markovits, 2003). These two bodies of work were selected for closer examination because they serve to highlight the two broad classes of cases and provide an interesting contrast to the question "What is a case?"

Exemplars: Highlighting Key Ideas about Mathematics Teaching and Learning

The narrative cases created by Smith and her colleagues are *exemplars* or what Shulman (1996) would call *paradigm* cases. That is, they instantiate a broader, more general set of ideas about teaching and learning and are intended to concretize complex practices. These cases draw on data, frameworks, and empirical findings from QUASAR (Quantitative Understanding: Amplifying Students Achievement and Reasoning), a national project in the United States aimed at improving mathematics instruction for students attending middle schools in economically disadvantaged communities in ways that emphasized thinking, reasoning, problem solving, and the communication of mathematical ideas (Silver, Smith, & Nelson, 1995; Silver & Stein, 1996). The project sought to both support instructional improvement efforts in local settings and to carefully document and study classroom instruction and student learning outcomes.

Three keys ideas about mathematics teaching and learning emerged from this research and provide the core set of ideas that are exemplified in the cases: 1) cognitively challenging mathematical tasks provide the greatest opportunities for students to develop the capacity to think and reason; 2) the cognitive demands of tasks can (and frequently do) change during a lesson (i.e., a task that starts out as challenging might be transformed during instruction to a less rigorous exercise);

and 3) a teacher's actions and interactions with students during classroom instruction are crucial in determining the extent to which students were able to maintain a high level of intellectual engagement with challenging mathematical tasks (Stein, Grover, & Henningsen, 1996; Henningsen & Stein, 1997).

To date, Smith and her colleagues have written four casebooks (Stein et al., 2000; Smith et al., 2005a, 2005b, 2005c) each of which contains 4-6 rich narratives that take you into one of the QUASAR middle school classrooms and serve to exemplify key features of instruction associated with the implementation of challenging mathematical tasks. The materials in these volumes are intended for use with both prospective and practicing teachers at all levels K-12. The casebooks can be used as the foundation for courses or individual cases can be used in other teachers' professional development programs.

Characteristics of the Exemplars
Specifically, each case-episode portrays the events that unfold in an urban middle school classroom as the teacher engages his or her students in solving a cognitively demanding task that has the potential to engage students in high level thinking about important mathematical ideas (Stein, Grover, & Henningsen, 1996; Stein & Smith, 1998; Smith & Stein, 1998; Stein et al., 2000). For example, Marie Hanson (the teacher featured in one of the cases in Smith et al., 2005a) and her students explore several candy jar problems that involve constructing equivalent ratios of discrete objects and finding the missing value in proportions when one of the quantities is not given (see Figure 2). Since students in Ms. Hanson's class have not previously learned a procedure for solving missing-value problems, they must invent their own strategies rather than applying memorized rules that have no meaning to them.

Each case begins with a description of the teacher, students, and the urban middle school, so as to provide a context for understanding and interpreting the portrayed episode. It then goes on to describe the teacher's goals for the lesson and the unfolding of the actual lesson in a fairly detailed way. Each case depicts a classroom in which a culture has been established over time by the implicit and explicit actions and interactions of a teacher and her students. Within this culture, a set of norms have been established regarding the ways in which students are expected to work on a task (e.g., being willing to take risks, being respectful toward members of the classroom community, being accountable for exampling a solution method).

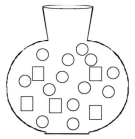

1. This jar contains Jolly Ranchers (the rectangles) and Jawbreakers (the circles).
   a. What is the ratio of Jolly Ranchers to Jawbreakers in the candy jar?
   b. Write as many ratios as you can that are equivalent to the first ratio that you wrote down.
2. Suppose you have a larger candy jar with the same ratio of Jolly Ranchers to Jawbreakers (5 to 13), but it contained 100 Jolly Ranchers? How many Jawbreakers would you have?

Figure 2. Candy Jar problems from the Case of Marie Hanson.

The cases illustrate authentic practice – what really happens in a mathematics classroom when teachers endeavor to teach mathematics in ways that challenge students to think, reason, and problem solve. As such they are not intended to be exemplars of best practice to be emulated but rather examples to be analyzed so as to better understanding the relationship between teaching and learning. In some case-episodes, like the Case of Marie Hanson, the cognitive demands of the task are maintained as the task is actually enacted; in such cases, various classroom-based factors can be identified which support students' high-level engagement with the task (e.g., pressing students to provide explanations, modeling high-level performance, scaffolding students' thinking). For example, in the Case of Marie Hanson the teacher consistently requests that her students provide explanations for their solutions and ideas and often allows students to use the overhead projector at the front of the room in order to do so publicly. In addition, the teacher also asks students to further explain ideas presented by others (e.g., "I asked if anyone could come to the front of the room and help April put the finishing touches on what was the start of a well-thought out strategy", "I asked the class if anyone had any questions about Jerry's work so far"). By asking students to do the explaining and sense-making she is sending the implicit message that she believes they are capable of such work and that she expects them to do it.

In other case-episodes, the cognitive demands of the task decline as the task is enacted; in these cases, other classroom-based factors – factors that serve to inhibit students' ability to engage with the task at the intended level – can be identified (e.g., the teacher specifies the exact procedures or steps that students need to follow). As such, the cases highlight a set of classroom-based factors that can support or inhibit student engagement with important mathematical ideas in an effort to help teachers develop a reflective and analytical stance towards their own practice (see Henningsen & Stein, 1997).

In addition to highlighting a set of pedagogical moves (i.e., factors) that support (or inhibit) student learning, each of the three more recent casebooks (Smith et al., 2005a, 2005b, 2005c) also highlight a key set of mathematical ideas in a particular domain (i.e., rational numbers and proportionality, algebra, geometry and measurement) and explicitly call attention to the ways in which pedagogy supports or inhibits students' learning of specific mathematical ideas.

Take, for example, the case mentioned earlier in which Marie Hanson and her students are working on the candy jar problems (Smith et al., 2005a). Ms. Hanson selected the problems to build on students' earlier experiences with ratios and has sequenced the problems in a way that helps students to develop increasingly sophisticated proportional reasoning strategies. As students work on the tasks individually and in small groups, the teacher closely monitors their work, noting the approaches they are using and the difficulties they are having. When it is time to share solutions with the entire class, the teacher selects students to present specific strategies. During the whole class discussion the teacher presses students to provide explanations, encourages communication between students, and asks questions that provide opportunities for students to make conceptual connections and analyze mathematical relationships. In the following excerpt from the case we see students trying to make sense of the incorrect strategy for problem 2 that has been presented by Jordan – "since you have to add 95 to get to 100 Jolly Ranchers, I did the same thing to the Jawbreakers – I added 95, so the answer is 108."

> Does everyone agree with Jordan?" I asked. Jerry volunteered that he did not because "the problem specifically said that the new candy jar had the same ratio of Jolly Ranchers to Jawbreakers and that in Jordan's new jar the ratio was almost one to one." He went on to say he didn't know why Jordan's way was wrong, but he was sure that he was. Still unfazed, Jordon asked Jerry how he did the problem. Jerry came up to the overhead and said that he went back to his old strategy of 1 Jolly Rancher to 2.6 Jawbreakers. He wrote his solution while he explained: "If one Jolly Rancher turns into 100 Jolly Ranchers, it must have been multiplied by 100. And so, the 2.6 Jawbreakers also have to be multiplied by 100." He put the pen down and appeared to reflect for a moment. "I guess I did the same thing to both numbers, too. But I multiplied. You added," he concluded.
>
> At this point, I invited the class as a whole to reflect on Jerry's new jar versus Jordan's new jar, "Which jar has the same ratio of Jolly Ranchers to Jawbreakers as our first jar?" (Smith et al., 2005, p. 34)

There are several noteworthy aspects to this excerpt. First, the teacher (Marie Hanson) has selected a student to present a strategy that is incorrect and she invites the class to take a position – do they agree with Jordan or not. Second, Jerry and

Jordan seem more than capable of carrying on a discussion without any intervention from Ms. Hanson. Finally, Ms. Hanson poses a question that builds on Jerry's observation regarding the new ratio and challenges the class to examine the two solutions using these criteria.

The Case Discussion

It is important to note that learning from cases is not self-enacting. Reading a case does not ensure that the reader automatically will engage with all the embedded ideas or spontaneously will make connections to their own practice. In order to learn from cases, teachers must engage in two types of processes: analysis and generalization. Analysis involves the careful examination of the case, focusing on the teacher's decisions and interactions with students in light of the goals that she wants to accomplish with respect to student learning. Generalization involves viewing the particularities of case-based episodes as instantiations of a broader set of ideas about mathematics, about teaching, and about learning.

Through our work with cases, we have found that readers of a case need to engage in specific activities related to the case in order to maximize the opportunities for learning. These activities include: solving and discussing the mathematical task on which the case is based, reading the case guided by a framing question, engaging in small and whole group discussions of the case centered on the framing question, and generalizing beyond the case to one's own teaching practice and to a larger set of ideas about mathematics teaching and learning. Each of these activities will be discussed in more detail in the sections that follow.

Solving the mathematical task. Having teachers complete and reflect on ways of solving the task that is at the heart of the case is critical to a rich and successful case discussion for several reasons. First, teachers go on to read the case with much more interest and confidence if they first engaged with the mathematical ideas themselves. Also, engaging in the tasks allows misconceptions that the teachers themselves may have to surface. Second, teachers are "primed for" and able to recognize many of the solution strategies put forth by students in the case. This way, teachers' understanding of the multiple pathways to solving the problems becomes strengthened and their perception of student thinking becomes sharper. Finally, Steele (2008) argues that working on the task and then engaging in a discussion of the case provides teachers with the opportunity to integrate their knowledge of mathematics with their knowledge of pedagogy and "create a more powerful learning experience than either activity might have afforded individually" (p. 15). Towards this end it is critical that teachers engage in a mathematic discussion that serves to support *their* learning.

In solving the second candy jar problem shown in Figure 2, teachers generally use one of four strategies: (1) factor-of-change (i.e., since there are 20 times as many Jawbreakers in the new candy jar, there must be 20 times as many Jolly Ranchers); (2) scaling-up (i.e., generate ratios equivalent to 5:13 such as 10:26, 100:260 using a ratio table or some other means); (3) unit rate (i.e., the strategy used by Jerry in the excerpt previously presented; and (4) cross-multiplication. During a discussion of the task, the facilitator presses teachers to compare the various strategies and discuss the ways in which different strategies are related. While this appears to be a simple task, it often uncovers misconceptions teachers have regarding the nature of multiplicative relationships (referred to earlier) and reveals their limited understanding of the cross multiplication algorithm. Research shows that teachers have difficulty differentiating situations in which the comparison between quantities is multiplicative rather than additive, tend to use additive strategies when multiplicative approaches would be appropriate, and do not recognize ratios as a multiplicative comparison (Post, Behr, & Lesh, 1988; Simon & Blume, 1994; Sowder et al., 1998). Hence problems like the Candy Jar task can provide an opportunity to closely examine the relationships between quantities and to consider approaches that would help one make sense of the situation (Boston, Smith, & Hillen, 2003).

Reading the case. Reading the case with a framing question in mind appears to lead to more "active" reading of the case and more thoughtful and focused participation in the case discussion. The framing question is intended to highlight what each case can best contribute to teachers' investigation of teaching and learning. These questions generally focus on identifying key pedagogical moves made by the teacher during the lesson and the impact these moves have on students learning of mathematics. The key here is not to focus solely on what the teacher is doing, but rather how the teachers' actions and interactions impact students' opportunities to engage in and learn mathematics. For example, as teachers read the Case of Marie Hanson, we ask them to identify ways in which her pedagogy appeared to support students' learning of mathematics throughout the lesson. Teachers are likely to generate a list that includes (but is not limited to) some of the following ideas: the teacher gained knowledge about concepts and how students think about them prior to the engaging students in the lesson; the teacher asked an open-ended question; the teacher was flexible – she did not decide on exactly what the homework would be until she determined what students would be ready for; the teacher monitored students' understanding; the teacher selected students in a particular way; the teacher used the "wrong" answer as an opportunity to expose the fallacy of an approach; and the teacher chose students wisely (she knows her students).

Discussing the case. The case discussion is intended to help participants analyze the mathematical and pedagogical ideas in the case. The question that framed the initial reading of the case can serve as a starting point for discussion. Facilitating a case discussion itself is skill that teacher educators need to learn. A complaint sometimes raised about case discussions is that they can be "all over the board", with the facilitator appearing to have only loose control over what gets talked about and how. Facilitators must listen intently to the participants and learn how to steer the conversation in useful directions. Toward this end, it is important for the facilitator to have specific learning goals in mind for the case discussion.

With respect to the case of Marie Hanson, a facilitator may want teachers to be able to learn how to interpret and selectively use various student-generated strategies (such as those presented by Jordan and Jerry) in whole-class discussions. To accomplish this goal, the facilitator would not only pose tasks that provided opportunities for teachers to notice how Marie Hanson used students responses, but would also listen carefully during the case discussion to the teachers' analyses of what occurred in Marie Hanson's class. A good facilitator would highlight and reinforce those comments that related to Marie Hanson's productive use of student responses, would acknowledge but not extend or elaborate those comments that took the discussion in different directions, and would summarize across relevant comments in order to emphasize the points that could be taken away from the case related to her goal.

Consider, for example, a discussion of the Case of Marie Hanson that took place in a content-focused methods course (Stein, Engle, Hughes, & Smith, 2003). The teachers in the course consisted of four practicing teachers working on their master's degrees (two certified for elementary teaching and two for secondary mathematics), and thirteen prospective teachers serving as full-time teaching interns while completing a Master of Arts in Teaching program (twelve seeking elementary certification, and one seeking secondary mathematics certification). During class, the teachers were asked to consider the following question: "What did Marie Hanson do to support student learning?" They were asked to back up their claims with evidence from the case in the form of paragraph numbers, which had been marked on the case itself.

Through this discussion, the facilitator wanted to draw teachers' attention to a set of practices that Marie Hanson employed in order to orchestrate a whole-class discussion in which the mathematics of the lesson was made salient to the students. In particular the facilitator wanted teachers to identify five specific practices in which Ms. Hanson engaged that supported her students learning: 1) anticipating student responses to the bag of marbles task, including the incorrect additive strategy; 2) monitoring students' work on and engagement with the tasks and noting who had used what methods; 3) selecting particular students to present their mathematical work such as Jordan; 4) sequencing the student responses that will be displayed in a specific order, such as beginning the second problem with an incorrect strategy; and 5) helping the class make connections between different students' strategies used and between the responses and key mathematical ideas.

Teachers discussed the question in small groups for approximately 22 minutes, followed by a 34-minute whole-class discussion, which was videotaped and transcribed. Each of the five practices was discussed at least once in the course of this discussion and at least 5 of the 17 items that came up in the discussion were specifically relevant to one or more of the target practices. The discussion of the practices accounted for about 33% of discussion time. While the facilitator recorded all the contributions made by teachers during the discussion, she probed and questioned more on the items that were directly related to her goals for the lesson.

Generalizing beyond the case. Following the analysis of each case, teachers are invited to engage in one or more activities in which the mathematical and pedagogical ideas discussed in the case are connected to their own practice or to other related ideas and issues regarding mathematic teaching and learning. According to Stein and her colleagues (Stein et al., 2000, p. 34):

> In order to "grab hold" of classroom events, to learn from examples, and to transfer what has been learned in one event to learning in similar events, teachers must learn to recognize events as instances of something larger and more generalizable. Only then can they accumulate; only then will lessons learned in one setting suggest appropriate avenues for actions in another.

This often begins immediately following a case discussion by having teachers consider the lessons learned from the case that applies to teaching more broadly. This helps teachers see particular events that occurred during the analysis of a specific case as instantiations of something more general. In addition, there are three types of connections to practice in which we ask teachers to engage: enacting high-level tasks in their own classrooms, analyzing their own teaching, and working on specific issues that were raised for them during the case reading and analysis. These activities are intended to invite exploration of and critical reflection on a teacher's own practice.

Returning to the example presented in the last section in which teachers in a content-focused methods course had the opportunity to learn about five practices for orchestrating a productive mathematics discussion, we consider whether or not teachers were able to generalize the ideas beyond the case. In an assignment given near the end of the term, participants in the course were asked to analyze the similarities and differences between the teaching of the two case teachers (of the four that had been analyzed during the course), to consider the implications of these differences for student learning, and then to discuss the lessons they had learned for their own teaching from doing this. More than half of the teachers in the course selected Marie Hanson as one of the teachers to be analyzed and made many statements in the "lessons learned" section to make it clear that they found the practices relevant not just to the case study teacher, but also to what they planned to do in their own classrooms. Thus it appeared that participants had begun the process of appropriating the practices from the case study teacher to their own instruction.

The Outcome: What Teachers Learn

An important question to consider is what teachers learn from their participation in these case discussions and related activities. Given the amount of time it requires to prepare for and conduct the activities described herein, the outcome needs to match the investment of resources. While our work in this area is ongoing, several studies we conducted provide evidence of teacher learning from engagement in cases and related activities. Specifically, the research indicated that the cases we have created have helped teachers develop a deeper understanding of mathematics content (e.g., Henningsen, 2008; Steel, 2008), a broader range of pedagogical practices (e.g.,

Hillen & Hughes, 2008; Stein, Engle, Hughes, & Smith, 2003), an understanding of the relationship between teaching and learning (e.g., Smith, 2003) and the capacity to reflect on and learn from the analysis of practice (e.g., Henningsen, 2008).

For example, in the study of teacher learning of the five practices described earlier, Stein and her colleagues (Stein et al., 2003) concluded that: (a) course participants recognized the five practices as a valuable aspect of what they had learned from the course; (b) course participants could learn to identify the five practices when they were embedded in various teaching contexts; and (c) some of the course participants had begun learning to apply the five practices to new pedagogical situations. Hence these studies provide evidence that teachers can learn important aspects of *mathematics knowledge for teaching* (Ball, Thames, & Phelps, 2005) through the analysis of cases and related activities. A key question that we are currently exploring is how teacher learning impacts their instructional practices and, ultimately, the learning outcomes of their students. Towards this end additional research is needed.

Problem Situations: Highlighting the Dilemmas of Practice

The cases created by Markovits and Even are what have been referred to as problem situations. The first cases were created for workshops with practicing junior high school teachers (Even & Markovits, 1991, 1993) and focused on the concept of function. Research on the use of these cases indicated that they raised teachers' awareness of students' ways of thinking (Even & Markovits, 1993). This was followed by the development of cases for workshops with practicing elementary school teachers (Markovits & Even, 1994, 1999a, 1999b). In order to enable teacher educators to use the cases in a more systematic way, a casebook was written (Markovits, 2003) for elementary school teachers. The book includes the cases, the analysis of each case (from the mathematical point of view and from the didactical point of view) and suggestions for the facilitator on how to work with the cases. The cases are now being used in courses for prospective teachers and in courses and workshops for practicing teachers.

Characteristics of Problem Situations

Mathematics Classroom Situations (MCS) are cases that focus on specific problematic teaching situations (Barnett, 1998). They are characterized as classroom situations involving mathematics, in which a problem, a dilemma, a debate, or some tension is involved (Markovits & Even, 1999a). They may be real events that took place in a classroom, or hypothetical situations, based on students' ways of thinking and conceptions as identified by research and personal experience. In each situation the teacher is invited to respond to a student's hypothesis, question or idea. The MCS are relatively short and do not include detailed background data, leaving it to the teachers' imagination to complete the background details according to their own experience. These cases invite teachers to suggest ways of responding to the student, based on their understanding of the student's thinking. Examples of MCS are shown in Figure 3 (Markovits, 2003).

All of the situations encourage teachers to elaborate pedagogical content issues such as: what does the student understand or not understand, how the teacher should respond to the student and which response will be the more efficient. Some of the situations also raise mathematical issues that might be challenging for or unclear to teachers. Thus the focus on such situations is also on mathematical content knowledge. For example, in the Division with Remainder situation (shown in Figure 3) teachers might argue that the student is correct and the equal sign should be used since the two answers are the same. Others, although understanding that the situation shows an incorrect placement of the equal sign, might suggest that the student is correct if he is in the lower grades of elementary school since he does not know how to divide without stating the remainder. The Height situation focuses on beliefs about mathematics as well, and also raises issues such as: the connection between mathematics and everyday life, the possibility of having two different answers--one in mathematics and one in everyday life, and the integration of everyday life into school mathematics.

The Missing Number
A student was asked to solve the following exercise:
$$35 - [\ \ ] = 12$$
The student told the teacher: I will do $35 + 12$ because you have here "minus", and I need to use the reverse operation, so I use the "plus."
How would you respond?

Division with Remainder
A student was asked to fill in the correct sign $<$ or $=$ or $>$,   in the following:
$$59 \div 42 \boxed{\ \ \ \ } \ 359 \div 342$$
The student said he will write the equal sign because:
  "$59 \div 42 = 1$ remainder 17
  $359 \div 342 = 1$ remainder 17
So in both exercises the answer is 1 and the remainder is 17, and that's why they are equal."
How would you respond?

Height
A student was asked the following question:
"The height of a 10 year old boy is 1.5 m. What do you think his height will be when he is 20?" The student answered: "In mathematics it will be 3 meters, because $1.5 \times 2 = 3$, and in everyday life it will be about 1.80 meters."
How would you respond?

Figure 3. Examples of core versions of Mathematics Classroom Situations.

The fact that MCS are relatively short might be seen as a disadvantage, since unlike the exemplars discussed earlier, no context information is provided. In MCS there is no information about the grade level of the student who produced the response, there is no description of what happened prior to the situation, there is no further explanation about what the student says or does, and there is no further conversation between the student and the teacher or between the student in the situation and other students in class. But all of these missing factors might be seen as an advantage, allowing teachers to think about the situation according to their own knowledge and experience. Teachers might argue about the grade level of the student and prepare different responses for students of different ages. They might suggest different scenarios which could lead to the present situation. They need to be very careful in analyzing the student's idea or question in order to understand what the student meant. The fact that the situation does not describe any action taken by the student's teacher forces the teachers to develop their own reactions. Thus, MCS put teachers in a situation in which they have to struggle with both pedagogical and mathematical issues, in which they need to be creative, to think in different directions, to try and understand what is "going on in the student's head" and to come up with several possible responses.

The MCS also have an extended form that includes responses that are presented as if they were given by other teachers. Some of these responses were actually suggested by teachers during MCS discussions while others were written by the author in order to highlight various issues with which teachers were intended to grapple. The teachers are asked to react to these "other teacher responses." Figure 4 presents responses that accompany the Division with Remainder situation in its extended form.

The first purpose of such responses is to enrich and expand the issues raised by the core form of MCS. Usually some of the responses raise issues limited to the situation presented, while others raise more general issues regarding mathematics teaching and learning. In the example of the Division with Remainder Situation (Figure 4) each of the first three teacher responses introduces a different possible mathematical mistake. The fourth response raises a dilemma: is the answer right if the student is in the third grade, but incorrect if he is in the sixth grade? In other words, does the correctness of the answer depend on the student's age? The fifth response is given by a teacher who knows the mathematics involved but does not understand what the student does not understand. The teacher in the last response puts the finger on the exact difficulty expressed by the student and uses small numbers and pizzas to explain the meaning of the remainder. In order to focus participants' reaction to the "other teacher responses" the following criteria are used (Markovits & Even, 1999a):
- Is there any problem regarding mathematical content knowledge?
- Does the teacher understand what the student does not understand?
- Does the teacher's response concentrate on the student's misconception?
- Does the teacher's response emphasize rituals? Does it pertain to meaning?
- Is the response teacher-centred? Student centred?

1. We will accept the answer. The student was asked to fill in the correct sign. He was not asked to explain but he added a reasonable explanation. Maybe if he would think in a different way, he could find the answer without using calculations. He could notice the numbers:

   $$59 \qquad 42$$
   $$359 \qquad 342$$

   The same number (3) was added to the divisor and the dividend. So we get the same answer.

2. The answer you have is correct, but you should solve the exercise like this:

   $$\begin{array}{cc} 1.17 & 1.17 \\ 59 \div 42 & = \quad 359 \div 342 \end{array}$$

3. The student is wrong. I will explain that the answer to this problem is:

   $$59 \div 42 = 1\frac{17}{59}, \quad 359 \div 342 = 1\frac{17}{59}, \text{ because we divide the remainder}$$

   as well.

4. A student in the second or third grade can fill in the equal sign, but a student in a higher grade should know that the division of 17 into 42 is not the same as the division of 17 into 342.

5. Before we check if the answer is correct or not I will ask the student and the whole class: Which one is bigger $\frac{1}{2}$ or $\frac{1}{4}$ and why. When the student will claim that $\frac{1}{2} > \frac{1}{4}$ I will ask which one is bigger and why: $\frac{10}{40}$ or $\frac{10}{20}$? The students will answer: When the nominators are equal the fraction with the smaller denominator is bigger. Now I will ask: Which is bigger $\frac{17}{342}$ or $\frac{17}{42}$? The answer will be, of course, $\frac{17}{42} > \frac{17}{342}$. The conclusion is that $59 \div 42 > 359 \div 342$ and thus the student's response is incorrect.

6. In my opinion the student does not understand the meaning of the remainder. Even if the student is in the third grade, it is important to work with him on the meaning of the remainder but with examples which involve small numbers. For example: $3 \div 2 = 1$ and remainder 1, $5 \div 4 = 1$ and remainder 1. I will talk with him about pizzas. If I have 3 pizzas and I want to divide them between 2 children or I have 5 pizzas which I want to divide between 4 children. Will the children in both cases eat the same amount of pizza? In both cases each child will get one whole pizza but in the first case each child will get another one half while in the second case only one quarter. I think that even a kindergarten child can understand this.

Figure 4. Extended form of the Division with Remainder situation.

Not all teacher responses can be analyzed according to all criteria. For each situation some criteria are more relevant than others and some additional criteria may be taken into consideration.

The second purpose for the use of "other teacher responses" is to involve in the discussion participants who might not feel comfortable in suggesting their own response. Some participants may be concerned that their own response to the situation might turn out to be a not very good one, and even may be criticized by other participants. Some might find among the "other teacher responses" the response they were thinking about but hesitated to say out loud. Thus the analysis of an "other" response may actually be an analysis of *their own* response which is done without the identification of the participant.

Work with MCS

MCS can be used in a variety of ways (e.g., as the focus of a one or two semester course, during a short workshop, integrated into didactic courses) with diverse groups of teachers (e.g., practicing teachers, teachers preparing to become mentors at the elementary level, prospective teachers in their last year of study, mixed groups of prospective and practicing teachers, groups of elementary school teachers and junior high school teachers as part of a program devoted to the transition from elementary school to junior high school). In addition, MCS can also be used during mathematics lessons in elementary school classrooms. The teacher presents the core form of the situation to her students saying that "a student from another class was given ..." and invites the students to react (Markovits, 2008). The purpose of using MCS with students is to confront them with the mathematical dilemma in the situation and to encourage them to explain the mathematics involved and justify their answers.

The core version of MCS together with the "other teacher responses" provides a variety of options in working with teachers. Teachers can be asked to respond to the situation in a number of different ways, each of which serves a different purpose:

Individual response – participants can be asked to respond individually (either orally or in writing). In this way, each participant has to decide how she or he would react before listening to other opinions. The individual reaction might then serve as a basis for the whole group discussion.

Small group discussion – participants can be asked to react during a small group discussion that enables the exchange of opinions among a small number of participants. In such settings, participants can disclose their thoughts without hesitation since they will be heard only by a few peers. During small group discussions participants can be asked to try and come up with one reaction that reflects the opinion of all or of most of the group members. Next, one member from each group can present the small group's opinion to the whole group, or several opinions if the members did not agree. Also the arguments can be shared.

Whole group discussion – during whole group discussions a variety of ideas are made public, thus providing the opportunity for the facilitator to move the discussion in different directions. But not all participants can (due to time) or will (due to disposition) explicitly express their viewpoints. Thus, some participants might become passive, waiting for others to express their opinion rather than offering to share their perspectives. Whole group discussions are not a threat to the participants who might hesitate to express their ideas. They can listen to others and compare the ideas expressed during the discussion to their own reactions.

Work with MCS can start with individual responses, move to small group discussions, and proceed to a whole group discussion. Following the whole group discussion, individuals could again be asked for their individual opinion. The individual opinions given prior to and following the whole group discussion could then be compared. Alternatively, a facilitator can start with whole group discussion, continue the discussion in small groups and then conclude by asking for individual opinion. The analysis of "other teacher responses" can be done individually, in small groups or as a whole group, either after the participants have given their individual opinion or after the discussion. Again, the participants can compare their individual opinion before and after the analysis of the "other teacher responses."

The time devoted to one MCS may also vary. Facilitators can deal with two or three different situations in one meeting or devote the whole period of time to only one situation. Of course this decision will dictate the depth at which the situation will be treated. When several situations are presented during one meeting they may have something in common (e.g., they all might focus on the number zero) or they may deal with different mathematical topics and pedagogical aspects. The form and depth of work with MCS is mainly a factor of the situation itself, the participants, and the facilitator.

Example from Working with MCS
The following example is drawn from a whole group discussion on the Height Situation (see Figure 3) that took place during a semester course focused on MCS. The participants were 20 elementary school teachers who participated in a two-year program designed to prepare mentors at the elementary level. The discussion was held during one of the first meetings. Prior to the discussion the participants were asked to indicate in writing how they would respond to the student who produced the solution presented in the MCS.

The discussion began by having teachers report on what they had written individually. Some teachers suggested that the student featured in the MCS was correct in giving two answers and thus separating mathematics and everyday life. Other teachers suggested that the first part of the student's response ("in mathematics it will be 3 m") was incorrect.

T1: I think the student gave a good answer.
T2: The answer was given by a bright child. He did not start from 0. He knows that the growth is not linear.

T3:   He explains, but I would not like him to fall into this mistake. Many students see two numbers, so they multiply, divide, add or subtract.

T4:   I am teaching both math and science. Although the thinking in the first part of the answer might be correct I would not accept it because not everything we do in math exists in life.

T2:   I think the child is trying to act clever. He knows this [the first part] is nonsense.

T5:   I think he gave a wonderful answer. He knows how to separate mathematics and reality. He gave a beautiful answer.

Class: Many calls of yes.

Although the participants were asked to consider how they would respond to the student, most of them focused on whether the student was right or wrong and continued to struggle with this issue without actually addressing the question posed. Even when T8 suggested weight as another context, T9 went back to the issue of whether the answer is correct or not as shown in the following excerpt:

T6:   I was a little disturbed by the separation he did. Like there is no connection between mathematics and reality. I liked the answer of T2.

T5:   What I meant was that he was able to separate between mathematics and everyday life in this case.

T7:   I am thinking of estimation here. Estimate the height of people around you.

Class: He did it already.

T8:   I would start like T2. But I would use weight and start with a baby born which is about 3 or 4 kilograms, and after one year his weight is growing about 3 times. And what will happen after two years? Then I will go back to heights.

T9:   … I think that the student has made a mathematical mistake here, by saying that it is 1.5x2=3, because nobody said that he grew at the same rate. So it is incorrect to say in mathematics it is 1.5x2=3. It is right but not with these data.

At this point, the facilitator tried to move the discussion toward the initial question that had been posed by asking teachers: "So what would you say to the student?" T9 indicated that she would say "that the ratio is not constant." This lead to a discussion of whether or not such a problem should be used during mathematics lessons since it could "mislead" students as shown in the following exchange:

T10:   The child might think the teacher is trying to mislead him. She gave twice the age, so what does she want us to do: to multiply by two.

T11:   It is like forcing the mathematics on something incorrect.

T4:   The child thinks "You tried to mislead me but look this is not true in everyday life."

T11:   There are so many situations in which we can use mathematics. I would not give a problem like this.

T12:   When a teacher gives a problem like this as part of mathematics lesson she has a purpose. If she gives such a problem and knows that the answer to it is that she shouldn't give such a problem, what exactly is her purpose?

T6:   To check if the children separate or do not separate mathematics from everyday life.

T12:   Why is this in a mathematics lesson?

T13:   I think that almost all of us, if we were in class we would tell the student that he gave a good answer, he separated mathematics and everyday life, I mean the student is thinking. To come now and say why you multiplied by 2, maybe now we teachers think about this, in class there is no time to think so I would say to him: Good for you! You know how to separate, it did not look reasonable to you so you used estimation, it's good you did not relate to the given numbers only.

The teachers continued to discuss the issue of the two answers given by the student. The facilitator did not interfere, but stopped the discussion after a few more minutes and presented a new situation. In the next meeting "other teacher responses" for the Height situation were presented and analyzed and the discussion was opened again.

The comment of T13 sheds light on the importance of cases in teacher education, suggesting that in class, in real time, there is not enough time to think about and come up with good answers to students' questions or ideas. Cases provide an opportunity for teachers to take the time to think deeply about a situation, to discuss a situation with other colleagues, to react to "other teacher responses" and to rethink the situation from several angles. By going through this procedure with many and different MCS, teachers can enrich their repertoire of situations and become more ready to deal with MCS when they occur in real time in their classrooms. Moreover, they become aware of the potential of such situations to enhance learning, and start looking for rich MCS in their own classrooms by turning students' questions or ideas into Mathematic Classroom Situations. The characteristics of a good MCS are captured in the reflection of a teacher at the end of course:

A good Mathematics Classroom Situation is a situation which questions the teacher's self confidence just for a moment or two .... no matter if what the student said is right or wrong. A good situation raises a dilemma, an uncertainty, and a need for discussion. The teacher has to think about the way he would explain to the students why this was so and so. The explanation cannot be immediate and just be pulled out as can be done with routine issues in which the answer is immediate and trivial. A good Mathematics Classroom Situation is not forgotten at the end of the meeting but it keeps rolling in the head and almost always is driven by a desire to discuss it with other teachers.

The Outcome: What Teachers Learn

Our research with practicing teachers showed that MCS enhanced teachers' mathematical content knowledge and pedagogical content knowledge, encouraged them to rethink their teaching, sharpened their attention to students' explanation and focused teachers' responses on what the student did not understand (Even & Markovits, 1991, 1993; Markovits & Even, 1994, 1993a, 1993b). The following are some excerpts of elementary teachers (prospective and practicing) who were asked "What is the most important thing you take from the MCS course?"

"I learned that it is not enough to know the mathematics. The teacher has to understand the difficulties students have and to be able to supply an immediate answer. Also the didactical courses should be changed by bringing in the class reality, same as we did here."

"As a teacher I have to be aware of the way students think and to try and find out what exactly he was thinking in a given situation so that I know how to respond. Also, I need a deep knowledge of mathematics so I can relate to the mistakes made by the student and to the correct mathematical facts."

"The teacher has to be very professional. He has to know a number of explanations for the same material, thus if the student has difficulties in understanding one explanation, the teacher can explain in a different way."

"I learned to look at the student at a different angle, to try and understand him and his way of doing mathematics."

"Following the situations we had in class I started to pay attention to situation that 'happen' to me when I am teaching in class. I started to pay more attention to the ways students solve problems, what I have to do in class, and how can I encourage students to reach the correct solution by themselves without my explanation."

DISCUSSION

Shulman (1986) argued that to call something a case is to make a theoretical claim – that is, that any story that is called a case must be a case *of* something. In this chapter we have attempted to explicate the essential attributes of a case and to explore two different visions of what the foci of a case can be – complex teaching practices (in the case of exemplars) and the problematic aspects of performance (in the case of problem situations). These two types of cases make salient the range of ways in which complex classroom events can be used in teacher education settings as contexts for developing the knowledge and skills needed to respond to the complexities and demands of real-time teaching.

A key issue in selecting a case is not the length, the context, or even the foci. Rather, it is the extent to which the material can engage teachers in analyzing authentic problems of practice that will help to build their capacity to make sound judgments in the classroom that matters most. Toward that end, the success of a case depends in large measure on the skill of the facilitator in highlighting the question, "What is this a case of?," thus stimulating learners "to move up and down, back and forth, between the memorable particularities of cases and the powerful generalizations and simplifications of principles and theories" (Shulman, 1996). Like an experienced teacher, a facilitator must decide "when to let students struggle to make sense of an idea or problem ..., when to ask leading questions, or when to tell students something" (NCTM, 1991, p. 38). The choices made by the facilitator have an influence on the direction of the discussion, on the depth and range of issues that are brought to the fore, and on the opportunities participants have to gain new insights, question current practices, and to continue to learn and develop as professionals.

Awareness of the vital role facilitation plays in the case method is evidenced by the growing availability of both specific and general materials for facilitators. For example, many of the casebooks described earlier (e.g., Smith et al., 2005a, 2005b, 2005c; Markovits, 2003) provide extensive materials for facilitators (e.g., identification and analysis of key mathematical and pedagogical ideas in a case, questions to stimulate discussion and reflection, sample responses from previous participants) that are intended to help them to use the specific case materials productively. More general advice for case facilitators is available from the experts from Harvard Business School (Barnes, Christensen, & Hansen, 1994) in a book aimed at helping facilitators "learn more about the skills and knowledge essential to case method teaching" and a seminar program "to help case method instructors become more adept in their craft" (p. 1).

Cases, regardless of how carefully they are selected or how skillfully they are facilitated, are not a panacea for all the shortcomings of teacher education. We must be aware of the potential pitfalls as well as the promise of these materials. Ball (2001) cautions us to remember that the analysis of cases (and other artifacts of practice) is intended to help teachers in their ability to make instructional decisions in the classroom, not to help teachers become more skillful at performing analysis for its own sake. Avoiding this pitfall requires keeping the work of teaching as a focus and making connections between the task at hand (analysis of a case) and the real work that teachers do (teaching children in classrooms).

CONCLUSION

Although only twenty years have passed since Shulman proposed "case knowledge" as a component of "teacher knowledge," and less than fifteen years have passed since the first mathematics cases were published, much progress has been made in integrating case methods into teacher education. Of course much more needs to be done. First, more cases are needed. Most of the cases currently available were developed for teachers in the elementary and middle grades. Few cases currently exist that focus on mathematics teaching in the early grades (PreK-2) or on high school mathematics. Teachers at all levels need opportunities to develop their knowledge base for teaching through critique, inquiry and investigation into the work of teaching--a task for which cases are particularly well-suited.

Second, we need to continue to design teacher education experiences that make use of case-based methods and other pedagogies and study what teachers learn from these experiences. According to Sykes and Byrd (1992), the selection and sequencing of cases with other elements of teacher education is a complex curricular issue. Ball and Cohen (1999) caution us to design professional education experiences so as to avoid "simply reproducing the kind of fragmented, unfocused, and superficial work that already characterizes professional development" (p. 29).

Finally, Griffin (1999) states that research on case use "is fragmented and fragile" echoing a concern expressed by many in the field that "enthusiasm for case use in teacher education comes primarily from advocacy" (p. 138). Hence additional research is needed to further explore issues of teacher learning (e.g., what do teachers learn from different types of cases and how they learn it) and how what teachers learn impacts their teaching performance.

REFERENCES

Ball, D. L. (2001, January). *A practice-based approach to teacher education: The potential affordances and difficulties.* Paper presented at the annual meeting of the Association of Mathematics Teacher Educators, Costa Mesa, CA.

Ball, D. L., & Cohen, D. K. (1999). Developing practice, developing practitioners: Towards a practice-based theory of professional education. In L. Darling-Hammond, & G. Sykes (Eds.), *Teaching as the learning profession: Handbook of policy and practice* (pp. 3–32). San Francisco: Jossey-Bass.

Ball, D. L., Thames, M. H., & Phelps, G. (2005, April). *Articulating domains of mathematical knowledge for teaching.* Paper presented at the annual meeting of the American Education Research Association, Montreal, Canada.

Barnett, C. (1991). Building a case-based curriculum to enhance the pedagogical content knowledge of mathematics teachers. *Journal of Teacher Education, 42*, 263–272.

Barnett, C. (1998). Mathematics teaching cases as a catalyst for informed strategic inquiry. *Teaching and Teacher Education, 14*, 81–93.

Barnett, C., & Ramirez, A. (1996). Fostering critical analysis and reflection through mathematics case discussions. In J. Colbert, K. Trimble, & P. Desberg (Eds.), *The case for education: Contemporary approaches for using case methods* (pp. 1–13). Boston, MA: Allyn & Bacon.

Barnett, C., Goldenstein, D., & Jackson, B. (Eds.). (1994). *Fractions, decimals, ratios, and percents: Hard to teach and hard to learn?* Portsmouth, NH: Heinemann.

Barnes, L. B., Christiensen, C. R., & Hansen, A. J. (1994). *Teaching and the case method: Text, cases and reading.* Cambridge, MA: Harvard Business School Press.

Boston, M., Smith, M.S., & Hillen, A. F. (2003). Building on students' intuitive strategies to make sense of cross-multiplication. *Mathematics Teaching in the Middle School, 9*, 150–155.

Broudy, H. S. (1990). Case studies – Why and how. *Teachers College Record, 91*, 449–459.

Carter, K. (1999). What is a case? What is not a case? In M. A. Lundeberg, B. B. Levin, & H. L. Harrington (Eds.), *Who learns what from cases and how? The research base for teaching and learning with cases.* Mahwah NJ: Lawrence Erlbaum Associates.

Even, R., & Markovits, Z. (1991). Teachers' pedagogical knowledge: The case of functions. In F. Fuginghetti (Ed.), *Proceedings of the 15th Psychology of Mathematics Education* (Vol. 2, pp. 40–47), Assisi, Italy.

Even, R., & Markovits, Z. (1993). Teachers' pedagogical content knowledge of functions: Characterization and applications. *Journal of Structural Learning, 12*(1), 35–51.

Grant, R. (1997). A claim for the case method in the teaching of geography. *Journal of Geography in Higher Education, 21*(2), 171–185.

Griffin, G. A. (1999). Commentary on "Learning from videocases". In M. A. Lundeberg, B. B. Levin, & H. Harrington (Eds.), *Who learns what from cases and how? The research base for teaching and learning H.L. with cases* (pp. 137–139). Mahwah NJ: Lawrence Erlbaum Associates.

Harrington, H. (1995). Fostering reasoned decisions: Case-based pedagogy and the professional development of teachers. *Teaching and Teacher Education, 11*(3), 203–21.
Henningsen, M. A. (2008). Getting to know Catherine and David: Using a narrative classroom case to promote inquiry and reflection on mathematics, teaching, and learning. In M. S. Smith & S. Friel (Eds.), *Cases in mathematics teacher education: Tools for developing knowledge needed for teaching* (pp. 47–56). Fourth Monograph of the Association of Mathematics Teacher Educators. San Diego, CA: Association of Mathematics Teacher Educators.
Henningsen, M., & Stein, M. K. (1997). Mathematical tasks and student cognition: Classroom-based factors that support and inhibit high-level mathematical thinking and reasoning. *Journal for Research in Mathematics Education, 29*, 524–49.
Herried, C. F. (1997). What is a case? Bringing to science education the established teaching tool of law and medicine. *Journal of College Science Teaching, 27*, 92–94.
Hillen, A. F., & Hughes, E. K. (2008). Developing teachers' abilities to facilitate meaningful classroom discourse through cases: The case of accountable talk. In M. S. Smith & S. Friel (Eds.) *Cases in mathematics teacher education: Tools for developing knowledge needed for teaching* (pp. 73–88). Fourth Monograph of the Association of Mathematics Teacher Educators. San Diego, CA: Association of Mathematics Teacher Educators.
Lundeberg, M. A., Levin, B. B. & Harrington H. L. (Eds.). (1999) *Who learns what from cases and how? The research base for teaching and learning with cases.* Mahwah NJ: Lawrence Erlbaum Associates.
Markovits, Z. (2003). *Analysis of mathematics classroom situations.* MOFET: Institute for Research, Curriculum and Program Development for Teacher Educators.
Markovits, Z. (2008). Is 1 1/4 the consecutive of 1/4? Mathematics classroom situations as part of math lessons. *Mathematics in School, 37*(1), 10–12.
Markovits, Z., & Even, R. (1994). Teaching situations: Elementary teachers' pedagogical content knowledge. In J. P. de Ponte,& J. F. Matos (Eds.), *Proceedings of the 18th International Conference for the Psychology of Mathematics Education* (Vol. 3, pp. 239–246). Lisbon, Portugal.
Markovits, Z. and Even, R. (1999a). Mathematics classroom situations: In-service course for elementary school teachers. In B. Jaworski, T. Wood, & A. J. Dawson (Eds.), *Mathematics teacher education: Critical international perspectives* (pp. 59–67). London: Falmer Press.
Markovits, Z. and Even, R. (1999b). The Decimal Point Situation: A close look at the use of mathematics-classroom-situations in teacher education. *Teaching and Teacher Education, 15*, 653–665.
McGinty, S. M. (2000). Case method teaching: An overview of the pedagogy and rationale for its use in physical therapy education. *Journal of Physical Therapy Education, 14*(1), 48–51
Merseth, K. K. (1991). *The case for cases in teacher education.* Washington, DC: American Association of Colleges of Teacher Education.
Merseth, K. K. (1996). Cases and case methods in teacher education. In J. Sikula, T. J. Buttery, & E. Guyton (Eds.), *Handbook of research on teacher education* (pp. 722–744). New York, NY: Macmillan.
Merseth, K. K. (1999). A rationale for case-based pedagogy in teacher education. In M. A. Lundeberg, B .B. Levin, & H. Harrington (Eds.), *Who learns what from cases and how? The research base for teaching and learning H.L. with cases* (pp. ix–xv). Mahwah, NJ: Lawrence Erlbaum Associates.
Merseth, K. K. (2003) *Windows on teaching math: Cases of middle and secondary classrooms.* New York, NY: Teachers College Press.
Merseth, K. K., & Lacey, C. A. (1993). Weaving stronger fabric: The pedagogical promise of hypermedia and case methods in teacher education. *Teaching & Teacher Education, 9*(3), 283–299.
National Council of Teachers of Mathematics (1991). *Professional standards for teaching mathematics.* Reston, VA: Author.
Patel, V. L., & Kaufman, D. R. (2001). Medical education isn't just about solving problems. *The Chronicle of Higher Education.* Feb 2, B12.

Post, T. R., Behr, M. J., & Lesh, R. (1988). Proportionality and the development of pre-algebra understandings. In A. F. Coxford & A. P. Shulte (Eds.), *The ideas of algebra, K-12: 1988 Yearbook* (pp. 78–90). Reston, VA: National Council of Teachers of Mathematics.

Richardson, V. (1996). Forward II. In J. Colbert, K. Trimble, & P. Desberg (Eds.), *The case for education: Contemporary approaches for using case methods* (pp. 197–217). Boston, MA: Allyn & Bacon.

Schifter, D., Bastable, V., & Russell, S. J. (1999). *Number and operations, Part 2: Making meaning for operations.* Parsippany, NJ: Dale Seymour Publications.

Schifter, D., Bastable, V., & Russell, S. J. (2002). *Geometry: Measuring space in one, two, and three dimensions.* Parsippany, NJ: Dale Seymour Publications.

Schifter, D., Bastable, V., & Russell, S. J. (2007). *Patterns, functions, and change.* Parsippany, NJ: Dale Seymour Publications.

Seago, N., Mumme, J., & Branca, N. (2004). *Learning and teaching linear functions: Video cases for mathematics professional development* (pp. 6–10). Portsmouth, NH: Heineman.

Shulman, L. S. (1986). Those who understand: Knowledge growth in teaching. *Educational Researcher, 15*(2), 4–14.

Shulman, L. S. (1992). Toward a pedagogy of cases. In J. Shulman (Ed.), *Case methods in teacher education* (pp. 1–29). New York, Teachers College Press.

Shulman, L. S. (1996). Just in case: Reflections on learning from experience. In J. Colbert, K. Trimble, & P. Desberg (Eds.), *The case for education: Contemporary approaches for using case methods* (pp. 197–217). Boston, MA: Allyn & Bacon.

Silver, E. A., & Stein, M. K. (1996). The QUASAR Project: The "revolution of the possible" in mathematics instructional reform in urban middle schools. *Urban Education, 30*, 476–521.

Silver, E. A., Smith, M. S., & Nelson, B. S. (1995). The QUASAR project: Equity concerns meet mathematics education reform in the middle school. In W. Secada, E. Fennema, & L. B. Adajian (Eds.), *New directions for equity in mathematics education* (pp. 9–56). New York, NY: Cambridge University Press.

Simon, M. A., & Blume, G. W. (1994). Mathematical modeling as a component of understanding ratio-as-measure: A study of prospective elementary teachers. *Journal of Mathematical Behavior, 13*, 183–197.

Smith, M. S. (2003). Developing teacher leaders in mathematics education. *Math & Science Collaborative Journal, 9*, 30–39.

Smith, M. S., & Stein, M. K. (1998). Selecting and creating mathematical tasks: From research to practice. *Mathematics Teaching in the Middle School, 3* (5), 344–350.

Smith, M. S., Silver, E. A., & Stein, M. K. (2005a). *Improving instruction in rational numbers and proportionality: Using cases to transform mathematics teaching and learning, Volume 1.* New York, NY: Teachers College Press.

Smith, M. S., Silver, E. A., & Stein, M. K. (2005b). *Improving instruction in algebra: Using cases to transform mathematics teaching and learning, Volume 2.* New York, NY: Teachers College Press.

Smith, M. S., Silver, E. A., & Stein, M. K. (2005c). *Improving instruction in geometry and measurement: Using cases to transform mathematics teaching and learning, Volume 3.* New York, NY: Teachers College Press.

Sowder, J., Armstrong, B., Lamon, S., Simon, M., Sowder, L., & Thompson, A. (1998). Educating teachers to teach multiplicative structures in the middle grades. *Journal of Mathematics Teacher Education, 1*, 127–155.

Steele, M. D. (2008). Building bridges: Cases as catalysts for the integration of mathematical and pedagogical knowledge. In M. S. Smith & S. Friel (Eds.), *Cases in mathematics teacher education: Tools for developing knowledge needed for teaching* (pp. 57–72). Fourth Monograph of the Association of Mathematics Teacher Educators. San Diego, CA: Association of Mathematics Teacher Educators.

Stein, M. K., Grover, B. W., & Henningsen, M. (1996). Building student capacity for mathematical thinking and reasoning: An analysis of mathematical tasks used in reform classrooms. *American Educational Research Journal, 33*(2), 455–488.

Stein, M. K., & Smith, M. S. (1998). Mathematical tasks as a framework for reflection: From research to practice. *Mathematics Teaching in the Middle School, 3* (4), 268–275.

Stein, M. K., Smith, M. S., Henningsen, M. A., & Silver, E. A. (2000). *Implementing standards-based mathematics instruction: A casebook for professional development*. New York, NY: Teachers College Press.

Stein, M. K., Engle, R. A., Hughes, E. K., & Smith, M. S. (2003). *Orchestrating productive mathematical discussions: Helping teachers learn to better incorporate student thinking*. Paper presented at the annual meeting of the American Educational Research Association, Chicago, IL.

Sykes, G., & Bird, T. (1992). Teacher education and the case idea. In G. Grant (Ed.), *Review of Research in Education, 18*, 457–521.

Zvia Markovits
Oranim Academic College of Education
Israel

Margaret Smith
University of Pittsburgh
USA

CAROLYN A. MAHER

3. VIDEO RECORDINGS AS PEDAGOGICAL TOOLS IN MATHEMATICS TEACHER EDUCATION

Teachers do not ordinarily have the opportunity to closely observe students' learning mathematics in their own classrooms. Studying well-chosen video recordings can serve as a seminal resource for understanding how students represent mathematical ideas and reason about them. Analyzing videos of students engaged in doing mathematics can be helpful to teachers in recognizing how mathematical ideas develop in learners as well as how valid justifications for solutions to problems are built by learners. Video episodes that illustrate various forms of student mathematical reasoning can help teachers become better aware of the unrealized potential of their own students' thinking.

This chapter focuses on the use of videos in teaching. It is organized in five sections. The first section provides an overview and rationale for using videos as pedagogical tools in studying learning and teaching - both from the perspective of using videos from collections and by making new videos to study one's own practice. In the next two sections, examples are provided of how video collections have been used as pedagogical tools for teacher education and professional development and for the study of learning and teaching. The next section gives examples of the use of an extensive video collection at Rutgers University for teacher education and provides an example of a secondary school teacher's study of videos of children's reasoning. In the final section future directions in the collaborative use of videos for teacher education are suggested and a summary for the use of videos as a tool for teaching is offered.

INTRODUCTION

Video recordings can be effective pedagogical tools for enhancing teacher learning in mathematics teacher education. Whether one studies the videos of one's own teaching or the teaching of others, video recordings invite conversations about student learning and teacher actions. They can illustrate a variety of classroom conditions for learning and teaching. In addition, video collections containing extensive sets of classroom teaching and learning are influential in mathematics teacher development.

Since videos can capture aspects of the emerging processes of learning, they can serve to engage prospective and practising teachers in new strategies for effectively teaching mathematical concepts to a range of students. Another significant feature in the use of videos for improving teacher practice is that videos make possible the study of teaching moves that play an important role in influencing learning outcomes. Teacher educators and prospective and practising

D. Tirosh and T. Wood (eds.), Tools and Processes in Mathematics Teacher Education, 65–83.

teachers can use videos as tools to study how students build new knowledge and how teacher actions affect student learning.

STUDYING SELECTED VIDEOS OF TEACHING

Particular circumstances that form the learning environment often establish the conditions for teaching. In studying videos, one can attend to student learning in different settings - individual, small group and whole class - and gain detailed knowledge across the milieu in which education occurs. Videos can reveal how student understanding is built by individual learners and collaboratively, and demonstrate how that knowledge is shared, as well as how it travels within the classroom. Studying video recordings affords teachers access to knowledge that might otherwise be unavailable. For example, students who are hesitant to engage in large group exchanges can be observed in videos of their learning in small group settings, where they may be more comfortable communicating and expressing their ideas with peers. Similarly, the contributions of students who are culturally and linguistically diverse and whose ideas when expressed are not readily recognizable to teachers because of cultural and language differences can be studied through video analysis. Thus, teachers, through video study, can gain knowledge of how students contribute to and engage in collaborative learning.

Video Study of Effective Teaching

Successful teaching draws on many components of teacher knowledge. While it is becoming increasingly recognized that knowledge of the content and how it is generated and structured in the discipline are fundamental components for quality teaching (Bruner, 1960), it is less clear how a teacher's pedagogical content knowledge is used effectively in classrooms (Shulman, 1986, 1987). Video recordings can capture how certain content is learned and how a teacher's knowledge of the subject for teaching influences the learning of that content during mathematics lessons.

Certain teaching techniques are useful in following the development of student mathematical knowledge. When used successfully, techniques such as questioning to elicit understanding and justification of ideas, enable the teacher to follow student learning as it unfolds (Martino & Maher, 1999). Studying video recordings of successful and unsuccessful questioning can be helpful in learning about effective ways to guide students in building on and extending their ideas. Moreover, studying video recordings of skillfully conducted individual interviews of children can provide even more detail into their thinking and reasoning and the role of skillful teacher questioning. As video recordings capture conversations between and among learners and the teacher, one can gain insight into the complexity of the intersection of a teacher's pedagogical content knowledge and the application of this knowledge in practice.

Video Study of One's Own Teaching

Video recordings are useful in studying one's own teaching. Teachers can evaluate whether or not certain interventions were beneficial and timely for student learning and reflect upon their practice. By studying video recordings of their own teaching, certain interventions can be reviewed and their consequences considered. Teacher moves can become the object of public discussion in which consideration of alternative approaches can be proposed and, under similar conditions, later tried. Depending on one's goals, video recordings are powerful tools for the detailed study of learning and teaching.

Teachers, after reviewing their teaching through the study of classroom video data, can become more aware of their practice. An example of the use of video recordings for this purpose is *video clubs* as employed by Sherin (2007). She used a video club format to study the professional development of a group of middle-school mathematics teachers who met monthly over a year to share segments of video recordings of their lessons. Together, the teachers observed excerpts of their video recordings. Prompted by a facilitator who asked them about what they noticed, the teachers responded by drawing attention to certain events. According to Sherin, this format evoked discussion and reasoning about certain events. She reported that teachers developed new ways of reasoning about student conceptions, thus showing development in the teachers' professional vision of students' mathematical understanding.

Using videos as a tool to evaluate and improve one's practice, teachers can plan and implement lessons, study the videos of the lessons, and analyze students' developing understanding as they take into account their role as facilitators in the process. Teachers can also reflect on the extent and quality of their probing of student understanding (Martino & Maher, 1999). Video recordings of lessons can capture the explanations teachers give to students and the responses they offer to student questions. In this way, teachers can observe and learn from their own practice and the practice of others in their community. By studying their lessons, teachers can become more aware of their classroom behavior. They can reflect on the moves they make and then consider and discuss with others whether or not certain moves are effective (Alston, Potari, & Myrtil, 2005).

In comparison with other evidence of students' learning, such as verbal statements and explanations, written work, and other forms of evaluation, video recordings offer the opportunity for studying subtle details of students' evolving learning. Obstacles and creativity in individual learning can be captured for later examination and review.

Video Portfolios

Another advantage of using video recordings to study one's practice is the potential for building *video portfolios* of student learning and teaching for later study. Included in video portfolios might be the collection of different kinds of data centered at an episode or a series of episodes of interest. These data sources may include: (a) video "cuts" of critical events of student learning; (b) video "cuts" of

67

critical teaching episodes; (c) associated written work of students; and (d) teacher and researcher notes documenting the mathematical activity that provide a 'trace' or pathway of the development of a mathematical idea (Maher & Martino, 1996a). An example of the use of video data to trace a student's cognitive evolution from pattern recognition to theory posing is contained in Maher and Martino (2000).

VIDEO COLLECTIONS OF MATHEMATICS TEACHING AND LEARNING

Collections of video recordings provide a database for careful analysis and reflection on student learning and on pedagogical practice. As these resources become increasingly more available through website access, links to storage areas and public repositories, mathematics teacher educators and professional developers can incorporate their use, taking into account language, cultural and context differences, into learning opportunities for teachers. A valuable feature is their availability for multiple viewings of consecutive lessons. Revisiting episodes of classroom lessons makes possible group discussion and personal reflection on one's own practice. It provides access to a variety of teaching styles in orchestrating classroom environments and the ways in which students respond to these. Multiple viewings provide for in depth analysis and reflection on the developing ideas and growth in conceptual knowledge of learners, as well as the obstacles they encounter in their learning. In this section, examples are given of projects that use video collections as tools for teacher education and professional development.

VIDEO CASES

A review of the use of video cases in general teacher education and mathematics teacher education specifically suggests that these videos are at least as effective as other methods (including live observation) in teacher training and are more effective than other approaches in helping prospective teachers learn teaching strategies and content (Grossman, 2005; Philipp, et al., 2007) (see also Seago, Volume 3, for a discussion of video cases as a means for practising teachers to develop as professionals). Video cases, specifically, make use of more advanced technology such as hypermedia in order to link certain video recordings to other artifacts. Examples of the use of video cases for teacher education and the study of students' learning are Derry and Hmelo-Silver's STELLAR System, Lampert and Ball's University of Michigan 'library collection', and Maher et al.'s longitudinal video cases described in the Private Universe Project in Mathematics (PUP-Math).

The STELLAR System

An example of an arrangement using video cases is STELLAR, a system that contains a collection of 11 video cases that are approximately 25 minutes long and indexed to a learning sciences hypermedia. The cases were collected primarily for use in learning sciences courses with students from multiple disciplines, including mathematics teacher education. Students using the system can examine which learning sciences concepts (e.g., transfer, cognitive apprenticeship) might be relevant to a particular video case. Also, for each learning sciences concept, students can link to all the video cases that exemplify that concept. These video cases were used as part of a problem-based learning (PBL) approach to instruction, in which the video cases are used as contexts for instructional design problems. A study of learning outcomes for prospective teachers in this PBL course demonstrated that students using video cases integrated with the online STELLAR system developed deeper understanding of targeted learning sciences concepts than students in a comparison class (Derry, Hmelo-Silver, Nagarajan, Chernobilsky, & Beitzel, 2006).

University of Michigan 'Library Collection'

Lampert and Ball conducted pioneering work in using video cases for teacher preparation and professional development by creating a video library in the domain of mathematics education. The library is a set of hypermedia materials based on their own teaching for an entire school year of instruction in third and fifth grades. The National Council of Teaching Mathematics (2000) *Principles and standards for school mathematics* were included in the hypermedia materials but, because of technical limitations at the time of development, the video and NCTM (2000) Standards are not cross-referenced (Lampert & Ball, 1998).

Much of the video used for professional development at the University of Michigan was collected originally for research purposes by Lampert and Ball to support the study of their 'reform-based' teaching. The resulting materials for use with teachers contain not only videos cases but also additional artifacts, transcripts, records of students' work, and their teacher journals. Using these video cases as a tool in teacher preparation, the prospective teachers were able to investigate how student ideas developed over the course of a year and how the teacher/researchers (Lampert & Ball, 1998) facilitated the process. An outcome of the project was a database for the sequence of classes, some of which were edited because of storage limitations. The organization of the collection was by day and unit of instruction, as compared, for example, with organization by mathematical concepts.

Private Universe Project in Mathematics

The Private Universe Project in Mathematics (PUP Math), *"Problems and Possibilities"*, is a video workshop for K-12 educators investigating how mathematics teaching can be structured to resonate with children's own mathematical ideas – many of which are surprisingly complex. The video cases of children's reasoning drawn for the video workshops come from the collection at the Robert B. Davis Institute of Learning, Rutgers University. Accompanying the six, one-hour video programs are materials for users (Maher, Alston, Dann, & Steencken, 2000). The Annenberg Channel broadcasts PUP-Math materials to schools, colleges, libraries, public broadcasting stations, public access channels, and other community agencies, 24 hours per day, 7 days per week, reaching 89 million households, 91,000 schools (with broadcasting licenses), with 19,000 total site registrations for workshops. Through the Annenberg Channel and national public television, practising teachers from more than 400 schools have utilized these materials and teachers from at least 43 states have participated in web-based workshops studying the video cases and the accompanying materials. The video cases highlight the impressive reasoning and problem solving of students in the first 12 years of the Kenilworth longitudinal study (Maher 2005, 2002), and shows the incredible potential of learners. Sample video case studies from the longitudinal study are accessible worldwide through the Harvard-Smithsonian National Digital Library.

VIDEO COLLECTIONS ORIGINALLY MADE FOR RESEARCH

In addition to these video cases, there are video recordings that were initially developed for research purposes beyond teacher self-study, but are now frequently being used in teacher education. Examples of these video collections include the Third International Mathematics and Science Study [TIMSS] (Stigler & Hiebert, 1999) and the Rutgers longitudinal study of student learning (Maher, 2005). These two collections illustrate diversity in setting and practice and include a broad range of grade levels.

TIMSS Classroom Study

The TIMSS Videotape Classroom Study was originally developed in order to better understand how teachers construct and implement eighth-grade mathematics lessons in three countries involved in the TIMMS, Germany, Japan, and the United States. The study is unique in that it was the first time video was used to collect cross-national data on teaching (Stigler, Gonzales, Kawanaka, Knoll, & Serrano, 1999). Also, included in the data collection are teacher responses to questionnaires and textbook pages and worksheets corresponding to lessons video recorded. The cross-national study produced 231 eighth-grade mathematics videotaped lessons used to survey teaching practices in these three countries. Studying video recordings of these lessons serve as useful windows into the practice of mathematics teachers in classrooms of a variety of cultures.

Longitudinal Study of Student Learning at Rutgers University

In a 20 year longitudinal research study, Maher and colleagues traced the mathematical thinking and reasoning of a randomly selected group of students from the low SES community of Kenilworth, New Jersey in the United States. The video recordings captured a focus group of students doing mathematics since first grade throughout their elementary, secondary, and (for some) tertiary schooling, along with follow up through graduate studies and current employment. The longitudinal design made it possible to explore the relationship of students' early grade mathematical ideas and insights to their justifications and building of proofs in later grades. Drawing from this data and parallel studies in school and informal, after-school settings, a collection of over 3500 hours of digitized video produced an extensive video library. Included in the collection are transcripts, tasks (organized by strand), student work, and researcher notes (Francisco & Maher, 2005). The various mathematical content areas addressed in the study emphasized counting and combinatorics, early algebra, probability, and pre-calculus, with a focus on the development of reasoning by student learners. The digitized video data are now housed at the Robert B. Davis Institute for Learning (RBDIL), Rutgers University.

VIDEO COLLECTION FOR TEACHER EDUCATION

The video collection at Rutgers University (described above) contains unique and valuable video data and artifacts such as transcripts of video recordings, coding schemes, students' work, observational and research notes, analytic commentaries) on how students build mathematical ideas and ways of reasoning over time in a variety of diverse school settings and across all grade levels, in several content domains. Drawing from the longitudinal and parallel cross-sectional studies in urban and suburban contexts, a collection of videos has evolved that captures the development of children's reasoning, early proof making, and how students build isomorphism between and among problems of the same structure (Maher, 2002, 2005; Maher, Muter & Kiczek, 2006; Maher & Martino, 1998; Maher & Martino, 1996; Maher & Davis, 1996; Maher, Davis, & Alston, 1992). This collection provides a useful resource for interdisciplinary teaching and research (Maher, 2005; Powell, Francisco, & Maher, 2003, 2004; Speiser, Walter & Maher, 2003; Maher & Speiser, 1997). The collection has the potential to be extraordinarily useful for mathematics teacher education.

The knowledge required to teach mathematics from the perspective of developing thoughtfulness and meaning in student learning requires that teachers have a deep understanding of the mathematics they are expected to teach and knowledge of the cognitive development of children in those areas. A model for use with prospective and practising teachers that has evolved using video recordings from the Rutgers archive involves: (1) teachers studying mathematics by working on strands of tasks; (2) teachers collectively studying their own solutions; (3) teachers viewing and analyzing video recordings of children working on the same or similar tasks; and, (4) teachers implementing and analyzing, together, the same or similar lessons in their own classrooms. In both undergraduate and graduate courses at Rutgers University, the videos are used to supplement classroom investigations, readings, and discussions. Prior to studying video data, prospective and practising teachers engaging in doing mathematics together, sharing their solutions to the problems, and learning about the contextual background and setting of the video episode they will be viewing. An example of this process is provided in the section that follows.

Doing Mathematics: Building Towers and Making Pizzas

As a component of teacher development, participants worked together on the following investigations: Building Towers and Making Pizzas. Following their collaborative work, teachers were invited to share their solutions to the problems. These problems were:

> Building Towers: *Build all possible towers four cubes tall when two colors of unfix cubes are available; then provide a convincing argument that all possible arrangements have been found.*

> Making Pizzas: *A local pizza shop has asked us to help design a form to keep track of certain pizza choices. They offer a cheese pizza with tomato sauce. A customer can then select from the following toppings: peppers, sausage, mushrooms, and pepperoni. How many different choices for pizza does a customer have? List all the possible choices. Find a way to convince each other that you have accounted for all possible choices.*

Studying Videos of Children Doing Mathematics

Following the activity of working on the tasks and sharing solutions, the teachers work together to study and analyze pre-selected videos episodes. As an example, consider the video, *Brandon and the Pizza Problem,* from Workshop 3, of PUP Math, in which nine-year-old Brandon explains the isomorphism between the 4-tall Tower Problem and the 4-topping Pizza Problem (Greer & Harel, 1998). See www.learner.org/channel/workshops/pupmath, Workshop 3.

THE CASE OF MANJIT, A HIGH-SCHOOL MATHEMATICS TEACHER

Manjit is in her seventh year of teaching in a suburban high school near Rutgers University. Over the years, she taught a variety of classes from remedial to honors-level mathematics. Last year, she began participating in off-campus courses as a component of a district-wide professional development program that emerged as a partnership between her school district and the University. She now is pursuing a graduate degree while teaching.

As a component of a counting/combinatorics strand on mathematical reasoning and justification (Workshops 1-3, PUP-Math), Manjit built solutions to the Tower and Pizza problems, and then viewed several videos from the PUP-Math Workshops. Manjit reported her ideas about this work in e-mail correspondence that is described below. She produced representations of her own and of the children's problem solving as displayed in the tables and drawings she provided.

Manjit's Description of Solutions to Pizza and Tower Problems

Manjit worked in class with her group on the 4-tall tower and 4-topping pizza problems. She reports below on her solution to each of the problems. She wrote:

> When I was assigned the Pizza and Towers problems, I organized my information in a table each time. For the pizza problem I found all the possible pizzas that can be made choosing from four different toppings by grouping the pizzas by the number of toppings each pizza had. The categories I used were pizzas with 0 toppings, 1 topping, 2 toppings, 3 toppings, and 4 toppings. When I started working out the problem I realized that I needed to account for 16 pizzas due to the binomial nature of the problem (because each topping can either be on or off and there are 4 toppings thus total number of pizzas equals $2^4 = 16$) I was able to convince my group that I had found all the pizzas by organizing all the cases by groups as shown in the table below. (See Figure 1)

Possible Pizzas	Pepperoni	Mushroom	Sausage	Onion	TOTAL
0 Toppings					1 pizza
1 Toppings	X				
		X			
			X		
				X	4 pizzas
2 Toppings	X	X			
	X		X		
	X			X	
		X	X		
		X		X	
			X	X	6 pizzas
3 Toppings	X	X	X		
	X	X		X	
	X		X	X	
		X	X	X	4 pizzas
4 Toppings	X	X	X	X	1 pizza

Figure 1. Manjit's solution for the 4-topping pizza problem.

> *When I was assigned the problem to find all towers possible that were 4 tall choosing from blocks of two colors, I again accounted for all the towers in a tabular format by controlling how many red blocks were used in a given tower. As I was making the table, (see Figure 2), I realized that the towers with one red block can also be thought of as towers with 3 blue blocks.*

Group	1st place	2nd place	3rd place	4th place	Group	Total
0 Red					All Blue	1
1 Red	X				3 Blue	
		X				
			X			
				X		4
2 Red	X	X			2 Blue	
	X		X			
	X			X		
		X	X			
		X		X		
			X	X		6
3 Red	X	X	X		1 Blue	
	X	X		X		
	X		X	X		
		X	X	X		4
All Red	X	X	X	X	0 Blue	1
						16

Figure 2. Manjit's solution of the 4-tall tower problem.

Manjit's Recognition of the Isomorphism to Pascal's Triangle

In describing the relationship of the tower and pizza problems and their relationship to Pascal's triangle, Manjit wrote:

> *As I finished making the table, I was able to see the fourth row of the Pascal's Triangle in the total number of towers for each category just as I was able to see this same row in the pizza problem solution. The solution for the towers problem is shown in the table (see Figure 3) below.*

```
                    1                        Row 0
                 1     1                     Row 1
              1     2     1                  Row 2
           1     3     3     1               Row 3
        1     4     6     4     1            Row 4
     1     5    10    10     5     1         Row 5
```

Figure 3. Manjit's representation of Pascal's Triangle.

Manjit's Analysis of the video of Brandon's Problem Solving

After studying the videos of Brandon, a ten-year old fourth-grade student, and his interview about his solution to the 4-tall pizza problem, Manjit remarks on Brandon's *aha*, and his recognition of the isomorphism between the two problems.

After we presented our solutions to the class we had an opportunity to watch Brandon's explanation of his solution for the Pizza problem, which involved coming up with all possible pizzas if you had four toppings available. In this clip Brandon explains how he made his table by number of toppings on each pizza. He uses a "1" to show the presence of a particular topping and a "0" to show its absence. Figure 3 shows Brandon's table that he made in the class. A month later Brandon was interviewed about his solution for the pizza problem and he recreates the pizzas by groups, which are controlled by the number of toppings in each group. He methodically lists his pizzas by zero toppings group which only has one possibility which he records by putting a "0" under every topping heading to show that topping's absence. For his one topping group he starts off with assigning a "1" to the peppers column and making the remaining three columns "0". He then moves to the mushroom column and puts a "1" under that column and "0" in the other positions. He continues this pattern until he has a "1" under each column as shown in Figure 4. For the two toppings group Brandon again uses a very systematic way of recording his pizzas. He starts off with "1" under the first two columns and "0" in the next two columns. For the next pizza in this category, he keeps the first column constant and now puts a "1" under the third column and puts a "1" in the last column. Then he puts "1" under both the second and third column and "0" in the other spots. Next row he keeps the "1" under the second column and now pairs it with the last column. Using this scheme he is able to account for all possible pizzas.

Brandon's organization of the possible pizzas	P	M	S	Pepperoni	Number of pizzas in each category
0 toppings	0	0	0	0	1 pizza
1 topping	1	0	0	0	
	0	1	0	0	
	0	0	1	0	
	0	0	0	1	4 pizzas
2 toppings	1	1	0	0	
	1	0	1	0	
	1	0	0	1	
	0	1	1	0	
	0	1	0	1	
	0	0	1	1	6 pizzas
3 toppings	1	1	1	0	
	1	1	0	1	
	1	0	1	1	
	0	1	1	1	4 pizzas
4 toppings	1	1	1	1	1 pizza

Figure 4. Manjit's analysis of Brandon's solution for 4-topping pizza

Manjit's Description of Brandon's Problem Solving

Manjit observed from the video of Brandon's interview, that he re-constructed his original solution to the towers problem. She describes how Brandon's representation of the pizza problem solution inspired him to re-organize the towers by cases, similar to that of the pizzas, leading him to recognize the equivalent structure of both problems, and build an isomorphism. She wrote:

When Brandon was asked if the pizza problem reminded him of any other problem he had work on, he replied that it did remind him of the tower problem he had worked on earlier. At this point he reconstructed all the towers by opposites as shown in Figure 5 below.

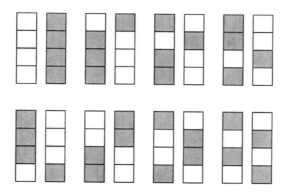

Figure 5. Brandon's replication of his first 4-tall towers solution[1]

Brandon then proceeded to regroup his towers by controlling the number of yellow blocks in each tower. The groups he used matched the groups he had used for the pizza problem, namely towers with 0 yellow blocks, with 1 yellow block, with 2 yellow blocks, with 3 yellow blocks, and with 4 yellow blocks. This is illustrated in Figure 6.

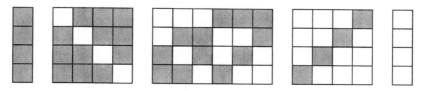

Figure 6. Manjit's description of Brandon's re-organization of towers from opposite pairs to cases.

To show that the two problems were essentially the same Brandon explains that the yellow blocks behaves like the "1" in his table for pizza problem and the red behave like the "0". He further demonstrates this by putting each tower side ways on his pizza table to show how all the "1" places match the yellow blocks and how all the "0" places match the red blocks. This correlation is demonstrated by the following diagram (see Figure 7).

---

[1] For the tower diagrams (Figures 5–8) shaded blocks represent red and white blocks represent yellow.

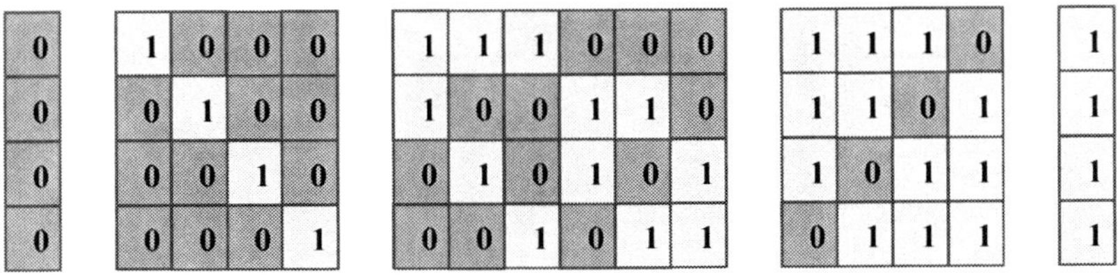

0		1	0	0	0
0		0	1	0	0
0		0	0	1	0
0		0	0	0	1

1	1	1	0	0	0
1	0	0	1	1	0
0	1	0	1	0	1
0	0	1	0	1	1

1	1	1	0		1
1	1	0	1		1
1	0	1	1		1
0	1	1	1		1

Brandon's organization of the possible pizzas	P Corresponds to the top block	M Corresponds to the second block in the tower	S Corresponds to the second block in the tower	Pepperoni Corresponds to the second block in the tower	Number of pizzas in each category
0 toppings	0	0	0	0	1 pizza
1 topping	1	0	0	0	
	0	1	0	0	
	0	0	1	0	
	0	0	0	1	4 pizzas
2 toppings	1	1	0	0	
	1	0	1	0	
	1	0	0	1	
	0	1	1	0	
	0	1	0	1	
	0	0	1	1	6 pizzas
3 toppings	1	1	1	0	
	1	1	0	1	
	1	0	1	1	
	0	1	1	1	4 pizzas
4 toppings	1	1	1	1	1 pizza

Figure 7. Manjit's rendition of Brandon's isomorphism between pizzas and towers

He goes even further (see Figure 8) by explaining that the problem could have been solved even if we assigned the value of "1" to the red blocks instead of the yellows (see Figure 8). He justifies this statement by rearranging his towers in the following fashion.

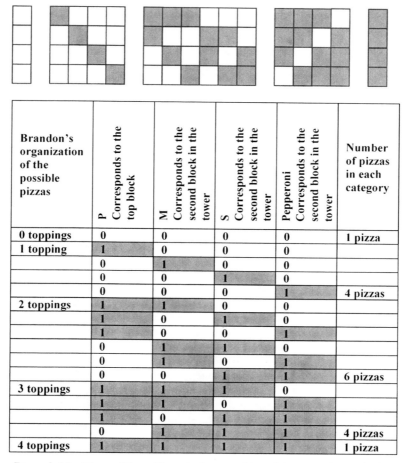

Brandon's organization of the possible pizzas	P Corresponds to the top block	M Corresponds to the second block in the tower	S Corresponds to the second block in the tower	Pepperoni Corresponds to the second block in the tower	Number of pizzas in each category
0 toppings	0	0	0	0	1 pizza
1 topping	1	0	0	0	
	0	1	0	0	
	0	0	1	0	
	0	0	0	1	4 pizzas
2 toppings	1	1	0	0	
	1	0	1	0	
	1	0	0	1	
	0	1	1	0	
	0	1	0	1	
	0	0	1	1	6 pizzas
3 toppings	1	1	1	0	
	1	1	0	1	
	1	0	1	1	
	0	1	1	1	4 pizzas
4 toppings	1	1	1	1	1 pizza

Figure 8. Manjit's rendition of Brandon's recognition of the equivalence of colours.

Manjit's Study of Video Data

In her analysis of the video of Brandon's reasoning, Manjit pointed out his use of notation, his organization by cases, and his recognition of the structural equivalence of both Pizza and Tower problems. Her detailed analysis of the video data enable her to recognize the depth of Brandon's problem solving, recognize the isomorphism he built, and relate her representation of the solution by cases to a row in Pascal's triangle. She writes as follows:

This explanation by Brandon for the Pizza and the Towers problems is a stellar example of an isomorphism that was invented by the student. This shows an extremely deep level of understanding of these two problems. I have watched many other students come up with brilliant explanation for their answers and they are able to justify their answers which in my opinion builds a strong bases for life long learning for these students.

It is noteworthy that the problem solving of a nine-year old student triggered such rich mathematical thinking from a secondary school teacher. By studying the representations, heuristics and ways of reasoning displayed on video recordings of young children, teachers and those preparing to be teachers, can, like Manjit, also think deeply about the rich mathematical ideas stimulated not only by Brandon's problem solving but their own problem solving as well.

SUMMARY AND FUTURE DIRECTIONS

Studying video cases and video data as a single video, video cases, or from large-scale collections can assist teachers to grow in their pedagogical content knowledge. The videos have invaluable potential for developing an awareness of how students use existing ideas and build new ones. Video research data can suggest new instructional strategies and ways of working with children and assist those who are learning to teach and those who want to improve their teaching. Certain teaching and learning episodes can be helpful to visualize abstract ideas, and provide access to phenomena and evidence that can help influence learning (Davis, Maher, & Martino, 1992; Derry, Wilsman, & Hackbarth, in press; Maher, 1998; Powell, Francisco, & Maher, 2003, 2004; Philipp et al., 2007).

While large-scale projects often collect large amounts of video data, often only a small subset of these data is relevant for addressing particular questions of learning, teaching and other areas of interest. Video repositories can store video that was carefully selected in a systematic way and illustrate particular critical events in learning and teaching. The events, when selected and edited, tell a story or make a point. A future vision for video use is for teachers and researchers to have access to video stored across multiple distributed servers so that they can contribute their interpretations and analyses of the videos. An outgrowth is to establish communities of collaborators who, together, have the potential to advance knowledge about learning and teaching (Goldman, 2007; MacWhinney, 2007; Pea and Hoffert, 2007). The Robert B. Davis Institute at Rutgers is working to build such a collaboratory.

A decade ago, Goldman-Segall challenged us to continue to grow through active engagement in building new meanings as we study videos and share our interpretations with others. Still worthy of reflection today is the notion that:

The learner of the future is a constructor of knowledge, a meaning-maker; the digital culture has made us more aware of our being meaning-makers. We are not only beholders and readers, we are creators. We create our truths, our meanings, through our points of viewing; and we do this while making new meanings both for ourselves and for other. However, we cannot make meaning from the plethora of choices we are offered each moment in an electronic environment if we are passive about exploring our own and others' point of viewing. The purpose of making our perspective clear is to invite others to explore how we see the world. In other words, our goal is to create a platform encouraging full participation in this wondrous exploration. We do not end our search by understanding our own perspectives; that is where we begin our journey. We build out from the center to fringes that may, in turn, become new centers. And we continue learning by looking for new perspectives that deepen and broaden our ways of looking at the world around us. (1998, p. 27)

In depth study of videos, through the establishment and use of new collaborators, suggests a new direction for research and practice in education. These collaborators have the potential of building new communities to share important video collections that support both basic research and professional development. They offer invitations for researchers and practitioners to interact and collaborate on research. They offer new ways to disseminate research and invite multidisciplinary perspectives from a variety of fields, including the learning sciences, developmental psychology, and mathematics education. Video-based technological advances hold great promise for the future.

REFERENCES

Alston, A. S., Potari, D., & Myrtil, T. (2005). An analysis of teachers' mathematical and pedagogical activity as participants in lesson study. *Proceedings of the Twenty-seventh Annual Conference of the North American Chapter of the International Group for the Psychology of Mathematics Education.* Roanoke, VA: Publisher.

Bruner, J. (1960). *The process of education.* Cambridge, MA: Harvard University Press.

Davis, R. B., Maher, C. A., & Martino, A. M. (1992). Using videorecordings to study the construction of mathematical knowledge of individual children working in groups. *Journal of Science, Education, and Technology, 1*(3), 177–189.

Derry, S. J., Hmelo-Silver, C. E., Nagarajan, A., Chernobilsky, E., & Beitzel, B. (2006). Cognitive transfer revisited: Can we exploit new media to solve old problems on a large scale? *Journal of Educational Computing Research, 35,* 145–162.

Derry, S. J., Wilsman, M. J., & Hackbarth, A. J. (in press). Using contrasting case activities to deepen teacher understanding of algebraic thinking, student learning and teaching *Mathematical Thinking and Learning, 9*(3), 305–329.

Francisco, J. M. & Maher, C. A. (2005). Conditions for promoting reasoning in problem solving: Insights from a longitudinal study. Special Issue: Mathematical problem solving: What we know and where we are going (Guest Editors: Cai, J., Mamona-Downs, J. & Weber, K.). *The Journal of Mathematical Behavior, 24*(3–4), 361–372.

Goldman, R. (2007). Video representations and the perspectivity framework: Epistemology, ethnography, evaluation, and ethics. In R. Goldman, R. Pea, B. Barron, & S. Derry (Eds.), *Video research in the learning sciences.* Mahwah, NJ: Erlbaum.

Goldman-Segall, R. (1998). *Points of viewing children's thinking: A digital enthographer's journey.* London: Lawrence Erlbaum Associates.

Greer, B., & Harel, G. (1998). The role of isomorphisms in mathematics cognition. *The Journal of Mathematical Behavior, 17,* 5–24.

Grossman, P. (2005). Research on pedagogical approaches in teacher education. In M. Cochran-Smith & K. Zeichner (Eds.). *Studying teacher education: The report of the AERA panel on research and teacher education* (pp. 425–476). Mahwah NJ: Lawrence Erlbaum Associates.

Lampert, M., & Ball, D. L. (1998). *Teaching, multimedia, and mathematics: Investigations of real practice.* New York: Teachers College Press.

MacWhinney, B. (2007). A transcript-video database for collaborative commentary in the learning sciences. In R. Goldman, R. Pea, B. Barron, & S. Derry (Eds.), *Video research in the learning sciences* (pp. 537–546). Mahwah NJ: Lawrence Erlbaum Associates.

Maher, C. A. (1998). Kommunikation och konstruktivistisk undervisning [Communication and constructivist teaching]. In A. Engrstom (Ed.), *Matematik och reflektion: En introduktion till konstruktivismen inom matematikdidaktiken* (pp. 124–143). Lund, Sweden: Studenlitteratur.

Maher, C. A. (2002). How students structure their own investigations and educate us: What we've learned from a fourteen year study. In A. D. Cockburn & E. Nardi (Eds.), *Proceedings of the Twenty-sixth Conference of the International Group for the Psychology of Mathematics Education* (Vol. 1, pp. 31–46). Norwich, UK: School of Education and Professional Development, University of East Anglia.

Maher, C. A. (2005). How students structure their investigations and learn mathematics: Insights from a long-term study. *The Journal of Mathematical Behavior, 24*, 1–14.

Maher, C. A., Alston, A., Dann, E., & Steencken, E. (2000). *Private universe project in mathematics series content guide: A professional development workshop series for K-12 teachers of mathematics.* Produced by Harvard-Smithsonian Center for Astrophysics and the Robert B. Davis Institute for Learning. Cambridge, MA: Smithsonian Institution Astrophysical Observatory, Available at www.learner.org.

Maher, C. A. & Davis, R. B. (1996). Children's explorations leading to proof. In *Proceedings of the Mathematical Sciences Institute of Education Conference on Proof.* London: University of London.

Maher, C. A., Davis, R. B., & Alston, A. (1992). Teachers paying attention to students' thinking. *Arithmetic Teacher, 39*(9), 34–37.

Maher, C. A., & Martino, A. M. (1996a). The development of the idea of mathematical proof: A 5-year case study. *Journal for Research in Mathematics Education, 27*, 194–214.

Maher, C. A., & Martino, A. M. (1996b). Young children invent methods of proof: The gang of four. In P. Nesher, L. P. Steffe, P. Cobb, B. Greer, & J. Golden (Eds.), *Theories of mathematical learning* (pp. 431–447). Mahwah, NJ: Lawrence Erlbaum Associates.

Maher, C. A., & Martino, A. (1998). Brandon's proof and isomorphism. In *Can teachers help children make convincing arguments? A glimpse into the process* (Vol. 5, pp 77–101). Rio de Janeiro, Brazil: Universidade Santa Ursula (in Portuguese and English).

Maher, C. A., & Martino, A. M. (2000). From patterns to theories: Conditions for conceptual change. *Journal of Mathematical Behavior, 19*, 247–271.

Maher, C. A., Muter, E. M., & Kiczek, R. D. (2006). The development of proof making by students. In P. Boero (Ed.), *Theorems and proof in schools: From history, epistemology and cognition to classroom practice* (pp. 197–208). Rotterdam, the Netherlands: Sense Publishers.

Maher, C. A. & Speiser, R. (1997). How far can you go with block towers? Stephanie's intellectual development. *The Journal of Mathematical Behavior, 16*, 125–132.

Martino, A. M., & Maher, C. A. (1999). Teacher questioning to promote justification and generalization in mathematics: What research has taught us. *Journal of Mathematical Behavior, 18*, 53–78.

National Council of Teachers of Mathematics (2000). *Principles and standards for school mathematics.* Reston, VA: Author.

Pea, R., & Hoffert, E. (2007). Video workflow in the learning sciences: Prospects of emerging technologies for augmenting work practice. In R. Goldman, R. Pea, B. Barron, & S. Derry (Eds.), *Video research in the learning sciences* (pp. 427–460). Mahwah NJ: Lawrence Erlbaum Associates.

Philipp, R. A., et al. (2007). Effects of early field experiences on the mathematical content knowledge and beliefs of prospective elementary school teachers: An experimental study. *Journal for Research in Mathematics Education, 8*, 438–476.

Powell, A. B., & Francisco, J. M, & Maher, C. A. (2004). Uma abordagem à análise de dados de vídeo para investigar o desenvolvimento das idéias matemáticas e do raciocínio de estudantes [An analytical model for studying the development of mathematical ideas and reasoning using video recorded data]. BOLEMA: *O Boletim de Educação Matemática* [BOLEMA: *The Bulletin of Mathematics Education*], *21*, 81–140.

Powell, A. B., Francisco, J. M., & Maher, C. A. (2003). An analytical model for studying the development of learners' mathematical ideas and reasoning using videotape data. *Journal of Mathematical Behavior, 22*, 405–435.

Sherin, M. G. (2007). The development of teachers' professional vision in video clubs. In R. Goldman, R. Pea, B. Barron, & S. Derry (Eds.), *Video research in the learning sciences* (pp. 383–395). Mahwah NJ: Lawrence Erlbaum Associates.

Shulman, L. S. (1986). Those who understand: Knowledge growth in teaching. *Educational Researcher, 15*(2), 4–14.

Shulman, L. S. (1987). Knowledge and teaching: Foundations of the new reform. *Harvard Educational Review, 57*, 1–22.

Speiser, R., Walter, C., & Maher, C. A. (2003). Representing motion: An experiment in learning. *The Journal of Mathematical Behavior, 22*, 1–35.

Stigler, J. W., Gonzales, P., Kawanaka, T., Knoll, S., & Serrano, A. (1999). *The TIMSS Videotape Classroom Study: Methods and Findings from an Exploratory Research Project on Eighth-Grade Mathematics Instruction in Germany, Japan, and the United States* (Research and Development Report No. NCES 99-074). Washington, DC: U.S. Department of Education, National Center for Education Statistics.

Stigler, J. W., & Hiebert, J. (1999). *The teaching gap: Best ideas from the world's teachers for improving education in the classroom.* New York: The Free Press.

Carolyn A. Maher
Robert B. Davis Institute for Learning
Graduate School of Education, Rutgers University
USA

83

MAKOTO YOSHIDA

4. EXPLORING IDEAS FOR A MATHEMATICS TEACHER EDUCATOR'S CONTRIBUTION TO LESSON STUDY

Towards Improving Teachers' Mathematical Content and Pedagogical Knowledge

Lesson study, a professional learning process that originated in Japan, helps improve teachers' content knowledge and pedagogical knowledge. Although the process of conducting lesson study seems simple on the surface, learning to conduct lesson study effectively is not an easy task. This chapter begins by describing the system and process of lesson study as it is conducted in Japan. In addition, an integral part of the lesson study process, kyozaikenkyu (instructional material investigation) is examined in detail. The merits of conducting lesson study and the important role it plays in the development of teachers is discussed next. Finally, ideas for conducting effective lesson study as well as the involvement of mathematics teacher educators in the lesson study process will be explored.

INTRODUCTION

Lesson study, called *jyugyokenkyu* in Japanese, is a process of professional learning that Japanese teachers engage in continuously throughout their careers to examine systematically their instructional methods, teaching content and curriculum, as well as their students' processes of learning and understanding in order to achieve their educational goals. One of the key features of lesson study is that teachers collaboratively study instructional materials and design a small number of *research lessons* that are implemented in actual classrooms with students. These research lessons are observed and discussed with teacher-colleagues and other educators to determine the effects of the lessons on student learning and understanding. This practice of lesson study has a long history in Japan. As a consequence, recent research on the instructional style of classroom teaching in Japan shows a significant shift from "teaching as telling" to "teaching for understanding" (Lewis & Tsuchida, 1998; Stigler & Hiebert, 1999; Yoshida, 1999).

The idea of lesson study was introduced to the U.S. from Japan in the late 1990s, and in 1999 a number of schools, districts, and teachers in the U.S. began conducting lesson study. There is no concrete data on how many sites or groups are actively engaged in lesson study in the U.S. at this time; however, the Lesson Study Research Group (LSRG) at Teachers' College, Columbia University has reported on their website that at least 150 self-registered lesson study

D. Tirosh and T. Wood (eds.), Tools and Processes in Mathematics Teacher Education, 85–106.

clusters/groups across 32 states, as well as approximately 130 school districts and 340 schools, are conducting lesson study as of May 2004.[1] Currently, lesson study is recognized as one of the most important professional learning approaches in the U.S. and national educational organizations such as the National Council of Teachers of Mathematics (NCTM) and the National Staff Development Council (NSDC) are promoting it as one of their recommended approaches to professional learning. In addition, groups such as the Mathematics Learning Study Committee supported by the National Research Council has recognized lesson study as one of the professional learning approaches that helps teachers develop proficiency in teaching mathematics as identified and recommended for students in order to advance and succeed in modern society (e.g., Kilpatrick, Swafford, and Findell, 2001). Additionally, the trend towards learning about and conducting lesson study is not only evident in the U.S., but also many countries in Asia and Europe have begun to recognize the importance of lesson study for improving classroom teaching and learning.[2]

Many of the ideas for professional learning processes, such as lesson study, place more emphasis on providing on-the-job opportunities for practicing teachers to focus on improving their classroom teaching and learning; however, use of lesson study with prospective teachers is not as evident. In order to improve lesson study at different stages of teacher education, reflection on the supportive role provided by mathematics teacher educators is vital. In this chapter, firstly the system and process of lesson study in Japan will be described. Secondly, one of the important parts of the lesson study process, *kyozaikenkyu* (instructional material investigation), crucial to improving the quality of learning, will be explained. Thirdly, the merits of conducting lesson study and what it provides for teachers is discussed. Fourthly, background for the introduction of lesson study will be provided. Lastly, using ideas for improving mathematics lesson study gained from U.S., lesson study experiences will be used to discuss the implications for how mathematics teacher education can contribute to lesson study in order to improve teachers' professional learning.

THE SYSTEM AND PROCESS OF LESSON STUDY: AN OVERVIEW

In Japan, lesson study is conducted in many forms and venues. Although the types of lesson study vary, they all involve three main activities: 1) establishing a lesson study goal; 2) engaging in a lesson study cycle to develop, implement, observe, and reflect on research lessons; and 3) reflecting on the whole lesson study process by producing a written report.

---

[1] The website is now moved to the new web address: www.lessonstudy.org. Unfortunately the data has not updated since May, 2004.

[2] Asia-Pacific Economic Cooperation is one of the organizations actively involves promoting lesson study. (http://www.criced.tsukuba.ac.jp/math/apec/)

Establishing a Lesson Study Goal

The first of the three activities that teachers undertake when conducting lesson study is establishing a *lesson study goal* (or a *lesson study research theme*). A lesson study goal is usually aligned with a school-wide research theme, a school improvement plan, a mission goal or a recently-introduced educational idea. Teachers who are involved in the lesson study process then conduct it with these goals in mind. This helps the teachers provide a systematic, coherent, and consistent education for all students at the school.

The process of setting a lesson study goal involves initial discussions among all team members of the group; these discussions are often held at the beginning of each school year. The lesson study goal is usually established by identifying a gap between the current state of student learning and understanding and the aspirations teachers have for their students, followed by a discussion on how to fill the gap. Teachers often look at past student performance data as well as observations and experience of working with current students in their classrooms. In addition, teachers often discuss how they want to close the performance gaps between students.

The process of establishing a lesson study goal is one of the most difficult parts of lesson study because it identifies the focus for educational improvement through lesson study activities. Lesson study goals are similar to hypotheses and action plans for improvement of instruction and learning in classrooms. In addition, lesson study goals are important in order to measure the success and effectiveness of lesson study activities, particularly the research lessons teachers conduct in classrooms (Fernandez, Cannon, & Chokshi, 2003, Lewis, 2002; Yoshida, 1999). According to Yoshida (2005):

> Having a [lesson study] goal is very important to planning a better lesson. How we want to connect the various goals relates to how to plan the lesson. Clear goals lead to planning more focused, logical, and coherent lessons with measurable outcomes; they also lead to a better understanding of and support for our students, as well as better discussion and evaluation of the lesson. Clear goals can help us evaluate whether we have achieved our objectives. All of this leads to better learning by students and teachers. (p. 33)

Since lesson study goals are similar to a research hypothesis established by a group of teachers, depending on the different forms and methods of lesson study, one group might come up with a different type of lesson study goal than another. For example, in a school-based lesson study setting at an elementary school, the lesson study group might choose a lesson study goal such as the following: "fostering students' problem solving as a development of their responsibility for learning" and investigate it in mathematics and other subject areas. However, in a mathematics-focused cross-district lesson study setting, teachers might establish a lesson study goal such as "fostering students' ability to express, interpret, and communicate mathematical thinking through mathematical expressions and equations."

Engaging in a Lesson Study Cycle

After teachers establish a lesson study goal, the teachers specify the subject areas in which they will investigate it (e.g., mathematics, science, etc.). Then the teachers will be divided into some subsets as teams or groups (e.g., grade level teams or subject area teams) and will engage in a *lesson study cycle* (see Figure 1).

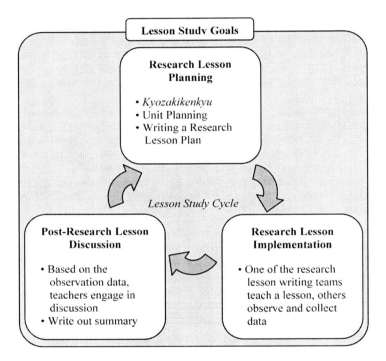

Figure 1. Lesson study cycle.

These teams are also often called *research lesson writing teams*. It is often said that an effective size for a team is 4 to 6 people. Each team discusses and chooses an appropriate topic by considering the current state of student learning. After the teams decide on the topic, a team of teachers engages in a lesson study cycle to develop, implement, observe, and reflect on a research lesson. Firstly, the team investigates instructional materials such as textbooks, teachers' manuals, state standards, manipulatives, etc. This process is called *kyozaikenkyu* in Japanese and I will discuss it in detail later. Then, a unit plan is developed and a detailed lesson plan is created. Secondly, the research lesson is taught by one of the team while the others observe the lesson and collect data. Thirdly, after observing the lesson the team engages in a post-lesson discussion to determine the effect of the lesson on student learning and understanding. The insights gained from the discussion are often incorporated into a revision of lesson. Fourthly, the revised research lesson is implemented in a different classroom and observed by the team members. Finally, the team engages in another post-lesson discussion and compiles all the results gained from the lesson study cycle experiences in order to write a detailed report.

Reflecting on the Process of Lesson Study and Writing a Report

After each research writing team has completed a lesson study cycle, the team writes up a summary report. Usually the report contains the research lesson plan and a summary of insights the team gained from the research lesson observation and discussions. Sometimes teachers include examples of student work and pictures from the lessons (e.g., students using manipulatives, different student solutions, blackboard organization). In order to write a comprehensive report of the lesson study cycle, it is important for the teachers to take detailed observation and discussion notes, as I mentioned earlier. At the end of the year a school might want to compile all individual teams' reports into one file and create an end of year report. The report becomes a portfolio of the team's or school's lesson study and an important resource for teachers to improve their practice in the future.

Different Forms and Venues of Lesson Study in Japan

Teachers in Japan use different forms of lesson study for different purposes. There are three main forms of lesson study in Japan. They are *school-based lesson study*, *district-wide lesson study*, and *cross-district lesson study* (see Table 1).

Table 1. Different forms of lesson study

	Description	Purpose
School-based lesson study (*Konaikenshu*)	• All staff members at a school are involved. • A school-wide lesson study goal is set up that aligns with the school mission goal or improvement plan. • Work done in several sub-groups under the lesson study goal.	• To create a common vision and strategy among staff members for educating students. • To develop and provide a systematic, coherent, and consistent approach to instruction to enhance student learning.

District-wide lesson study	• Intra-school lesson study model within a district. • Subject focused groups (e.g., mathematics). • A district wide research theme is set up. • Research lessons are developed with teams or individuals. • Teachers meet once or twice a month on 1/2 day professional development.	• To improve instruction and learning in the district as a whole. • To explore new ideas for teaching. • To develop communication among schools and exchange ideas.
Cross-district lesson study	• Cross-district or national-wide model. • Voluntarily organized groups of enthusiastic practitioners. • Research lessons are often developed by individuals and new ideas are proposed through the lessons. • Teachers meet once or twice a month on weekends or holidays.	• To present/propose new ideas for teaching and learning and engage in discussion. • To investigate curriculum (sequence and content). • To developing new ideas for improving curriculum. • To disseminate new ideas for teaching and learning.

Lesson study that is conducted as a part of *school-based lesson study* is called *konaikenshu* in Japanese. This type of lesson study is a whole-school research model that involves all school staff members. This is the most popular form of lesson study found in elementary schools (grades 1-6).[3] Some of the purposes of conducting lesson study in this form are that it helps establish a common educational vision and strategy among the staff members at a school as well as develops and provides systematic, focused, and consistent instruction to enhance student learning. Isolation of teachers in a school is a formidable barrier to developing a systematic and consistent school-wide improvement effort. The school-based lesson study model in particular provides a system and a framework for teachers to work as a unit in order to cope with this problem.

Another form or method of conducting lesson study in Japan is *district-wide lesson study*. Each teacher in the district decides a subject for their professional learning. Once or twice a month on a half-day professional development day, teachers meet in different schools in the district that are assigned in different subject areas to engage in lesson study. Depending on the district, the frequency of meetings varies. Each subject group establishes a lesson study research theme. Under the research theme, research lessons are developed with teams or individuals and the lessons are taught in the classrooms and observed. Since this is a district-wide lesson study setting, usually a large number of teachers observe the research lessons. In addition, many outside district educators such as university professors, school district subject specialists, and principals who are particularly interested in

---

[3] School-based lesson study is not commonly practiced in middle and high schools in Japan. However, many enthusiastic teaches engage in cross-district lesson study (voluntary organized group).

the subject are invited for the day.[4] Because district-wide lesson study is organized by subject groups (e.g., a mathematics group) and many teachers with extensive teaching and lesson study experience participate, the discussions tend to be serious and critical. The purposes of conducting this form of study are: 1) improving teaching and learning in the district as a whole; 2) exploring new ideas for teaching; and 3) developing communication among schools and exchanging ideas. New teaching methods and ideas for learning are often proposed through research lessons and this form of lesson study functions to help disseminate those ideas to all schools in the district.

Another form of lesson study is *cross-district lesson study*. Cross-district lesson study is usually organized by voluntarily organized groups of very enthusiastic lesson study practitioners. These teachers are committed to improving teaching and learning and curriculum in a particular subject area. Teachers often meet once or twice a month on days that school is closed such as Saturdays. Many of these groups are small (sometimes called 'circles') but some are fully developed as organizations that even host annual conferences which often include public research lessons. The Japan Society of Mathematical Education (JSME) is one of the well-established organizations that also host national and regional level conferences that include public research lessons. In addition, national university-attached elementary schools (laboratory schools) such as Tsukuba University Attached Elementary School, often host public research lesson events. These events are crowded with educators from all over Japan. Some lessons are taught in a large auditorium with nearly 500 people observing the lessons and participating in the post-lesson discussion often using panel discussion format. Some functions of this form of lessons study are: 1) exposing new ideas for teaching and learning that are proposed by educators and engaging in discussions; 2) investigating curriculum sequences and content through observing and discussing proposed research lessons; 3) developing new ideas for improving curriculum; and 4) disseminating new ideas for teaching and learning.

In Japan, these different forms of lesson study are used for varying purposes but each type is intended to contribute to improving classroom teaching and learning. In addition, teachers in Japan have, throughout history, created a well-established lesson study system and provided many opportunities for teachers to conduct or participate in lesson study activities. Yoshida's research (1999) reported that teachers in the western region of Hiroshima prefecture typically have an average of 10 opportunities per year to observe and discuss lessons that are developed through lesson study with other colleagues in and outside of their own schools. This means that for a 10 year teaching career, teachers will have the opportunity to observe and discuss an average of 100 research lessons. The well-established lesson study

---

[4] Principals in Japan are usually very experienced classroom teachers and they are often very experienced lesson study practitioners. They are expected to be instructional leaders of the schools and they often involve in lesson study activities with in and out side of schools.

system in Japan makes a fundamental contribution to change in and the improvement of the culture of classroom teaching and learning.

Lastly, in Japan, in order to support aspiring and novice teachers as they enter the teaching profession, as well as continuous education of teachers, lesson study is also incorporated into first-year teacher education, prospective teacher education programs, and master's degree programs for practicing teachers. In the first-year teacher education program, a first-year teacher is expected to work with a mentor teacher for about 60 days while she/he is also teaching a full load of classes (Shimahara & Sakai, 1995). In this program, the teacher often observes other teachers' lessons with the mentor teacher and engages in discussions on classroom teaching, student thinking and understanding, as well as the curriculum. In addition, the teacher conducts lesson study with the mentor teacher and teaches the lesson several times. Some of these lessons are taught as part of school-based lesson study, providing all teachers at the school an opportunity to observe those lessons and engage in discussion.

As for lesson study as it is conducted with prospective teachers, they are expected to conduct lesson study during student teaching. A student teacher is assigned a mentor teacher at an assigned school and collaborates with his/her mentor teacher to use lesson study to develop lessons. A university professor and the mentor teacher usually oversee the student teaching process and observe and participate in the discussion of research lessons.

To prepare students for student teaching, universities provide method courses that often focus on topics such as: understanding instructional materials; understanding points and processes of planning and conducting lessons; and understanding student thinking and understanding processes. For the master's degree program, students are expected to write a thesis on their research areas. For example, mathematics teachers in the program are expected to develop original mathematics teaching materials by studying curriculum, instructional materials, and recent research on the topics. They then implement the lesson in an actual classroom and collect data to investigate changes in student learning and understanding. Mentor professors and a few educators might observe the lesson and engage in discussion, similar to the way a lesson study cycle works. Data and findings from research through the lesson study project are compiled and a research paper is written. These graduate students are expected to develop deep content and pedagogical knowledge on the research topic, keen eyes to look at student thinking and understanding processes, as well as research skills to help them become the next leaders in curriculum development and teacher educators. (Isoda, Stephans, Ohara, & Miyakawa, 2007). Engaging in lesson study is an integral part of being a teacher in Japan and it is often mentioned by teachers as having contributed significantly to their professional growth (Fernandez & Yoshida, 2004; Lewis & Tsuchida, 1998; Isoda, Stephens, Ohara, & Miyakawa, 2007; Yoshida, 1999).

Kyozaikenkyu (Instructional Material Investigation)

As I mentioned above in the description of lesson study cycle, teachers engage in the investigation of instructional materials as a part of developing a research lesson. This process is very important for developing a coherent unit plan and research lesson. This process is called *kyozaikenkyu* in Japanese and it is usually translated into English as *"investigation of instructional materials."* Instructional materials here encompass not only textbooks, teacher manuals, and manipulatives, but a wider range of materials, including the course of study (standards), the educational context, learning goals, tools, research and case study publications, lesson plans and reports from lesson study open houses, and ideas gained from research lesson observations. *Kyozaikenkyu* also includes investigation of students' prior knowledge, learning experiences, state of learning and understanding, which makes it possible for teachers to be able to anticipate student reactions and solutions to the problems students undertake during the lesson. To do *kyozaikenkyu* teachers often study the scope and sequence of the topics that relate to the topic the team is developing as a research lesson. Mathematics is a subject for which students need to build upon their knowledge and skills based on a foundation of what they have learned before, so it is very important for teachers to look at the curriculum (e.g., textbooks) and understanding how the mathematical ideas students learn build upon other related topics they learned previously. .

To make this *kyozaikenkyu* process more concrete and easy to follow I present a hypothetical example based on my observations of a Japanese lesson study cycle conducted by fifth- and sixth-grade level teachers who plan a research lesson on finding the area of triangle. These teachers might start by looking at the textbooks that they are using at school in order to engage in *kyozaikenkyu*. In the Japanese fifth-grade textbook,finding the area of a triangle appears in the unit called "Area of Quadrilaterals and Triangles". By studying the unit, the teachers learn that the instructional sequence proposed in the textbook for learning about area of a plain figure starts with parallelograms and then moves to triangles, as is shown in the bottom half of Figure 2. After triangles, the students study the area of various quadrilaterals including trapezoids.

Some of the teachers in the team might recall learning about area of a triangle in a different sequence when they were students. These teachers might have learned about the area of triangles first, before learning the area of parallelograms or other figures. Also these teachers might remember the relationship between the area of a rectangle and a right triangle. If the teachers take the time to look at another textbook series, they might find this sequence.

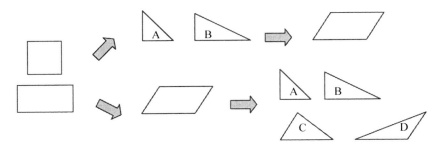

Figure 2. Different sequences for learning about area of different figures.

This type of investigation of textbooks provides an opportunity for teachers to engage in discussions of why one textbook uses one sequence and another uses a different sequence and how this affects student learning. Through this type of discussion, the teachers might find answers to their questions, but also might want to investigate more by reading research or resource documents related to this topic. For example, through the investigation, teachers might find that studying the area of a parallelogram first helps the students to find the area of triangles, such as triangle C and D, in Figure 2. Although the area of triangles C and D cannot easily be related to the area of a rectangle, it is easy to recognize that the areas of triangle C and D are half of the parallelogram. Also, because the students will have already learned how to find the area of a rectangle, square, and parallelogram, prior to learning about the area of triangles, they can relate all triangles, A, B, C, and D, to their prior learning. If we follow this argument, teaching the area of triangle before learning the area of a parallelogram might limit the students' ability to find the area of a variety of triangles. This discussion may also lead teachers to want to know more about how students learn area at different grade levels. For example, in Japanese textbooks, the teachers might find that students learn about the area of rectangles and squares in the fourth grade, the area of a circle after they learn area of triangles and quadrilaterals in the fifth grade, and the surface area of solids in the sixth grade. By doing so the teachers may start to question how the area of a circle is introduced similarly or differently from the area of triangles and quadrilaterals. Teachers may also wonder how students' learning experience of the area of quadrilaterals and triangles provides a foundation for learning about the area of circles. This type of investigation also helps to develop a coherent unit plan the research lesson will fit. One lesson alone cannot help students acquire a solid understanding of a concept and its application. Thus, it is very important for the teachers to plan a coherent unit before developing a research lesson. In addition, understanding vertical articulations of curriculum (not only within the grade level, but also across several grade levels) is very important because understanding the curriculum helps teachers have a very clear understanding of how mathematical ideas are presented instructionally and how this helps to meet individual students' needs (Takahashi, Watanabe, Yoshida, & Wang-Iverson, 2005; Watanabe, Takahashi, & Yoshida, 2007).

The curriculum is another instructional document the teachers investigate during *kyozaikenkyu*. For example, the Japanese Course of Study states that students need to develop formulae for area of various plane figures through investigation activities. In addition, this document describes how students need to find ways to figure out the area of new plane figures using what they have previously learned. Many teachers may have learned formulas for area of various plane figures by observing their teacher's demonstrations and simply memorized them without an in-depth understanding of them. In addition, for teachers, these formulae were most likely taught as something to be remembered or memorized and emphasis was placed on using them to find correct answers. Using *kyozaikenkyu* to study standards and textbooks is now a critical part of implementing new educational ideas for classroom teaching.

Lastly, in the *kyozaikenkyu* process, teachers have to consider the students' thinking and their processes of understanding. To investigate more thoroughly how students might think to solve a problem teachers often do the problems themselves and try to anticipate student responses, including multiple solutions and potential student misunderstandings and errors. Using these predictions, teachers think about what strategies they might use for leading discussions and how to help students compare certain solutions. For example, in the case of area of triangle, students might solve a problem in a variety of ways (see Figure 3).

By knowing students' anticipated solutions, teachers can use the first four solutions to show how mathematical expressions can be generalized as a formula. Teachers might also decide that the first solution is the one all the students in the class need to understand, including the lower achieving learners, because it is the most simple way to find the area of the triangle. In addition, teachers might notice that the first two solutions involve doubling original area while other two solutions require decomposing the original triangle and recompose into the shape the students already know without changing the area.

If teachers conduct *kyozaikenkyu* effectively, they are likely to acquire strong content knowledge that will aid them in helping students learn and lead to understanding and more advanced mathematics for themselves. In addition, good quality *kyozaikenkyu* helps to improve the teachers' planning, observation, and discussion processes in lesson study. As a result, it also helps to improve teachers' overall learning experience from lesson study. In order for lesson study to be a professional learning process, *kyozaikenkyu* has to be effective. *Kyozaikenkyu* is a difficult process even for Japanese teachers who have been conducting lesson study for many years. Yoshida (1999) reported that Japanese teachers or schools might say with confidence that they are conducting lesson study, but the same confidence is not there when asked about conducting *kyozaikenkyu* as a part of lesson study.

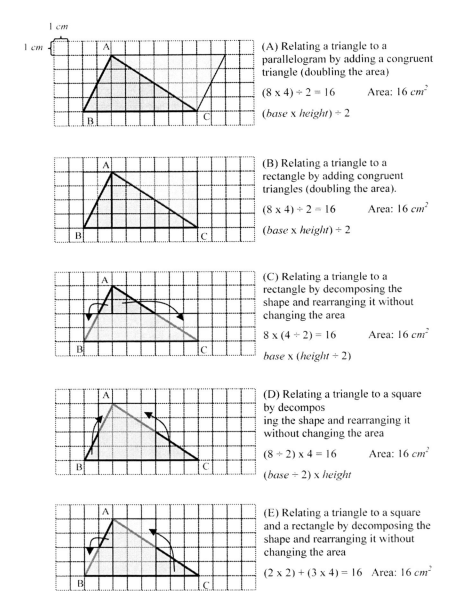

1 cm

1 cm

(A) Relating a triangle to a parallelogram by adding a congruent triangle (doubling the area)

$(8 \times 4) \div 2 = 16$ Area: $16 \ cm^2$

(*base* x *height*) ÷ 2

(B) Relating a triangle to a rectangle by adding congruent triangles (doubling the area).

$(8 \times 4) \div 2 = 16$ Area: $16 \ cm^2$

(*base* x *height*) ÷ 2

(C) Relating a triangle to a rectangle by decomposing the shape and rearranging it without changing the area

$8 \times (4 \div 2) = 16$ Area: $16 \ cm^2$

base x (*height* ÷ 2)

(D) Relating a triangle to a square by decompos
ing the shape and rearranging it without changing the area

$(8 \div 2) \times 4 = 16$ Area: $16 \ cm^2$

(*base* ÷ 2) x *height*

(E) Relating a triangle to a square and a rectangle by decomposing the shape and rearranging it without changing the area

$(2 \times 2) + (3 \times 4) = 16$ Area: $16 \ cm^2$

Figure 3. Different students' anticipated solutions for area of a triangle.

WHY LESSON STUDY? WHAT DOES IT PROVIDE?

The question might be asked: why are many researchers and educators recommending lesson study? One of the obvious reasons is that it enhances collaboration between teachers to create a learning community. The idea of collaboration in professional learning is not new. In fact many programs introduced as *powerful design* by NSDC all share the quality of collaboration to develop learning communities (2004).[5] Collaboration helps to reduce isolation of teachers that commonly exists in U.S. schools and develop a coherent, consistent, and systematic approach to improving instruction and learning in schools. It also helps teachers to share their knowledge (e.g., content and pedagogy) and experience as well as provide them opportunities to influence each other to develop professionalism. Moreover, collaborative interactions with other teachers help the teachers to reflect on their own subject content and pedagogical knowledge. Good collaborative effort in a learning community will help teachers become life-long learners and problem solvers. In addition, it also helps teachers become independent thinkers and autonomous learners by acquiring knowledge and experience from other collaborators.

Through the collaboration of teachers, lesson study establishes a learning community that is led by teachers. Teachers can own the professional learning and actively be involved in the process of instructional change and curriculum development. The traditional professional development approach often puts teachers as passive recipients of knowledge and skills and they are asked to figure out how to use the knowledge on their own. According to Wilms (2003), this type of professional development system was based on a mass-production system that education in the U.S. inherited from industry a century ago and it is a cultural barrier (habitual pattern of behaviour) to improving education.[6]

Lesson study also provides a good structure or system for teachers to collaborate and investigate how to improve classroom instruction and learning. Teachers might learn new educational ideas from workshops or conferences such as problem solving and differentiating instruction. They can investigate the effect of new instructional ideas for improving student learning with colleagues by planning, observing, and discussing a research lesson through lesson study. Because planning and teaching lessons are the centre of lesson study activities, it is natural for teachers to engage in the process. Lesson study activities provide a more concrete

---

[5] Few examples of the powerful design that NSDC promoting are: Action Research, Critical Friends, Peer Coaching, and Mentoring. Standards such as Principles and Standards for School Mathematics (2000) by NCTM and National Board for Professional Teaching Standards (2002) are also enthusiastically promoting teacher collaboration.

[6] Companies successfully transformed from mass-production model to continuously improving work system that are lead by workers are remaining competitive edge against successful foreign companies. The same principles are found in lesson study and it might provide great impact on improving education in public schools that are also modelled after the mass-productions model.

approach to improving their practice. In addition, the structure of lesson study and the collaboration process create a systematic way for teachers to pass on a generation of wisdom and experience to a new generation of teachers.

Another feature of lesson study is that it puts students at the heart of the professional learning activity. Improving student learning and understanding is the focus of lesson study, so it is important for the teachers to have as many opportunities as possible to carefully observe and discuss changes in student learning and understanding through classroom practices. Taking time to observe and reflect on how students learn and understand (and sometimes misunderstand) is a very important exercise in order for the teachers to develop the ability to meet the individual needs of students. Moreover, trying to figure out what type of instruction provides better results on student learning with colleagues on many occasions in your career is bound to help teachers improve instruction.

Lesson study is a form of research that teachers can conduct collaboratively. To conduct lesson study, teachers set a lesson study goal or research lesson theme. Then the teachers develop a research lesson plan to achieve the goal. The research lesson is the hypothesis and action plan and it is implemented in the classroom with students in order to determine the effect of the lesson on student learning. To do so the teachers collect data through their observation of the lesson and it is analysed and discussed during the post-lesson discussion. By practicing lesson study teachers can therefore develop research skills over the course of their careers that helps them acquire the ability to look at the student learning and understanding processes in the classroom. In addition, lesson study will help them develop a more constructive and systematic approach to improve their teaching practice.

Finally, lesson study provides teachers with opportunities to contribute to curriculum development. For example, teachers can investigate ways to introduce new topics recently added to their curriculum, use of different manipulatives, sequences of curriculum, and use of different instructional methods through lesson study. Because of the existence of lesson study, mathematics textbooks in Japan are written by experienced lesson study practitioners (teachers), mathematics educators, and mathematicians and they contain generations of their wisdom and experience that has been accumulated through a long history of participation in lesson study.[7]

INTRODUCING JAPANESE LESSON STUDY TO THE U.S.

No systematic studies about Japanese teachers' professional development were conducted in Japan or the U.S. until the late 1990s. However, there have been

---

[7] English translated version of a Japanese elementary textbook series, Tokyo Shoseki's Mathematics for Elementary School (Grades 1-6), are now available at www.globaledresroouces.com. Many lesson study practitioners in the U.S. are using it as part of *kyozaikenkyu* to improve their content and pedagogical knowledge in elementary and middle school mathematics in the U.S.

several studies that have looked at how Japanese teachers learn 'on the job' (e.g., Shimahara and Sakai, 1995), and some researchers have pointed out the importance or uniqueness of lesson study[8] (e.g., Sato, 1993; Shimahara 1991; Stigler & Stevenson, 1992). For example, Stevenson and Stigler (1992) pointed out that:

> Asian [Japanese and Chinese] lessons are so well crafted that one can notice a very systematic effort to pass on the accumulated wisdom of teaching practice to each new generation of teachers and to keep perfecting that practice by providing teachers the opportunities to continually learn from one another. (p. 46)

Toward the end of the 1990s, three important research documents were published that led to the beginning of the movement to bring lesson study to the U.S. Lewis and Tsuchida (1998) reported that in Japan research lessons conducted in classrooms made a significant contribution to changing elementary school science instruction and student learning. This article described the system and process used to conduct research lessons and provided some examples of the merits of lesson study. For example, Lewis and Tsuchida explained that lesson study (and research lessons) improves classroom practice and infuses new content and instructional methods.[9] It also provides a system for teachers to collaborate, connect classroom practice and broader goals such as school improvement goals, and honours the teachers and role of classroom teaching by placing them at the heart of the professional learning.

Stigler and Hiebert (1999), lead researchers of the Third International Mathematics and Science Study (TIMSS) video study, made recommendations regarding educational reform in the U.S. They concluded that in spite of a decade of reform efforts in the U.S. there was not much evidence of significant change in classroom teaching. Moreover, the majority of instruction was still found to be focused on a very narrow band of procedural skills followed by practicing the skills with actual problems. However, the researchers found that Japanese lessons better exemplified current reform ideas than did U.S. lessons, and because Japanese teachers made instructional changes through the process of lesson study, they recommended that educators and policy makers rethink the existing approaches to professional development in the U.S. Additionally, the researchers pointed out that implementing professional development that is collaborative, systematic, and for

---

[8] The word lesson study was not use until Stigler and Hiebert's book was published. Sato and Shimahara used terms such as "in-house workshops" and "informal in-service workshops" and "voluntary study groups" to describe lesson study system in Japan.

[9] At the beginning of introduction of lesson study in the U.S. may different words were used to describe it. As more publication started to come out researches and educators start using *lesson study* as a whole professional learning process and *research lessons* as the lessons developed through lesson study process.

which classroom instruction and student learning is the central focus (like lesson study in Japan), is needed.

Yoshida's (1999) ethnographic research project on elementary school mathematics lesson study in Japan provided a very descriptive and comprehensive view of how the Japanese teachers conduct lesson study, what kind of supportive structures exist, and what lesson study provides for the teachers and students. His insights from the process of conducting lesson study include, for example, how the Japanese teachers collaborated in order to develop a research lesson, what they discussed during the process, and what they looked at in order to understand how students were constructing understanding through the research lesson. These insights were important for educators and researchers to understand how teachers work collaboratively during lesson study.

At the same the time as these three seminal documents were published, there was another book that contributed significantly, although more indirectly, to the lesson study movement in the U.S. This was the book by Ma (1999). Although the book does not address lesson study in particular, it does describe that teachers in China often meet as a group to study the textbook they are using to teach; this practice allows teachers an opportunity to develop strong content and pedagogical knowledge by studying instructional materials together, sharing each other's experiences, and engaging in discussion on classroom instruction and learning. Results from this research and Chinese students' superior performance in international studies (e.g., Stevenson and Stigler, 1992) brought to the fore the need for improving the mathematics content knowledge of elementary and middle-school teachers and the need for changes in mathematics teacher preparation, professional development, and mathematics education in general (e.g., curriculum) in the U.S.

To summarize, in the U.S., the majority of lesson study sites are focused on the topic of mathematics; however, there is a growing interest in expanding lesson study to other subject areas. Every year more and more new lesson study sites are experimenting conducting lesson study in new subject areas. This is due, in part, because lesson study was first introduced by TIMSS researchers, Stigler and Hiebert (1998), who focused on mathematics and science. It was also fuelled by the general and political concern about the performance of U.S. students in mathematics and science compared to students in other nations. In Japan, however, lesson study is conducted on other topics, such as language arts, science, social studies, even other subjects such as gym, art, and music (Lewis & Tuschida, 1998; Yoshida, 1999).

IDEAS FOR INVOLVEMENT OF MATHMATICS TEACHER EDUCATORS' FOR IMPROVING LESSON STUDY

The system and process of lesson study looks very simple at first glance and the merits of conducting lesson study seem convincing and promising for improving mathematical classroom instruction and student learning. However, conducting lesson study effectively and producing a good outcome is not an easy task. In fact, as the lesson study movement expands in the U.S., uncertainties have begun to emerge about how lesson study can effectively improve classroom practice, teacher content knowledge, teacher abilities to observe student thinking and learning, and their ability to promote student understanding. Educators and researchers are also trying to figure out what support mechanisms are necessary in order for teachers to conduct lesson study and sustain the professional learning for years to come.

One of the most important aspects of lesson study that makes it effective in Japan is its role as a vehicle to foster teachers' mathematical content knowledge and pedagogical knowledge by considering student learning. Imagine a picture of a team of teachers conducting lesson study without strong mathematical content knowledge. What kind of outcome can be expected from this lesson study? The team went through the steps of a lesson study cycle, have a research lesson plan and have implemented it in the classroom. These teachers might say they enjoyed the collaboration and aspect of observing a lesson they planned in the classroom. However, what can we say about what they learned from conducting lesson study? It is conceivable that such a group might never be engaged in deep discussions about the mathematics that they taught and how or what exactly their students learned. There are many reported cases of teachers looking only at surface improvement in lessons, such as planning a motivational introduction to the lesson, using interesting student manipulatives, and creating representations to help students memorize procedures. We need to recognize that lesson study in the U.S. is still in the early stages of implementation and problems of effectiveness still exist at a large number of lesson study sites (Takahashi and Yoshida, 2004; Fernandez, Cannon, Chokshi, 2003).

NCTM's *Principles and Standards for School Mathematics* (2000) and their new document called *Curriculum Focal Points for Pre-kindergarten through Grade 8 Mathematics* (NCTM, 2006) suggests that teachers should focus on student learning of a small number of significant mathematical topics in each grade level. These topics are chosen because they will help students build their knowledge base of the mathematics necessary to understand in order to learn more advanced mathematics in later grades. In addition, the Mathematics Learning Study Committee (MLSC) at the National Research Council published a book entitled *Adding It Up* (Kilpatrick, Swafford, & Findell, 2001) to introduce a vision of student mathematical proficiency (e.g. conceptual understanding, procedural understanding, strategic competence, adaptive reasoning, and productive disposition). These documents strongly suggest that teachers need to acquire integrated knowledge about the mathematics they are teaching. What they refer to is not just knowledge of mathematics, it also includes a knowledge of how curriculum sequences build up student understanding of mathematics, how student mathematical understanding develops, and how different instructional methods help to develop different types of mathematical proficiency among students in classrooms. Therefore, the question is, how can we help teachers conduct lesson study with the goal of developing a strong integrated knowledge about the mathematics they are teaching so that classroom instruction and learning will be improved?

The first idea for fostering teachers' mathematical content and pedagogical knowledge is improving the *kyozaikenkyu* (instructional material investigation) process in lesson study as described earlier in this chapter. If teachers can conduct *kyozikenkyu* successfully, they can gain mathematics content and pedagogical knowledge. In addition, if *kyozaikenkyu* can be improved, the quality of the research process in the lesson study cycle will increase significantly. Teachers would be able to produce a well-thought-out research lesson plan with a clear hypothesis, a clear plan to implement the lesson, clear outcomes, and clear evaluation methods. Observation and data collection become more purposeful and the post-lesson discussion becomes focused and deep. This would help teachers learn more from lesson study, which in turn will help increase teacher motivation for continuing lesson study.

More specifically, teachers need to learn how to conduct *kyozaikenkyu* on a deep level, not just scraping the surface of the materials that are investigated. An effective way to start *kyozaikenkyu* might be to provide teachers with the best available curricular materials that are grounded in strong content and pedagogical knowledge. This will help teachers conduct the process in a way that can support their lesson study work to achieve the visions that mathematics educators put forth.

One place to start this *kyozaikenkyu* process is to focus on finding out if the current textbooks the teachers are using in their classrooms represent well the recommendations advocated by reform. Developing a new curriculum is too challenging a place to start for teachers, therefore the focus should be on teachers examining their current curriculum deeply and thinking about a way to incorporate the recommendations for improving classroom practice through lesson study.

Another idea is conducting *kyozaikenkyu* with materials that have been developed in other countries that are also grounded in the strong mathematical content and pedagogical knowledge that is in accord with the new recommendations mentioned above. Textbooks from countries such as Singapore and Japan, highlighted in the TIMSS, might be a good resource for *kyozaikenkyu*. These textbooks have been shown to be coherent and focused. Japanese textbooks in particular are developed by lesson study practitioners (teachers), mathematics educators, and mathematicians in Japan, and they contain many ideas gained from *kyozaienkyu* and lesson study. Topics in Japanese textbooks are focused and coherently sequenced and the teachers' manuals provide clear rationales for the topics covered, how they are sequenced, how student prior knowledge is fostered through lessons on new concepts, what are typical student misunderstandings that become barriers to their learning, etc. (Takahashi, Watanabe, & Yoshida, 2003; Takahashi & Yoshida, 2004). Investigating such textbooks through *kyozaikenkyu* may help U.S. teachers as well as teachers in other countries expand and deepen their mathematical content and pedagogical knowledge.

The second idea for fostering teacher's mathematical content and pedagogical knowledge is making sure the teachers work with *knowledgeable others* who are knowledgeable about mathematics content, pedagogy, and the student learning and understanding process. The support from knowledgeable others enhances the level of investigation of the mathematics they are teaching. Knowledgeable others can provide helpful questions to lead teachers to think deeply, as well as resources for the teachers to study. I believe that good facilitation and input from these knowledgeable others are another very important link to improving *kyozaikenkyu*.

Many of the participants of lesson study (practitioners, leaders, specialists, knowledgeable others, etc.) in the U.S. are still novices with very little actual experience conducting *kyozaikenkyu* and lesson study. It is therefore very important for the lesson study community to think about increasing the number of knowledgeable and experienced lesson study practitioners (leaders) and knowledgeable others who can support effective lesson study. In Japan, there are mainly two types of knowledgeable others. One of the types of knowledgeable others often evolve from lesson study practitioners who have many years of experience teaching and conducting lesson study and have worked with many teachers. These knowledgeable others have a lot of experience working with lesson study groups, teaching research lessons, and observing and discussing them. The second type of knowledgeable others are university professors who are well informed about content and pedagogy, research in instruction and learning, and have vast experience working with teachers and schools supporting lesson study. Collaborating with teachers by thinking and working seriously together to make changes in classroom instruction and learning through lesson study is an important way to improve skills working within lesson study communities. For this reason, many knowledgeable others seek the opportunity to work with schools and teachers. Moreover, knowledgeable others can learn a lot from working with teachers and they can share the knowledge they gain with other lesson study groups. In addition to fostering knowledgeable others, developing lesson study leaders who have quality experience conducting effective lesson study is very important. These lesson study practitioner-leaders can use their experience to educate other teachers, as well as promote the ideas of lesson study for improving classroom teaching and learning.

To improve teachers' mathematical content and pedagogical knowledge, mathematics teacher educators must be involved in lesson study and help improve lesson study and *kyozaikenkyu*. There are two ways for mathematics teacher educators to be involved in lesson study. The first way is serving as *knowledgeable others* to support lesson study. In order to do this, mathematics teacher educators also need to work with teachers to conduct lesson study. Understanding of importance of working together with teachers to conduct lesson study in order to improve teaching and learning in the classroom is a one quality necessary for mathematics teacher educators to have. In addition, by working together, providing support for improving *kyozaikenkyu* is vital. The second way is to provide courses for supporting lesson study. Courses improving lesson study and the *kyozaikenkyu* process are very important. Learning about content and pedagogical knowledge is important for the courses but helping teachers learn how to conduct *kyozaieknkyu* is crucial. Through the course, teachers need to learn how to investigate instructional materials, plan a research lesson, observe it, and discuss it.

A related idea for how mathematics teacher educators can support lesson study is the development of a systematic teacher education system that supports lesson study. In Japan, as I described before, lesson study is incorporated as part of prospective teachers' education. As a part of student-teaching, aspiring teachers conduct lesson study in collaboration with professors at their university, their classmates, and classroom teachers (usually very experienced lesson study practitioners) who are assigned as mentors at the schools with student teachers. Through this system, aspiring teachers also have opportunities to observe and participate in other classmates' research lessons as well as lessons taught by mentor teachers. Student teachers often report that conducting lesson study during student teaching was very hard to do mentally and physically but they recognized that it was the most rewarding experience in their pre-service education (Shimahara and Sakai, 1995; Yoshida 1999). This is a place where mathematics teacher educators also contribute. Working with student teachers and their mentor teachers, mathematics teacher educators can support *kyozaikenkyu* and the lesson study process. Supervising the lesson the students are developing, observing the lesson they teach, and participating in the discussion to support their learning is important. If mathematics teacher educators can provide strong support for lesson study by making these courses available, and they can be involved in lesson study in schools, a systematic approach to improving lesson study in order to improve teacher's content and pedagogical knowledge and classroom teaching and learning can be built.

CONCLUSION

As discussed in this chapter, the process of lesson study looks simple on the surface and simply going through the motions of a lesson study cycle may not be difficult. However, conducting lesson study effectively in order to improve teacher mathematical content and pedagogical knowledge, so that the teachers can see significant changes in classroom instruction and learning, is no easy task. In order to make lesson study more effective, teachers need to learn how to conduct *kyozakenkyu* in mathematics effectively so they can improve the research lesson planning, observation and discussion of the lesson. Effective lesson study helps foster more committed teachers because the experiences and learning they gain is highly valuable to their professional learning. To ensure that teachers experience effective and meaningful professional learning in their professional career, teachers also need to receive strong support from knowledgeable others. Their questions and suggestions from knowledgeable others will lead to higher quality lesson study. Mathematics teacher educators can serve as knowledgeable others to support ongoing lesson study, provide courses for improving lesson study and *kyozikenkyu*, and connect the student teaching process with lesson study. In order to provide quality support for lesson study efforts, mathematics teacher educators also need to learn and experience lesson study and look at themselves as part of the lesson study community working together with teachers to improve classroom teaching and learning.

REFERENCES

Fernandez, C., Cannon, J., & Chokshi, S. (2003). A U.S.-Japan lesson study collaboration reveals critical lenses for examining practice. *Teaching and Teacher Education, 19*(2), 171–185.

Fernandez, C., & Yoshida, M. (2004). *Lesson study: A Japanese approach to improving mathematics teaching and learning.* Mahwah, NJ: Lawrence Erlbaum Associates.

Isoda, M., Stephens, M., Ohara, Y., & Miyakawa, T. (Eds.), (2007). *Japanese lesson study in mathematics: It's impact, diversity and potential for educational improvement.* Singapore: World Scientific Publishing.

Kilpatrick, J., Swafford, J., & Findell, B. (Eds.), (2001). *Adding it up: Helping children learn mathematics.* Washington, DC: National Academy Press.

Lewis, C. (2002). *Lesson study: A handbook of teacher-led instructional change.* Philadelphia, PA: Research for Better Schools, Inc.

Lewis, C., & Tsuchida, I. (1997). Planned educational change in Japan: The case study of elementary science instruction. *Journal of Educational Policy, 12*(5), 313–331.

Lewis, C., & Tsuchida, I. (1998). A lesson is like a swiftly flowing river: How research lessons improve Japanese education. *American Educator*, 12–17, 50–52.

Ma, L. (1999). *Knowing and teaching elementary mathematics: Teachers' understanding of fundamental mathematics in China and the United States.* Mahwah, NJ: Lawrence Erlbaum Associates.

National Council of Teachers of Mathematics (2000). *Principles and standards for school mathematics.* Reston, VA: Author.

National Council of Teachers of Mathematics (2006). *Curriculum focal points for pre-kindergarten through Grade 8 mathematics.* Reston, VA: Author.

Sato, M. (1992). Japan. In H. Leavitt (Ed.), *Issues and problems in teacher education: An international handbook.* New York, NY: Greenwood Press.

Shimahara, N. (1991). Teacher education in Japan. In E. Beauchamp (Ed.), *Windows on Japanese education.* New York, NY: Greenwood Press.

Shimahara, N., & Sakai, A. (1995). *Learning to teach in two cultures: Japan and the United States.* New York, NY: Garland Publishing.

Stevenson, H., & Stigler, J. (1992). *The learning gap: Why our schools are failing and what we can learn from Japanese and Chinese education.* New York, NY: Summit Books.

Stigler, J., & Hiebert, J. (1998). Teaching is a cultural activity. *American Educator*, 1–10.

Stigler, J., & Hiebert, J. (1999). *The teaching gap: Best ideas from the world's teachers for improving education in the classroom.* New York, NY: The Free Press.

Takahashi, A., Watanabe, T., Yoshida, M., & Wang-Iverson, P. (2005). Improving content and pedagogical knowledge through Kyozaikenkyu. In P. Wang-Iverson & M. Yoshida (Eds.), *Building our understanding of lesson study.* Philadelphia: Research for Better Schools.

Takahashi, A., & Yoshida, M. (2004). Ideas for establishing lesson-study communities. *Teaching Children Mathematics, May.* 436–443.

Watanabe, T., Takahashi, A., & Yoshida, M. (2007). *Kyozaikenkyu: A critical step for conducting effective lesson study and beyond.* Kennesaw State University.

Wilms, W. W. (2003). Altering the structure and culture of American public schools. *Phi delta Kappan. 84*(8), 606–615.

Yoshida, M. (1999). *Lesson study: A case study of a Japanese approach to improving instruction through school-based teacher development.* Unpublished doctoral dissertation, The University of Chicago, Chicago.

Yoshida, M. (2005). Lesson study goals and their purposes. In P. Wang-Iverson & M. Yoshida (Eds.), *Building our understanding of lesson study.* Philadelphia, PA: Research for Better Schools, Inc.

Makoto Yoshida
Center for Lesson Study
William Paterson University
USA

SECTION 2

TASKS IN MATHEMATICS TEACHER EDUCATION

ANNE WATSON AND PETER SULLIVAN

5. TEACHERS LEARNING ABOUT TASKS AND LESSONS

In this chapter we suggest that mathematics teacher educators can use the obvious interest of prospective and practising teachers in planning and teaching lessons as a way of drawing their attention to key aspects of student learning. We argue that different tasks have different purposes and that consideration of those purposes can be an effective way of educating teachers. We also argue that converting tasks to lessons is complex and that the structure of lessons should also be purposeful in supporting the type of task and its purpose. We discuss four types of tasks, those that: foster conceptual understanding; develop mathematical fluency; create opportunities for focus on strategic competence; and, create opportunities for use of adaptive reasoning. We also suggest templates for mathematics lessons that support each type of task. These tasks and templates can be incorporated critically into mathematics teacher learning opportunities.

INTRODUCTION

In this chapter we examine ways in which the study of classroom tasks and mathematics lessons can be used to enhance teacher learning. We outline some of the affordances of classroom tasks that address four overlapping aspects of mathematics, and illustrate these with four different templates to indicate how such classroom tasks can be used as the basis of lessons.

We use 'teachers' to mean prospective and practising teachers involved in deliberate formal learning situations who we assume are thinking about how to teach their students. We use 'students' to refer to children and adolescents in schools who are being taught mathematics by teachers. We use 'lessons' to convey the units of learning and teaching used in schools for organisational purposes.

We use 'classroom tasks' to refer to questions, situations and instructions that teachers might use when teaching students, and 'tasks for teachers' to include the mathematical prompts, many of which may be classroom tasks, that are used as part of teacher learning. We are not offering these as definitions, rather they are our attempt to narrow the use of the word 'task' to designate *the starting point of mathematical activity*, whether it is by students in classrooms or by teachers in educational settings, for the purpose of this chapter. This means we are not going to deal explicitly with tasks for teachers such as 'compare how students P and Q responded to this task', although these too are tasks in mathematics teacher education but we assume that everything we discuss is taking place within an educational context in which such pedagogic tasks are the norm.

D. Tirosh and T. Wood (eds.), Tools and Processes in Mathematics Teacher Education, 109–134.

USING CLASSROOM TASKS TO PROMPT TEACHER LEARNING

Tasks for teachers have multiple purposes in teacher education. Teachers' engagement with such tasks can have the following purposes:

Purpose 1.   To inform them about the range and purpose of possible classroom tasks.

Purpose 2.   To provide opportunities to learn more about mathematics.

Purpose 3.   To provide insight into the nature of mathematical activity.

Purpose 4.   To stimulate and inform teachers' theorising about students' learning.

Teacher educators commonly combine these purposes and provide mathematical tasks, both of familiar and unfamiliar kinds, for teachers so that their engagement as learners is genuine (Watson & Mason, 2007). They might learn, for example, about how unfamiliar task types provide different ways of engaging with mathematics, or they might learn how different learners respond to familiar task types. Such learning may be mathematical, pedagogic, or a mixture of both depending on how task goals, discussion and reflection are structured in the teaching session, with a degree of familiarity relating to mathematical content, or task-type, or expected ways of working.

Teachers in educative settings often want tasks or task-types that can be used in their own classrooms with minimal transformation, while teacher educators might seek to offer tasks which influence teachers' learning. Here we combine these aims by concentrating on how teachers can be educated about classroom tasks through reflective engagement with such activities. The starting point for our considerations is to think about how particular types of tasks offer the potential for students' learning, since that is the shared concern of teachers and their educators. By starting with this as the focus, the four purposes listed above can be achieved in ways which support effective teaching, and which recognise and build on existing pedagogic strengths, whatever the systemic constraints within which teachers work. We also extend this to include what Stein, Grover, and Henningsen (1996) termed the task 'as set up' by the teacher in the classroom, that we take to be the lesson.

Our starting point is from the teachers' decisions about the nature of mathematical learning, then what kinds of tasks can promote such learning, followed by the creation of tasks or their selection and adaptation from published materials, and finally the use of the task in the creation of a lesson which incorporates it into a sequence of events in a classroom.

CONNECTING TASKS TO LEARNING

Doing tasks does not guarantee learning. Stein et al. (1996) show that it is possible for teachers and students to act together to reduce a classroom task to a sequence of things to do towards completion, and for students to trail through those 'things to do' without engaging with meanings, purpose or ideas. The connection between task and learning is non-deterministic and far from simple. Hiebert and Wearne (1997) propose that "what students learn is largely defined by the tasks they are given" (p. 395) but, while this may be true, Christiansen and Walther (1986) report that "even when students work on assigned tasks supported by carefully established educational contexts and by corresponding teacher-actions, learning as intended does not follow automatically from their activity on the tasks" (p. 262). Christiansen and Walther go on to distinguish between the task as set and the activity that follows, including students' interpretations of the purpose of the task, ways of working, teacher interventions, how language and symbols are used and what is seen as valuable mathematical action.

Gibson's (1977) notions of *affordance* and *constraint* are useful to help us focus on what becomes possible when the task is set (Watson, 2004). The setting of a task opens up the potential for learning – it gives students things to hear, look at, read, think about, make sense of, relate to previous experience, and so on. These responses include rejection, confusion, misreading of symbols and other unhelpful responses. The design of a task can constrain these responses so that it is more likely that students will focus on the mathematics intended by the teacher, and will draw on the knowledge, actions, and generalities which the teacher hopes will inform the ensuing activity. In addition the idea that students are attuned, through past experience, disposition and enculturation, to respond in certain ways, to transform tasks into certain kinds of activity, helps teachers think about how far the task can go to prompt learning.

In this chapter, we think about ways to work with tasks so that the desired learning is more likely to take place. For teachers and their students to achieve learning goals, whatever they are and however they are described, the task must at least afford those goals to be pursued. Different classroom tasks afford different kinds of mathematical activity, and students' experiences of different kinds of activity indicate different kinds of mathematical learning. When teachers decide to use particular tasks, and types of tasks, they are making choices about the nature of mathematical activity and learning that might take place, and about mathematics. In our reading of the literature we found that these aspects which give the tasks purpose and meaning are often implicit. For example, there is a significant body of research about observing and replicating worked examples (Atkinson, Derry, Renkl, & Wortham, 2000; Moreno 2006); about the design of complex problematic situations (Brousseau, 1997; Freudenthal, 1973); and about tasks which address cognitive development (e.g., Swan 2006). Results from these sources of research can be interpreted to conflict rather than form a cohesive whole. This is mainly because these results lack explicitness about their *pedagogic* purpose.

New teachers, and some experienced teachers, often fail to make distinctions about the kinds of cognitive activity likely to be prompted by a task and may adopt attractive resources because they provide fun contexts, quiet work, material for discussion, or practical activity, without analyzing the nature of learning afforded. Any agenda for teachers associated with choice and use of classroom tasks needs to offer distinctions about learning. Teachers need to select and adapt tasks which make it more likely that particular pedagogical goals are achieved, whether these goals are about learning methods; understanding concepts, ideas, and relationships; working, thinking and reasoning mathematically; becoming a better learner;

knowing more about mathematics; and so on (Mason & Johnston-Wilder, 2006). In this chapter, the distinctions we make about the nature of learning mathematics in school classrooms are structured around the five strands of mathematical learning described by Kilpatrick Swafford, and Findell, (2001). We use four of their strands as they present them, but have adapted their second strand, 'procedural fluency', to include factual and conceptual knowledge which comes to mind fluently when appropriate, calling this entire repertoire of readily usable knowledge 'mathematical fluency'. We agree with them that conceptual understanding provides the coherent networks which inform suitable choices and the means to reconstruct what cannot be recalled, but also wanted to emphasise that definitions, names, facts, theorems and canonical examples often need to be available rapidly alongside procedures. Their strands, with our one adaptation, are:

- *conceptual understanding* – 'integrated and functional' (p. 118) comprehension of mathematical concepts, operations, and relations;
- *mathematical fluency* – skill in carrying out procedures flexibly, accurately, efficiently, and appropriately, and, in addition to these procedures, factual knowledge and concepts that come to mind readily;
- *strategic competence* – ability to formulate, represent, and solve mathematical problems (p. 124);
- *adaptive reasoning* – capacity for logical thought, reflection, explanation, and justification (p. 129); and
- *productive disposition* – habitual inclination to see mathematics as sensible, useful, and worthwhile, coupled with a belief in persistence and one's own efficacy (p. 131).

Within each of the first four strands we show how teachers can learn more about tasks, mathematics, activity and learning. In addition we show how including tasks in some standard lesson templates can raise further educative questions for teachers, and can also enrich the mathematical affordances of tasks. We do not address the fifth strand explicitly since it is connected to the tasks and lessons addressing each of the other strands; we discuss tasks and lessons with the assumption that they allow for the development of a productive disposition over time, and we describe the contribution certain lesson templates might make to this. While these strands help to organise our thinking, and the chapter, it is important to stress, as do Kilpatrick et al., their integrated and overlapping nature. They are different emphases, not separate categories, but for them all to be present as affordances in mathematics lessons, teachers have to plan specifically for each and not merely offer tasks which tend towards one strand in the hopes that other strands will somehow develop automatically. For this reason we adopt a critical approach in our use of the strands, because overemphasis at a superficial level (such as might happen if these, or similar, 'strands' are used to categorise parts of a curriculum, or as assessment foci, or as criteria for 'good' teaching) can lead to ineffective teaching.

FROM TASKS TO LESSONS

Because most teachers in the world need to 'fit in' to existing cultural and political practices in terms of teaching methods and assessment regimes we do not assume anything about so-called traditional or reform paradigms. Instead, we show how teachers can incorporate tasks that afford the development of all five strands within a range of lesson structures. A lesson needs to provide the structure within which the task is more likely to initiate and fulfil mathematical activity of the complex kind described above.

So far we have emphasised the centrality of having a learning purpose in mind when selecting, adapting and designing classroom tasks, and have pointed out that the accompanying pedagogic choices make a significant difference to whether students merely 'do' tasks or whether they learn mathematical ideas in the associated activity. Mathematics teachers in our countries (U.K., Australia), for a variety of reasons, tend to focus on individual lessons rather than individual classroom tasks. Planning real or imaginary lessons is seen by teachers as practical and authentic, a worthwhile way to spend time, and helps to provide a direct connection between theoretical considerations and practical imperatives. By considering the effect of stringing various tasks together to form a lesson with overall mathematical coherence, the tendency to simplify task intentions described by Stein et al. (1996) can be addressed, along with the long term aim of developing a productive disposition. A classroom culture that fosters productive disposition can be developed and sustained over time through task choice and lesson design which takes into account these elements:

- the level of implied student choice, in that student choice of focus, approach, and difficulty contributes to motivation (e.g., Middleton, 1995);
- the potential for prompting communication, in that communication can contribute to effective learning (e.g., Wood, 1995), and is more productive if there is more to discuss than the correctness of the answer;
- the degree of risk, recognising that not all students respond well when they are uncertain on how to proceed or the risk of failure is high (e.g., Doyle, 1986; Dweck, 2000); and
- the 'level' of potential student engagement, described by Fredericks, Blumfield, and Paris (2004) in terms of behavioural, emotional, and cognitive responses. They argued that engagement is enhanced by tasks that are authentic, meaning whether or not students can engage with tasks with the whole of their current sense of self – they do not need to leave their personalities and dispositions at the classroom door in order to participate in mathematical activity. Thus lessons must provide opportunities for students' sense of ownership and personal meaning, fostering collaboration, drawing on diverse talent, and providing fulfilment and empowerment.

In each of the following sections we discuss an aspect of mathematical learning from four strands. In each section we elaborate the nature of the learning associated with the strand, showing critical perspectives that challenge simplistic categorisation. We then offer illustrative tasks that mathematics teacher educators can use with teachers, and propose a template of a lesson structure to which tasks within that strand can be adapted.

The templates are a device to facilitate discussion of the key elements of lessons which address the various aspects of mathematics as exemplified in the Kilpatrick et al. strands. The templates are not recipes to be enacted, nor are they algorithms to be followed stepwise. Rather they are an attempt to articulate the key features or phases in the respective lessons. Describing the key features and phases in this way not only provides prospective and practising teachers with a language that can be used to describe action with the phases, but also gives indication that the respective phases are indeed important for the success of the particular type of lesson. The templates also signal that there is not one type of mathematics lesson, just as there is not one type of mathematics learning. The templates are particularly useful with prospective teachers in that often guidelines they are offered in general courses on pedagogy do not provide structures that can assist in their creation of mathematics lessons. For each strand we offer an illustrative template noting that there are, of course, other possible lesson structures and possibilities in each case.

STRAND 1: CONCEPTUAL UNDERSTANDING

In this section we discuss some task types which are generally familiar in schools and argue that 'chalk-and-talk' methods, or whole-class teacher-led discussions, can be done in ways which enable students to engage with the meaning of concepts. The conceptual understanding of mathematics can be problematised with teachers in at least three ways. The first is for teachers to develop greater insights into the mathematical thinking that is encapsulated in their own understandings. The second is for teachers to work with topics which are hard to teach and easy to confuse because of their conceptual nature. The third is to know that relational understanding (Skemp, 1977) is always a possibility in mathematics and that this has implications for the way they teach. To work on the first of these, teachers need to become articulate and explicit about how they came to understand concepts; for the second, they need to recognise that mathematics is littered with inherent cognitive difficulties for students; for the third, teachers need to see that their own knowledge might be limited, and what they know as procedures might be reconceptualised as expressions of generalities about relationships. These three ideas are elaborated next.

Insight into the Mathematical Thinking Encapsulated in Their Existing Understandings

Using concepts which are well-understood by teachers, it is possible to unpack the essential relationships and reconstruct them as 'discovery' tasks to show how mathematics derives from general relationships and behaviours. For example, teachers can be asked to use a calculator to demonstrate the effects of entering any number, using the 'x^2' button, then using the '$\sqrt{}$' button. Once the technicalities of using the calculator are sorted out, school students typically make observational statements such as 'it's just the same' or, if they entered a negative number, 'it doesn't work'. Teachers are aware of the relationship between squaring and square-rooting, but the use of the calculator helps them re-engage with this relationship as learners might. However, the crucial issue to discuss with teachers is how to help students shift from these superficial observations to the notion of inverse, forms of conventional notation, and other representations which might explain what is happening, and also, why negative numbers are different. These discussions help teachers appreciate the conceptual depth of topics they already 'know', show how simple 'exploration' tasks can valuably be incorporated into the curriculum, generate mathematical discussion about 'why negatives don't work', and suggest that reasoning about patterns in results is something all learners can do at an appropriate level. Teachers bring their existing knowledge to the task, but may well end up with richer understandings of concepts (in this case, of 'inverse') and of the domains of applicability of concepts.

Topics Which Are Hard to Teach and Easy to Confuse Because of Their Conceptual Nature

Swan (2006), working within a cognitive perspective, devised task types which structure conceptual understanding of hard-to-teach and easy-to-confuse topics. His tasks scaffold the processes of making and refining distinctions, resolving ambiguity, and enacting the mathematical discipline which characterise the interface between conceptual learning and general human endeavour. Some of these tasks require learners to:
- classify objects using properties, definitions, language, distinctions;
- interpret multiple representations by making links between them and forming mental images;
- evaluate mathematical statements, deciding if they are always, sometimes or never true, and generating examples, counterexamples and arguments to justify such decisions;
- create mathematical problems to understand reverse and inverse processes;
- analyse other people's reasoning and solutions by comparing methods, solutions, diagnosing errors, and identifying chains of reasoning.

His research shows that these tasks can generate talk about the mathematical ideas and meanings involved. For example, matching fraction, percentage and decimal representations of proportion can to some extent be done using instrumental knowledge, but students can be asked to develop such a task further by making up objects which are 'hard' to calculate and 'hard' to match (using their own definition of 'hard'), or by being asked to place things in order and provide missing objects. Similar tasks for use with teachers could be set up with functions and methods of integration; or with polynomials and lists of roots. Thus teachers explore the extent of their own mathematical understandings, while at the same time seeing that the ordinary human activities of sorting, ordering, classifying, naming and so forth can be harnessed through such tasks to help students learn mathematics. Often a mathematical idea is hard to teach and learn because it is

115

easily confused with something already known, so questions which encourage learners to make distinctions for themselves are especially valuable.

Relational Understanding Is Always a Possibility

The type of relational understanding that Skemp (1977) described is about meaning, about making connections between different expressions of a mathematical idea, about connecting an idea to other known ideas. Relationally understood ideas are easier to remember than instrumentally learnt ideas, and they are more likely to be seen as useful in unfamiliar contexts. New teachers can be helped to realise that the way they learned to multiply a decimal number by 10 by moving the decimal point to the right, or divide by a fraction ("invert the guy and multiply"), or that negative times negative makes a positive, or how to differentiate, might not make sense, and these are just rules applied to get a correct answer in the short term. The task of the mathematics teacher educator is to indicate that achieving this relational understanding is worth the effort, and that using this understanding in their teaching is crucial.

An Illustrative Task for Teachers: Comparing Affordances and Constraints of Classroom Tasks

In many current curriculum cultures teachers perceive themselves as having to maintain a balance between tasks that promote engagement with concepts and those that focus on testable fluency. The discussion above focuses deliberately on tasks that contribute to curriculum 'coverage' and also offer teachers a context for looking at their existing knowledge from a conceptual perspective, thus addressing purposes 2 and 3 as well as offering task types (purpose 1).

We now offer an example of a task that mathematics teacher educators can use with teachers to compare how conceptual understanding might develop differently when teachers follow different kinds of curriculum guidance, here comparing a 'realistic' approach to a more abstract cognitive approach. This comparison draws attention to the fact that different kinds of mental activity can be generated by different kinds of task. The task of comparing classroom tasks addresses purposes 1 and 4.

The following two classroom tasks are each concerned with simultaneous linear equations. Teachers can be asked to say what different kinds of activity could follow from each task, and what different sorts of learning might be prompted. Teachers could be invited to consider what types of intervention might be necessary to ensure students shift from 'doing' to 'conceptualising' in each case, and come to know ways to recognise and solve simultaneous equations using these tasks as starting points.

"Realistic" task

Solve the following problem:

Two rounds of drinks were bought, one by Anne and one by Peter. Anne bought three coffees and two fruit juices and the bill came to £6.70; Peter bought one coffee and three juices and the bill came to £4.80. Now they want to get the money back from their friends so need to know the cost of coffees and juices.

Compare your methods for working this out.

Later, they had to buy drinks for a larger group and Anne's bill for 13 lemonades and 6 cokes came to £26.20 while Peter's bill for 20 lemonades and 13 cokes came to £43.70. This time, what do lemonades and cokes cost?

What methods could you use to work out similar problems in future?

"Abstract" task

Using a graph-plotter to help you, find, where possible, two equations in set A which go through each of the coordinate points in set B. Where it is not possible, invent new equations to make it possible.

Set A

$y = x$	$y + x = 6$	$y - x = 6$
$y + 2x = 6$	$2x + 3y = 6$	$3x + 2y = 6$
$y = 6x + 2$	$6y = x + 2$	$x + y = 1$

Set B

(3,3)	(0, 6)	(2,2)
(0, 3)	(2, 0)	(4, -3)

Make up more sets of mathematical objects which can be matched up like this.

The first of these classroom tasks presents a "realistic" context, while the second affords the possibility of generalising from the patterns identified by the students. Each type offers an opportunity to understand that solving simultaneous equations is not just a matter of applying methods, but involves the intersection of relationships. But it is possible to do both tasks without thinking much about solving equations at all. Both need purposeful interaction to shift students towards conceptual and relational understanding. The central questions are: what kinds of experience do learners need so that they can generalise? and, how can they be led to develop appropriate abstractions?

The teacher development activity of comparing classroom tasks (as above) is most effective if teachers have first done the tasks themselves. It allows teachers to engage with their own knowledge at a relational level (thus incorporating purposes 2 and 3), and also to understand that 'relational' does not only mean 'applicable'. This extra turn of the wheel not only brings the discussion into the arena of their professional interest (what can I do in my classroom so that these tasks promote appropriate mathematical activity?) but also enables them to talk about how tasks promote learning through mathematical activity (purpose 4). The pedagogic choices to be made, and which teachers can discuss, include:

– what will students see in terms of visual impact, layout and diagrams?
– will they handle actual objects?
– how much familiarity do they need to have with notations and conventions?

- what questions can be asked about their experiences (such as what changes and what stays the same; what is the same and what is different)?
- what key words and ideas can the teacher offer to influence thinking?

An Illustrative Template for a Lesson Focusing on Conceptual Understanding: Active Teaching

How can tasks that foster conceptual understanding can be used as the building blocks of a lesson? Again, we take a pragmatic view that new teachers cannot be expected to teach lessons that are very different from what already happens, and from what students expect, so the overriding question is 'how can I include a conceptual focus in my ordinary teaching?' The following template, adapted from Sullivan (2007), is similar to the lesson structure that is representative of mathematics teaching in the U.S., which is similar to that described by Good, Grouws, and Ebmeier (1983) as "active teaching". It specifies particular familiar activities including: daily review of homework; development (including addressing prerequisite skills, lively presentations by the teacher, assessment of comprehension, and controlled practice); seatwork; and homework assignment, with the teacher having an active role at each stage. What we hope to show here is how such a lesson can afford significant engagement with concepts, rather than focus solely on technical proficiency. We note that this template is basically what could be considered 'traditional' mathematics teaching. The key is that it is possible to structure such lessons so that advantage is taken of the possibilities of developing conceptual understanding, and it is also possible to miss such possibilities. Given that such lessons are common, at least in the U.K., U.S., and Australia, this familiarity allows their critical study.

To illustrate the elements or phases of the template, suppose a teacher wants her class to learn that it is possible to multiply any number by 99 mentally by first multiplying by 100, then subtracting the number. The lesson can build conceptual understanding of ways of calculating, and to illustrate a purpose for the distributive law notation. The left hand column of Table 1 is a description of how the template might work in this example. The right hand column in the table is intended to apply to lessons of a similar structure.

The template is characterized by limiting student choice, in that the focus and pace are decided by the teacher; there are few opportunities for prompting communication, in that it is either correctness or a particular approach that is of interest; the experience is low in risk for students in that the teacher guides the lesson; the engagement is through the energy, activity, and explanations of the teacher, or perhaps through a student's innate desire for competence. There is some opportunity early on for students to suggest methods and later to extend the lesson to consideration of the general ways of writing such calculations.

Table 1. The active teaching template

In this example ...	Key lesson element
The teacher poses some examples such as 600-6, and 1100-11 to check student facility with the pre-requisite skills.	The teacher revises pre-requisite content with students, using carefully chosen special examples, and assesses current understandings, so that the lesson can build on understanding rather than only on skills.
Teacher poses some examples like 5×99, 8×99, and asks students to work out the answers. Some students explain what they have done. The teacher emphasises the method: $5 \times 99 = 500 - 5 = 495$	Teacher uses lively methods to illustrate aspects of mathematics or procedures, possibly building on suggestions from students, emphasizing relational understanding and making connections with previous learning. The teacher gives one or two carefully varied practice examples, which are reviewed.
Further questions are posed, in sets of similar cognitive demand. The first set might be like 6×99, the next set like 11×99, and the next set like 25×99, and then perhaps extending to 110×99.	Individually or in small groups, students complete further examples, tasks or problems designed for practice and consolidation of content. Teacher monitors work of students, noticing solution strategies, adapting the questions if necessary.
The students' responses to set exercises are corrected, and some further examples (e.g., 4×99) are posed to check both their accuracy and capacity to explain the process they used. The teacher can also draw out the key mathematical points involving the distributive law $5 \times 99 = 5 (100 - 1)$ etc. It can also be extended to questions such as 4×98.	The teacher reviews the methods and answers of the students, and attends to particular problems or responses that assist in consolidating the purpose of the lesson. Students might propose questions of their own, and suggest extensions to the technique. A key feature of this template is the careful preparation of examples that address specific aspects of a concept, so procedural and conceptual development proceed together.

For all teachers, new and experienced, such a template is familiar. Thus the lesson template provides a frame for the teacher-task of imagining alternative choices, and the activity they would afford. It is instructive for teachers to analyse specific parts of a lesson, identifying exactly where task choices might make a difference to overall learning, such as choosing to extend beyond the use of 99, or choosing to use the bracket notation. Marton's (2006) variation theory shows the significant advantages in offering variation of different aspects. In the lesson we gave above, the early examples involve only single digit multiplication, before moving to two digits. Further variation in the question, and even the use of formal representation, is left until the basic technique can be carried out competently. Another significant choice is in the nature of questions posed for individual work. In this lesson, students are asked to imitate or reconstruct the procedure on sets of questions, but it would also be possible to match questions to answers, to work backwards from answers to questions, to sort questions into 'easy' or 'hard', or 'those that can/cannot be done by this method'. In this section we have deliberately used a type of lesson familiar to many teachers to show how example choice and task design can lead to a focus on conceptual understanding, even within a paradigm normally associated with mathematical fluency.

STRAND 2: MATHEMATICAL FLUENCY

As with Kilpatrick et al. (2001), we see the development of fluency as one of the goals of mathematics teaching, although we wish to be more explicit about the inclusion of recall of names, facts and definitions in such fluency. Teaching which takes mathematical fluency as the learning aim generally focuses on minimising the difficulty and effort required for learners to perform algorithms correctly. Task designers in this tradition tend to seek to reduce *cognitive load* by identifying what is intrinsic and what is extraneous (see Bransford, Jones, & Cocking, 1999). The underlying theory for this view is that working memory cannot process too much input so complexity leads to inefficient learning (Baddeley & Hitch, 1974). The instructional aim, therefore, is to offer students 'worked examples' from which smooth performance can be imitated or inductively followed. Typically, instructional designers, from this view, are concerned with how many examples and of what kind learners need to see before they can successfully do similar examples for themselves. These approaches to teaching have been challenged on the basis that they do not address the need for learners to develop conceptual understanding through problem solving and to develop mathematical fluency in conjunction with conceptual understanding. Yet teachers everywhere whose students are subject to high-stakes examinations need to know ways to help their students to achieve fluency, and addressing this strand requires thought about how learners might perceive the examples, experiences and exercises teachers offer, and how (and what) they might later recall. For example, it has been found that showing students a problem before demonstrating a similar example is more effective for complex ideas than offering a worked example without learners knowing why they might need to pay attention to it (Sweller, 2006). One explanation for this is that having a purpose for watching and listening to something helps to focus attention on what is necessary to achieve that purpose. Hewitt (1994) designs teaching sequences which ease learners' fluent enaction of routines by using repetition and pattern (aural, visual and physical), thus engaging sight, sound and action as a united experience.

We are, again, deliberately talking about forms of teaching which are conventional in some countries to show how learning to perform mathematical procedures, and learning to reproduce memorised mathematical facts, can be made easier for students if teachers choose examples and design demonstrations with fluency as the goal. Therefore, this does not have to be in contradiction with the development of understanding.

An Illustrative Task for Teachers: Comparing and Adapting Textbook Exercises

A standard way to address mathematical fluency is for the teacher to provide worked examples and to give students follow-up practice exercises. When teachers use sequences of worked examples and exercises they have to anticipate what learners might attend to so that examples give enough information about generality, without too much irrelevant information and without displaying common features which are unhelpful (Atkinson et al., 2000). Literature in the cognitive tradition pays important attention to what students *can* perceive when mathematics is communicated to them in symbolic and diagrammatic forms.

New teachers often assume that exercises will automatically 'provide' learning without analysing how the whole set is structured and hence what kinds of mathematical activity will be prompted. Such assumptions can be challenged by asking teachers to compare the purposes of, say, three textbook exercises which purport to address the same content and to describe how the tasks and questions vary and whether such variation provides affordances or constraints to students' development of mathematical fluency; how it provides affordances or constraints to conceptual understanding.

As with other tasks for teachers, this is more effective when teachers actually do the tasks and appreciate for themselves how the variations affect them. What is important here is not whether doing exercises in general supports this or that kind of fluency, or this or that kind of understanding, but that teachers think critically about learners' experience in doing a particular exercise, beyond whether they will merely be able to do individual questions.

Teachers can also reorganise textbook questions into orders which (a) make mathematical fluency more likely or (b) make conceptual understanding more possible. They can then alter given exercises so that they might be more effective in developing conceptual understanding or fluency, and discuss whether it is possible to achieve both. These tasks for teachers address purpose 4 (thinking about how students learn) and also develop critical skills for selection and adaptation of textbook tasks (purpose 1).

It is not only repeated experience that develops memory. Many teachers offer memory aids, but teachers often report that they find it harder to recall how to use 'SOHCAHTOA'[1] than to remember the 'word' itself. When working on this with teachers we often find it hard to keep discussion focused on classroom tasks – because the discussion becomes peppered with aids teachers 'give' or 'tell' their students which might just become 'more things to remember'. More suitable classroom task types to address the development of repertoire include: devising

---

[1] A mnemonic, widely-used in the English-speaking world, for recalling that Sine is Opposite over Hypotenuse, and so on.

personal (rather than adopting given) mnemonics, creating visual and audio representations of mathematical ideas, concept mapping, comparing similar concepts, keeping a record of typical and atypical examples and definitions, and creating their own 'obscure' examples of ideas. Sorting out those aids which support memory without masking mathematical meaning is a useful thing to do with groups of teachers, and the resulting discussion develops purpose 3 through creating a need to make clear distinctions.

The word 'practice' is often used loosely to mean 'doing several examples' but it is not always clear what this 'doing' is supposed to achieve. Many teachers use games and investigations which require repetition of procedures to enable automatisation through subordination of repetitive tasks to the more complex task (e.g., Kirkby, 1992) – the mathematical equivalent of becoming a faster and stronger cyclist by taking on a newspaper delivery job. We illustrate this kind of task embedded in a supportive lesson template.

*An Illustrative Template for a Lesson Focusing on Mathematical Fluency:
Purposeful Games and Puzzles*

Purposeful games and puzzles (PGP) (see Sullivan, 2007) have the potential to form a basis for meaningful experiences which focus on the development of mathematical fluency. It is suspected, though, that mathematical learning does not occur optimally merely as an incidental component of engaging in these PGPs. In this case, the intent of the template is not only to emphasise the mathematical purpose of the PGP, but also to facilitate development of mathematical fluency in ways that has potential for future use.

The following is an example of a mathematical puzzle, adapted from Swan (no date). The puzzle involves a set of rectangular term (or number) cards and arrow operations cards, a subset of which could be:

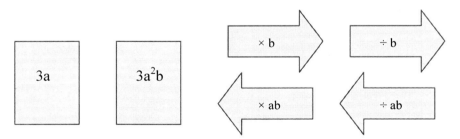

In this case, the puzzle is to choose the two operation cards that can be placed between the two term cards to represent the connection. The point is that students have to look for the appropriate operation card to connect the terms and, by doing so, evaluate a range of possible operations simultaneously. It is also self correcting, in that there are unique operations connecting the terms. A generic lesson template for using such puzzles, and possible actions for this particular puzzle, is presented in Table 2. Note that fluency is not the only likely learning outcome of such a lesson.

Table 2. Lesson elements for purposeful games and puzzles template

In this example ...	Key lesson element
The teacher explains that there are cards on which are mathematical terms, and arrows on which there are operations. The intention is to connect the terms using the operation cards. The teacher might model the process using different but related cards.	After explaining the rules and purpose of the PGP, the teacher demonstrates the PGP to the class.
After the students have worked for a while on the task, there can be a teacher facilitated class discussion of the processes for deciding which operation card is placed where, after which the students can continue with the puzzle. Students can be invited to describe how they made decisions on operations.	Students engage in the PGP for a short while, after which there is a teacher-led class discussion of the strategies and or mathematical point of the PGP (also rules and possibilities may need to be clarified)
The teacher monitors the students' work as they arrange the cards of the puzzle. It is possible to have both harder and easier sets of cards, for those who finish quickly, and those for whom the puzzle, as it is, is too difficult. Some cards sets might just involve numbers, or easier operations such as addition and subtraction. If necessary, it may be helpful to pose questions such as $$3a \times ? = 3a^2 b$$	The students are then offered further opportunity to engage with the PGP. There can be additional discussion and activity as needed. The teacher or the students can suggest variations, such as making the PGP more challenging for some, or less complex for others. It is possible to group students based on their success at the PGP, so that, for example, students who complete the activity quickly might be grouped together for the next implementation of the PGP.
The students can be asked to complete a set of practice exercises on operations with like terms with the goal of emphasizing fluency, and/or students can be asked to create their own sets of term and operation cards.	The teacher leads a discussion of the mathematics of the PGP. Specific problems can be posed that allow either fluent practice that focuses on the mathematical point, or extension of thinking.
The teacher can ask for the students to suggest rules that can guide operations using algebraic terms, and to illustrate how the principles used in choosing the operation to connect $3a$ and $3a^2b$ can be extended to other operations.	The teacher summarises the main mathematical ideas. The teacher has an active role to find commonalities, patterns, and principles that can form the basis of the formalisation of the intuitive insights developed during the engagement with the PGP.

A games format, by generating a need for efficiency and optimisation, encourages adaptation and conceptualization as well as fluency. The PGP template focuses explicitly on the importance of the development of mathematical fluency, including remembering certain facts and strategies. There is student choice in the strategy to be used, in that students choose not only the game or puzzle strategy but also the ways they solve the mathematical aspect of the game or puzzle; it is a medium for prompting communication, so the teacher must take an active role in encouraging students to talk to each other about the choices they make; it is low in risk in that students have some degree of choice and the format is self correcting, and engagement is through the competition or challenge associated with the activity or game.

As before, imagining tasks in a lesson context enables teachers to anticipate possible problems and choices. For instance, the template reminds teachers to discuss the mathematics with the students, and not to merely let them solve the puzzle or play the game and celebrate the outcome with prizes or congratulations. It also offers the possibility that designing a new 'game' might be as valuable in conceptual terms as doing some practice exercises.

While it is possible for teachers to take this template straight into a classroom, discussion of the affordances of different choices is important because neither the puzzle, nor the game, nor the PGP template, address fluency without this becoming explicit for the teacher and students. This is also true of the use of textbook exercises. For most teachers in most schools in most of the world, textbooks (or similar internet resources) are the main teaching and learning tool. Critical comparison of the fluency and understanding afforded by different task-types, and the relationship between these, needs to be included in mathematics teacher education.

STRAND 3: STRATEGIC COMPETENCE

Strategic competence refers to the ability to formulate, represent, and solve mathematical problems (Kilpatrick et al., 2006, p. 124). This does not refer to questions posed in textbooks, often in the form of words, or embedded in an artificial context, which require application of techniques. Rather it applies to situations which could be treated mathematically, including the initial mathematisation, in order to be explored and, possibly, resolved. New teachers often talk of presenting mathematics as 'relevant' and 'applicable' to motivate learners, and when asked to elaborate this often means the provision of 'real-life' contexts in which conventional mathematical techniques can be used. This oversimplifies the relationship between application of school-learnt techniques and the strategic use of mathematics in contexts outside school. For example, the school use of shopping as a context for exact subtraction is unrealistic – in real shops 'counting on' might be more common, or the till (cash register) might perform a subtraction, and the purchaser might be working with estimates rather than exact amounts. To develop strategic competence, therefore, learners have to experience a variety of authentic problems, including problems within mathematics, and discuss explicitly how to work with them.

There are various approaches to developing such problem-solving skills. Anderson and Schunn (2000) claim that efficient problem-solving has to be preceded by learning some prerequisites, namely the difference between declarative and analogical knowledge; knowledge about application and how to acquire new knowledge; knowing structures of knowledge and how to use them in practice. Others from a mathematical background, such as Polya (1981) and Freudenthal believe that one learns to solve mathematical problems by solving problems: Freudenthal (1973, p. 110) states "[t]he best way to learn an activity is to perform it". In our experience, a combination of the two approaches makes sense in addressing the needs of teachers: experience of using mathematical knowledge strategically is central to understanding how to create lessons in which learners have to do this themselves, but an understanding of the kinds of activity which take place during such tasks is also helpful in thinking about how to help learners without telling them exactly what to do. For example, recognition that looking for similarities with other experiences can be turned into the pedagogic question 'have you seen anything like this before?', and knowing how structures are manifested in complex situations, and what structures are likely to show up, are useful for teachers. We shall not elaborate these combinations in detail here (see Mason, Burton, & Stacey (1982) for demonstrations of how problem-solving can be combined with an awareness of mathematical knowledge, structures and processes); instead we assume that these are familiar aspects of working with tasks and look critically at how teachers might incorporate such tasks in a content-led curriculum.

Teachers can combine conceptual and strategic aims by providing:
i) situations which require thoughtful application of known procedures – for example, in the puzzle described in the previous section;
ii) situations which generate a need to know new procedures in-the-moment; and
iii) situations for which students might create methods of solution.

Complex multistage problem-solving tasks do not always offer new mathematical insights without the teacher's intervention to draw attention to significant features, as we saw in the 'realistic' task in strand 1. More often, solutions are *ad hoc*, locally relevant and robust, and learners become better at situated problem solving, rather than learn more conventional mathematics. For teachers the tension is that learners may focus on finishing the task as posed, which may include choosing to pursue it in ways not predicted by the teacher, while teachers may want some mathematical content to somehow 'come out' of it.

The following comparison between tasks illustrates some of the challenges in such teaching. Each task engages learners in exemplifying and in constructing algebraic generalisations, well-known mathematical strategies. Each task affords the comparison of different algebraic representations and discussion of how these representations relate to the physical properties of the situations. Each task offers extension possibilities to, in the first case, other possible designs and, in the second

125

case, other polygons. The second case, however, also offers knowledge from the conventional mathematics repertoire, a useful fact which is likely to be called on in many future contexts. The first case may give insight into a relationship between triangle numbers and square numbers (although this is masked by the extra dot), itself a mathematical fact but not one which is drawn on much in school mathematics.

Pattern seeking and using:

How many dots? How many ways to count them? Compare ways of counting them.

Represent one dimension by n. How many ways can you express the total in terms of n?

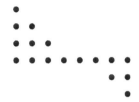

Internal angles of polygons:

How many triangles? Use the fact that the internal angles of a triangle add up to 180 degrees to find the sum of internal angles in this polygon. Use the same method to find internal angle sums of other convex polygons.

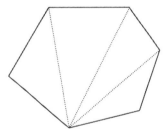

An emphasis on problem-solving skills may confuse the issue further, in that teachers may not see that successful solving of a problem has not, by itself, led to mathematical or intellectual progress. Our experience has been that, despite the advice about argumentation and class reporting (Wood, 1995), the review of student work, in which important mathematical understandings are emphasised and named, is a challenge for teachers. Yet it is through serious review, in which the teacher really listens to what students are saying, that the teacher can recognise what, if any, progress has been made in mathematical knowledge or power. The mechanics of review can be an explicit focus of teacher learning sessions – how can a teacher orchestrate students' ideas and steer towards mathematical progress while still valuing the varieties of strategy used in the problem? This focus can include the educator modelling a review of the teacher learning, and even initiating a collective critique of the teacher educator's own actions in such a review.

An Illustrative Task for Teachers: Thinking about Building on the Learning of the Students

In a particular lesson review, practising teachers were posed the task to develop advice, in the form of a mnemonic, for beginning teachers on key actions in reviewing student work after a complex, multi-stage task. One group came up with the mnemonic TEACHER:

Talk with, not at, the students

Explain any unknown concepts

Acknowledge and attribute any progress

Challenge them further by questioning

Highlight what is known by the group as a whole rather than individuals

Explore the concept further

Revisit the original idea

We present this mnemonic not as something to be used in itself, but as an example of how teachers working explicitly on a pedagogic issue can raise each others' awareness and make different teaching skills available.

An Illustrative Template for a Lesson Focusing on Strategic Competence: Imagined Representations

The *Imagined Representation* lesson template (Sullivan, 2007) is similar to what is often presented as a "Japanese lesson" (Stigler & Hiebert, 1999; Yoshida, this volume) and is suited to investigations that use a realistic, practical, or pseudo-practical context seeking to foster strategic competence. Table 3 provides a frame for task-types which do not offer students something obvious to do, and supports teachers who are learning how to use less structured tasks than those they may be used to, while emphasising the importance of the review in connecting what has been achieved strategically to the development of mathematical knowledge.

The name, *Imagined Representations,* relates to the key element of problem solving associated with imagining possibilities.

For example: The height of the Statue of Liberty is 46.05 metres. How long would you expect the arm to be?

While it is difficult for the teacher to predict what will happen, this particular activity provides a context for introduction of proportional reasoning and probably for application and reinforcement of estimation and measurement of length. It contributes to students' awareness not only of the different potentials of multiple strategies, but also the usefulness of planning.

There is student choice of strategy, since they suggest which strategy to use; it is high in potential for prompting communication, in that students would be keen to explain what they found and how they found it; there would be medium risk in that, while the students have some degree of choice, what they are required to do is ambiguous; and the engagement would be through both the potential for choice, and the inherent interesting nature of the task.

Again, the right-hand column is intended to apply to all tasks and lessons of this type. The left-hand column is how this might work for this particular task:

Table 3. Lesson elements for imagined representations template

In this example ...	Key lesson element
The teacher asks the students to record an estimate of the length of the arm on the statue. The estimation engenders interest in the answer.	After posing and clarifying the problem, the teacher asks the students to record an estimate.
After discussion, some groups might suggest comparing the length of the height and the arm on a photograph, others might suggest measuring a sample of people to get a common ratio of height to arm length, and others might suggest using ratios used by artists when representing people.	Students are invited to think about what strategies they might use to calculate an answer, first individually, then brainstorming in a group, and the groups describe their strategies to the class.
Groups of students follow different solution strategies, preferably those they have suggested. Using whatever resources are required, they implement the particular strategy and prepare a report.	Groups choose (or are allocated) a strategy, they implement the strategy to find an answer, and discuss how they will describe what they did to the rest of the class. The teacher monitors the work of the groups, ensuring that all students are involved in the strategy implementation, and anticipating groups who might report at the next phase.
The students report on their strategy including indicating their estimate of the length of the arm. The teachers can ask questions about the most accurate method, desired levels of accuracy, and the most efficient method.	The teacher leads a review of responses, including attending to issues such as efficiency of a strategy, and appropriateness of the degree of accuracy. The teacher selects a few groups to report, those that are most likely to contribute to the purpose of the activity.
Some similar ratio tasks can be posed that allow students to practise the skills, or prompt for transfer to alternate situations.	Students complete more problems or exercises that consolidate the principles identified in the investigation or prompt transfer to a related context.
The teacher emphasises the process for calculating ratios, which is the purpose of posing the task in the first place, as well as the steps necessary to ensure that data collected are accurate.	The teacher summarises the main mathematical ideas addressed in the activity. One key aspect of the teacher's role is to emphasise the "dimensions of variation" (Marton, 2006) inherent in the range of strategies and modes of communication of solutions that arise.

This lesson template is applicable to any practical or realistic task that requires investigation or consideration of strategy by the students, especially where there is a need for students to imagine a representation. It also gives the teacher the role of identifying important mathematical ideas and providing ways to engage further with them.

As we said earlier, teachers need to work through such tasks, perhaps with others, to fully understand the affordances and constraints (and perhaps developing their own mathematics (purpose 2) and hence what kinds of learning might take place (purposes 3 and 4). After this, it can be useful to pool teachers' conjectures about how students might respond (or observe videos of what happens in real classrooms), and what to do with particular kinds of response. There is a difference between lessons in which teachers are listening *for* certain anticipated responses, and lessons in which teachers are genuinely listening *to* students, but a role play offering certain responses can at least prepare teachers for some of the possibilities. This template also includes the important task of comparing strategies, in terms of their relative power, rather than merely valuing all student-generated methods equally. In conjecturing or observing students' differing responses, purposes 1 and 3 can be addressed. Typically, some students can do well in tasks like this who may not do so well in more conventional tasks. In discussion, this observation can be used to challenge theories of mathematical learning which assume fixed 'ability' (purpose 4) and instead verify that different task-types promote different kinds of learning.

STRAND 4: ADAPTIVE REASONING

Adaptive reasoning refers to the capacity for logical thought, reflection, explanation, and justification, including the power of mathematics to provide its own verification methods. For students to develop this we need classroom tasks that have adaptive reasoning as the main focus, rather than answers, methods, fluency and memory. Task types which focus on reasoning could be used as isolated questions, but are probably more appropriately combined and embedded in complex tasks, as elements of overall design. Whereas a concept-focused task might use 'sameness and variation' as an intellectual tool to get at particular features of some objects, the same task, but with a reasoning focus, might be about developing the use of 'sameness and variation' as a way of acting on *any* mathematics. If the aim is to learn a concept, then the teacher will emphasise the concept; if the aim is to develop reasoning, then the teacher will talk about the purpose of identifying sameness and difference. When the focus is on developing the skills of mathematical enquiry, teachers typically are not interested so much in content knowledge or curriculum coverage, but in the development of being mathematical, a culture of mathematics, within the social world of classrooms. For new teachers, experience of working with such task structures for themselves provides a way to become more articulate about reasoning, and hence to be able to encourage reasoning with their students through language.

Reasoning can be included as a focus throughout teaching, so that new teachers can fulfil existing school expectations of curriculum coverage yet also enrich the existing ways of teaching in the school. Teachers need a repertoire of the specific reasoning skills of mathematics in order to embed them throughout their teaching. such as: asking about sameness and difference (Brown & Coles, 2000); talking about how an example represents a whole class of objects (Mason & Pimm, 1984); asking students to create their own examples (Watson & Mason, 2006); asking students to conjecture about other possibilities (Brown & Walter, 1983/2005); and playing with extreme examples. Cuoco, Goldenberg, and Marks (1996) offer a further list: justifying claims, proving conjectures, seeing logical necessity; analysing answers and methods, visualising, interpreting diagrams, translating between representation, looking for invariants, generalising, seeking similarities in structure, and developing inner sayings about relationships and methods.

An Iillustrative Task for Teachers: What Sorts of Thinking Did I Do When ...?

A suitable task for teachers is to pose situations which require them to learn new mathematics, or at least to engage with known mathematics in new ways. When teachers work together exploring some mathematics which is new to them, they can generate descriptions of the mental acts of adaptive reasoning, such as those listed above, for themselves, although sometimes this has to be 'seeded' by the teacher educator naming what they are saying. For example, a teacher might say 'I tried a few numbers...' and the teacher educator might name that as 'exemplifying'; another teacher might say 'I looked to see what would happen if...' and the teacher educator might call this 'controlling variables'. In our experience, the more these language forms become habitual among teachers, and between new teachers and their tutors and mentors, the more likely the language forms are to inform planning and classroom discourse. Without this 'habituation' they stay as 'more to do' and can be lost beneath the pressures of curriculum coverage. Describing the mathematical activity prompted by a classroom task engages directly with purposes 2 and 3.

An Illustrative Template for a Lesson Focusing on Strategic Competence: The What If? Template

The *What if?* template is useful for open-ended and mathematically-focused investigative tasks. Such tasks can engage students in productive exploration (Christiansen & Walther, 1986), enhance motivation through increasing the students' sense of control (Middleton, 1995), and encourage pupils to investigate, make decisions, generalise, seek patterns and connections, communicate, discuss, and identify alternatives (Sullivan, 1999). The term "what if" is used to highlight the role of the teacher in prompting the dimensions of variation inherent in such tasks (Brown & Walter, 1983/2005; Marton, 2006).

The following is an example of a task suitable for this template:

You have a box that needs 1 m of string to tie it up like this. What might be the dimensions of the box?

Assume that 30 cm is needed to make the bow.

The generic lesson template, and possible actions for this example task, are as presented in Table 4. The template focuses on adaptive reasoning although there are also possibilities for fostering conceptual understanding and strategic competence. Notice that the template assumes that exploratory work will be maintained over at least one lesson, but the prompts towards adaptive reasoning that we give above can be inserted during any lesson.

There is student choice in the strategy to be used, in that they can choose the degree of difficulty, and the mode of representation; it is a good task for prompting communication, in that students have the products of their own explorations to contribute; it is low in risk in that students have choice in strategies and the level at which they work; and the engagement is through their choice of strategy and the challenge of the task.

Table 4. Lesson elements for the What If? template

In this example …	**Key lesson element**
The teacher might pose the problem, clarifying terms and meanings. The students might be invited to record their answers systematically. The teacher might pose a preliminary problem such as "how might you calculate the length of the string on this box without untying it?"	Teacher poses and clarifies the purpose and goals of the task. If necessary, the possibility of multiple responses can be discussed.
The teacher monitors the work of the students. For students who have difficulty answering the initial question, the teacher might prepare some boxes and loose string for students who might need to tie up a box, or a box covered in a streamer that could be cut into sections. For students who produce one or more correct responses, the teacher might ask them to find as many answers as possible, the smallest box, the nicest box, etc.	Students work individually, initially, with the possibility of some group work. Based on students' responses to the task, the teacher poses variations. The variations may have been anticipated and planned, or they might be created during the lesson in response to a particular identified need. The variations might be a further challenge for some, with some additional scaffolding for students finding the initial task difficult.

131

Some students with simple strategies might be invited to demonstrate those to the class. Next, the teacher might choose a student who had produced an organised response to summarise their answers to the whole group. Students who have different responses can be invited to contribute.

The teacher leads a discussion of the responses to the initial task. Students, chosen because of their potential to elaborate key mathematical issues, can be invited to report the outcomes of their own additional explorations.

Finally, the teacher can summarise the successful strategies and the collective responses. Again this is the key part of the lesson for drawing out the patterns, commonalities, and generalisations.

The teacher finally summarises, with the students' input perhaps, the main mathematical ideas.

CONCLUSION

Effective mathematics teaching requires the alignment of a variety of complex factors, and education of mathematics teachers should ideally prepare teachers for the challenge of addressing each of the factors. Basically we have argued in this chapter that, while there are many other aspects of teaching to learn, both prospective and practising teachers can benefit from the study of the affordances of classroom tasks, and the ways that these might be incorporated into lessons. The four purposes of task use with teachers, listed at the start of the chapter, have been met in various ways in our treatment of the four strands. Many of our suggested tasks for teachers are also classroom tasks; the rest require critical comparison of classroom tasks. All of them offer opportunities to learn more about mathematics, in particular to revisit familiar knowledge in new ways. The tasks for teachers all focus on what kinds of mathematical activity are afforded, and all these purposes are nested within a critical approach to how different strands of mathematical proficiency are, and might be, developed in classrooms.

Finally, we placed typical task-types into lesson templates in recognition of the practical needs of teachers. We did not elaborate the ways that such lesson templates could be used in teacher education, except to suggest the discussion of ways in which they can be varied, since we assume that the development and study of lessons is already part of all initial teacher education and many in-service programmes and so take it that our suggestions can be incorporated into those existing programmes.

REFERENCES

Anderson, J. R., & Schunn, C. D. (2000). Implications of the ACT-R learning theory: No magic bullets. In R. Glaser, (Ed.), *Advances in instructional psychology: Educational design and cognitive science* (Vol. 5, pp. 1–34). Mahwah, NJ: Lawrence Erlbaum Associates.
Atkinson, R., Derry, S., Renkl, A., & Wortham, D. (2000). Learning from examples: Instructional principles from the worked examples research. *Review of Educational Research, 70,* 181–214.

Baddeley, A D., & Hitch, G. J. (1974). Working memory, In G. A. Bower (Ed.), *The psychology of learning and motivation: Advances in research and theory* (Vol. 8, pp. 47–89). New York: Academic Press.

Bransford, J. B., Brown, A. L., & Cocking, R. R. (Eds.). (1999). *How people learn: Brain, mind, experience, and school*. London, National Research Council.

Brousseau, G. (1997). *Theory of didactical situations in mathematics*. Dordrecht, the Netherlands: Kluwer Academic Press.

Brown, L., & Coles, A. (2000). Same/different: A 'natural' way of learning mathematics. In T. Nakahara & M. Koyama (Eds.), *Proceedings of the 24th Conference of the International Group for the Psychology of Mathematics Education* (Vol. 2, pp. 153–160). Hiroshima, Japan: IGPME.

Brown, S., & Walter, M. (1983/2005). *The art of problem posing*. Hillsdale, NJ: Lawrence Erlbaum Associates.

Christiansen, B., & Walther, G. (1986). Task and activity. In B. Christiansen, A. G. Howson, & M. Otte (Eds.), *Perspectives on mathematics education* (pp. 243–307). Dordrecht, the Netherlands: Reidel.

Cuoco, A., Goldenberg, E. P., & Mark, J. (1996). Habits of mind: An organizing principle for mathematics curriculum. *The Journal of Mathematical Behavior, 15*, 375–403.

Doyle, W. (1986). Classroom organization and management. In M. C. Wittrock (Ed.), *Handbook of research on teaching* (pp. 392–431). New York: Macmillan.

Dweck, C. S. (2000). *Self theories: Their role in motivation, personality, and development*. Philadelphia: Psychology Press.

Fredericks, J. A., Blumfield, P. C., & Paris, A. H. (2004). School engagement: Potential of the concept, state of the evidence. *Review of Educational Research, 74*, 59–110.

Freudenthal, H. (1973). *Mathematics as an educational task*. Dordrecht, the Netherlands: Reidel.

Gibson, J. J. (1977). The theory of affordances. In R. Shaw & J. Bransford (Eds.), *Perceiving, acting, and knowing: Towards an ecological psychology* (pp. 67–82), Hillsdale, NJ: Lawrence Erlbaum Associates.

Good, T. L., Grouws, D. A., & Ebmeier, H. (1983). *Active mathematics teaching*. New York: Longmans.

Hewitt, D. (1994). *The principle of economy in the learning and teaching of mathematics*. Unpublished doctoral dissertation, The Open University, Milton Keyes.

Hiebert, J., & Wearne, D. (1997). Instructional tasks, classroom discourse and student learning in second grade arithmetic. *American Educational Research Journal, 30*, 393–425.

Kirkby, D. (1992). Games in the teaching of mathematics. Cambridge: Cambridge University Press.

Kilpatrick, J., Swafford, J., & Findell, B. (2001). *Adding it up: How children learn mathematics*. Washington, DC: National Research Council.

Marton, F. (2006). Sameness and difference in transfer. *Journal of the Learning Sciences, 15*, 499–535.

Mason, J. H., Burton, L., & Stacey, K. (1982). *Thinking mathematically*. London: Addison Wesley.

Mason, J. H., & Johnston-Wilder, S. J. (2006). *Designing and using mathematical tasks*. St Albans, UK: Tarquin Publications.

Mason, J., & Pimm, D. (1984). Generic examples: Seeing the general in the particular. *Educational Studies in Mathematics, 15*. 227–289.

Middleton, J. A. (1995). A study of intrinsic motivation in the mathematics classroom: A personal construct approach. *Journal for Research in Mathematics Education, 26*, 254–279.

Moreno, R. (2006). When worked examples don't work: Is cognitive load theory at an impasse? *Learning and Instruction, 16*, 170–181.

Polya, G. (1981). *Mathematical discovery* (combined edition). New York: Wiley.

Skemp, R. (1977). Relational understanding and instrumental understanding. *Mathematics Teaching, 77*, 20–26.

Stein, M. K., Grover, B., & Henningsen, M. (1996). Building students' capacity for mathematical thinking and reasoning: An analysis of mathematical tasks used in reform classrooms. *American Educational Research Journal, 33*, 455–488.

Stigler, J., & Hiebert, J. (1999). *The teaching gap: Best ideas from the world's teachers for improving education in the classroom*. New York: The Free Press.

Sullivan, P. (1999). Seeking a rationale for particular classroom tasks and activities. In J. M. Truran & K. N. Truran (Eds.), *Making the difference. Proceedings of the 21st annual conference of the Mathematics Educational Research Group of Australasia* (pp. 15–29). Adelaide, Australia.

Sullivan, P. (2007). Creating mathematics lessons. In S. Close, D. Corcoran, & T. Dooley (Eds.), *Proceedings of the Second National Conference on Research in Mathematics Education* (pp. 30–43). Dublin, Ireland.

Swan, M. (2006). *Collaborative learning in mathematics: A challenge to our beliefs and practices*. London: National Institute of Adult Continuing Education.

Swan, M. (no date*). Using percent to increase quantities (trial materials)*. London: The Standards Unit.

Sweller, J. (2006). The worked example effect and human cognition. *Learning and Instruction. 16*, 165–169.

Watson, A. (2004). Affordances, constraints and attunements in mathematical activity. In O. McNamara & R. Barwell (Eds.), *Research in Mathematics Education, 6*, 23—34. British Society for Research into Learning Mathematics.

Watson, A., & Mason, J. (2006). *Mathematics as a constructive activity: Learners generating examples*. Mahwah, NJ: Lawrence Erlbaum Associates.

Watson, A., & Mason, J. (2007). Taken-as-shared: A review of what is known about mathematical tasks in teacher education. *Journal of Mathematics Teacher Education, 10*, 205–215.

Wood, T. (1995). From alternative epistemologies to practice in education: Rethinking what is means to teach and learn. In L. P. Steffe & J. Gale (Eds.), *Constructivism in education* (pp. 331–339). Hillsdale, NJ: Lawrence Erlbaum Associates.

Anne Watson
Department of Education
Oxford University
United Kingdom

Peter Sullivan
Faculty of Education
Monash University
Australia

RINA ZAZKIS

6. EXAMPLES AS TOOLS IN MATHEMATICS TEACHER EDUCATION

My focus is on examples that increase teachers' mathematical understanding and their pedagogical sensitivity. I suggest that examples that persuade teachers to reconsider 'basic assumptions' used in teaching and learning of mathematics, or to become explicitly aware of these assumptions, serve as a means toward this end. By 'basic assumptions' I refer to assumptions related to mathematical content, rather than those related to the nature of learners or learning processes. That is, 'basic assumptions' are parts of information used in mathematical activity, but not mentioned explicitly in statements or tasks. I distinguish between different kinds of assumptions: mathematical conventions, shared understandings, and assumptions that present unintended constraints to problem solving. I exemplify and discuss each of these kinds in relation to the goals of teacher education. I argue that the presented examples extend teachers' example spaces and contribute to reconstructing their schemas in order to overcome dis-equilibration.

PROLOGUE

Examples as tools in mathematics teacher education…

After initial excitement with the opportunity to write a chapter with this stimulating title, I was lost. Everything appeared to be an example: an instructional activity became an example of instructional activities, a paradox became an example of paradoxes, and a cognitive conflict became an example of cognitive conflicts. In fact, anything that came to mind as a tool used in teacher education was an example of something. I shared my frustration with Dina Tirosh. "Narrow and define your scope", she suggested. What is presented below is an example of my attempts to follow this suggestion.

GOALS IN TEACHER EDUCATION

There are many goals we are trying to achieve in the mathematics education of teachers. With a focus on mathematics, the following are my main goals:

(a) to improve and enhance teachers' personal understanding of mathematics.
(b) to examine and introduce to teachers the variety of students' possible understandings or misunderstandings of mathematics.

In this chapter I focus on examples as tools in working towards these goals. More specifically, my focus is on examples that:

D. Tirosh and T. Wood (eds.), Tools and Processes in Mathematics Teacher Education, 135–156.

(a) increase teachers' awareness of underlying mathematical ideas; and

(b) increase teachers' awareness of students' possible mathematical ideas.

Opportunely, many of the examples presented below address both of these foci simultaneously.

WHAT IS AN EXAMPLE?

Watson and Mason (2005) list a wide variety of meanings that the word example may refer to. They "use the word example in a very broad way to stand for anything from which a learner might generalize" (p. 3). This includes, among others: illustrations of concepts and principles, placeholders used instead of general definitions, 'worked examples' as means of demonstrating specific techniques, 'exercises' as means to practice application of specific techniques, and *specific contextual situations that can be treated as cases to motivate mathematics*. This last interpretation is the one I use in this chapter.

EXAMPLES AS TOOLS

Tools for What?

Almost any activity in mathematics is, or can be, accompanied by examples. Bills, et al. (2006) provided an extensive overview of the role of examples in mathematics pedagogy, including its historical origins. In teaching mathematics examples can serve as tools for introducing ideas, for modeling techniques, as tools for verifying or refuting conjectures, for triggering investigation, for experimenting and for challenging one's intuitions or perspectives.

Acknowledging the centrality of examples, Rowland (2008) found it 'curious' that "reference to the role of examples in mathematics teaching, and to their pedagogical significance, has been notably and surprisingly absent from the teacher education literature". He focused on two uses of examples in teaching: "to embody abstract concepts and typify general procedures" (ibid.). As such, examples are seen as tools to provoke or facilitate abstraction, and to illustrate practice-oriented exercises. The latter is also referred to as 'worked examples' (Zhu & Simon, 1987). Rowland's research described different purposes for which teachers use examples in elementary mathematics teaching and discussed teacher's awareness of different aspect of their choices. Zaslavsky and Lavie (2005) defined 'instructional example' as an example offered by a teacher within a context of learning a specific topic. They investigated teachers' perceptions of 'good' instructional examples and the considerations that influenced teachers' choices of these examples. They further analysed changes in teachers' practice as a reflection on their choices of examples.

Connecting research on examples with research on mathematics teacher education can be interpreted two ways: One way is to focus on teachers' practice, examine instructional examples used by teachers and guide them towards mathematically or pedagogically more appropriate choices. Another way is to focus on teachers as learners and examine what instructional examples – used by mathematics educators – can be beneficial for professional development. While Rowland (2008) and Zaslavsky and Lavie (2005) focused on the former, my focus is on the latter. In accord with my goals identified above, in mathematics teacher education examples are used as tools for re-examining one's mathematical ideas, and for increasing pedagogical sensitivity to mathematical ideas of learners. However, this use of tools in teacher education is still very general and calls for a tighter focus.

Defining the Focus

The focus that I define here is on *examples that are tools for examining basic assumptions that guide mathematical activity.* When saying 'basic assumptions' I refer to assumptions related to mathematical content, rather than those related to the nature of learners or learning processes. In what follows I distinguish between different kinds of assumptions: assumptions that are mathematical conventions, assumptions that are shared understandings, and assumptions that present unintended constraints to problem solving. I exemplify and discuss each of these kinds of assumptions in relation to the goals identified above.

ASSUMPTIONS SHAPED BY CONVENTIONS

Facing Basic Assumptions: Upside Down World

Consider the following problem, "Imagine that there is a map of the world drawn in a rectangle, and covered with a blank sheet. Put a pin where you think your home town is located."

Figure 1. Approximate location of Vancouver, BC as identified by teachers.

137

My students, who are prospective teachers in Vancouver BC, Canada all pointed somewhere close to the area identified by the X in Figure 1. (Vancouver is found in Western Canada, on the Pacific Ocean, close to the border with the USA.)

Then I uncovered the map, shown in Figure 2.

"You turned my world upside down!" commented one of the students. Looking more carefully at the map, he added – "ending up somewhere on the Great Barrier Reef isn't that bad after all."

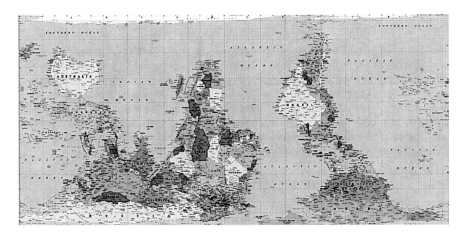

Figure 2. "Upside down" world.

I use this example as a starting point in a sequence of examples that lead prospective teachers to re-examine and bring to the fore their implicit assumptions. We – or at least those of us educated in the Northern hemisphere – take for granted that on the map of the world Americas are on the left, Eurasia is on the right and Australia is somewhere close to the bottom right quadrant, so called "down under". The basic assumption in an attempt to locate Vancouver, BC – that no one questioned – was that the map was presented in Eurocentric tradition, with North at the top. Reference to the world map in a certain position was driven by convention. Conventions are choices made and agreed upon, within a certain group, to assure successful communication. Of course, conventions are to be respected. There is no need in changing assumptions, but there is a need to become aware of them. Further, in mathematics teacher education it is important to understand not only the nature but also the sources of our assumptions.

Following this introductory example, I ask students to exemplify of what conventions related to mathematics they are aware. For example, the choice of 'right' as a positive direction on a number line is a matter of convention. Initially, there appears to be difficulty in distinguishing between conventions, such as order of operations, properties, such as commutativity, or definitions, such as $a^0 = 1$ (for $a \neq 0$), driven by the need for consistency. Then students note that the symbols we use in mathematics are based on convention, and, surprisingly, some of these choices are not universal. For example, there is no universal consistency for how to separate the whole part of a number from its decimal part; the symbol ':' means ratio in some countries and division in others; the multiplication 'dot' can be placed in the middle of the row or at the bottom, and the latter placement causes significant confusion with decimal representation for those familiar with the former. Eventually, someone in the group observes that everything that guides our communication – either written or oral – from assigning meanings to words, or sounds to letters – is based on convention. With this understanding, I focus in the next section on conventions that are particular to school mathematics.

Examining Basic Assumptions

Consider the following examples:
   (a) The sum of interior angles in a triangle ABC is 280 degrees
   (b) The graph of a function $y=x$ is a parabola.
   (c) A number is divisible by 5 if and only if the sum of its digits is divisible by 5.
When presented to a class of prospective secondary mathematics teachers, without an explicit hint given in the title of this section, there seemed to be an agreement that all three statements 'did not make sense' or simply were false. There was a tendency to consider the elements that did not fit as misprints or typographical errors and therefore to make some corrections, like taking x to the second power in (b), changing 5's to 3's in (c), and changing 280 to 180 in (a). After a short discussion and general agreement on how to alter the above examples so that they present true statements, prospective teachers were asked to consider another set of examples:
   (a) The sum of the interior angles of a triangle is always 180 degrees.
   (b) A graph of a function $y=x$ is a straight line.
   (c) A number is divisible by 3 if and only if the sum of its digits is divisible by 3.
The first reaction to each of these statements was, "Sure! Every ninth grader has already learned that!" Then the prospective teachers were guided to recognize some hidden assumptions in their immediate response. The statement (b) is true, if the function is represented with Cartesian coordinates. The statement (c) is true, if we take it for granted that the number is represented in the base ten number system. The statement (a) is true only if we assume that the triangle lies on the Euclidean plane.

   But what if not? What if we vary these conventions? It makes no sense to restate the obvious assumption if one has never experienced the environment in which these assumptions do not hold. Following Brown and Walter (1983), a powerful tool in mathematics teacher education is to apply the 'what if not' strategy to some of the fundamental assumptions of school mathematics. I argue that examples that invite teachers to examine the implicit assumptions are valuable on two counts:

first, they create a valuable mathematical experience for teachers; and second, they help in obtaining a perspective on students' work.

In what follows the three topics alluded to above – non-Euclidean geometry, non-Cartesian coordinates and non-base-ten representation – are treated with a different degree of attention. I discuss in detail the example of positional representation in bases-other-than-ten, presenting possible mathematical engagements and several research results associated with this example. I then discuss briefly the examples of graphical representation with coordinates-other-than-Cartesian, presenting research results of one particular variation. However, I do not discuss at all geometries-other-than-Euclidean. These choices, I believe, are in inverse proportion to the time allocated to these topics in a typical undergraduate mathematics curriculum: My assumption is that in the mathematical background of secondary mathematics teachers non-Euclidean geometry has been explored, non-Cartesian coordinates have been occasionally introduced, but teacher education is the main place presenting the opportunity to examine non-decimal positional representation.

Varying Basic Assumption: Bases Other Than Ten

Dienes (1960, 1965) advocated for the use of multi-base arithmetic to reinforce understanding of the base ten positional system. With the rise and subsequent fall of the 'new math' movement, the topic was introduced to and subsequently eliminated from the school curriculum. However, there is a renewed interest in this topic at the college level, for education of prospective mathematics teachers. For example, Hungerford (1992) suggested and strongly encouraged a new instructional approach for teaching "new arithmetic", with positional numeration different from base ten, since it "seems to improve students' understanding of the mathematics involved". On the other hand, Freudenthal (1983), arguing with "innovators", who "like to do structures on other bases", claimed that "if compared with mathematics resulting from pondering more profoundly the subject matter and its relations to reality, unorthodox positional systems are a mere joke" (p. 132). Even so, Freudenthal did not exclude other-than-ten bases for "remedial use", and actually stated that "it is a good didactics to motivate pupils by jokes, and an unorthodox positional system may even be a good joke" (ibid.).

Regardless of what one may call the learning/teaching engagement with bases other-than-ten – be it an example of a powerful tool or merely a "good joke" – I appreciate its value for teachers as a topic leading to rich and deep mathematical investigations, and as a topic assisting in acquiring deeper understanding of place value numeration and multidigit structures. Examples of engagement with bases other than ten usually include the following:

- Counting in different bases, (For example, in base four the first numerals are 1, 2, 3, 10, 11, 12, 13, 20, 21, 22, 23, 30, 31, 32, 33, 100, 101... The task is much more challenging if pursued orally)
- Conversion from different bases to base ten and vice versa

• Operations with numbers represented in different bases

The work of elementary teachers with numbers in bases other than ten provides them with an enriched understanding of numeration and with a more informed perspective on learners' difficulties. With a simple procedure of counting in base four, while it is clear what comes after 2, there is usually a 'moment of thinking' to determine what number comes after 3, or 33. The process – implicit for some while challenging for others – is to attempt, almost by inertia to count 32-33-34-no-40-no-100, realizing anew that there is "no digit 4 in base four". Rather often we witness young children learning to count by chanting nine, ten, eleven, twelve... and later attempting larger numbers, such as twenty-eight, twenty-nine, twenty-ten, twenty-eleven, twenty-twelve, and so on. For a teacher, a similar personal confusion when working with base four or five, adds appreciation for the children's difficulties. Moreover, the difficulty of counting in different bases can be increased when teachers are asked to count backwards or to skip-count. Again, the process they go through to decide what number comes before 1000_{three} enhances their understanding of numeration. Skip-counting in base ten is almost automatic, but skip-counting – for example by 3's in base five or base seven – introduces discussion of different strategies, such as addition or 'silent skipping' which, in turn, will be helpful when similar strategies are explored with young learners and base ten. Freudenthal (1983) noted that "counting may or may not be accompanied by insight into the structure of the counting system" (p. 86). He further pointed out that structure of the system is better understood by counting backwards or skip-counting. My suggestions for teachers are in accord with these observations.

Performing addition and subtraction in bases-other-than-ten creates an appreciation of previously learned and blindly followed algorithms, and a more profound understanding of 'borrowing' and 'trading'. And what about multiplication? While addition and subtraction in other bases usually appears for most prospective teachers as feasible but slow, performing multiplication in bases other than ten for many is close to impossible. This fact often surprises and provokes interesting discussion. The difference between addition and multiplication is that addition facts in other bases, while not a part of our basic repertoire, are easily derived, while deriving multiplication facts is much more complicated. For example, adding 4 and 5 in base six can be thought of as the total of 9 units which are 1 group of 6 and additional three units. That is, if one thinks in base ten (as most do) while operating in base six, converting the result to base six is relatively simple as it involves separating only one 'base group'. However, multiplication will involve converting 20 to base six, which is more complicated as more 'base groups' are involved.

Is there value in memorizing multiplication tables? Asking teachers to perform multiplication in bases-other-than-ten provides a convincing answer. Lack of knowledge of basic multiplication facts in other bases, combined with the fact that deriving them is not immediate, makes multiplication tedious and prone to errors. Having multiplication facts available makes the task accessible. To increase further the appreciation of availability of basic multiplication facts, I invite teachers to create their own 'times tables' for base five or base six and use these tables on

141

several examples. This experience shifts the conversation from "should we make kids memorize multiplication tables?" to "what are the best possible ways in helping young learners memorize multiplication tables?"

In addition to the above listed topics that are rather frequently practiced in mathematics teacher education courses, I introduced the example of 'non-decimal decimals' (Khoury & Zazkis, 1994; Zazkis & Khoury, 1993, 1994; Zazkis & Whitkanack, 1993). These are fractional numbers, such as 12.34_{five} or 121.22_{three}, that similar to decimal fractions are written in one line, but that lack the main ingredient of decimal fractions, which is base ten representation. Examples of non-decimals lead to a variety of activities. For elementary school teachers these activities involve mainly conversion from different bases to base ten and numerical operations. For secondary school teachers there are possibilities of engagements that employ more advanced mathematics. For example, how to convert a repeating non-decimal to base ten? While converting finite non-decimals is mainly based on assigning corresponding place values, converting repeating non-decimals can be approached using limits or geometric sequences. Additional questions may come up: How to represent 1/5 or 1/7 in base three? Or in general, how to represent any fraction at any base? Is it possible to determine whether a given fraction has a finite or repeating representation in a given base? Some of these problems are explored in Zazkis and Whitkanack (1993).

I suggested in prior research (Zazkis & Leikin, 2007) that learner-generated-examples – the tool that Watson and Mason (2005) introduce as a powerful pedagogical activity – can be also used as a research tool. This connection between pedagogy and research is likely not limited to learner-generated-examples. That is, if a certain example is a tool valuable in achieving pedagogical goals, it could be valuable as a research tool as well. Without making such an elaboration explicit, in Zazkis and Khoury (1994) we used the example of non-decimals as a tool for investigating prospective teachers' understanding of place value and multidigit structure of positional representation of numbers. When invited to convert 12.34_{five} to base ten, about half of the participants made a correct assignment of place values to digits and performed a corrects conversion, such as:

$$12.34_{five} = 1 \times 5 + 2 \times 1 + 3 \times 1/5 + 4 \times 1/25 = 7 = 7.76$$

Other participants invented strategies that corresponded to their understanding of non-decimals, revealing their understanding of decimal representation. An elaborated list of strategies was compiled in Zazkis and Khoury (1994). I introduce here three approaches that I found rather popular in my subsequent use of this conversion example with prospective teachers. Many teachers choose to convert 12 and 34 separately, and then 'glue' them together, separating by point:

$$12_{five} = 7_{ten} ; \quad 34_{five} = 19_{ten} \quad 12.34_{five} = 7.19_{ten}$$

This is likely influenced by a popular reference to this number as "twelve-point-thirty-four", rather than "twelve-and-thirty-four-hundredths". Also, even a correct "reading" of the number, without pondering its meaning, appeared problematic. Assigning the lowest place value – hundredths – to all the decimal part is possible only because 3/10 and 4/100 equal 34-hundredths. However, following the analogy of "hundredths", and an understanding that in base five the analogue of 1/100 is 1/25, some teachers assign this place value to the fractional part. That is, they convert 0.34five to be 34/25. The fact that the result is bigger than one can make some teachers reconsider their approach while it can be totally ignored by others.

Further, a popular error is to assign to 3 (in 12.34^{five}) a correct place value of 1/5 and then to assign to 4 a place value of 1/50 , rather than 1/25. This is definitely influenced by the analogy of moving from 1/10 to 1/100. While "adding" zero has the same effect as dividing by the base in base ten, it is not applicable in bases-other-than-ten. This strategy shows that the analogy is drawn using syntactic reference rather than a semantic one.

I suggest that attention to these erroneous examples – of prospective teachers themselves or their classmates – and identifying the reasons for their possible sources equips teachers with a more solid understanding of mathematics. When in turn the concepts related to decimal representation and place value are taught following this experience, it is more likely that the meaning and the multiplicative structure of the basic place value sequence – ... 1000, 100, 10, 1, 0.1, 0.01, 0.001 ... – will be attended to, rather than its superficial structure of appending or removing zeros.

There are many different systems of numeration. However, while exposure to Roman, Mayan or Hebrew numeration simply exemplifies the repertoire of possibilities, exposure to positional systems with bases-other-than-ten achieves more than that. It exemplifies the power of place-value assignment and invites prospective teachers to relive their elementary school experience by personally facing an increasing complexity – from counting, to multiplication, to decimal fractions – in acquiring basic arithmetic skills. This experience achieves a double goal of increasing personal mathematical awareness as well as increasing awareness of potential difficulties for students.

Varying Basic Assumption: Coordinates Other-Than-Cartesian

There are many different coordinate systems. In what follows I mention a few briefly, but then focus on Affine coordinates on a plane. This choice is similar to the choice of positional systems in bases-other-than-ten: while exposure to some coordinate systems simply introduces the possible variety, engagement with Affine coordinates induces a more profound understanding of the Cartesian convention. In particular, I attend to orthogonal coordinate systems in which the units on the axes are of different length (Zaslavsky, Sela, & Leron, 2002).

Polar coordinates are likely the most familiar among the non-Cartesian ones. In addition, Friedlander and Dreyfus (1991) list and name the following: bidirectrix, bipolar, bifocal, and focus-directrix coordinate systems. In each of these systems a graph of a function or equation is considered in terms of loci. In a bidirectrix system, for example, the graph of $y=x$ is the locus of points equidistant from two perpendicular lines, say p and q. In the same system the graph of $y=2x$ is the locus of points whose distance from p is twice the distance from q. In bifocal and bipolar systems the loci are considered in terms of distances from two fixed points or angles from two fixed rays respectively.

Among the systems mentioned above, the focus-directrix system is worthy of particular attention because of its connection to several curricular areas. In this system a locus is defined in terms of distances from a fixed point and a fixed line. An investigation could start with a simple task of graphing $y=x$, $y=2x$, $y=3x$, $y=(1/2)x$ and $y=(1/3)x$ (see Figure 3).

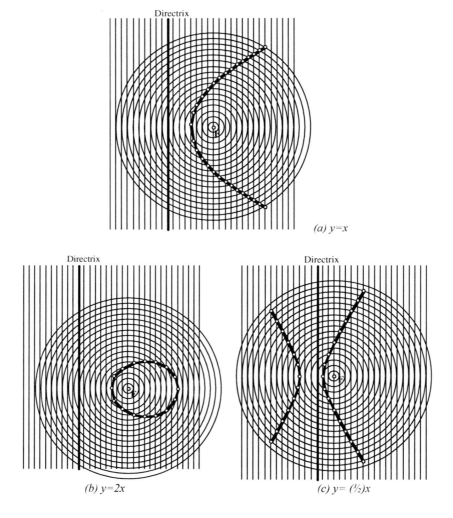

Figure 3. Graphs in Focus-directrix coordinate system.

An observation that some of these graphs look like ellipses, others look like hyperbolas and only one looks like a parabola invites a discussion of conic sections and their definitions in terms of loci. An 'AHA! Effect' is a common reaction when teachers notice that what is defined in the focus-directrix coordinate system by $y=x$ is a set of points that are equidistant from a chosen line (directrix) and a chosen point (focus), which is, surprisingly or not, one of the definitions of a parabola.

How can different parabolas be obtained? – is a question that motivates further investigation. Another interesting issue to be explored is the relationship between the distance from the focus to the directrix and the shape of the graph of the function. The initial graphing of the functions in the focus-directrix coordinate system can be made on a special grid, as shown in Figure 3, in which concentric circles intersect parallel lines. For a further investigation of possible variations and relationships, Dynamic Geometry software, such as Geometer's Sketchpad or Cabri, can be helpful. It allows the user to define a locus of points under given constraints and then to investigate a change in this locus as the constraints change.

The Cartesian coordinate system is an orthogonal homogeneous system, that is, on a plane it is defined by a choice of two perpendicular lines, of a positive direction on each line and of a unit that is equal on both lines. This coordinate system induces one-to-one correspondence between ordered pairs of real numbers and points on the plane. However, the Cartesian system of coordinates is only one particular example of Affine coordinates, that can be neither orthogonal nor homogeneous. Affine coordinate system is defined on a plane by any three non-collinear points (O, I, J). Lines OI and OJ establish two axes intersecting at the origin O, directed segments OI and OJ determine a positive direction and a unit on each one of the axes (Fehr, Fey & Hill, 1973). Coordinates of a point on a plane are found by parallel projection, that is, drawing parallel lines to the axes through this point, and noting points of intersection of these lines with the axes (Figure 4).

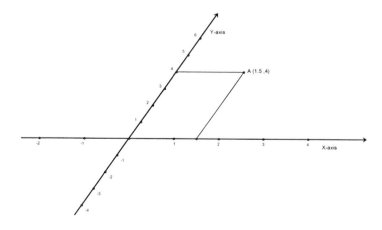

Figure 4. Locating Affine coordinates of a point.

145

Among the first tasks presented to teachers when introducing an Affine coordinate system is to assign a correspondence between points on a plane and their coordinates. But even this simple task is challenging at first to individuals 'stuck' in Cartesian plane. For example, in describing how to find the coordinates of a point on a plane, many teachers attempt to "draw a perpendicular from the point to the axes". Of course this description is valid only when the axes are orthogonal. Facing limitation of this description, and striving for an appropriate one, can be a starting point for a proof, that within Affine system of coordinates, every point on a plane has a unique representation as an ordered pair of numbers and vice versa.

After becoming familiar with plotting points and assigning coordinates, teachers attend to graphs of polynomials of the first degree, or so called 'linear' equations. This may be a good opportunity to reconsider their knowledge of linear equations plotted with the Cartesian coordinates and to decide what holds for any Affine coordinate system. What is defined by parameters m and b in $y=mx+b$? Do two lines have a unique point of intersection? Does a graph of $y=x$ form a 45 degrees angle with a positive direction of the X-axis? If not, how can this angle be determined? What predicts how steep the slope is?

Additional discussion can look at Affine coordinates as a transformation of the Cartesian plane. Following Klein's Erlangen Program, we take a view that what defines geometry is invariance under a group of transformations. What are the invariants here? Do straight lines remain straight lines? Do triangles remain triangles? Squares? Circles? Conic sections? If yes - why? If not, what do they become? Investigation of these issues followed by a class discussion has the potential to be fruitful and enlightening.

Of particular interest is the orthogonal non-homogeneous system, that is, the system of coordinates where the axes are perpendicular but the unit is different on each axis. This system is of significant importance as current graphing technology allows for the choice of different scale on different axes. Zaslavsky, Sela & Leron (2002) investigated the perception of students, teachers and mathematics teacher educators of the notion of 'slope', and its connection to the angle between the graph and the X-axis. In their study participants were asked to consider the slope of the function $y=x$ when graphed with homogeneous and non-homogeneous coordinates, as shown in Figure 5. The particular question of interest was "Should the slope of the function as presented in Figure 5(b) be considered 1 or 1/3?"

The task was set "to examine people's behavior when some specific default assumptions are violated" (p. 138). Zaslavsky, Sela and Leron (2002) presented a thorough analysis that drew a distinction between 'visual slope' and 'analytic slope'. They concluded that the task "prompted the participants to rethink and deepen their understanding if the underlying assumptions beneath the coordinate systems in which they are accustomed to represent functions" and "led to re-examination and refinement of the assumptions concerning basic notions as slope, scale and angle" (p. 138). They further suggested that the task was suitable mainly for teachers, both prospective and practicing. This thought-provoking example is constantly present in my courses as a tool for examining basic assumptions.

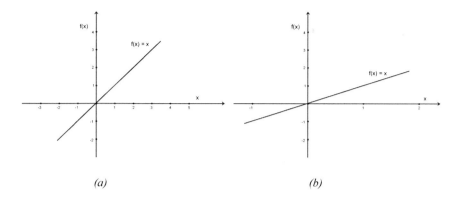

Figure 5. f(x) = x in (a) homogeneous and (b) non-homogeneous system.

An additional basic notion that invites re-examination with the help of Affine coordinates is that of length. In my research I asked teachers to prove the famous theorem about the medians in a triangle by using the sides of a triangle to assign the system of Affine coordinates (see Figure 6).

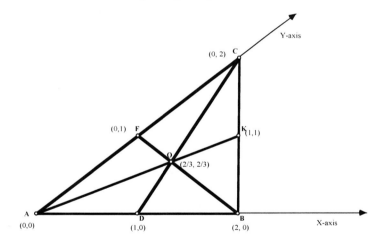

Figure 6. Affine coordinates determined by a triangle.

In particular, after calculating the coordinates of the intersection O, teachers had to prove that AO:OK = BO:OF = CO:OD = 2:1 . Surprisingly or not, most teachers used the 'distance formula' ($d = \sqrt{(x_1 - x_2)^2 + (y_1 - y_2)^2}$) to determine the lengths of the segments. This led to an exciting conversation of the origins of the formula, its

147

scope of applicability, and the notion of 'length' in general. In this particular case the unit of length is determined only with the reference to the particular axis, and therefore there cannot be a numerical assignment as the length of a given segment. Nevertheless, comparison of length in terms of ratios is possible by attending to the difference in X and Y coordinates respectively. However, this correct statement was proven using an incorrect method. Why did this 'work'? – This question can prompt another powerful conversation with teachers.

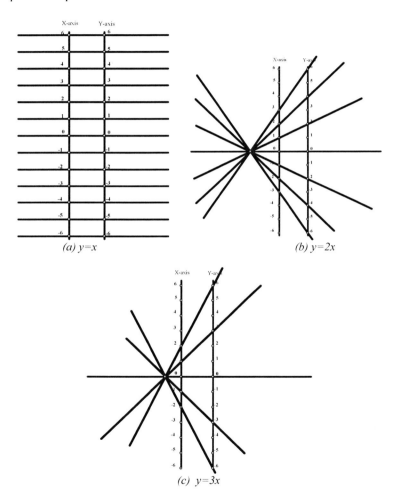

(a) y=x

(b) y=2x

(c) y=3x

Figure 7. Examples of graphs in a system of parallel axes.

Our only constraint in the choice of Affine axes was that they must intersect, to define the origin of (0,0). However, a pair of parallel lines can also be seen as a system of coordinates (Arcavi & Nachmias, 1990; Friedlander, Rosen, & Bruckheimer, 1982; Nachmias & Arcavi, 1990). The graph of the function $y=f(x)$ is attained by drawing lines connecting x on the X-axis with $f(x)$ on the Y-axis. Figure 7 presents sketches of graphs of $y=x$, $y=2x$, and $y=3x$ in the system of parallel axes. The graph of $y=x$ is a set of parallel lines, while each of the graphs for $y=2x$ and $y=3x$ is a burst of lines intersecting at one point, called the focus. Of course the diagram can show only several out of infinitely many lines in each graph of a linear function.

Observation of these diagrams invites several questions. Do all graphs of linear functions, where $m \neq 1$, have a focus? The answer to this question is positive and a proof is based on consideration of similar triangles and proportional segments.

High school students often struggle with a task of assigning equations to graphs in the Cartesian coordinate system, when specific coordinates are not marked on the axes. A similar challenge – assign a possible function to the given focus point – can be presented to mathematics teachers when working with a system of parallel axes (Figure 8).

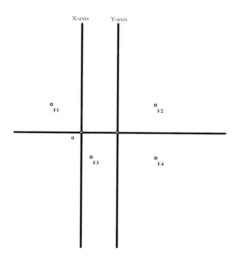

Figure 8. To what functions can these foci correspond?

However, in order to face these challenges, there are a few questions that must be addressed. Does every point on a plane determine a focus of some linear function? How can this equation be found? Is it unique? To be prepared for this investigation it is beneficial to engage first in a task of finding what parameters m and b in $y=mx+b$ determine. More specific questions to consider are: Where one should expect to find the focus of the graph, if m (or b) is positive, negative, between 0 and 1, between 0 and -1? What happens to the focus when m (or b)

increases or decreases? For what values of m and b is the focus to the left of both axes? To the right of both axes? Between the axes? When observing the examples in Figure 8 and noting that the focus is to the left of the axes, the most common conjecture is that for the negative values of m the focus will be to the right of the axes. However, further investigations refute this conjecture. For what values of m and b is the focus below, above or exactly on the 'zero' line, which is the line connecting 0 on one axis to the 0 on the other axis? Can the focus be on one of the axes? What can be said about the equation then? If three foci are collinear, what can be said about the corresponding equations? These are just a few examples of the investigations that parallel axes generate.

Graphing functions is one of the central topics in school mathematics at any level. Activities with alternative coordinate systems shed a new light on the topic. They assist in constructing richer understanding of conventional mathematics as well as creating bridges to other mathematical topics, such as geometry, transformations, loci, and more.

ASSUMPTIONS SHAPED BY COMMON UNDERSTANDINGS

Further to assumptions shaped by conventions, there are constraints that are embedded within conventional understanding of situations. Consider, for example, the following:

- Grandma baked 12 cookies for three of her grandchildren. How many cookies will each child have?
- 280 students of ABC elementary school will go to a field trip by buses. There are 40 seats on a bus, how many buses are needed?

Most learners will automatically state the result. Greer (1997) showed that students solve mathematical word problems by simply applying operations to the numbers in the text and with apparent disregard for the reality of situations described in these problems. He explained that this is due to the traditional instructional treatment of such problems that is a part of the school mathematics culture. Some learners may struggle with one of the problems or with both. It could be the case that a learner's inability to solve these problems is in their insufficiently developed concept of division, either partitive division or measurement division. However, it may also be the case that a leaner is lost in considering different options, being unaware of the shared assumed understanding. After all, the expected correct solution is not the only possibility. Should the cookies be shared equally?

This assumption underlies many textbook problems, but is almost never stated explicitly. In 'real life' a more likely case is that one of the grandchildren does not like grandma's cookies or that grandpa steals a few of them. As for the field trip, do the 40 seats include the bus driver? Are teachers and parents joining the trip? All these considerations usually do not play out when examples like these are considered in elementary school.

When trying to present elementary mathematics as applicable to the 'real life' context, we are stripping it from a real life complexity, at times explicitly and at times subconsciously. However, complexity is everywhere around, where learners are caught in a discord between mathematics classroom and the 'real world'. If you buy a shirt that cost $12 and a pair of shoes that cost $29, you will not pay $41 for your purchase, at least not in Canada, where taxes are not included in the price, but are added to your bill. If you want to exchange 100 Euros for Canadian currency, and exchange rate is 1 EUR = $1.4 CAD (at the time of writing this chapter), you will not get $140 CAD for your $100 Euros. You are likely to get about $132, depending on the commission deducted by the exchange facility. And if you are to drive at the maximum permitted speed of 90 km/hour, not exceeding it, for the distance of 180 kilometres, it is not likely that you will arrive at the destination in 2 hours. So the expected correct answers to so called 'real life' problems do not always correspond to reality. Greer (1997) called for "an alternative conceptualisation of word problems, as situations calling for mathematical modeling" (p. 293). I am not advocating here for a reality-based modeling approach. I bring these examples up for consideration in order to increase teachers' awareness of our shared understandings that are seldom examined.

Choose a number between 1 and 10. I will not make a strong claim that most people chose 7. My only comment is that no one will chose π or 4.35. Is it a self-imposed constraint or preferred convenience? Mary had 3 blouses, 4 jackets and 5 skirts. How many outfits can she make? The expected correct answer assumes that the outfit consists of exactly one of each of these items. This is a rather conservative fashion statement.

Another shared understanding is often utilized when dealing with proportion problems. Consider the following examples:

- I ate healthy foods for 2 weeks and lost 7 pounds. How many pounds will I loose if I eat healthy foods for 20 weeks?
- Jake bought a 12-pack of beer and paid $10.44. He then decided that he needed two more cans of beer. How much will it cost him?

In addition to unreasonably optimistic data with respect to results of dieting and over-taxed Canadian prices of alcohol, these examples possess the structure of standard problems approached by proportion: If X results in Y, what will be the result of Z? The expected solution assumes a constant ratio, that is, if Z = kX, then the solution is given by kY. The degree to which the assumption of a constant ratio is reasonable, is never examined.

In modelling 'real world' in school we are eliminating 'noise'. There are no traffic lights and no sales tax. Growth has a constant rate and everything is shared equally – friendly utopia. Examples of word problems used in mathematics classrooms are supposed to indoctrinate students to the assumptions that are shared by teachers and textbook writers. Examples of word problems used in mathematics teacher education serve as a tool to re-examine these implicitly shared assumptions. For teachers it is important to understand that some learners are unsuccessful not because of their lack of mathematical ability, but because of their inability to ignore the 'noise' around the presented examples.

ASSUMPTIONS AS CONSTRAINTS

- Can you cut a given cardboard square into 10 squares, using all the material?
- Can you plant 4 trees such that there is the same distance between each two of them?

Though both examples are embedded in 'real life', there is little debate about the respective mathematical models. The cardboard example is interpreted as drawing segments within a square, so that the resulting regions present non-overlapping squares. The trees example is interpreted as locating 4 points such as the segments connecting each two have the same length.

For an inexperienced problem solver, at first glance, both problems appear unsolvable. However, both examples can be seen as variations on the famous psychological experiment that invites to connect 9 dots in a square arrangement by 4 lines. People are confined by the frame these dots determine, and find the task impossible. However, the task becomes simple once the confinement to the frame is recognized as self-imposed constraint, which is not a part of the original task. Once this constraint is removed, the solution is obvious (see Figure 9).

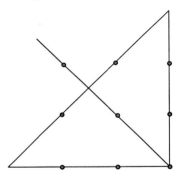

Figure 9. Connecting 9 dots with 4 segments.

Back to our examples: What self-imposed constraints impede a successful solution? In the cardboard square the constraint is in the expectation that the cut-out squares must be of equal sizes. This makes the solution immediate for 4 or 9 squares, but the example mentions 10. With the realization that equal size is not the expectation, several possible solutions emerge, as shown in Figure 10.

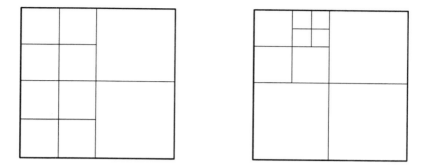

Figure 10. Cutting a square into 10 squares.

In the four trees example the constraint is that the trees are to be planted on the same level, or the points to be found on the same plane. In this case, 'out of the box' thinking leads to a third dimension. The solution is possible if the points are vertices of a tetrahedron or one of the trees is planted on a hill. What is exemplified by these examples? I attend to this question in the next section.

WHAT IS EXEMPLIFIED?

Everything is an example of something. As stated in the introductory paragraphs, the meaning of 'example' employed here is *a specific contextual situation that can be treated as a case to motivate mathematics.* As such, when used in different contexts the examples explored in this chapter exemplify different things. Examples related to 'conventional assumptions', when used with students in school, exemplify challenging extensions of the material or extra-curricular activities. However, when used in mathematics teacher education, the intended exemplification is different. They exemplify a rich variety of possibilities and extend the boundaries of teachers' *example spaces*, an idea proposed by Watson and Mason, (2005) that I discuss below. In addition, they exemplify processes – such as multi-digit addition or assigning coordinates to points – that have become automated within conventional experiences. Further, they exemplify issues of difficulty for students by having teachers examine their personal pitfalls in working with unconventional structures.

Examples related to 'shared assumptions', when used in school, represent typical exercises for drill and practice. When used in mathematics teacher education, they become tools for raising awareness of what is implicitly taken for granted and what can be problematic for learners. Similarly, examples related to 'assumptions as constraints', if used in school, exemplify riddles or brain-teasers, with a variable degree of difficulty in each. In mathematics teacher education they are intended to exemplify how human thinking is guided by constraints and how an important part of problem solving is to recognize these constraints within oneself and become aware of their existence. In turn, this self-awareness will be beneficial in guiding students.

ON EXAMPLE SPACES AND SCHEMAS

Watson and Mason (2005) introduced the idea of 'example spaces', which are collections of examples that fulfil a specific function. They distinguished, among others, between personal example spaces, shaped by individual experiences, and conventional example spaces, as "generally understood by mathematicians and as displayed in textbooks" (p. 76). Being shown or developing new mathematical objects, and realizing new applications of familiar things are some of the ways of extending personal example spaces. As such, any instructional example, if attentively explored, enriches learners' example spaces. The obvious role of examples, as tools in mathematics teacher education, is to extend teachers' personal and potential example spaces. However, I suggest that examples presented in this chapter not only extend teachers' example spaces, but also restructure them. Skemp's (1971) notion of schema is helpful in illustrating this restructuring.

According to Skemp, "to understand something means to assimilate it into an appropriate schema" (p. 46). A question that pertains to mathematics teacher education is how can one understand better what has been already understood, that is, assimilated. I extend Skemp's claim by suggesting that to understand something better means to assimilate it in a richer or more abstract schema. I suggest that a richer schema is constructed when a mathematical concept in one's mind becomes a particular example of a more general mathematical concept. This happens, for example, when familiar numbers become an example of a numeration system or when familiar X-Y axes become an example of possible coordinate systems.

What can stimulate a construction of a richer schema? A central tenet of Piaget's theory is that an individual, disequilibrated by a perceived problem situation in a particular context, will attempt to re-equilibrate by assimilating the situation to existing schemas or, if necessary, reconstruct particular schemas in order to enable the individual to accommodate to the situation. I argue that examples presented in this paper disequilibrate teachers and therefore create a need for reconstruction of their schemas.

Introducing Black Swans

Until recently, I believed that swans were white. Of course, influenced by some exposure to zoology from the Ugly Duckling, by Hans Christian Anderson, I knew that cygnets were gray, and that they turned to white as they grew. My visit to Australia dramatically changed this belief. I saw black swans. Not only did these birds look like swans, but also the sign in front of their habitat at a wild life reserve identified them as 'swans'. This put my doubts to rest. Before this experience the only black swan I ever encountered was the evil Odelia from Tchaikovsky's Swan Lake, who pretended to be the lovely Odetta and almost stole the heart of Prince

Zigfrid. But the existence of black swans outside of the fairy tale dancers was no more real than the existence of enchanted girls who turned into swans at daylight.

In this example my initial schema was constructed by exposure to examples of a certain kind, and later was reconstructed following the exposure to a different set of examples. This non-mathematical example illustrates and summarizes the main role of examples as tools in mathematics teacher education. Examples are tools for reconstructing schemas, and this is achieved mainly by extending example spaces of individuals. However, initial concepts and images thereof may prevail, despite the awareness of their limitations. That is, whenever I imagine a swan it is still white.

REFERENCES

Arcavi. A., & Nachmias, R. (1990). Desperately looking for the focus. *Mathematics in School, 19*(2), 19–23.

Bills, L., Dreyfus, T., Mason, J., Tsamir, P., Watson, A., & Zaslavsky, O. (2006). Exemplification in mathematics education. In J. Novotná, H. Moraová, M. Krátká, & N. Stehlíková (Eds.), *Proceedings of the 30th Conference of the International Group for the Psychology of Mathematics Education* (Vol. 1, pp. 125–154). Charles University in Prague, Czech Republic.

Brown, S., & Walter, M. (1983). *The art of problem posing.* Philadelphia, PA: Franklin Press.

Dienes, Z. P., & Jeeves, M. A. (1965). *Thinking in structures.* London: Hutchinson.

Dienes, Z. P. (1960). *Building up mathematics.* New York: Humanities Press.

Freudenthal, H. (1983). *Didactical phenomenology of mathematical structures.* Dordrecht, the Netherlands: Reidel.

Greer, B. (1997). Modeling reality in mathematics classrooms: The case of word problems. *Learning and Instruction, 7*(4), 293–307.

Hungerford, T. W. (1992). An experiment in teaching prospective elementary school teachers. *UME Trends, 4*(1).

Fehr, H., Fey, J., & Hill, T. (1973). *Unified mathematics.* Menlo Park, CA: Addison Wesley.

Friedlander, A., Rosen, G., & Bruckheimer, M. (1982). Parallel coordinate axes. *Mathematics Teaching, 99,* 44–48.

Friedlander, A., & Dreyfus, T. (1991). Is the graph of y=kx straight? *Mathematics Teacher, 84,* 526–531.

Khoury, H., & Zazkis, R. (1994). On fractions and non-standard representations. *Educational Studies in Mathematics, 27*(2), 191–204.

Nachmias, R., & Arcavi, A. (1990). A parallel representation of linear functions using a microcomputer-based environment. *The Journal of Computers in Mathematics and Science Teaching, 9*(4), 79–88.

Skemp, R. (1971). *The psychology of learning mathematics.* City: Penguin Books.

Rowland, T. (2008, in press). The purpose, design and use of examples in the teaching of elementary mathematics. *Educational Studies in Mathematics.*

Watson, A., & Mason, J. (2005). *Mathematics as a constructive activity: Learners generating examples.* Mahwah, NJ: Lawrence Erlbaum Associates.

Zaslavsky, O., & Lavie, O. (2005, May). *Teachers' use of instructional examples.* Paper presented at the International Commission for Mathematical Instruction (ICMI) 15, *The professional education and development of teachers of mathematics.* Áquas de Lindòia, Brazil.

Zaslavsky, O., Sela, H., & Leron, U. (2002). Being sloppy about slope: The effect of changing the scale. *Educational Studies in Mathematics, 49,* 119–140.

Zhu, S., & Simon, H. A. (1987). Learning mathematics from examples and by doing. *Cognition and Instruction, 4,* 137–166.

Zazkis, R., & Khoury, H. (1994). To the right of the decimal point: Preservice teachers' concepts of place value and multidigit structures. *Research in Collegiate Mathematics Education, 1*, 195–224.

Zazkis, R., & Whitkanack, D. (1993). Non-decimals: Fractions in bases other than ten. *International Journal of Mathematics Education in Science and Technology, 24*(1), 77–83.

Zazkis, R., & Khoury, H. (1993). Place value and rational number representations: Problem solving in the unfamiliar domain of non-decimals. *Focus on Learning Problems in Mathematics, 15*(1), 38–51.

Zazkis, R., & Leikin, R. (2007). Generating examples: From pedagogical tool to a research tool. *For the Learning of Mathematics, 27*(2), 15–21.

Rina Zazkis
Faculty of Education
Simon Fraser University
Canada

MARCUS NÜHRENBÖRGER AND HEINZ STEINBRING

7. MANIPULATIVES AS TOOLS IN MATHEMATICS TEACHER EDUCATION

In this chapter we elaborate the following important theoretical perspectives on the role that manipulatives play as tools in mathematics teacher education. A basic view is that manipulatives are not simply tools that function automatically in teaching and learning abstract mathematical knowledge, but that it is necessary to be aware of the symbolical and structural character of manipulatives in coping with mathematical knowledge. Further, this fundamental epistemological nature of manipulatives has implications for mathematics teacher education in a twofold manner. First it is necessary to see prospective teachers as learners themselves, i.e., they have to develop a careful and critical understanding of the specific epistemological character of manipulatives when learning mathematical knowledge for themselves. Second, it is necessary that prospective teachers become more and more expert in assessing students' learning and understanding of mathematical knowledge with the help of manipulatives – not as mechanical devices but as symbolical tools.

INTRODUCTION

The use of manipulatives in mathematics instruction – especially in primary schools – is wide spread. In particular, there seems to be a very extensive – and at times uncritical – use of manipulatives in Anglo-American countries; in any case these working materials are strongly recommended as essential learning aids by publishing companies and in (mathematic-didactical) textbooks (O'Shea, 1993). Our chapter is not about presenting and examining the great variety of existing manipulatives for mathematics learning systematically for the different mathematical subject areas. Rather, we will develop a theoretical-critical perspective towards the fundamental conditions and possibilities of the use of manipulatives for learning abstract mathematical knowledge based on relations and structures. Our analysis and concerns are similar to the critical questions raised by Deborah Ball (1992) in her article: *Magical Hopes – Manipulatives and the Reform of Math Education*, in which she writes:

> My main concern about the enormous faith in the power of manipulatives, in their almost magical ability to enlighten, is that it will be misled into thinking that mathematical knowledge will automatically arise from their use. (p. 18)

We understand manipulatives to be working and visualisation materials on the one hand, and visual charts and diagrams as a means to represent mathematical knowledge as manipulatives on the other hand. Concrete materials and

D. Tirosh and T. Wood (eds.), Tools and Processes in Mathematics Teacher Education, 157–181.

representations need different forms of practice in relation to their physical nature. The use of a manipulative seems to be more like the use of a *tool*. No one would expect a tool to do the work on its own, but an appropriate *use* of the tool leads to desirable results. The same seems to apply to manipulatives. But in a mathematical context the power of a tool consists not only in the right and appropriate use, the tool needs to be generically structured. When the structure can be interpreted one can use the tool as a mental object. In this sense a mathematical tool seems to be like a ruler. On the one hand, the ruler is a technical tool which can be used to measure; on the other hand one can use the ruler as a mental object, as a thinking tool. The ruler is well structured and the measurement structure has a symbolic significance, which can be interpreted with regard to key ideas of measurement (Nührenbörger, 2001). Thus, the value of manipulatives depends on the relation of the object to the mathematical relations and structures it represents. As Fischbein points out the generic structure of materials:

> Material objects have to elicit mathematical thinking, they must do it by their inner, specific properties [...] Concrete models are not necessarily initiating techniques in the teaching of mathematics. Their efficient use depends on their nature and on their relationships with the corresponding mathematical concepts. (1977, p. 163f)

For mathematics instruction in preschool (kindergarten), in primary school as well as in secondary school I (grades 1 to 10, ages; 5/6 to 16) manipulatives are in many regards an indispensable means to learn and to understand the abstract and symbolic mathematical knowledge.

Often, however, the following belief and assumption about the use of manipulatives is acted upon in instruction practice – the concrete working materials encourage the acquisition and the insightful understanding of mathematical knowledge in an easy and direct way. Artfully constructed material seemingly guarantees success for the students' understanding. In the history of mathematics instruction and into today's world, new constructions as well as new inventions of mathematical manipulatives are an important area of mathematic-didactical and school-practical work. The development and the sale of partly comprehensive collections of mathematical learning materials has become a large and extensive industry (which we will not discuss in this chapter). In this context it is interesting to note that Fischbein (1977) 30 years ago argued that it is important to try to start, as early as possible, to encourage students to reason without manipulatives.

In the frame of mathematics teacher education manipulatives have a dual role. On the one hand, prospective teachers need to get to know these manipulatives, for example, which ones are used in the different school years of mathematics instruction. They need to understand the didactical objective of these materials and to develop a competent evaluation of these materials in order to be able to use them appropriately with students in situations for mathematics learning. Furthermore the prospective teachers must develop diagnosis abilities in order to adequately analyse the students' learning processes when using manipulatives. On the other hand, manipulatives are learning objects for the teacher-students *themselves*, in the sense that exemplary manipulatives serve to encourage prospective teachers' learning and understanding processes and for acquiring a professionally founded understanding of essential elements of mathematic-didactical teacher knowledge.

In the centre of our theoretical analysis of the role of manipulatives within mathematics teacher education is the relation between »Manipulatives <—> Mathematical Knowledge«. The requirement of an appropriate understanding of this relation exists in the fact that manipulatives and mathematical knowledge are not identical, but that they are nonetheless in a close relationship to each other within learning and understanding processes. The relation between these two elements is always produced by a person (a student, the practicing teacher or a researcher), by means of constructing interpretations about the manipulatives as the explanation basis for (new) mathematical knowledge. In the basic form we are thus dealing with the following triangular scheme:

Figure 1. Manipulatives as an epistemological learning medium for students and prospective teachers.

The student (see Figure 1) in mathematics instruction produces his own interpretations of (concrete) working materials for understanding mathematical knowledge. In the place of the student, of course, can also be the prospective teacher, who uses and interprets working materials for his professional teacher knowledge. A further interesting constellation consists with prospective teachers in their education – respectively the practicing teacher in instruction – carrying out a didactical reflection about how the students use (concrete) working materials in the instruction. This situation can be represented in the following triangular scheme (Figure 2):

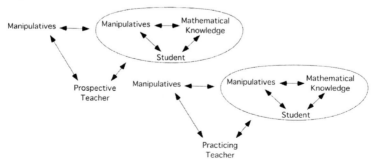

Figure 2. Manipulatives as an epistemological learning medium for prospective and practicing teachers.

A fundamental thesis for our considerations is the following:

> Manipulatives are not simply concrete elements out of an extensive tool kit, with which one can directly construct the mathematical knowledge in question according to given, simple rules (this applies to students in instruction as well as to the prospective teachers in their education);
> Manipulatives and mathematics are initially separated from each other and a relation between them can only be productively constructed by the learner's own considerations and interpretations in order to actively develop mathematical understanding and insights. The relation »Manipulatives <—> Mathematical Knowledge« is a relation to be built theoretically and consciously; it does not emerge spontaneously and automatically (what this means in detail shall be elaborated in the following paragraphs).

In the following section the first perspective towards the role of manipulatives within mathematics instruction is discussed: *What are the particular didactical and epistemological aspects of manipulatives* which are mainly used in the different school years of mathematics instruction? In the next section, the second perspective shall be dealt with: *What importance do common manipulatives,* which are traditionally and widely used in the curricula and in the schools, *have for the development of professional didactical teacher knowledge in the frame of teacher education?* Due to space limitations not all materials and visualisations can be addressed in detail. Thus, for the elaboration of a theoretical characterisation of the essential epistemological conditions of manipulatives we will concentrate on those materials and visualisations, which have a central function for the development of the decimal structure of the number concept in grades 1 to 10.

THE ROLE OF MANIPULATIVES IN MATHEMATICS TEACHING (GRADES 1–10)

A large number of manipulatives is used in mathematics lessons with the claim that they facilitate and extend students' learning of mathematical concepts and operations. These are: coloured reversible chips, cubes and multi-system blocks, Cuisenaire rods, abacus, point fields such as fields of 20 or 100, number boards such as boards of 20 and 100, numberline, empty numberline or place value tables. The use of different manipulatives for the illustration of numbers and number relationships, of operations and operation relations as well as for argumentation and for the proof of basic mathematical ideas is an important integral part of mathematics lessons in grades 1 to 10 (Scherer & Steinbring, 1998).

With the help of manipulatives mathematical concepts are assumed to be made "comprehensible". Analyses of school textbooks or teaching experiments give the illusion that, especially at primary school, empirical references are very intensively and rightly used for this purpose (Lorenz, 1998). In everyday mathematics lessons, however, manipulatives are often treated as equivalent to the mathematical objects. Children are far too quickly supposed to have taken in mathematical concepts and operations just by the concrete work with manipulatives. However, the empirical collection cannot be unambiguously correctly interpreted from a mathematical point of view – they are rather "empirically ambiguous" (Lorenz, 1998; Steinbring, 1994a). Furthermore, the stress on empirical references must not result in a neglect of relational views. Mathematical concepts are relational from the start with regard to their empirical meaning structure and are to be increasingly reflected and interpreted in a more differentiated and diverse manner.

Based on a "copy-theory" point of view it was assumed for a long time that mathematical knowledge was a copy of external seeing and acting in the mind of a child and was transmitted as such from the teaching to the learning person (Lorenz, 1998). The external 'seeing' of mathematical concepts and operations in manipulatives could therefore lead to the development of an analogous internal seeing. Based on manipulatives, mathematical ideas were initially demonstrated by the teacher in a concrete-acting and linguistically accompanied manner which was followed by a practicing, passively imitating repetition by the students (Figure 3).

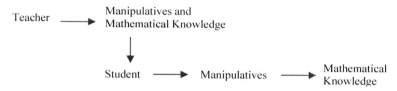

Figure 3. Manipulatives as a "teaching medium" (traditional view I).

This copy-theory point of view does not correspond to the idea of learning mathematics through an active, subject-related constructional process which is influenced by the experience, emotions and knowledge of the teacher. Based on concrete work with manipulatives, mathematical concepts are, therefore, not to be taken in passively. They are actively discovered and internalised in the form of mental images and operations (Aebli, 1980; Piaget & Inhelder, 1979). With regard to the development of children's thinking Bruner (1974) makes a distinction between three modalities of the representation of mathematical concepts and operations: enactive – iconic – symbolic. In present-day mathematics lessons these three modalities are frequently found in an almost formalistic application in a sequence of three steps: The introduction of a mathematical concept starts with the acting-enactive acquisition using concrete manipulatives – this is followed by activities at the visual-iconic level – and finally exercises are carried out exclusively at the symbolic-linguistic level using abstract signs (see Figure 4). These three steps are based on the "naive conviction" that, especially primary school children, need to work actively with manipulatives at the start of a mathematical learning process while children at higher grades can do without these and increasingly use images and diagrams instead. Moreover, it is assumed that children with mathematical learning problems must be allowed more time for the concrete-enactive work with manipulatives than other 'normal' children.

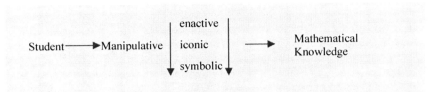

Figure 4. Manipulatives as an "unambiguous learning medium" (traditional view II).

This instructive idea of manipulative as a learning medium is to be critically questioned, however. A strict separation of the three modalities "enactive – iconic – symbolic" cannot be maintained because the respective context in which the manipulative is used affects the interpretation of the manipulative. As Söbbeke illustrates:

> Based on the example of the reversible chips […] it becomes obvious that the active work with the concrete material may also have a highly symbolic character. A chip in the place value table not only symbolizes a '1', for instance, but, depending on its location in the place value table, possibly also a '100' or even '1,000,000'. Three chips which have been sorted into the ones and hundreds columns can be interpreted as a quantity of 3 chips, but at the same time – and this is the special feature of symbolic material – they may represent the figure '102'. If a chip is then moved from the column of ones to the column of tens a new interpretation, a reinterpretation of the material will be required – although 3 chips are still available. (2005, p. 16, this quotation refers to Figure 5)

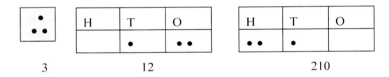

Figure 5. Different interpretations of three chips.

Even if for the educationalist or teacher the mathematical structure is "obviously" represented in the manipulatives, there is no direct way which takes the students from the process of looking and acting to the desired mental picture.

> The work with a given illustration material does not for all students in the same manner lead to the development of the cognitive procedures and structures aimed at by the producers of the visualization aid. (Lorenz, 1998, p. 1)

The manipulatives are rather interpreted in distinct ways by different children. This may lead to students' problems in understanding and in the long term to rule-guided work with manipulatives which corresponds to the apparently obvious (to

162

the adult) conventions. Particularly, if desired interpretation patterns and rituals are largely standardized, confirmed and continued and there is no space is allowed for students to reveal unexpected and undesired interpretations, an "unambiguous interpretation culture" is developed in which students learn to point out to each other the "correct" and especially the "obviously visible" interpretation for all.

However, openness to alternative interpretation attempts which corresponds to the epistemological value of manipulatives is required (Söbbeke, 2005). Manipulatives are symbolic representations in which mathematical relationships, structures and patterns are contained which can be actively interpreted, exchanged within the discursive context and checked with regard to plausibility (Figure 6).

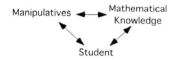

Figure 6. Manipulatives as an "epistemological learning medium".

Manipulatives have two essential aspects in common:
- Manipulatives embody mathematical knowledge materially, but the embodiment is based on the internal structure of the manipulatives and has symbolic character. The idea of representation rests on the internal structure on which the manipulatives are based. On the basis of his/her "old knowledge" the learning person is to interpret the respective mathematical structure by active dealing with the manipulatives.
- The manipulatives represent the theoretical mathematical concepts and operations without, at the same time, reflecting them empirically. The students can work with manipulatives at the concrete level but need to interpret them with regard to the mathematical concept.

The relation between the abstract mathematical concept and the concrete manipulative which refers to the concept but at the same time also has symbolic character is described by Duval (2000) as the "paradoxical character of mathematical knowledge". Within the genetic framework illustration aids have no didactic but an epistemological status; they represent embodiments of mathematical structures which are open in principle and represent a field of action for comprehensive, structured activities of the learning person. In other words, illustration aids are not instruments of the teacher but a means of cognition in the hands of the learning person (Wittmann, 1993). This particular requirement for the work with manipulatives provides potential for their use.

In mathematics lessons the structural relations contained in manipulatives are to be deliberately picked out as a central theme so that students learn to unfold a relational view of the mathematical concepts and operations when working with the manipulative. Manipulatives are "theoretically ambiguous" (Steinbring, 1994b) so that by means of a change of perspective new relations can be considered (see Figure 8, from Steinbring, 1994b, p. 17f for an example).

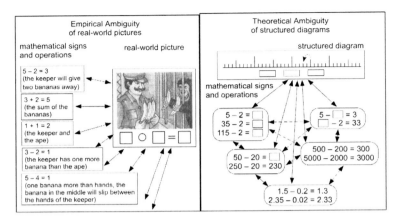

Figure 8. Empirical and theoretical ambiguity.

It is of particular significance that students will have the opportunity during the lesson to take different views and interpretations, to discuss the use of symbols with others and to change their views subsequently. It is therefore necessary to continuously examine actions in which iconic and symbolic interpretations are structurally developed. Even if the concrete work with manipulatives is indispensable, the child must not permanently remain at the empirical level. This would lead to mathematical knowledge which is exclusively validated empirically.

> Through interaction with structured external representations in the learning environment students' internal representational systems develop. The students can then generate new external relations. Conceptual understanding consists in the power and flexibility of internal representations, including the richness of the relationships among different kinds of representations. (Goldin & Shteingold, 2001, p. 8)

The example of the allocation of numbers in the 100-table below is given to demonstrate how openness to manipulatives develops the class discussion about mathematical relations in a new way and also illustrates how the discussion during the lesson is characterized by the tension between expected views and individual interpretations. In the following transcript students of grades 1 and 2 (6–7 years) discuss the position of the number '0' in the 100-table after several numbers have already been placed in the table.

1	Teach	Someone just asked, Is there also a zero?
2	Stud	Where does the zero go then?
3	Teach	Where should it go? Kira?
4	Kira	The one should go here *(points to the field next to 1)*, the zero should go here *(points to the field in which the 1 is fixed)*.
5	Teach	That means, you would do it like this? *(removes the 1 and sticks the 0 in its place)* Would anybody do it differently?
6	Stud	No!
7	Teach	What has Kira done correctly? (...) Louis?
8	Lou	She stuck it in the hundred-field. The sequence is correct then.
9	Teach	Mmh. I know what you mean. Mmh. Mia?
10	Mia	(.) Em, (.) she stuck it next to the one.
11	Teach	Not behind it.
12	Mia	In front of it!
13	Teach	Exactly. That is correct. It must go <u>before</u> the one. But?
14	Lou	Now there's no room for the two.
15	Teach	Exactly, and therefore it does not go into the field but on the side of the field.
16	Mar	Otherwise the sequence would be hidden, then the ten would have to go under the one.
17	Teach	Correct. Then we would have to move them all (...) That's also possible. What else will then happen in another place of the hundred-field? If we move them all. The zero goes here, where Kira put it. The one, the two, the three, the four, five, six, seven, eight, <u>nine</u> (.) ten, eleven, twelve, what else will happen?
18	Flo	Then the hundred will be here *(points to the bottom next to the hundred-table)*.
19	Teach	Then <u>it</u> would have to go on the side. Did you want to say that, too? (..) Great. So that means, both of them don't fit on it, one of them has to be thrown off. I have to decide at the start whether or not to begin with the zero.

(...) = 3 seconds, (..) = 2 seconds, (.)= 1 second

0	1				7		9	10
			15					
			35					
								100

In this scene the students discuss the consequences of placing the zero into the 100-table and take up different views. The interpretation relating to the position of the "0" leads to the fact that the teacher abandons her conventional, quickly regulating idea (line 15) and, contrary to conventions, allows beginning the 100-table with a zero (line 19). Here the zero is correlated to the other numbers without exclusively putting the emphasis on an empirical interpretation. In this kind of communicative culture of mathematics lessons the epistemological value of manipulatives can be discussed. Interpretation attempts are not made spontaneously here but deliberately on the basis of a constructive relation between manipulatives and the mathematical knowledge so that (new) mathematical insights can be obtained.

The relational character of mathematics is emphasized by manipulatives which are structured in themselves and are at the same time "semi-concrete". "Semi-concrete" means that interchangeable concrete features which are not significant for mathematical activities are pushed into the background and more general, neutral aspects come to the fore so that the manipulatives can be understood as representatives of other objects. For the mathematical cognition process a certain vagueness of the manipulatives in this respect is a guarantee for a basic "openness" which is indispensable for the use of manipulatives. Wittmann compares these manipulatives with amphibians which are "concrete and abstract and are therefore ideal mediators between reality and mathematical theory" (1994, p. 44).

In this chapter we concentrate on manipulatives which can be used for the development of the number concept and for the insight into the decimal structure of our number system. For this purpose both reversible chips (e.g., white on one side and black on the other) and structured diagrams (e.g., the place value table) can be used which, in the sense of theoretical ambiguity, allows for discussion that make different references to the mathematical world and therefore also establishes mathematical relations between empirical elements of the factual situation.

Example 1: Reversible chips

In initial arithmetic lessons reversible chips often serve only as counting objects. It is of elementary significance, however, that already at the start of school a relational view of numbers and operations is opened up and unfolded so that in further years effective strategies for elementary arithmetical operations can be progressed.

Reversible chips for the representation of numbers and number relations: During lessons the reversible chips are primarily used as counting objects. In this context a number can be "assigned" to each chip. The number "5" would be represented by five chips, 5% and/or 1/20 by 5 black and 95 white chips (see Figure 9a). At the same time the number "5" can also be seen as the difference between three and eight chips and as the addend in 3 + 5, which is illustrated by five white chips and/or by the reduction of a number (see Figure 9b). The discussion of the different reduction options opens up an increasingly differentiated interpretation process of abstract mathematical relations and structures already at the start of school.

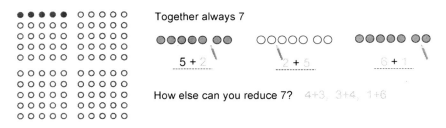

Figure 9a. The number 5, 5% or 1/20.

Figure 9b. Decomposition tasks with number 7 (from Wittmann & Müller, 2004, p. 34.)

Reversible chips for the representation of arithmetical operations and operative relations: If reversible chips are linked with number fields, arithmetical relations can be explored by means of the chips. Based on their concrete work with the material the students discover mathematical relations and operative variations. For example, the problem $7 + 6$ can be shown in different ways in the 20-field; e.g. consecutively as $7 + 3 + 3$, as $5 + 5 + 2 + 1$ or underneath each other as $7 + 7 - 1$.

Reversible chips for the representation of patterns and for establishing proof: The large variety of options for the geometrical arrangement of the reversible chips facilitates the exploration of mathematical relations and patterns and their discussion, justification and generalization. Especially triangular, square and rectangular numbers are well-known here. The relation between square numbers and the sum of a sequence of odd numbers can be illustrated by means of reversible chips (see Figure 10); for instance, by
— showing each new square of odd numbers as a line of towers increasing in size which can be rearranged by changing a part of the towers into squares,
— showing each new square number by a new angle which doubles a line and column (top and right) and increases it by a corner point.

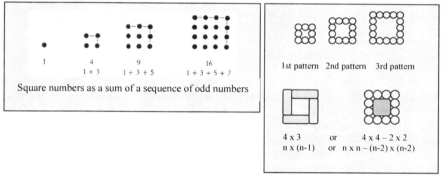

Figure 10. Different views on patterns (see Böttinger, 2007).

Example 2: Place value table

The place value table, just like the reversible chips, has the "character of variables" (Jahnke, 1984, p. 35) and can be read and used in many different ways. It therefore not only shows what is already known but encourages pupils to make further explorations due to its symbolic and ambiguous character.

The place value table for the representation of numbers and number relations: In principle the place value table consists of different columns which are assigned to different places within our base ten number system. A number is divided into individual digits which are given a certain value in the respective column. The number thus symbolizes mathematical relations. If a number is missing in a column this points to the fact that this place value is not "occupied" and that the respective

167

place is empty. The zero has a special quality here. It does not stand for a missing empirical object but for a mathematical relation between different place values. The decimal place value table can be used in different number areas and number systems. It can be extended both to the left and to the right so that not only larger numbers but also decimal numbers can be explored.

In connection with the place value table the character of variables of the reversible chips is particularly emphasized because they have different values depending on their position. A chip in the tens column has a different value than one in the ones column. The representation of numbers in the place value table by means of a given number of chips (1, 2, 3 ... chips) on the one hand facilitates explorations between the numbers and on the other hand promotes combinatory discoveries. Particular focus is on the relations between numbers in the decimal systems if the numbers are to be shown analogously in the million and thousand table (see Figure 11). The number "111" as a "related" number can be laid not only as a "111" in the million table but also as a "111 000" or multiplied by ten as "1 110" or as "101 010" etc.

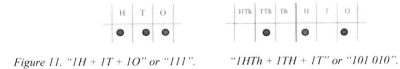

Figure 11. "1H + 1T + 1O" or "111".   *"1HTh + 1TH + 1T" or "101 010".*

The place value table for the representation of arithmetical operations and operative relations: Calculation methods can be introduced by means of the place value table. Especially for the preparation of the written addition the transformation between the place value of hundreds, tens and ones can be practiced in the lesson by entering also two-digit numbers in the place value table and transforming them. Two-digit numbers in the place value table can be described as riddle numbers because they do not correspond to the decimal system.

The interpretation of the respective manipulatives such as reversible chips or place value table in the context of a targeted setting of tasks serves as an explanation utility for the construction of (new) mathematical knowledge. Students must therefore have the opportunity to create relations between the manipulatives and their mathematical knowledge in order to actively develop mathematical understanding and insight.

THE ROLE OF MANIPULATIVES IN MATHEMATICS TEACHER EDUCATION

The epistemological characterisation of the role of manipulatives for mathematics instruction, which was developed in the last section, is itself a subject in the education of prospective teachers. Like any theoretical knowledge, this didactic-epistemological knowledge about the role of manipulatives for mathematics instruction is no mere collection of finished facts or recipe knowledge, which could be directly passed on to the learners. Theoretical – professional – knowledge for prospective-teachers can only be elaborated in one's own active discussion with this knowledge and by means of one's own interpretations and analyses (Steinbring, 2003). The essential epistemological conditions for the relation »Manipulatives <—> Mathematical Knowledge« have been elaborated in the last paragraph especially on the example of working and presentation materials for the development of the base 10 place value structure. This exemplary reference to essential manipulatives for the number concept development shall be continued in this paragraph.

If one wants to focus on the goals, requirements and constraints for the education of prospective teachers for a didactical, competent use of manipulatives in mathematics teaching, one has to consider in particular the following duality. On the one hand, prospective teachers have their own explicit and implicit conceptions, imaginations and knowledge elements about the relation »Manipulatives <—> Mathematical Knowledge«. From their own school time they have such or similar manipulatives still in mind and additionally they have partial experiences in the use of manipulatives in their own mathematical learning processes. These brought subjective experiences and views about manipulatives which sometimes predefine the prospective teachers' opinion about the use of these manipulatives. They often ascribe to manipulatives a too simple and direct positive effect on learning abstract mathematics (Ball, 1992). They also believe concrete working materials have to be unambiguous, colourful and visually stimulating in order to work well with students. These naïve views about the effect of manipulatives on mathematics learning are often unconsciously so deep-seated that it becomes difficult to call them into question, and then to develop a more differentiated conception about the particular epistemological requirements when using manipulatives in mathematics teaching.

With this the other side of the required dual role of manipulatives in teacher education comes into view. Opposite to the subjective and individual conceptions about the relation »Manipulatives <—> Mathematical Knowledge«, it is necessary to confront prospective teachers in their education with essential theoretical aspects of (also very concrete, material) manipulatives in order to cause cognitive conflict and thus to encourage changes in existing subjective conceptions and to stimulate further developments. The addressed duality can be represented in the following diagram as shown in Figure 12:

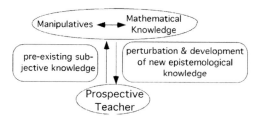

Figure 12. Subjective and objective knowledge about the relation between Manipulatives and Mathematical Knowledge.

This dual perspective of the role of manipulatives as tools in mathematics teacher education shall in the following be elaborated and described in more detail and several examples illustrate the use of typical materials for the number concept development.

In primary school concrete materials play a central role for the »embodiment« of mathematical knowledge, especially arithmetical knowledge (see the paragraph above as well as Lorenz, 1998; Wittmann, 1993, 1994). A central material for the representation of (natural) numbers is two-sided coloured chips (described in the previous section). These materials – as with all manipulatives – have, depending on the user – students or prospective teachers – different roles and functions. They can be used as very concrete materials or also as abstract symbols. How prospective-teachers can insightfully perceive this important interpretation range shall be explained with several accurate examples from mathematic-didactical education.

Example 3: The rule of the divisibility by 9

> (...) The so-called rule of nine, which states that *whether we divide the integer or its digital sum by 9, the remainder is the same. In particular, a number is divisible by 9 if and only if 9 divides its digital sum.* (Dantzig, 1954, pp. 263–264)

A proof of this rule can occur in an arithmetical way by means of a typical number example and be partially generalized. In order to do this one can carry out the following consideration for an example number $z = 3681$ (DS means digital sum of a natural number z): $3681 = 1000 \cdot 3 + 100 \cdot 6 + 10 \cdot 8 + 1 = 999 \cdot 3 + 99 \cdot 6 + 9 \cdot 8 + (3 + 6 + 8 + 1) = 999 \cdot 3 + 99 \cdot 6 + 9 \cdot 8 + DS(3681) = 999 \cdot 3 + 99 \cdot 6 + 9 \cdot 8 + 18 = 9 \cdot (111 \cdot 3 + 11 \cdot 6 + 8) + 18$

This consideration of a number example can be transferred to any natural number z: $z = 1000a + 100b + 10c + d = 999a + 99b + 9c + (a + b + c + d) = 999a + 99b + 9c + DS(z)$. A number z is divisible by 9 exactly when DS(z) is divisible by 9. One can furthermore discover that a number z is divisible by 3 exactly when DS(z) is divisible by 3.

In contrast to this arithmetical justification of the rule of nine by an operative proof (Winter, 1985; Wittmann, 2006), the use of chips in the place value table (manipulative) is presented and with this the role of manipulatives in teacher education discussed. The confirmation of the rule of nine with the help of concrete material is given as a problem for one's own active work to the prospective teachers by the following problem:

– Put the number 3681 with chips in a place value table!

Example:

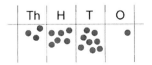

Th	H	T	O

- Consider what it means in the place value table to form the digital sum with the help of the chips! Example: All chips are moved under the One (O).

Th	H	T	O
			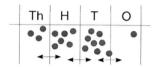

- How does the number, represented by chips, change when a chip is moved from one place value position to a neighbouring position? Example: The value of the number changes when moving it by 9, 90, 900, etc. (less or more).

Th	H	T	O

- Formulate with your own words in a consistent way a justification for the nine rule, which expresses the generality of the rule and which considers the use and the interpretations of the concrete material.

Example: Formulation of an operative principle (Wittmann, 2006): The initial number decreases through the moving of the representing chips from a place value position to the right neighbouring position by a multiple of 9; when the sum of all chips in the One position – the checksum of the initial number – is divisible by 9 (resp. by 3) exactly then also the initial number is divisible by 9 (resp. by 3).

Possible theoretical interpretations of manipulatives, which prospective-teachers can learn autonomously when working on this problem is:
- Chips do not directly and immediately represent numbers; by moving the chips between the place value positions the numbers represented by the chip change
- Concrete materials such as chips, which are actively dealt with – touching, moving etc. – do not simply have a function as concrete material: The use as well as the concrete actions with the material do have to be actively interpreted by the learner with regard to their symbolically intended representations.
- The changes carried out concretely with the material are not merely the ›concrete‹ and acting confirmation of the divisibility of the number 3681, but this work contains at the core the relations and structures for the general proof of the rule of nine (Müller & Wittmann, 1988).

Example 4: Variation and generalisation – numbers in place value tables represented by chips

The place value table together with the numbers represented by chips can be varied, changed and expanded in many ways. For instance the place values Ones, Tens, Hundreds, etc. can be expanded to the right by tenths, hundredths, thousandths, etc. (in this way also decimal numbers are represented, see part 2).

Usually a chip represents the value of a power of ten (10^n, n = 0, 1, 2, ...) in the place value. The basis b = 10 of the common ten system can, however, also be changed to other bases (e.g. b = 2, 5, 12 or other values). In the following arithmetical questions shall be presented exemplarily in the frame of the binary system (b = 2), which make clear which mathematic-didactical and epistemological insights and knowledge prospective teachers can acquire in their education about the role of manipulatives in this number system when using chips (see more about this from among others, Gardner, 1974; Steinbring, 1994a).

Addition and subtraction of natural numbers in the binary system with the help of chips:

Exercises for prospective-teachers when working with the binary abacus:

– Place the two natural numbers 19 and 53 in the binary abacus with the help of chips and add them in the binary abacus!

The example numbers 19 and 53 are to be added; in order for this they are placed in the binary abacus with chips as follows:

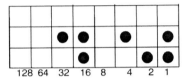

The addition of the two numbers happens by ›moving together‹ the chips. This "form of addition" reminds of the very original meaning of addition as "putting together" of numbers or of quantities of different objects, which represent numbers.

– Which representation does the sum of the two numbers 19 and 53 have in the binary abacus? Consider how you can receive an *unequivocal* representation of the sum!

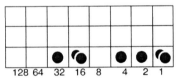

Explanations: In the first representation of the sum 19 + 53 there are "double allocations" of place values. For the production of the "unequivocal" representation in the binary system, one needs the following rule.

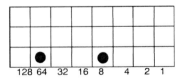

Rule for the production of an unequivocal representation: At any position there may only be one chip: two chips in one position mean that for this, a chip is introduced one position higher and both chips are taken away.

– Consider at the example of the two numbers 53 and 19 how the subtraction 53 – 19 can be carried out by chips in the binary abacus!

Explanations to this exercise: The subtraction can occur by a comparison of the chip relation of the two numbers (53 upper line and 19 lower line). When the chip representation is in such a way that in every position, in which there is a chip for the subtrahend (19), there is also a chip of the minuend (53) in the same position; then this chip can be taken away for the minuend as well as for the subtrahend, without the difference changing. Behind this concrete action the *law of the constancy of the difference* (e.g. $53 - 19 = 50 - 16$) is hidden.

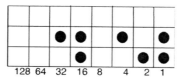

Thus for carrying out the subtraction it is important that the condition is met that "above" each chip for the representation of the subtrahend there is also a chip at the minuend. When this is NOT the case, one can accomplish this by applying the rule of the unequivocal representation stated above "backwards".

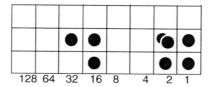

Then these chips are taken away, the resulting number has been "moved downwards".

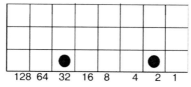

By taking away one chip from the minuend and subtrahend each in those positions where one chip is present in both representations, one acquires the subtraction result by concrete acting with the chips (34 or 100010_2).

Further possible theoretical interpretations of manipulatives, which prospective teachers can autonomously learn when working on this problem:

– Actions with chips can mean different forms of arithmetical operations, e.g. concrete putting together for addition, or a relational, structural comparison at the example of subtraction
– Chip configurations do not simply represent concrete objects and materials, they can only be understood when the structure represented by them is observed (e.g., the respective place values for a chip, relations between neighbouring positions, on which chips are placed, the rule for the production of an unequivocal representation of the number, etc.)

- The arithmetical operations carried out by concrete actions on the chip material (addition or subtraction) are based on underlying abstract arithmetical laws (e.g., the law of the constancy of the difference).

When working on this exercise the materiality of the manipulatives and the concrete way of acting with them vanish more and more into the background; the schematic operating with the chips in the binary abacus in order to carry out additions and subtractions is similar to the operations of a computer, which also can only be interpreted and understood as symbolic operations on the basis of abstract structures, relations and laws. These manipulatives do not work as concrete material with concrete ways of use, but as concrete symbols for mathematical relations and operations.

Example 5: Continuation of the abstraction process – negative numbers in place value tables represented by chips

Can negative base numbers also be used in order to represent numbers? (cf. Knuth 1969). Can one also in a place value table with a negative base number represent the numbers unequivocally? Example: $b = -2$:

$(-2)^7$ $= -128$	$(-2)^6$ $= 64$	$(-2)^5$ $= -32$	$(-2)^4$ $= 16$	$(-2)^3$ $= -8$	$(-2)^2$ $= 4$	$(-2)^1$ $= -2$	$(-2)^0$ $= 1$	
							●	1
					●	●		2
					●	●	●	3
					●			4
					●		●	5
						●	●	-1
						●		-2
				●	●		●	-3
				●	●			-4
				●	●	●	●	-5

Instead of the base $b = -2$ one can of course also use other negative numbers: $b = -3, -7, -11$, etc.

In their education the prospective-teachers also independently examine addition and subtraction (subtraction is carried out as an addition with the respective negative number) in the negative binary system. In the following the prospective-teachers are to examine multiplication and its particular rules with the exercise $(-5)\cdot(-7)$ in the negative binary abacus. (The prospective teachers know the multiplication of positive dual numbers in the positive binary abacus; the way of proceeding becomes clear with the following example.)

Exercise:
- Examine at the example $(-5) \cdot (-7)$ in the negative binary abacus the rules of multiplication of negative numbers!
- Explain why "$(-) \cdot (-) = (+)$" applies!

One can calculate the exemplary exercise $19 + (-52)$ as follows:

The prospective teachers know from the example of multiplication of positive numbers in the binary system that one first puts the two factors outside at the abacus, e.g., the −5 into the horizontal below, and the −7 in the vertical right. The multiplication is now carried out with chips in such a way that at the "coordinate points" in the abacus, where outside a chip of the two factors lies, a chip is included.

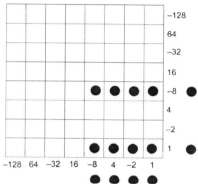

The chips lying in the abacus have to be added according to the positions: chips lying in different lines in the abacus have different place values. This happens by "diagonal moving together" of the chips.

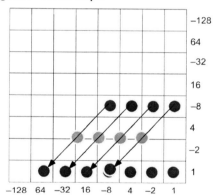

The result of the multiplication is in the lowest horizontal line, however not yet in the unequivocal, adjusted form. The rule for the production of an unequivocal representation in this place value system has to be modified:

Two chips in one position and **one** chip exactly one position higher together result in zero. $(2 \cdot (-8) + 1 \cdot (16) = 0)$ At both positions the chips are taken away accordingly.

Two chips in one position and **no** chip exactly one position higher mean that for this, one needs to put one chip one and one more (second) position higher.

With these rules one receives the result: $(-5) \cdot (-7) = 64 - 32 + 4 - 2 + 1 = 35$.

When working on this exercise prospective teachers can actively gather further important didactical and epistemological insights about the role and function of manipulatives for the learning of mathematics. Besides the necessity of constructing more and more general and abstract structures as basis for the manual operating with the chips, it becomes very clear that concrete manipulatives can not be equated with mathematical ideal objects. When negative numbers are represented by chips in the negative binary abacus, these chips as chip configurations in a mathematical structure have the character of *mathematical symbols* (they are not mere concrete materials).

When prospective teachers have developed a flexible theoretical understanding of the role of manipulatives themselves – for instance while working on problems as discussed above – they then are requested to "apply" their personal knowledge about manipulatives to teaching and learning situations where students in the classroom are working with such manipulatives or representations of mathematical structures. The following example of students working together with their teacher on arithmetical questions using a position table might provide an example of the way in which observation of classroom interaction illustrates how this activity can be used in teaching.

H	T	O
1	17	39

Without observing the diagram this riddle number can be interpreted as "11739". The placement of the numbers in the diagram opens up new interpretations, however: 1H + 17T + 39O= 1H + 10T + 7T + 30O + 9O= 1H + 1H + 7T + 3T + 9O= 2H + 10T + 9O= 2H + 1H + 0T + 9O= 3H + 9O= 309.

Based on the discussion between the teacher and the class about how a riddle number can be transformed, shows how the students' different interpretations of this riddle number in the place value table. First, the student, Jill, explains her view of the number: "*Here, where the 39 is, there's a 39, so that only 9 can remain here because the 3 must be added straight away, and only 9 of the ones are left.*" Some time later in the interaction, Jill points to the changes in the tens column and says, "*And then I have to calculate in that direction because this goes here* points to the 1 in the 17 in the tens column, then to the hundreds column *then a 10 has to go here* points to the tens column *because 3 plus 7 is 10, (...)* enters 10 in the tens column *and then we have to add 100 plus 100 here* points to the 1 in the hundreds column and the 1 of the 17 in the tens column *that comes to 200, then a 2 has to be entered here* enters a 2 in the hundreds column . *The result is then 219.*"

H	T	O
1	17	39
2	10	9

Jill interprets the numbers in the place value table in different ways. On the one hand, she can reduce 39 ones to 30 ones and 9 ones as well as to 3 tens and 9 ones as well as 17 tens to 1 hundred and 7 tens. On the other hand, she interprets 10 tens as 1 ten. Here the special role of the zero becomes apparent which for Jill holds the empirical character of "nothing" and is therefore not to be considered as a ten. Her classmate Anna brings in a new interpretation by saying that 10 tens correspond to one hundred *("Because the ten is 10 times 10 is 100. Therefore the hundred plus 200 must be 300.")*.

H	T	O
1	17	39
2	10	9
100+200=300		

While Anna interprets the tens according to their place value, she notes the hundreds as numbers in the hundred column. In the further course of the lesson this leads to different interpretations which are often developed in the context of "well-meant" representations if the decimal places are to be "clarified" by means of empirical objects. If blocks in the ones column, rods of 10 in the tens column, fields of 100 and cubes of 1000 are to be introduced underneath the designations of O, T, H and Th there will be a risk of providing an "over-materialized representation" which perturbs the students and may lead to a conflict with their symbolic interpretation such as: What do 5 fields under H mean? Do they mean 5 hundreds or 500 hundreds? This kind of put-on concrete specification devalues the material because it does not correspond with the interpretation possibilities of the students and does not allow any retrospection or further interpretation.

The problems for prospective teachers in the frame of their mathematical and didactical education in the example above try to meet the requirement that as student-teachers they must critically deal with the role and the interpretation of manipulatives for learning mathematics in two ways. First, prospective teachers need to experience and learn for themselves by means of concrete exercises that manipulatives do not work as concrete, material objects – even in an immediate, spontaneous way – as learning aids for abstract mathematical knowledge. Second, concrete material objects are only appropriate for the representation of mathematical knowledge in the form of symbols. Furthermore, it is important that on this basis prospective teachers then acquire professional didactical knowledge about how students in mathematics instruction (primary and secondary school) can learn in a sensible, structure-oriented interaction with manipulatives, in order to enhance and differentiate their mathematical views and ways of interpretation.

CONCLUDING REMARKS

The central idea about the role and meaning of manipulatives as tools in teacher education, which was developed in the previous paragraphs, states that the actual function and the particular use of manipulatives for learning mathematics does not consist in these manipulatives as concrete objects as being perceivable things, which seemingly are appropriate for directly and spontaneously gaining the understanding and the acquaintance of abstract mathematical knowledge. As pointed out in the introduction the productive view of manipulatives not only comprehends a discussion of didactical meaningful learning objects, but also a theoretical-critical analysis of the conditions and possibilities of the use of manipulatives for learning abstract mathematical knowledge based on relations and structures. The concrete didactical materials only become productive mathematical manipulatives in the context of their *use by the students* – they do not simply exist without an interpretation by the learner. In this sense one cannot evaluate manipulatives in an easy manner, however, there are a few guidelines and criteria, which help to distinguish them from common manipulatives (Schipper, 1996; Wittmann, 1993):

– In what way do the manipulatives embody basic – structured – mathematical ideas (like numbers, decimals, fractions, operations, decimal system, arithmetical rules and patterns)?
– Is it possible to continue with the manipulatives using the same structure in different school years?
– Is it possible to develop for different students individual approaches for using manipulatives for the elaboration and solution of the tasks with the?
– Is it possible to act with the manipulatives for developing operational strategies?
– Do the manipulatives support the abandonment of arithmetical counting strategies?
– Are the manipulatives well structured and manageable for students?

Manipulatives receive their particular meaning when they are seen and needed by the learners more and more in the form of material symbols which serve for representing mathematical structures, relations and patterns. The development of an appropriate use and an adequate interpretation of manipulatives occur by means of phases in the use of a concrete material and of working with these materials up to a more and more structural and abstract interpretation of manipulatives as quasi-symbolical representations of mathematical knowledge. This development plays a role

– within the mathematical learning process of students from the begin of the first grade up to higher mathematics education,
– within the education of future mathematics teachers at university, namely
– for their own profound understanding of the abstract nature of mathematical knowledge,
– for their professional mathematics teacher knowledge, which has to contain competent mathematic-didactical and epistemological knowledge about students' mathematics learning when using manipulatives.

The appropriate use of manipulatives when learning mathematics as well as the useful and beneficial interpretation of the manipulatives, which aim at the quasi-symbolical character, cannot be acquired as a subject matter step by step according to fixed rules. This knowledge about interpretations and use of manipulatives cannot be learnt as procedural mathematical knowledge; much rather evolves through interactive learning in order that the discussion and the comparison of different ways to use and interpret of manipulatives can occur. This interactive form of learning is essential for both mathematics instruction and for prospective teachers' education.

Manipulatives as tools in mathematics teacher education needs to be viewed under two perspectives alternately requiring each other:

– Manipulatives are, on the one hand, tools for prospective teachers in order to be able to work on mathematical problems and to understand mathematical concepts,

– Manipulatives are tools for students in schools, and prospective-teachers need to gain professional insights about students' mathematics learning with manipulatives.

These two central perspectives on manipulatives as tools in mathematics teacher education, however, require that the conception that manipulatives – in school mathematics instruction as well as in university teacher education – are not spontaneously working methods as means of help in order to directly understand abstract mathematics, but that they become, in the course of mathematical learning processes, quasi-symbolical representatives for mathematical operations, structures and concepts.

REFERENCES

Aebli, H. (1980). *Denken: Das Ordnen des Tuns* (Band 1) [*Thinking: The ordering of doing* (Vol. 1)]. Stuttgart: Klett.

Ball, D.L. (1992). Magical hopes–Manipulatives and the reform of math education. *American Educator, 16*(2), 14–18, 46–47.

Böttinger, C. (2007). Muster und Rechenaufgaben, Rechenaufgaben und Muster. *Die Grundschulzeitschrift, 21*(201), 30–41.

Bruner, J.S. (1974). *Entwurf einer Unterrichtstheorie* [*Toward a theory of instruction*]. Berlin: Berlin-Verlag.

Dantzig, T. (1954). *Number, the language of science*. London: Georg Allen & Unwin LTD.

Devlin, K. (1997). *Mathematics: The science of patterns*. New York, NY: Scientific American Library.

Duval, R. (2000). Basic issues for research in mathematics education. In T. Nakahara & M. Koyama (Eds.), *Proceedings of the 24th International Conference for the Psychology of Mathematics Education* (Vol. 1, pp. 55–69). Hiroshima, Japan: Nishiki Print.

Fischbein, E. (1977). Image and concept in learning mathematics. *Educational Studies in Mathematics, 8*, 153–165.

Freudenthal, H. (1973). *Mathematik als pädagogische Aufgabe* [*Mathematics as an educational task*]. Stuttgart: Klett.

Gardner, M. (1974). Mathematical games – How to turn a chessboard into a computer and to calculate with negbinary numbers. *Scientific American, 4*, 106–111.

Goldin, G., & Shteingold, N. (2001). Systems of representations and the development of mathematical concepts. In A.A. Cuoco & F.R. Curcio (Eds.), *The roles of representation in school mathematics* (pp. 1–23). Boston, VA: National Council of Teachers of Mathematics.

Jahnke, H.N. (1984). Anschauung und Begründung in der Schulmathematik [Visualization and explanation in school mathematics]. *Beiträge zum Mathematikunterricht. Bad Salzdetfurth*, 32–41.

Lorenz, J.H. (1998). *Anschauung und Veranschaulichung im Mathematikunterricht. Mentales visuelles Operieren und Rechenleistung* [*Visualization and illustration in mathematics teaching. Mental visual operations and arithmetical achievement*], 2nd print. Göttingen: Hogrefe.

Knuth, D.E. (1969). *The art of computer programming, Vol II, Seminumerical algorithms*. Reading MA: Addison Wesley Publishing Company.

Müller, G.N., & Wittmann, E.C. (1988). Wann ist ein Beweis ein Beweis? [When is a proof a proof?] In P. Bender (Ed.), *Mathematikdidaktik: Theorie und Praxis. Festschrift für Heinrich Winter* [*Mathematics education: Theory and practice. Festschrift for Heinrich Winter*] (pp. 237–257). Berlin.

Nührenbörger, M. (2001). Insights into children's ruler concepts – Grade-2-students' conceptions and knowledge of length measurement and paths of development. In M. van den Heuvel-Panhuizen (Ed.), *Proceedings of the 25th Conference of the International Group for the Psychology of Mathematics Education* (Vol. 3, pp. 447–454). Utrecht: Freudenthal Institute.

O'Shea, T. (1993). The role of manipulatives in mathematics education. *Contemporary Education, 65*(1), 6–9.

Piaget, J., & Inhelder, B. (1979). *Die Entwicklung des inneren Bildes beim Kind* [*The development of the child's inner image*]. Frankfurt: Suhrkamp.

Scherer, P., & Steinbring, H. (1998). Strategien und Begründungen an Veranschaulichungen – statische und dynamische Deutungen [Strategies and explanations using visualizations – static and dynamic interpretations]. In W. Weiser & B. Wollring (Eds.), *Beiträge zur Didaktik der Mathematik in der Primarstufe – Festschrift für Siegbert Schmidt* [*Contributions to mathematics education for primary teaching – Festschrift for Siegbert Schmidt*] (pp. 188–201). Hamburg: Dr. Kovac.

Schipper, W. (1996). Arbeitsmittel für den arithmetischen Anfangsunterricht – Kriterien zur Auswahl [Working tools in the early arithmetical classroom – Criteria for choice]. *Die Grundschulzeitschrift*/Sammelband "Offener Mathematikunterricht: Arithmetik II", 52–55.

Söbbeke, E. (2005). *Zur visuellen Strukturierungsfähigkeit von Grundschulkindern – Epistemologische Grundlagen und empirische Fallstudien zu kindlichen Strukturierungsprozessen mathematischer Anschauungsmittel* [*Elementary students' visual structurizing ability – Epistemological foundations and empirical case studies on children's structuring processes with visual materials*]. Hildesheim: Franzbecker.

Steinbring, H. (1994a). Symbole, Referenzkontexte und die Konstruktion mathematischer Bedeutung – am Beispiel der negativen Zahlen im Unterricht [Symbols, reference contexts and the construction of mathematical meaning – The case of teaching negative numbers]. *Journal für Mathematikdidaktik, 15*(3/4), 277–305.

Steinbring, H. (1994b). Die Verwendung strukturierter Diagramme im Arithmetikunterricht der Grundschule. Zum Unterschied zwischen empirischer und theoretischer Mehrdeutigkeit mathematischer Zeichen [The use of structured diagrams in the elementary arithmetics classroom. The difference between empirical and theoretical ambiguity of mathematical signs]. *Die Mathematische Unterrichtspraxis (MUP)*, (IV), 7–19.

Steinbring, H. (2003). Zur Professionalisierung des Mathematiklehrerwissens – Lehrerinnen reflektieren gemeinsam Feedbacks zur eigenen Unterrichtstätigkeit [The professionalization of mathematics teachers' knowledge – Teachers jointly reflect on feedbacks to their own teaching activity]. In M. Braun & H. Wielpütz (Eds.), *Mathematik in der Grundschule – Ein Arbeitsbuch* [*Mathematics in the elementary school – A working book* (pp. 195–219). Seelze: Kallmeyersche Verlagsbuchhandlung.

Winter, H. (1985). Neunerregel und Abakus – Schieben, denken, rechnen [The rule of nine and the abacus – Moving, thinking, calculating]. *Mathematik lehren* (11), 22–26.

Wittmann, E.C. (1993). 'Weniger ist mehr': Anschauungsmittel im Mathematikunterricht der Grundschule ['Less is more': Visual material in elementary mathematics teaching]. In K. P. Müller (Ed.), *Beiträge zum Mathematikunterricht*, Bad Salzdetfurth, pp. 394–397.

Wittmann, E.C. (1994). Legen und Überlegen: Wendeplättchen im aktiv-entdeckenden Rechenunterricht [Laying and considering: Coloured chips in an actively discovering arithmetical classroom]. *Die Grundschulzeitschrift* (74), 44–46.

Wittmann, E.C., & Müller, G.N. (2004). *Das Zahlenbuch 1 mit Lösungen* [*The number book 1 with solutions*]. Leipzig: Klett.

Wittmann, E.C. (2006). *Mathematics as the science of patterns – A guideline for developing mathematics education from early childhood to adulthood*, (EC Wittmann – irem.u-strasbg.fr: http://irem.u-strasbg.fr/php/publi/annales/sommaires/11/WittmannA.pdf)

Marcus Nührenbörger
Institute of Didactic of Mathematics
University of Duisburg-Essen
Germany

Heinz Steinbring
Institute of Didactic of Mathematics
University of Duisburg-Essen
Germany

MARIA G. BARTOLINI BUSSI AND MICHELA MASCHIETTO

8. MACHINES AS TOOLS IN TEACHER EDUCATION[1]

The aim of this chapter is to present some issues concerning teacher education, at both primary and secondary school levels, drawing on the activity of the Laboratory of Mathematical Machines at the Department of Mathematics of the University of Modena and Reggio Emilia (MMLab: www.mmlab.unimore.it). After having defined what are mathematical machines (geometrical and arithmetical machines, as well), we shall illustrate shortly the theoretical framework of semiotic mediation after Vygotsky, where the activity for prospective and practising school teachers is situated. We shall offer two examples. The first concerns arithmetical machines related to the meaning of place value in primary school and the second geometrical machines related to the meaning of axial symmetry in secondary school. Activity takes place in small size (25–30 students) laboratory settings for prospective and practising school teachers, according to the Italian standards for teacher education and to the implementation realized at the Faculty of Education of the University of Modena and Reggio Emilia.

INTRODUCTION

The Laboratory of Mathematical Machines of the University of Modena and Reggio Emilia is a well known research centre for the teaching and learning of mathematics by means of instruments (Maschietto, 2005; Larousserie, 2005). The name comes from the most important collection of the Laboratory, containing more than 200 working reconstructions (based on the original sources) of many mathematical instruments taken from the history of geometry. Briefly,

> a mathematical (or, better, a geometrical) machine is a tool that forces a point to follow a trajectory or to be transformed according to a given law.

Examples are the standard compass (that forces a point to go on a circular trajectory, see below) and the Dürer glass used as a perspectograph (that transform a point into its perspective image on a glass from a given point). However, the activities in the MMLab are not limited to the above kind of instruments. Also activities with physical machines concerning arithmetics are carried out. For brevity, we shall call them "arithmetical machines". Briefly,

---

[1] Research funded by MIUR (PRIN 2005019721): Meanings, conjectures, proofs: from basic research in mathematics education to curriculum (national coordinator: M. G. Bartolini Bussi).

D. Tirosh and T. Wood (eds.), Tools and Processes in Mathematics Teacher Education, 183–208.

an arithmetical machine is a tool that allows the user to perform at least one of the following actions: counting; making calculations; representing numbers.

Tools from ICT (Information and Communication Technologies, e.g. calculators, dynamic software) are available and frequently used in the MMLab, but, in this chapter they will not be considered. Rather, we shall focus on artefacts which, because of their very origin and the concrete constructions, foster both historical-cultural and manipulative approaches to mathematics.

Using effectively such artefacts in the mathematics classroom is a true challenges for teacher, as specific professional competences, which cannot be taken for granted, are required,. The complexity of these competences is consistent with the multidimensional feature of *mathematical knowledge for teaching* (Ball et al., submitted).

In all the research studies carried out by the team of the MMLab, at least three analytical components are present:

- an *epistemological component*, with attention to mathematical meaning;
- a *didactical component*, with attention to the classroom processes;
- a *cognitive component*, with attention to processes of learning (Arzarello & Bartolini Bussi, 1998).

This approach for activity in primary and secondary classrooms is carried out also in prospective and practising teacher education that takes place within the Faculty of Education at Reggio Emilia. According to the Italian governmental regulations issued in 1998, teacher education is organized around three main kinds of activities: *lectures* (for large groups of prospective teachers, up to 100 and more), *in-school apprenticeship* (individual participation in standard classroom activities, under the supervision of expert teachers) and *laboratories*.

The activities described in this chapter take place in the laboratory settings, which are the same size as a standard classroom (25–30 participants). In most mathematical laboratories, in our faculty, prospective teachers explore geometrical and arithmetical machines.[2] At the beginning, the teacher educator acts as the classroom teacher, whilst the prospective teachers act as the students: usually they are given tasks that are similar to the ones that could be used with primary and secondary students. Later metacognitive activity takes place, to make explicit the links between the mathematical activity, as experienced by the prospective teachers, and the theoretical framework. In this way the very tasks acquire a paradigmatic feature that allows the prospective teachers to give sense to the theoretical framework. We shall come back again to the differences between the activity with students and with prospective teachers in the conclusions.

In the following section, some elements of the theoretical framework will be summarized very briefly, drawing on the chapter by Bartolini Bussi and Mariotti (in press), before discussing some cases. In the mentioned framework, the artefacts

---

[2] In the Italian context this is consistent with the indications of the Mathematics curriculum (see the part on Mathematical Laboratory at http://umi.dm.unibo.it/italiano/Didattica/ICME10.pdf).

of MMLab are interpreted *as tools of semiotic mediation for the construction of mathematical meanings under the teacher's guide*. A Vygotskian framework is particularly suitable, because of the importance of the teacher's role and the focus on both the concreteness (that requires direct manipulation) and on the explicit historical reference of the artefacts.

THEORETICAL FRAMEWORK: AN OUTLINE

Artefacts

The word *artefact* is generally used in a very general way and encompasses oral and written forms of language, texts, physical tools used in the history of arithmetic (e.g., abaci and mechanical calculators) and geometry (e.g., straightedge and compass), tools from ICT, manipulatives, and so on. According to Rabardel (1995), an *artefact* is a material or symbolic object per se. The *instrument* (to be distinguished from the artefact) is defined as a hybrid entity made up of both artefact-type components and schematic components that are called *utilization schemes*. The utilization schemes are progressively elaborated when an artefact is used to accomplish a particular task; thus the instrument is a construction of an individual.[3] It has a psychological character and it is strictly related to the context within which it originates and its development occurs. The elaboration and evolution of the instruments is a long and complex process that Rabardel names *instrumental genesis*. Instrumental genesis can be articulated into two coordinated processes: *instrumentalisation*, concerning the emergence and the evolution of the different components of the artefact, drawing on the progressive recognition of its potentialities and constraints; *instrumentation*, concerning the emergence and development of the utilization schemes. "In the instrumentation process, the subject develops, while in the instrumentalization process, it is the artefact that evolves" (Rabardel, 1995, p. 12).[4] In the following, we shall illustrate how both

---

[3] An utilization scheme (Rabardel, 1995) is an active structure into which past experiences are incorporated and organized, in such a way that it becomes a reference for interpreting new data. As such, a utilization scheme is a structure with a history, which changes as it is adapted to an expanding range of situations and is contingent upon the meanings attributed to the situations by the individual. This concept allows for the identification of the processes through which an activity is adapted to the diversity of the outside world, in accordance with the particular content to which the scheme is applied

[4] Bèguin and Rabardel (2000) define *instrumentalization as*:

> "We can distinguish several levels of instrumentalization in the attribution of functions to one or more of the artefact's properties. At the first level, instrumentalization is local. It is related to a particular action and to the specific circumstances under which that action occurs. The artefact's properties are given a function temporarily. The artefact is momentarily instrumentalized. At the second level, the artefact's property is more permanently linked to a function that the instrument can perform within a class of actions, objects of the activity, and situations. The instrumentalization is lasting if not permanent. At both of these levels, the artefact itself does not undergo any material transformations. It simply takes on new properties as far as the subject is concerned, acquired either momentarily or more

(continued)

processes, that have been studied by Rabardel in cognitive ergonomy, apply to classroom activity.

The artefacts used in the MMLab and selected for this chapter are machines concerning geometry and arithmetic. Unlike some artefacts from ICT, they are to be concretely handled; they require motor abilities; they put up resistance to motion; and they need time to be explored. One might observe that using concrete manipulatives to teach mathematics is a long-established educational strategy, at least with young learners, based on theories claiming that children need concrete referents to develop abstract mathematics concepts (Piaget, 1966). This assumption has been often supported by the implicit or explicit claim that educational manipulatives are "transparent" for mathematical meanings (see also Chapter 7, this volume). We take the distance from this view in relation to the following two different issues:

- *The learners' age:* we claim that concrete manipulatives are to be used not only with children but also with older students, up to the tertiary level; we shall offer examples showing that some very sophisticated mathematical processes (e.g. the elaboration of definitions and the construction of proofs) can take advantage of a guided manipulation of concrete artefacts at all ages;
- *The transparency of the artefact:* we claim that artefacts are not transparent, rather they "become efficient, relevant, and transparent through their use in specific activities and in relation to the transformations that they undergo in the hands of users" (Méira, 1998). To Meira, transparency (if any) is not an inherent (objective) feature of the tool, but emerges through the very use of the tool itself. The artefacts used in the MMLab seem "transparent", as unlike the tools of the ICT, the functioning is completely accessible and there is no hidden engine or software inside. Yet, in spite of this functioning transparency, they are not "transparent" where mathematical meaning is concerned.

Cultural artefacts play an essential role in the Vygotskian approach. Vygotsky pointed out that, in the practical sphere, human beings use technological or concrete tools, reaching achievements that would otherwise have remained out of reach. In mental activities, human beings reach higher levels through mediation by artificial stimuli (signs or semiotic tools), that are referred to as psychological tools. In most of the further literature signs have been interpreted as linguistic signs, due to the greater importance attached by Vygotsky to language. Yet,

---

permanently. At the third level, the artefact can be permanently modified in terms of its structure so as to perform a new function" (p. 183).

In the same paper, Bèguin and Rabardel define *instrumentation* as follows:

"Utilization schemes have both a private and a social dimension. The private dimension is specific to each individual. The social dimension, i.e., the fact that it is shared by many members of a social group, results from the fact that schemes develop during a process involving individuals who are not isolated. Other users as well as the artefact's designers contribute to the elaboration of the scheme" (p. 182).

Vygotsky (1981) himself suggested other examples among which there are various systems for counting and mechanical drawings.

Example: the Compass

A simple, yet meaningful example for mechanical drawing, is given by the tool evoked by Hero in his mechanical dynamic procedural definition of circle, as

the figure described when a straight line, always remaining in one plane, moves about one extremity as a fixed point until it returns to its first position. (Heath, 1908, p. 184)

This tool (Figure 1) is a different version of the pair of compasses (Figure 2). In the former, the straight line is materialized by the piece of the bar (OC) between the two hands, whilst in the latter is given by the (not visible) base (OP) of the triangle formed by the legs.

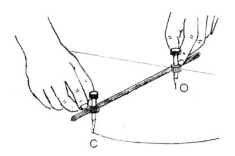

Figure 1. Beam compass.

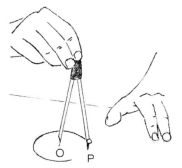

Figure 2. Pair of compasses.

As *technical tools*, both a beam compass and a pair of compasses (we shall use in both cases the word compass, for brevity) are used to produce round shapes: the ways of handling, evoked in the above figures, are different and are neither spontaneous nor simple, especially for young pupils. As a *psychological tool* either has the potentiality to evoke the peculiar feature of circles (i.e., the constancy of the radius) and to create the link with the geometrical static relational definition of Euclid:

A circle is a plane figure contained by one line such that all the straight lines falling upon it from one point among those lying within the figure are equal to one another. (Heath, 1908, p. 183)

As a technical tool it is *externally* oriented; as a psychological tool it is *internally* oriented (Vygotsky, 1978, p. 55). A compass may be used to produce a solution of the following construction problem, from Euclid's elements Book 1 (see, Heath, 1908, p. 241).

To construct an equilateral triangle on a given finite straight line.

In the proof, no compass is mentioned. Rather, among others, the third postulate is recalled:

Let the following be postulated: To describe a circle with any centre and radius.

In other words, what is important is not the very drawing of the circle carried out with some artefact, but the possibility to describe it and to use its peculiar properties. The original proof follows.

Proposition 1.
To construct an equilateral triangle on a given finite straight line.
Let AB be the given finite straight line.
Thus it is required to construct an equilateral triangle on the straight line AB.
With centre A and distance AB, let the circle BCD be described [post. 3];
Again, with centre B and distance BA let the circle ACE be described [post. 3].
And from the point C in which the circles cut one another, to the points A, B, let the straight lines CA, CB be joined [post. 1].
Now, since the point A is the centre of the circle CDB, AC is equal to AB [def. 15].
Again, since the point B is the centre of the circle CAE, BC is equal to BA [def. 15].
But CA was also proved equal to AB, therefore each of the straight lines CA and BC is equal to AB.
And things which equal the same thing also equalto one another [C.N. 1].
Therefore CA is also equal to BC.
Therefore the three straight lines CA, AB, and BC are equal to one another.
Therefore the triangle ABC is equilateral, and it has been constructed on the given finite straight line AB.

(Being) what it was required to do.[5]

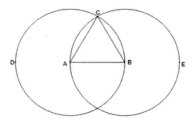

Figure 3. Euclid's Proposition 1: The drawing.

[5] The text refers to postulates (post.), definitions (def.) and common notions (C.N.), taken from Euclid's Book One.

In technical drawing lessons, secondary school students are taught a solution of the same problem (Figure 4), where two small signs are traced by means of the compass to find the third vertex of the triangle. They might be able to carry out the concrete operations with the compass and to describe it carefully (*how*), without being able to give any geometrical justification (*why*); when this happens, the students are using the compass only as a technical tool to produce a drawing, but not (yet) as a psychological tool, because they are not (yet) aware that the solution draws on the property of circle to be the locus of points at a given distance from a given point.

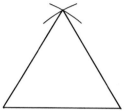

Figure 4. The construction of an equilateral triangle in technical drawing handbooks.

It might be considered only a first step in the construction of the meaning of circle, as soon as the students appropriate this meaning the above construction problem is not challenging any more and becomes a trivial exercise. The above discussion suggests a meaningful task to be introduced into teacher education, concerning the solution of a particular construction problem.

A task in teacher education. On a standard white (not squared) sheet of paper, two circles are drawn: the radii are 3 cm and 2 cm and the distance between the two centres is 7 cm. The problem is:

Draw a circle with a radius of 4 cm tangent to the given circles. You can use instruments. Explain clearly the method so that others can use it. Explain carefully why the method works

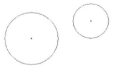

Figure 5. The drawing of the task.

The task is twofold as the learner is explicitly asked to produce both a correct solution (*how*) and a geometrical justification of the solution (*why*). The artefact "compass" is evoked by the hint to use instruments: it has the potential of suggesting both a solution and a justification, that is, on the one hand, functionally linked to the task and, on the other hand, explicitly related to mathematics knowledge. However this potential is not trivial to be exploited by learners, regardless of age and expected school education. We have tested this problem with both young students from grade 5 (Bartolini Bussi et al., 2007) and prospective teachers, who have enrolled in the college for primary teacher education. In the latter case, one might expect solutions referring to argumentation (as prospective teachers have studied some geometry in secondary school); yet the early solutions given by undergraduates are similar to the solutions given by children. In most cases the compass is used only to draw the new circle (with a 4 cm radius), and not to find the centre of that circle. Rather, the centre is found by trial and error, evidence is given by the many small holes that appear by transparency in the sheet of paper. Again, the compass is used as a technical tool and not as a psychological tool. The very formulation of the task (*how* and *why*) allows the teacher educator to raise some issues in the discussion of the solutions. When the solution is found, even by trial and error, it is easily recognized that the problem is equivalent to the problem of finding a triangle with given sides. Hence the position of C may be calculated by intersecting two circles (with radii (3 + 4) cm and (2 + 4) cm respectively, see the dotted circles in Figure 6). The justification for this solution (*why*) requires the student to call into play some particular features: the Euclidean definition of circle; the equality of the distance between the two centres of two (externally) tangent circles to the sum of the radii.

When either the primary school pupils (under the teacher's guidance) or the prospective teachers (under the teacher educator's guidance) become aware of the relationships between the definition of circle, the function of this definition in the solution of the problem and the use of the compass, the process of transformation of the compass into a psychological tool is started. The justification of the method assumes the form of a true mathematical proof, with explicit reference to the definition and to the property of tangent circles.

This process is neither spontaneous nor short. It is the responsibility of either the teacher or the teacher educator to guide this process, fostering the transformation of the students' texts (*situated* in the practical activity carried out with the artefact) into mathematical texts.

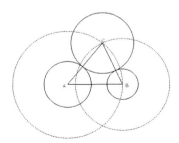

Figure 6. A solution by pair of compasses.

Semiotic Mediation

The process described above for the compass is similar to the process observed for other artefacts (Bartolini Bussi & Mariotti, in press) which can be linked, on the one hand, to meaningful tasks and, on the other hand, to some pieces of mathematics knowledge. In this paragraph we shall use the general term "teacher" to mean both the school teacher and the teacher educator and, similarly, the term "student" to mean both the pupil and the prospective teacher. The teacher, after having designed a meaningful task which refers to mathematics knowledge and may be solved by means of the compass (the left side of the diagram of Figure 6), has the responsibility of observing and analysing the situated texts produced by the students and of designing and implementing their transformation into mathematical texts (the right part of the diagram).

The word "text" is used in a broad sense, to include not only written texts, but also gestures and gazes (that sometimes cannot be easily transformed into words by the students), drawings and whatever sign is used to make sense of and to communicate the procedure. The teacher's role in this process may be described as follows: *he/she uses the artefact as a tool of semiotic mediation.* For a detailed presentation of semiotic mediation in accordance with a Vygotskian approach, the reader might refer to Bartolini Bussi and Mariotti (in press). In short, one might say that the artefact is drawn by the teacher into the solving process both as a technical tool and as a psychological tool. In fact, on the one hand, it allows the user (either the teacher or the student) to produce a solution, and, on the other hand, it may evoke the cultural elaborations that are deposited on it from the time of Euclid (e.g., the peculiar features of circle). Hence the utilization schemes of students evolve and the they construct the meaning of circle as a locus of points in the same plane, equidistant from a given point, to the extent to be able to mobilize this piece of knowledge in problem solving.

In Figure 7, the epistemological, the didactical and the cognitive components are articulated with each other. The *cognitive component* concerns the higher triangle "task – artefact – situated texts"; it is an evolutionary component, because, during time, the process of internalization in the zone of proximal development, enriches pupils' cognitive processes and changes the produced texts. The *epistemological component* concerns the left triangle "task – mathematics knowledge – mathematical texts". The *didactical component* concerns the right triangle "task, situated texts, mathematical texts", where teaching is in the foreground. In the last two a crucial function is played by the artefact, which, in this scheme, has been put in the centre.

191

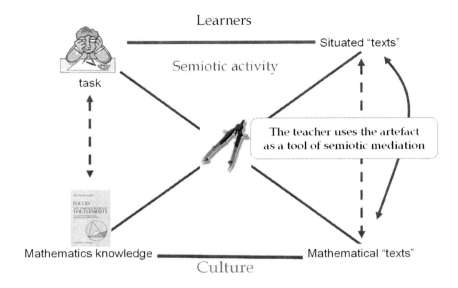

Figure 7. Semiotic mediation.

In the following sections, other examples will be discussed. All the machines are taken from case studies developed with primary or secondary school students, before being applied to teacher education. The differences between classroom and teacher education settings will be addressed in the conclusions.

PRIMARY SCHOOL: PLACE VALUE FOR NATURAL NUMBERS IN BASE TEN

The Object to Be Mediated

The representation of numbers is an immense field of research from the historical perspective (Menninger, 1958), from the anthropological perspective (Crump, 1992), and from the cognitive perspective (Tolchinsky, 2003). From a didactical perspective, the manipulation of written numbers and of operation algorithms is a general requirement in all the school systems, at least from primary school level on. The object to be mediated, in this case, is *the place value of digits:* this is an overarching meaning that is related to other meanings (e.g. one-to-one correspondence; numbers as operators) which will be mentioned below.

The Network of Artefacts

The worldwide interest in this topic and the age of the pupils involved has fostered the production of many manipulatives ("arithmetical machines"), which are still

192

merchandised for and used in primary schools. We have selected a network of artefacts, which are documented in the history of mathematics. We shall briefly describe them below, before analysing the related instrumentalisation and instrumentation processes. We use the term *network of artefacts* to mean that no individual artefact is sufficient to form the meaning of place value to the extent of constructing the arithmetic operations and algorithms; rather it is the very system of them that can form this meaning in the plane of user's consciousness, together with the awareness of the different features of each artefact.

Counting sticks (dating back to ancient China) are thin bamboo or plastic sticks: the sticks are counted, grouped and bundled (and tied with ribbons or rubber bands) into tens for counting up to hundred; ten-bundles are grouped and bundled into hundreds and so on .

Figure 8. Counting sticks.

The *spike abacus* consists of 3 spikes and 27 beads (or more). Each spike represents a particular position of a digit and can have a maximum of 9 beads. Another version (dating back to the Roman age) has no spike but grooves (the *grooved abacus*), where pebbles or other counters to represent numbers are placed.

The *pascaline*[6] is a mechanical calculator (see Figure 10), with a gear train (Maschietto and Ferri, in press). When the lower right wheel has turned a complete rotation, the upper right wheel makes the central wheel to go one step ahead. The same happens when the central wheel has turned a complete rotation: the upper left wheel makes the lower left wheel to go one step ahead. Digits from 0 to 9 are written on the lower wheels. The three small triangles on the bottom side point at a digit each, so that every 3 digit number is represented by the 3 pointed digits. The functioning is similar to the one of old mechanical odometers.

The above artefacts are modern reconstructions of traditional artefacts (Menninger, 1958); most were used for reckoning also before the place value of digits was established in writing. The explicit historical dimension differentiates them from other artefacts, such as the multibase blocks (Sriraman & Lesh, 2007) and the ICT tools. The teacher may benefit from introducing an historical discourse in the mathematics classroom, with even recourse to selected historical sources, to introduce the pupils into the flow of mathematics culture. This additional potential for the construction of mathematical meanings will not be explored in this chapter.

---

[6] The pascaline (called "zero+1") is a small (27 cm x 16 cm) plastic tool, produced and sold by the Italian company "Quercetti intelligent toys" (www.quercetti.it).

Figure 9. A spike (left) and a grooved (right) abacus.

Figure 10. The pascaline "zero+1".

Meanings

It is beyond the scope of this chapter to analyse in detail the mathematical meanings potentially attached to the above artefacts (Bartolini Bussi & Mariotti, in press; Bartolini Bussi & Boni, in press). In short:

One-to-one correspondence is in the foreground for the counting sticks and abaci (although for the spike or grooved abaci, it works only for a very limited number of beads, i.e., 9 in the base ten representation, afterwards, conventions about grouping, composing and exchange need to be used).

Grouping i.e. *composing (groups of ten)* is in the foreground for the counting sticks and abaci.

Number symbols are written only on the pascaline. In the shift from counting sticks and abaci to written representations of numbers, zero appears as a place holder, whilst in the pascaline zero is rather a label.

The generation of the written number sequence is in the foreground in the pascaline. It is generated by iterating the function "+1" concretized by one-tooth clockwise rotation of the right wheel. This is important when addition is at stake. With pascaline, the function of the two addenda is not symmetrical (the second one is an operator on the first one), whilst with counting sticks and abaci, the addition works as a binary operation. The above differences justify why it is not only better but necessary to refer to a network of artefacts rather than to a sole artefact: their complementarity is meaningful and suggests metacognitive tasks aimed at comparing their potential.

Instrumentalization

The difference between the artefacts (in spite of the similarity of meanings) makes this phase very important. Before the emergence of the evolution of the different components of the artefact, the given artefact is in the foreground. The quoted artefacts have some peculiar features: they consist of different parts with relationships with each other. A very simple example of instrumentalization is described by Bartolini Bussi and Boni (2003), concerning the spike abacus. In a mathematical discussion with second graders (7 year olds) about the function of abacus, the pupils had in front of them their personal abacus with four wires. The need for representing numbers beyond 9999 suggested the solution of placing side by side as many abaci as needed. The evolution of the artefact was progressive, from the juxtaposition of several abaci to the "mental" design of a new abacus with as many wires as needed.

Instrumentation

When a task is given, to be solved by means of one of the above artefacts, instrumentation is at work. Each individual learner constructs her/his own utilization schemes. A learner, while describing the process of using an artefact to solve a specific task, produces usually situated texts (see Figure 7), where metaphors and even gestures and gazes are very frequent and aim at conveying part of the meaning.

Examples of Tasks for Teacher Education

A small group of prospective teachers was given one of the above arithmetical machines together with rulers for measuring, and paper and pencil. Instrumentalisation tasks.

1   Produce a carefully written description of the artefact you have received, the parts, the size, the shapes, their spatial relationships, and so on. You can use words and drawings.
2.   Design with everyday materials an arithmetical machine that can be used in the place of the one that has been offered you.

195

Instrumentation tasks.

3.   *Represent the number 107 by means of counting sticks (or an abacus, or a pascaline). Describe carefully how you have realized the representation and why you are sure that it is correct.*

4.   *Compare the utilization schemes in the above task, when different artefacts are into play.*

5.   *Add 108 and 245 by means of counting sticks (or an abacus, or a pascaline). Describe carefully and justify your process.*

In the spike or grooved abaci, before using the conventional term "exchange" (ten beads with one bead in a different position, hence with a different value) or "compose", pupils and even prospective teachers are likely to use terms from everyday language, such as "pinch", "hide", "tie", and similar. Forcing the shift from these situated signs to mathematical signs is just what either the teacher or the teacher educator has to do in mathematical discussion to help learners construct mathematical meaning.

Task 1 aims at making the prospective teachers aware of the features of the given artefact. This is the first step, before being involved in task 2, that influences them to make the artefact evolve on the basis of teaching needs (see chapter 6, this volume).

Consider the "pasta" abacus (see Figure 11), designed by a pair of teachers within a training laboratory, as a variation of the grooved abacus. They had to solve problems met in their classrooms (e.g., the cost of individual teaching aids, the noise, trouble and danger of the falling marbles, the risk that younger kids may swallow beads, and so on). The choice of a very special kind of pasta was carefully discussed: some kinds of macaroni were discarded because a line of macaroni could have hidden the perception of the break between two of them. The size was discussed in order to meet the need of pupils' fingers. When the special shape of "wheels" was chosen, several exemplars were produced for classroom use.[7]

---

[7] Two different instrumentalisation processes have been described in this section: the juxtaposition of abaci to represent numbers beyond 9999 and the design of the "pasta" abacus as a variation of the grooved abacus. They are realized by different subjects (pupils vs. teachers). Several differences may be highlighted, with reference to different issues: e.g.,

  –   task: in the former the pupils are confronted by a mathematical task whilst in the latter the teachers are confronted by a mathematics education task, where all the domains of mathematics knowledge for teaching are at stake (Ball et al., submitted);

  –   meaning: in the former, the place value as meaning is in progress, whilst in the latter it is taken for granted;

  –   aim: in the former, the aim is to construct mathematical meaning, whilst in the latter the aim is to produce a tool for constructing mathematical meaning;

  –   concreteness: in the former, the concrete realization of the artefact must be overcome to represent larger and larger numbers, whilst in the latter the concrete realization is in the foreground;

  –   relationships: in the former the pupils are faced with a task, an ineffective artefact and a piece of mathematics knowledge, whilst in the latter the teacher are faced with a task, an artefact to be changed, a piece of mathematics knowledge and the pupils who are expected to use the new artefact.

(continued)

The tasks 3, 4 and 5, instead, concern the instrumentation process, and call into play the utilization schemes, that are briefly described below, in another set of tasks. The reader may complete the list for the other artefacts.

Tasks: Artefacts and utilization schemes

Find the utilization schemes of the counting sticks, the abacus, the pascaline for each of the following tasks: counting and storing data; representing a given number.

Task: *Counting and storing data.*

Counting Sticks

1a (one-to-one correspondence): to move a stick for each item to be counted

1b (counting all): to count all the sticks

2a (bind-tens): to bind with a ribbon or a rubber band ten sticks to obtain a ten-bunch;

2b (bind-hundreds): to bind with a ribbon or a rubber band ten bunches of ten-bunches etc.

Task: *Representing a given number.*

Pascaline

3a (iteration): to repeat the operation of pushing one step clockwise the wheel A on the right until you reach the number.

4a (decomposition) to push clockwise the unit wheel as many steps as needed, the ten wheel as many steps as needed, the hundred wheels as many steps as needed.

Figure 11. The "pasta" abacus.

The last issue is related to the different institutional roles played by pupils (who are expected to learn) and teachers (who are expected to teach). It explains why processes and outcomes are expected to be different when even the "same" task

> "Design with everyday materials an arithmetical machine that can be used in the place of the one that has been offered you"

is given to primary school pupils and to primary school teachers.

For prospective teachers, the careful analysis of arithmetical machines is the first move towards the design of a long term intervention project on the place value of digits at the beginning of primary school.

The Object to Be Mediated

Symmetry is a well known property of those plane figures, which show to be invariant in a mirror image. In geometrical terms, symmetry about an axis is a plane transformation that can be defined as follows:

Axial symmetry with axis a straight line r is a transformation that for each point P of a plane, defines a point P' such that the line segment PP' is perpendicular to the axis and the midpoint M of PP' is on the axis.

In procedural way, it may also be defined as follows:

Given a line r (symmetry axis), the image of a point P (not on r) in the symmetry about the axis r is a point P' obtained in the following way. Draw a line n perpendicular to r through P and say H the orthogonal projection of P on r. Choose the point P' on n, so that PH = HP' (being H a point of the line segment PP'). If P is on r, P'=P.

The second definition gives a construction that may be carried out by straightedge and compass.

The Network of Artefacts

Beside the pair "straightedge and compass", there are other artefacts that allow to construct the symmetrical point P' of a given point P by means of a direct operation.[8] In the following, two different artefacts will be illustrated.

The *geodreieck* is a small square (popular in German speaking countries) realized by an isosceles right triangle, where the axis of hypotenuse is traced and the hypotenuse contains two symmetrical number lines with origin in the middle point (Figure 12). Also the other sides of the triangles are graduated in degrees, referring to the inner goniometer. When the axis of the hypotenuse lies on given symmetry axis, two points on the hypotenuse, with the same numerical label, are symmetrical about the symmetry axis.

The *symmetry linkage* is a system of an articulated rhombus and a wooden board with a straight rail; two opposite vertices of the rhombus slide in the straight rail and the other two can carry two pens, in charge of tracing two symmetrical

---

[8] We shall not consider, in this chapter, paper folding which is, however, a popular way to approach symmetry with young pupils.

drawing in the plane of the linkage (Figure 13). It dates back to the French scientist C. E. Delaunay (1816–1872).

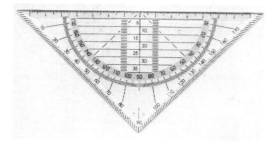

Figure 12. Geodreieck.   *Figure 13. The symmetry linkage.*[9]

Meanings

All the artefacts (straightedge and compass, geodreieck and linkage) work in a limited part of the plane (see Figure 19 to show the case of linkage). The first definition above, on the contrary, applies to whichever point of the plane. Both geodreieck and linkage evoke the procedural definition, drawing on:

-   measuring and coordinate system (geodreieck);
-   peculiar properties of rhombuses (in the linkage, diagonals are perpendicular to and bisecting each other).

Instrumentalization

The artefacts are quite different from each other. Geodreieck is a transparent triangle, with printed numbers, referring to the different measures (length and angle

---

[9] Figure 12 shows a frame of the java simulation of the concrete linkage used by young students in Figures 14 and 15 (http://www.museo.unimo.it/theatrum/macchine/simj/m117.htm: drag the green point to explore). The machines of the MMLab are made of wood and brass. They have different sizes: the large ones (about 70 cm x 50 cm) are used for large group explanations; the small ones (40 cm x 40 cm) are available in multiple copies for small group work. They can be bought or rented by schools (http://associazioni.monet.modena.it/macmatem/kit%20nuovi.pdf). Individual cardboard or plastic (e.g. geostrips with brass fasteners) models may be cut and assembled in the instrumentalization phase, although, for the instrumentation phase, they show limitations in functioning (they sag and lack holes for pens).

width); the linkage has no number at all. Yet a perceptual resemblance appears as also the linkage shows the symmetry axis and some isosceles triangles. Measuring by means of a ruler witnesses that it is a rhombus, within the limit of the measuring tool sensitivity.

Instrumentation

We shall analyse the instrumentation process, starting from some tasks in teacher education.

Tasks in teacher education. A small group of prospective teachers is given the above artefacts together with paper and pencil.

1) *Write the solution of the following task "to draw a pair of symmetrical points about the axis r", using straightedge and compass, the geodreieck and the linkage. Compare the three solutions.*
2) *Write the solution of the following task "to draw two symmetrical triangles about the axis r", using straightedge and compass, the geodreieck and the linkage. Compare the three solutions.*
3) *Write the solution of the following task "to construct the symmetrical triangle A'B'C' of a given triangle ABC about the axis r", using straightedge and compass, the geodreieck and the linkage. Compare the three solutions.*

To draw the symmetrical point of a given point by means of straightedge and compass, one must know the procedural definition of symmetry. On the contrary, some elements of the definition are embodied in the structure of the other artefacts: for instance, the choice of a rhombus for the linkage (although not necessary, see below Figure18) depends on the properties of rhombus. Yet, at the beginning, they are not transparent for the meaning of axial symmetry. With the geodreieck the utilization schemes may be partially guided by an intuitive idea of axial symmetry that may help the reading and the control of points in the two symmetrical number lines. Anyway, it is necessary either to have or to draw the axis on the sheet. It means that the planning of the solution needs a sophisticated consciousness of what is being done, to avoid an improper use of the small square. With the linkage, one must put a sheet on the wooden plate, know the holes where to put the pencil and draw two points; the axis is physical (the rail in the plate). Hence, it is possible to use the artefact by imitation, without being aware of the function of the rail.

To solve the task 2 by means of the geodreieck, the most effective way is to draw 3 pairs of symmetrical points (P, P'; Q, Q'; R, R') and, later, to draw the triangles PQR and P'Q'R'. One must seize the small square with one hand and draw one point at a time with the other as shown in Figure 14. Only at the end, after having drawn the triangles, the symmetry appears evident.

On the contrary, by means of the linkage, one can draw contemporaneously and continuously the two triangles, putting two pens at the two free vertices and piloting them one with the left and the other with the right hand (see Figure 15). If the rail is perpendicular to the subject, as shown in Figure 15, the muscle perception makes clear, during the process, that the two hands are going two symmetrical ways: this is more evident if the user closes the eyes and pays attention to the hand motion only.

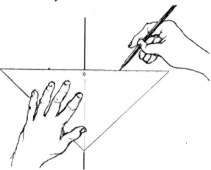

Figure 14. Using a geodreieck.[10]

In the solution of the task 3 (Figure 16) the muscle perception described above disappears and is substituted by the coordination of the gaze (which follows the triangle outline) with the motion of the hand which grips the pencil. This utilization scheme often requires the joint action of two students. The situation is different with the geodreieck.

Figure 15. The contemporaneous drawing of two symmetrical figures.

Figure 16. The drawing of a figure symmetrical to another one.

To solve the task 3, the geodreieck and the linkage confront students with some physical constraints of the artefact (the local feature of the transformation) which induce peculiar utilization schemes. In fact, the given triangle ABC must be drawn close enough to the axis to be accessible for either the hypotenuse of the

---

[10] Courtesy of Germana Bartoli.

geodreieck or the free vertex of the rhombus. Only one pencil is sufficient in both cases. One of the free points of the rhombus (pointer) follows the triangle ABC outline, whilst the pencil, placed in the other free point (plotter) draws the triangle A'B'C'.

Generally, in both task 2 and 3, the linkage seems to force students to draw the whole triangle in one motion, although this solution produces always inaccurate drawings (Brousseau, 1986). This is frustrating for many students who would aim to produce precise drawings (as usually required in the geometry lessons). The possibility of improving the precision, by using the linkage to draw only the vertices and by joining them later with a ruler is not usually considered, as if the dynamical feature of the artefact leads necessarily the user towards a global control of the triangle.

Meanings (again)

Until now we have analysed in parallel different artefacts for axial symmetry. In the following we shall analyse in more details different uses of the same artefact (the linkage) at different school levels, then drawing from them some implications for teacher education.

We have introduced the symmetry linkage in the third grade (8 year-olds) of primary school after some experiences with paper folding. In spite of the young age of the pupils, the geometrical structure of the linkage appeared both evident and relevant for meaning construction; the function of the axis and the properties of a rhombus are the main components of the meaning of axial symmetry. Yet a more important experiment was started during the 2006/2007 school year. A long-term teaching project[11] about geometrical transformations was started in grade 7 (12 year-olds (see Figure16). The main focus was on the elaboration of a definition, and this required pupils to draw on the notions of perpendicularity and parallelism.

This experiment was useful also to design the tasks for teacher education. In the laboratory setting of teacher education, prospective teachers are supposed to have learnt some definition of axial symmetry in secondary school: hence, the focus is on the revisitation of the definition and on the justification (*why*) of the linkage functioning. The working sessions are usually split into two parts:
- small group work on the linkage, by means of a working sheet, and
- collective work on the solutions for the given tasks.

Anothe Task in Teacher Education

A small group of prospective teachers is given the linkage, a working sheet with a drawing (see Figure 17) together with paper and pencil.
Answer the questions, writing carefully your answers.

---

[11] "Isometric and non-isometric transformations in the plane: a teaching project that makes use of mathematical machines" (Research project carried out by M. Maschietto and F. Martignone).

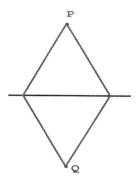

Figure 17. The machine drawing.

1. *Describe and represent the machine (How many rigid rods make up the full linkage? Describe the linkage system and measure the lengths of the individual rods…)*
2. *In the machine some vertexes are forced to move in a certain way (bounded vertexes) and other vertexes are free to move on the plane. Which vertexes of the linkage are free? Which ones are bounded? Which are these bounds?*
3. *The two vertexes that are free to move on the plane are called: "pointer" and "plotter". In your machine drawing the pointer is P and the plotter is Q. Put the pencil in the plotter hole and trace the drawing with the pointer* [the point P (the pointer) traces over a given curve or shape and the point Q (the plotter) draws the associated curve or shape (locus) as the linkage moves].

If the pointer (point P) traces out	the plotter (point Q) draws
a line segment (of length … …)	
a line segment perpendicular to the straight rail (of length … …)	
a line segment parallel to the straight rail (of length … …)	
a given triangle	

Compare the original figure as followed by the point P and the figure drawn out by the point Q – what do you notice?
4. *When the point P moves along a segment of a given figure, in a particular direction, does the point Q also move along the corresponding side of the plotted figure (locus) in the same direction sense?*
5. *Given a point A, design its correspondent B with the plotter. Explain how the point B can be obtained from the point A (without using the articulated system).*
6. *Try to give a definition of the final transformation produced by this linkage system.*

7. *Choose a Cartesian axes system: if we know the coordinates of the point A, write down the coordinates of the point B in terms of those in A.*

8. *Is it possible to use a different quadrilateral instead of the rhombus?*

9. *What are the shape of the corresponding regions?*

10. *Are there fixed points (i.e. points which have themselves as images)? Are there fixed straight lines (i e. lines which have themselves as images)?*

Questions 1 and 2 aim at highlighting the physical features of the given artefact (the emergence of the components in the instrumentalisation process) and offer elements to justify the functioning of the linkage. Moreover, question 2 concerns also the instrumentation process (as does question 3), as the manipulation of the linkage is required. Questions 3 and 4, however, aim at highlighting some features of transformation. The straight rail is put in evidence in the question 3 (table), as a reference line. Question 5 rouses the statement of an operative definition (*how*) of axial symmetry, when the linkage is not available any more (but the rail is still in the board). Question 6 asks for a definition.

The following questions, 7, 8, 9, and 10, may be either used in group work or left for the collective discussion. In particular, question 8 prompts a process of conjecture production (*what*) and proof construction (*why*) (Figure 18). It may foster the evolution of the artefact in the instrumentalisation process, by using another linkage to realize the same transformation. Question 9 focuses the limitation of the plane regions where the linkage works (Figure 19).

The limitation of the plane regions is an important constraint. While answering question 3, the students (or prospective teachers) often draw some figures that are too far from the rail and do not succeed in following the figure outline with the pointer. They erase the figure and start again. A new utilization scheme appears: they first look for a region which is close enough to the rail and then draw in that region. The questions about points and lines that have themselves as images are easy to be considered, because the pointer and the plotter may be moved in order to go very close to each other or may be exchanged with each other.

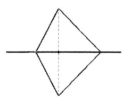

Figure 18. Not only a rhombus.

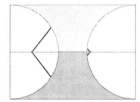

Figure 19. The two corresponding regions.

The collective part of the session concerns the shift from the texts produced by the students (or the prospective teachers) towards mathematical texts (definition and properties of symmetry). The different answers (given by different groups) to the question 5 and 6 allow for the start of deeper work on definition. Prospective teachers often bypass these questions and answer only "it is an axial symmetry".

Yet the question is different and concerns the elaboration of a definition. This process starts during group work and ends in the collective discussion, when the comparison between different definitions highlights linguistic issues and tacit assumptions.[12] A typical shift concerns the rail: the initial artefact sign (just "rail") has to be transformed into "symmetry axis", that is, a true mathematical sign; the fissure in the wooden board where the linkage is placed becomes, in drawings, a graphical sign with a very precise meaning. It is the only element of the artefact that is maintained in the definition of the transformation as the linkage disappears. Taking away the linkage (question 5) is a strategy to direct students and prospective teachers to focus on the peculiar features of the artefact, i.e., not so much the rhombus as the rail. This is not to be taken for granted. When students and prospective teachers are required to draw the artefact themselves, sometimes they draw only the rhombus (i.e., the most evident part, the element to be handled and moved) and not the rail, which at a first glance may appear non essential.

CONCLUSIONS

In this chapter we have discussed some cases of arithmetical and geometrical machines, showing their use in teacher education, within small size laboratories. The main features of the mathematical machines described in this chapter are the following. The artefacts are to be explored with hands and eyes, hence they exploit the potential of body activity that is at the core of present application of cognitive linguistic and neurosciences to mathematics education (Arzarello & Robutti, in press). The artefacts are taken from the historical phenomenology of mathematics (either arithmetic or geometry), hence they have already shown, in the history, the potential of fostering the construction of mathematical meanings, that have lived through the ages. The reading of historical sources might be placed beside the use of such tools, to make the users aware that they are taking part in historical process that is not individual but collective (Otte & Seeger, 1994).

In the mathematics classrooms, the recourse to physical manipulatives is becoming less frequent and too often substituted with ICT: virtual copies of manipulatives are more and more easily available also for primary school (e.g., http://nlvm.usu.edu/en/nav/index.html). We are not against virtual objects, as a typical task in the Laboratory of Mathematical Machines is the modeling of geometrical machines within a DGE. But we claim that this is only a part of the story and that concrete manipulation has to find a place both in the mathematics classroom and in teacher education. The example of the linkage for symmetry clearly shows some processes (e.g., the transformation of the rail into the axis) that are not expected to emerge in a simulation within DGE, where all the objects are

---

[12] When linkages concerning less known transformations are into play (e.g., translation), the amount of situated texts in small group work is larger. In these cases the collective work of writing a mathematical definition under the teacher's guide is an important moment of social construction.

drawn in the same way. ICT are not surrogates for concrete objects; rather they have their own place in mathematics education, because of the features that are partly different from the ones of physical artefacts.

Our genuine interest in ICT is witnessed by another circumstance, the Vygotskian theoretical framework that we have briefly mentioned (Bartolini Bussi and Mariotti, in press) has proved to be effective in the design, implementation and analysis of activities with different kinds of artefacts, i.e., not only classical technologies (as in this chapter, see also Maschietto & Martignone, in press) but also ICT (Bartolini Bussi & Mariotti, submitted).

As we have highlighted above, the tasks for teacher education have been designed drawing on teaching experiments in primary and secondary school, in order to make prospective teachers capable of planning and running effective classroom activities. The teacher educator's role in the laboratory for prospective teachers is similar to the teacher's role in the classroom, with, at least at the beginning, very similar tasks (and even similar solutions!) in spite of the difference in learners's age. There is, however, a big difference: working with prospective teachers, the process is disclosed and explicitly linked to the theoretical framework and its schematic representation in Figure 7, in order to function as a model of effective classroom activity to be implemented in the teaching profession.

If one assumes the perspective of a teacher educator, it is evident that this increases the complexity of the design of laboratory sessions for prospective teachers compared to laboratory sessions for students. This complexity is consistent with the multidimensional feature of *mathematical knowledge for teaching* (Ball et al., submitted). Actually different domains of knowledge are brought into play, such as:

- the *common content knowledge*, i.e., the mathematical knowledge at stake in the material to be taught (evoked in Figure 20 by the triangle "task – artefact – mathematics knowledge");
- the *knowledge of content and students,* related to the prediction and interpretation of students' processes when a task is given (evoked in Figure 20 by the "cognitive" or "learning" triangle "task – artefact – situated texts");
- the *knowledge of content and teaching*, related to the teacher's actions aiming at the students' construction of mathematical meaning (evoked in Figure 20 by the "teaching" triangle "task – situated texts – mathematical texts");
- the *specialised content knowledge* (evoked in Figure 20 by the "epistemological" triangle "task – mathematics knowledge – mathematical texts").

In each triangle a special function is played by the artefact, i.e., the mathematical machine introduced as tool for teacher education.

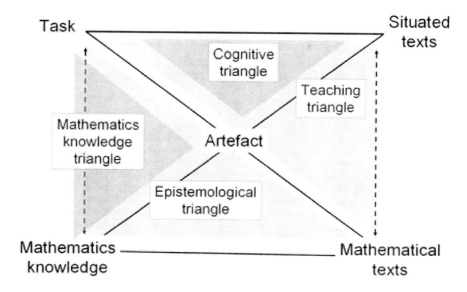

Figure 20. The scheme of Figure 7 revisited.

REFERENCES

Arzarello, F., & Bartolini Bussi, M. G. (1998). Italian trends in research in mathematics education: A national case study in the international perspective. In Kilpatrick, J. & Sierpinska, A. (Eds.), *Mathematics education as a research domain: A search for identity* (Vol. 2, pp. 243–262). Dordrecht, the Netherlands: Kluwer Academic Publishers.

Arzarello, F., & Robutti O. (in press). Framing the embodied mind approach within a multimodal paradigm. In English, L. et al. (Eds.), *Handbook of international research on mathematics education* (2nd edition), Mahwah, NJ: Lawrence Erlbaum Associates.

Ball, D. L., Thames, M. H., & Phelps, G. (submitted). Content knowledge for teaching: What makes it special? Available from http://www-personal.umich.edu/~dball/papers/index.html.

Bartolini Bussi, M. G., & Boni, M. (2003). Instruments for semiotic mediation in primary school classrooms. *For the Learning of Mathematics, 23*(2), 12–19.

Bartolini Bussi, M. G., & Boni, M. (in press). The early construction of mathematical meanings: positional representation of numbers at the beginning of primary school. In Barbarin, O. A. & Frome, P. (Eds.), *The handbook of developmental science and early schooling: Translating basic research into practice.* New York, NY: Guilford Press.

Bartolini Bussi, M. G., Boni, M., & Ferri, F. (2007). Construction problems in primary school a case from the geometry of circle. In P. Boero (Ed.), *Theorems in school: From history, epistemology and cognition to classroom practice* (pp. 219–248). Rotterdam, the Netherlands: Sense Publishers.

Bartolini Bussi, M. G., & Mariotti, M. A. (in press). Semiotic mediation in the mathematics classroom: artefacts and signs after a Vygotskian perspective. In English, L. et al. (Eds.), *Handbook of international research on mathematics education* (2nd edition). Mahwah, NJ: Lawrence Erlbaum Associates.

MARIA G. BARTOLINI BUSSI AND MICHELA MASCHIETTO

Bèguin, P., & Rabardel, P. (2000). Designing for instrument-mediated activity. *Scandinavian Journal of Information Systems, 12*, 173–190.
Brousseau, G. (1986). *Théorisation des phénomènes d'einseignement des mathématiques.* Thése d'etat, Université Bordeaux 1.
Crump, T. (1992). *The anthropology of numbers.* Cambridge: Cambridge University Press.
Heath, T. L. (1908). *The thirteen books of Euclid's elements,* Vol. I. New York, NY: Dover Publications.
Larousserie, D. (2005). Voir les maths pour comprendre. *Science et Avenir*, March, 80–85.
Maschietto, M. (2005). The laboratory of mathematical machines of Modena. *Newsletter of the European Mathematical Society, 57*, 34–37.
Maschietto, M., & Ferri, F. (in press). Artefacts, schèmes d'utilisation et significations arithmetiques. In Szendrei, J. (Ed.), *Mathematical activity in classroom practice and as research object in didactics: Two complementary perspectives*, Proceedings of the CIEAEM 59, Dobogókő (Hungary).
Maschietto, M., & Martignone, F. (in press). Activities with the mathematical machines: Pantographs and curve drawers. In *Proceedings of the 5th European Summer University on the History and Epistemology in Mathematics Education.* Univerzita Karlova, Prague (Czech Republic).
Meira, L. (1998). Making sense of instructional devices: The emergence of transparency in mathematical activity. *Journal for Research in Mathematics Education, 29*(2), 121–142.
Menninger, K. (1958). *Number words and number symbols. A cultural history of numbers.* Cambridge MA: MIT Press.
Otte, M., & Seeger, F. (1994). The human subject in mathematics education and in the history of mathematics. In Biehler, R., Scholz, R. W., Straesser, R. & Winkelmann, B. (Eds.), *Didactics of mathematics as a scientific discipline* (pp. 351–365). Dordrecht, the Netherlands: Kluwer Academic Publishers.
Piaget, J. (1966). *Psychology of intelligence.* Totowa, NJ: Littlefield, Adams & Co.
Rabardel, P. (1995). *Les hommes et les technologies — Approche cognitive des instruments contemporains.* Paris : A. Colin.
Sriraman, B., & Lesh, R. (2007). A conversation with Zoltan P. Dienes. *Mathematical Thinking and Learning. 9* (1), 59–75.
Tolchinsky, L. (2003). *The cradle of culture and what children know about writing and numbers before being taught.* Mahwah, NJ: Lawrence Erlbaum Associates.
Vygotskij, L. S. (1978). *Mind in society. The development of higher psychological processes.* Harvard, MA: Harvard University Press.
Vygotsky, L. S. (1981). The genesis of higher mental functions. In J. V. Wertsch (Ed.), *The concept of activity in Soviet psychology.* Armonk, NY: Sharpe.

Maria G. Bartolini Bussi
Dipartimento di Matematica Pura ed Applicata
Università di Modena e Reggio Emilia
Italia

Michela Maschietto
Dipartimento di Matematica Pura ed Applicata
Università di Modena e Reggio Emilia
Italia

SECTION 3

RESEARCH IN MATHEMATICS EDUCATION AS TOOLS IN MATHEMATICS TEACHER EDUCATION

PESSIA TSAMIR

9. USING THEORIES AS TOOLS IN MATHEMATICS TEACHER EDUCATION

This chapter presents three research segments, indicating that teachers' familiarity with Fischbein's theory and with the intuitive rule theory can promote their mathematical knowledge, their pedagogical knowledge and their teaching. It also addresses the questions: What theories should be presented in mathematics teacher education programmes? In what ways and at what stages (e.g., prospective teachers or practicing teachers) should theories be presented? How to assess the impact of teachers' familiarity with theories on their professionalism?

INTRODUCTION

In the last decades, the mathematics education community has been increasingly engaged in theorizing and reflecting on possible connections between theories on one hand, and research and reform in teacher education on the other. In their chapter on theory in mathematics education scholarship Silver and Herbst (2007) report on the intensifying attention to theory in mathematics education, and state that "Whereas the role of theory in mathematics education scholarship was usually tacit (at best) 30 years ago, it has become much more visible and important in contemporary scholarship" (Ibid., p. 40). Sowder (2007) provides a wide-ranging examination of issues related to the development of mathematics teachers, pointing to the growing recognition that teachers' professional development must be a priority. Additional indications of the emergent interest of the mathematics education community in these two issues can be found in reviews of academic activities that have taken place in major international conferences, such as PME (e.g., theories, Confrey & Kazak, 2006; Lerman, 2006; Tsamir & Tirosh, 2006; teacher education, Llinares & Krainer, 2006), International Congress on Mathematics Education (ICME) (e.g., theories, Arzarello, 2004; mathematics teacher education, Adler, 2004) and Conference of the European Society for Research in Mathematics Education (CERME) (e.g., theories: Bosch et al., 2007; Dreyfus et al., 2005; Furinghetti, 2001; Peter-Koop et al., 2003; teacher education, Carrillo et al., 2005; 2007; Furinghetti, 2001; Grevholm, 2003; Krainer & Goffree, 1998), in reviews of the literature, i.e., central journals (e.g., theories, Lerman & Tsatsaroni, 2004; teacher education, *Journal of Mathematics Teacher Education* (JMTE) Special Issue, 2006; Adler et al., 2005; and the creation of JMTE), books (e.g., theories, Brousseau, 1997; Fischbein, 1987; Stavy & Tirosh, 2000; teacher education, Cochran-Smith & Zeichner, 2005; Lin & Cooney, 2001; Wood, Jaworski, & Dawson, 1999), chapters in handbooks (e.g., theories, Mason & Waywood, 1996; Silver & Herbst, 2007; teacher education, Comiti & Ball, 1996;

D. Tirosh and T. Wood (eds.), Tools and Processes in Mathematics Teacher Education, 211–234.
© *2008 Sense Publishers. All rights reserved.*

Cooney & Wiegel, 2003; Jaworski & Gellert, 2003; Noddings, 1992; Sowder, 2007), as well as in various national and international documents. The time seems ripe to address the issue of "using theories as tools in mathematics teacher education".

It should be noted that various academic publications refer to "theory", "theorizing", or "theoretical" as well as "teaching", "teacher education" "teachers' knowledge" or "teacher professional development". Commonly, these publications analyse prospective teachers' and teachers' subject matter knowledge (SMK), pedagogical content knowledge (PCK) (cf., Shulman, 1986) and teaching by means of prevalent theories (e.g., Brown et al., 2007; Tsamir, 1999); they may alternatively describe researchers' attempts to formulate new, teacher-education specific theories, aimed at interpreting and characterizing the professionalization of mathematics teachers (e.g., Ball & Cohen, 1999; Jaworski, 2006; Rowland et al., 2005; Wood, 1999). In publications of both types, the theory generally serves explicitly as a tool only, used by researchers, who perform theory-based investigations of teacher-education related phenomena. The prospective teachers or practising teachers usually play the role of "investigated objects". As such, they do not share the theory-based interpretations of the occurrences.

Does this mean that teacher education programmes do not address theory? The answer is certainly not. Many mathematics teacher education programmes include various blends of compulsory (basic and specialization) and non-compulsory theory-oriented courses. For example, a brief survey of internet sites, of the "Mathematics Teacher Education Around the World" section in JMTE and of other JMTE papers, shows that programmes often include general theoretical courses such as *Developmental Psychology*, *Sociology of Education* and *Theory and Practice of Teaching* (see, for instance, the programme *Minor degree in mathematics education*, at the University of Cyprus, 2007). Other programmes occasionally include extensive discussions of specific theories that are strictly embedded in mathematics education. For example, at Concordia University in Montréal, Canada, Sierpinska gave theory-based mathematics education oriented lectures in the programme *Master in the Teaching of Mathematics*, where she discussed the *theory of didactic situations* (Sierpinska, 1999/2003; based on Brousseau, 1997) and the *theory of intuition in science and mathematics* (Sierpinska, 2001; based on the ideas of Fischbein, 1987); at Tel Aviv University, Israel, seminars on the intuitive rules theory were given to secondary school science and mathematics teachers and to prospective secondary school mathematics teachers. From interviews with a few participants the mathematics teacher educators concluded that "the impact of such a seminar on in-service teachers' knowledge of the intuitive rules theory and its effects on their actual teaching has not yet systematically been studied" (Tirosh et al., 2001, p. 81). That is, it is not clear how knowledge acquired in theory-related courses is translated into practice: Do the student teachers use these theoretical models in their learning and / or teaching, and if they do, how?

The purpose of this chapter is to examine whether theories can serve as tools to promote prospective teachers' and practising teachers' (1) mathematical knowledge (an SMK component), (2) knowledge about students' mathematical reasoning (a PCK component), and (3) knowledge about the formulation and sequencing of tasks (a PCK component). In the chapter I refer to expressions of prospective teachers' and teachers' knowledge, both during academic courses and when they actually teach. However, before addressing these questions, one may wonder what theories should be chosen for this purpose.

THEORIES IN TEACHER EDUCATION PROGRAMMES: DECISIONS AND CHOICES

There is wide agreement that mathematics education is situated at the crossroads of various academic domains, such as mathematics, psychology, sociology, anthropology, and linguistics (e.g., Sierpinska et al., 1993). Many theories in these fields were used in mathematics education (behaviorism, constructivism, radical constructivism, socio-cultural models, socio-political models) as researchers have reported (e.g., Johnson, 1980 in Silver & Herbst, 2007; Lerman & Tsatsaroni, 2004; Silver & Kilpatrick, 1994). Moreover, specific mathematics-education oriented theoretical models[1] were formulated, e.g., the instrumental-relational model (Skemp, 1971), the process-concept-procept model (Tall, 2005); the concept image-concept definition model (Tall & Vinner, 1981), the RBC abstraction-in-action model (Hershkowitz et al., 2001), the theory of didactic situations (Brousseau, 1997), and the socio-mathematical norms model (Yackel & Cobb, 1996). Comprehensive discussions and classifications of various mathematics-education related theoretical perspectives, and references to the diversity of theories, are offered, for instance, in Mason and Waywood (1996) and in Silver and Herbst (2007).

These theories are relevant to teacher education but only partly presented due to, for instance, time constraints. Clearly, the question of, which theories to include in a teacher education programme, is not trivial. Jaworski reported that in their discussions on a theoretical model which is suitable for teacher education programmes mathematics education scholars met difficulties even when having to decide what counts as a theoretical model.

In this chapter I focus on two of the theoretical models that I discussed with secondary school mathematics prospective teachers and with mathematics teachers in my courses at Tel Aviv University: Fischbein's theory, and Stavy and Tirosh's theory. I chose these particular theories for three reasons: (1) these theories were formulated "at home", i.e., at Tel Aviv University, and much related research has been conducted in our department; (2) the theories satisfy the set of evaluation-criteria offered by Schoenfeld (2002), i.e., both have descriptive power (to capture "what counts"), explanatory power (how and why things work), scope (to cover a wide range of phenomena), predictive power, ability to be falsified (the accuracy of the claims is tested empirically), triangulation (multiple sources of evidence), rigor

---

[1] The notions "theories" and "theoretical models" are used interchangeably.

and specificity, as well as being replicable, generality and trustworthiness; and (3) the theories provide two interesting perspectives to the analysis of mathematical performances: a content-oriented perspective, addressing the impact of learners' prior knowledge (Fischbein, 1987), and a task-oriented perspective, addressing the impact of certain tasks on learners' tendencies to respond in specific ways (Stavy & Tirosh, 2000). In the following sections I offer a brief description of the two theories, and then I present data regarding the impact of teachers' familiarity with these theories on their knowledge and practice.

Fischbein: Three Knowledge Components

Fischbein's (e.g., 1993) theoretical framework presents three components of knowledge: formal, intuitive and algorithmic. *Formal knowledge* is based on propositional thinking, which is characterized by rigor and consistency in deductive construction, being free of the constraints imposed by concrete or practical characteristics. *Algorithmic knowledge* is the ability to use theoretically justified procedures. *Intuitive knowledge* is a kind of persistent cognition, which is accepted directly and confidently as being obvious, imparting the feeling that no justification is required (see also Fischbein, 1987).

Each of the three components alone plays a vital part in students' mathematics performance, but their interrelations are not any less significant. Fischbein explained that "sometimes, the intuitive background manipulates and hinders the formal interpretation or the use of algorithmic procedures" (1993, p. 14). Consequently, he and his colleagues identified and investigated a number of algorithmic procedures, which he called *algorithmic models*, when referring, for instance, to methods of reduction in processes of simplifying algebraic or trigonometric expressions. For example, students' tendency to treat $(a + b)^5$ as $a^5 + b^5$ or $\log (x + t)$ as $\log x + \log t$ was interpreted by Fischbein as evolving from the application of the distributive law, which he identified as a prototype for simplifying algebraic and trigonometric expressions (Fischbein, 1993).

Fischbein paid significant attention to learners' primary intuitions, which "develop in individuals independent of any systematic instruction as an effect of their personal experience" (1987, p. 202). He explained that correct intuitions do not simply replace primitive, incorrect ones, because primary intuitions are usually extremely resistant and thus may rather coexist alongside new, scientifically acceptable ones. This is what often generates inconsistencies in the students' responses. In conclusion, Fischbein stated that "every instructional activity always has to cope with intuitive tendencies ..." and he thus recommended to teachers "to create 'alarm devices' which would alert the student each time he reaches a potential pitfall in his reasoning" (Fischbein, 1987, p. 38).

Stavy and Tirosh: Intuitive Rules

Stavy and Tirosh claimed that students tend to react in a similar, predictable manner to various, scientific, mathematical and daily tasks that share some external features (e.g., Stavy & Tirosh, 1996a, 1996b, 2000; Tirosh & Stavy, 1999) but are otherwise unrelated. The intuitive rules theory presents three rules considered to be intuitive since they entail Fischbein's (1987) major characteristics of "intuitive knowledge" (i.e., immediacy, self-evidence and confidence). Here I focus on the intuitive rules *more A–more B* and *same A–same B* which were identified in students' reactions to comparison tasks.

The intuitive rule *more A–more B* was identified when students were given tasks, presenting two entities that differ with regard to a certain quantity A ($A_1 >$ A_2), but asking to compare the entities with respect to another quantity B, where B_1 is not necessarily larger than B_2. Students tended to claim that "$B_1 > B_2$ because $A_1 > A_2$ or more A–more B". For example, Klartag and Tsamir (2000) found that high school students tended to claim that for any function f (x), if f (x_1) > f (x_2) than f ' (x_1) > f ' (x_2), or more A (value of f(x)) - more B (value of f ' (x)). These claims were evident even when students were presented with algebraic representations of specific functions, where it was easy to "substitute and refute".

The intuitive rule *same A–same B*, was found in students' reactions to tasks presenting two entities that are equal in respect to a noticeable characteristic A (A_1 = A_2), but asking to compare these entities with regard to another characteristic B, where ($B_1 \neq B_2$). A common response was "$B_1 = B_2$ because $A_1=A_2$, or same A–same B." For example, students tended to claim that any hexagon with equal sides necessarily has equal angles, that is, *same sides–same angles* (e.g., Tsamir, 2002). Stavy and Tirosh (2000) claimed that the intuitive rules theory may also serve as a means to both explain and predict students' responses to different tasks. Consequently, the researchers asserted that teachers' familiarity with the intuitive rules theory may improve mathematics and science teaching.

INVESTIGATING THE USE OF THEORIES IN TEACHER EDUCATION

In the following sections I present three research segments illustrating the impact of prospective teachers' and practising teachers' familiarity with the two theoretical models on their knowledge and practice (see also, Tsamir, 2006, 2007a, 2007b). *Research segment 1* illustrates prospective teachers' use of the intuitive rule theory as a tool to promote their SMK by increasing their control when dealing with sides and angles of polygons. *Research segment 2* illustrates prospective teachers' use of Fischbein's theory as a tool to promote their PCK, i.e., their knowledge of how and why students err when solving inequalities, and to build tasks to match students' difficulties. *Research segment 3* illustrates a prospective teacher's use of the intuitive rule theory and a practising teacher's use of Fischbein's theory in actual practice, when discussing integrals in their classes.

Research Segment 1: Promoting SMK and Control When Discussing Polygons

This segment presents the occurrences during two lessons. One lesson was held with 32 secondary school prospective teachers during the course *Psychological Aspects of Mathematics Education*; while the other lesson was conducted with 17 secondary school mathematics teachers during a seminar on *The Role of Errors in Mathematics Education* (the latter teachers were not familiar with the intuitive rules theory).

The Lessons. The initial occurrences in both classes were similar. I opened the lesson by asking the participants whether the statement: "In any triangle, if all the sides are equal, then all the angles are equal", is valid and if so, why. In both classes, the participants easily confirmed and explained the validity of the statement. Then, they were asked to formulate related statements by applying the what-if-not approach (see, for instance, Brown & Walter, 1983): i.e., changing at least one component of a statement and examining the impact of this change on the validity of the original statement.

In each of the classes, participants correctly designed and modified statements. For example, they suggested "reversing it" to the following valid statement: "In any triangle, if all the angles are equal, then all the sides are equal" or changing it to the invalid statement "In any quadrilateral, if all the sides are equal, then all the angles are equal". The classes effortlessly examined the validity of the statements and provided appropriate justifications to their related judgments.

The interesting events in each of these lessons took place when participants tried to determine whether the statement: "In any hexagon if all sides are equal, then its angles are also equal" is valid and why. In both classes, all participants viewed the statement as being valid, and – erroneously – "proved" it on the board (see Figure 1).

In both classes the seemingly-formal proof was enthusiastically accepted at first. Then some participants raised doubts regarding the unconditional possibility of "inscribing an equal-sided hexagon in a circle". But although they criticized the suggested proof, no participant made the next step of doubting the validity of the statement.

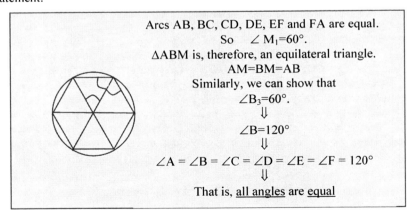

Arcs AB, BC, CD, DE, EF and FA are equal.

So $\angle M_1 = 60°$.

$\triangle ABM$ is, therefore, an equilateral triangle.

AM=BM=AB

Similarly, we can show that

$\angle B_3 = 60°$.

⇓

$\angle B = 120°$

⇓

$\angle A = \angle B = \angle C = \angle D = \angle E = \angle F = 120°$

⇓

That is, <u>all angles</u> are <u>equal</u>

Figure 1. Ben's solution.

216

Ben, a prospective teacher who "proved" it on the board, said:

> Ben: It might be problematic... maybe I limited the generality by inscribing the hexagon... I think IT IS possible [to inscribe the hexagon in a circle... It should be possible 'cause the sides... so the angles ARE equal... I must find a way of showing WHY it is always possible to inscribe the hexagon in a circle.

Here, Ben had some second thoughts about his proof, but rather than questioning its conclusion, he remained convinced that the angles ARE equal, and thus assumed that inscribing the hexagon in a circle must always be possible. On the whole, both the prospective teachers and the practising teachers felt no need to base their "sense of correctness" on proof. They said things like, "It's obvious" and "Sure, they are equal, because the sides are". The teachers were asked to investigate the statement in small groups, but they spent most of the time trying to prove "that it is equal". They were given a home assignment to prove or refute this statement in a mathematically acceptable and convincing way.

In the prospective teachers' class one participant, Ron came up with a counter example, which refuted the statement (see two steps of his explanation in Figure 2). This is what he said about his experience:

> Ron: At first I myself had wrong ideas... I had no proof...and suddenly, it struck me that my solution was INTUITIVE, I mean same-same, so... it might be nonsense... 'cause if the quadrilaterals do not follow same-same... why should the hexagon? So... I started to look for a counter example... I was amazed when I FOUND a counter example...

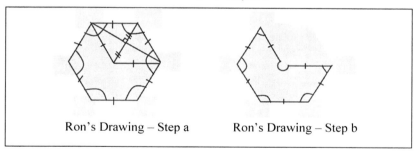

Ron's Drawing – Step a   Ron's Drawing – Step b

Figure 2. Ron's drawing.

Here, Ron communicated his awareness that "INTUITIVE, I mean same-same, might be nonsense...", and his awareness of having shifted from intuitive to formal reasoning. This critical thinking made him recall the invalid quadrilateral-statement and freed his mind to the search of a counter example. Then, another prospective teacher, Eran, who later presented a different counter example, told us that he had gone through a process similar to that of Ron.

Eran: I too was a hundred percent sure... at the beginning... that equal sides-equal angles... when Ron talked I realized "bang" it is just a same A-same B solution... I did not PROVE it... it was only that [giggled] I thought I was immune to such errors... especially when solving simple tasks... so I started to play with the drawing and I found... I'll show you...

Several participants went on voicing their reflections. For example, Anat said: "I had a same-same error in an EASY problem... I was completely sure that I was right here too... same-same intuitions", Hagar said: "I can't believe that I was so stuck with my intuitive solution", and Gal said that "Maybe, the main thing is to remain doubtful..." Anat added that they erred although they knew about intuitive solutions, "Obviously, high school students are going to err here". Here she expressed sensitivity to students' reasoning and to possible, logical bases underlying intuitive errors. Ron reacted excitedly:

Ron: HIGH SCHOOL STUDENTS? Hey, look here... WE erred... when WE are in class we must... consider the possibility of solving intuitively... so that WE won't make errors...

Ron concluded that before concerning themselves with their future students' mistakes teachers should be alert to their own intuitive thinking.

Participants' Reflective Notes. By the end of each of these lessons, participants were asked to hand in a brief summary of ideas, thoughts, comments and questions that were triggered during the lesson. The practising teachers' reflective notes, submitted by the end of this lesson, mainly included questions, e.g.: "Can every hexagon be inscribed in a circle?" "How can we prove it?" Some teachers asked: "Isn't it obvious that, when all sides of a polygon are equal, then the angles are also equal?" It should be noted, that by the end of the following lesson, after I presented a counterexample refuting the statement, 10 teachers reported that they had been confused: "I was probably confused" or "Last time the equal sides confused me", 3 added that it was "surprising to see a counterexample", and 2 others mentioned that "such tasks are never really discussed in [secondary school] classes".

The prospective teachers were much more critical in their reflective notes. They acknowledged the possibly problematic influence of intuition on their mathematical performance "...It's not only that I made an error: I was convinced it was actually correct. Like, intuition beats logic". They re-examined their initial assumption that high school mathematics topics are trivial to them and concluded that they would have to invest time in the relevant mathematics and in analyzing their intuitive ways of reasoning: "I feel that... we should invest efforts in deepening our knowledge of secondary school mathematics and in widening our familiarity with theories that might help in interpreting solutions." They drew some practical conclusions regarding the need to think critically and carefully about any solution that involved intuitive (and specifically intuitive rule-based) reasoning: "The intuitive rules theory actually offers a way to examine our own errors, why we err, why we come up with the erroneous solution and not with another, and why we feel so sure about its correctness".

Some Observations. The evaluation of participants' gains derived from these lessons was based on the lessons themselves and participants' end-of-the lesson reflective notes. The teachers in this segment were trapped in their erroneous, same-same solution (see also Tsamir, 2002, 2007a) until the end of the lesson. They did not solve the question "Can we always inscribe a hexagon in a circle?" In the following lesson, after being presented with a refutation of the statement, they related in their reflective notes to their errors but from a narrow perspective.

It seems, nonetheless, that the intuitive rules theory provided several prospective teachers with a framework for understanding some of their tendencies to err and for formulating related control strategies. Familiarity with the intuitive rule allowed Ron and Eran "to act on the spot" (cf., Mason & Spence, 1999): it served as a trigger to crack their absolute confidence in the correctness of their erroneous, same-same judgment, and as a tool for analyzing the fragility of their intuitive solution. Consequently, it freed them to search for a correct direction. In Schoenfeld's terminology, Ron and Eran managed to reject the guesses "that turn out not to be fruitful, and (eventually) to hone in on directions that seem to help" (Schoenfeld, 1987, p. 44).

Consequently, during the lesson prospective teachers used an intuitive rules-based analysis of their own errors, which led them to a sensitive theory-based approach to students' errors (Anat & Ron). The prospective teachers' reflective notes included four types of SMK-related observations: their awareness of (1) the fragility of their mathematical knowledge and the power of intuition, (2) the need to scrutinize intuitive solutions, (3) the need to continuously reinforce their secondary-school mathematics, and (4) the possible role of the intuitive rules in reflecting on their SMK. These aspects of SMK are regarded as important for professional teaching (e.g., Sowder, 2007). All in all, the prospective teachers' conclusions referred to the need to maintain awareness of the impact of intuition on our solutions and to regard intuitive solutions as a red light, calling for control (Fischbein, 1987; Stavy & Tirosh, 2000).

Research Segment 2: Promoting PCK when Discussing Inequalities

This segment presents an analysis of prospective teachers' written reactions to a student's solution to an inequality-task that was given twice in the course *Didactics of Secondary School Mathematics* - once at the beginning of the year (before attending the course, *Psychological Aspects of Mathematics Education,* which they took in parallel) and once at the end (towards the end of the courses). Twenty five prospective secondary school teachers answered the task at that first point in time, and 23 of them (2 were missing) handed at the second (Figure 3).

All prospective teachers accepted, both before and after the course, Danny's solution that "the statement is false". However, their analyses of "what Danny

PESSIA TSAMIR

knows" and their view of a "good next-task" significantly differed before and after the course.

Pre-Course Reactions. Before the course all prospective teachers expressed confidence in Danny's knowledge, with vague declarations that "Danny seems to know the topic", "Danny's knowledge is good", "Danny understands it".

The statement:

For any a in R $a \cdot x > 5 \rightarrow x > \dfrac{5}{a}$ is TRUE /FALSE (circle). Why?

Danny wrote:

The statement: for any a in R, $a \cdot x > 5 \rightarrow x > \dfrac{5}{a}$, is false.

The statement is false for a=0, so it is not true for ANY number.
One counterexample is sufficient. So, it's false.

In your view:

a.   Danny's solution is CORRECTS / INCORRECT
    If Danny's solution is correct -
        What does Danny know?

    If Danny's solution is incorrect -
        What does Danny know? What is his error?
        What are possible reasons for this error?

b.   What is a "good next-task" to present to Danny? Why?

Figure 3. The inequality task.

One prospective teacher wrote that "Danny knows inequalities". In this spirit, when addressing the "good next-task", 7 prospective teachers stated that they see no need in giving any additional task, because "this is a demanding task, and if Danny can answer such parametric-inequalities, then he can continue with the curriculum", or "this task looks short and simple, but it is not. If Danny managed to do this type of task correctly we can just continue teaching." Four prospective teachers generally suggested giving Danny a similar task: "It is very important to exercise much, so I would give him some more of this kind", or a more demanding one: "I would look for a more challenging task with parameters, to exercise". Fourteen prospective teachers did not suggest any task.

Post-Course Reactions. This task was not discussed with the prospective teachers during the course. After the course, 9 of them continued to have confidence in Danny's knowledge, offering explanations resembling their initial ones: "Danny seems to know". Three of them were indifferent to what task Danny should do next: "He dealt with a difficult problem, so we can give him anything." and one proposed to continue with the curriculum: "Time is limited, if he solved this task, we should move on to the next topic".

The other 14 prospective teachers were not sure that Danny "knows inequalities", although they clearly stated that Danny's solution was correct. Six of them expressed their view about what Danny does know, stating that "Danny certainly knows how to refute a general statement (for all). He knows that one counter-example is sufficient." Or "Danny has the formal knowledge (cf., Fischbein) about refutations of mathematical statements". However, they added reservations regarding "Danny's familiarity with the way [substitution of] negative numbers [for a] would work here". These prospective teachers based their arguments on Fischbein's theory of intuition, addressing the possible impact of Danny's prior knowledge about equations on his solutions to inequalities. Their explanations were, for example, "Danny only addressed zero, which would have been the only counter-example if this was an equation. He might intuitively think that it works like an equation. His explanation is correct, but that does not indicate whether he knows what happens for negative 'a's"; or "It may be that Danny has the image of equations, so it's possible that he thought that it is OK to divide both sides by any number that is not zero"; or more generally, "When students solve inequalities, they may intuitively think about equations, because it is the prior knowledge that seems relevant. As Fischbein said, they may have an intuitive equation-inequalities mix without knowing it".

When addressing the "good next-tasks", the fourteen prospective teachers who were not certain about Danny's knowledge of inequalities, tried to tackle the "special nature of zero" and the "negative coefficient" issue in different ways. Twelve of them offered presenting Danny with a "solve" inequality like, $\frac{3x+5}{2x+9} > 0$ or $\frac{9x+2}{3x+1} > 5$ or even simpler inequalities like $-5x > 20$ explaining that they want to see whether Danny would address the "negative option". One prospective teacher wrote:

> Since zero is a good counter-example here, and this may be intuitively related to equations, I need to find a similar task where zero does not work. I can offer doing it in two ways: (1) reverse the inequality, so that zero is no more a counter example, and (2) present the statement with an additional condition $a \neq 0$, and ask:
>
> 1. Is the statement for any a in R, $a \cdot x < 5 \rightarrow x < \frac{5}{a}$ true? Why?
>
> 2. Is the statement for any $a \neq 0$ in R, $a \cdot x > 5 \rightarrow x > \frac{5}{a}$ true? Why?

Another prospective teacher elaborated on her explanation, before offering the three next-tasks. She wrote:

I need to be careful in drawing conclusions about what a student knows when he solves a certain task correctly, because he might solve this task correctly, without showing any of the intuitive, mistaken-knowledge or incomplete-knowledge he actually holds. Usually, a correct solution to a certain task does not require the full picture of one's related knowledge. Here, zero was sufficient to refute, but it gave no indication about what Danny knows about negative coefficients. Bearing in mind that zero works also for equations, it might be that Danny intuitively thought about equations when solving this inequality. So, the next-tasks should be formulated to examine this. It is also important to remember that students are not always consistent and their solutions to different types of tasks may be different and even contradictory. So, I should prepare different types of tasks that examine these issues. For example:

1. Solve: $(x-13)(5-x) + x^2 > 7$ (Here Danny may reach $-8x > 72$)

2. Solve: $\dfrac{x+3}{x-3} > 9$ (Here we can see whether $x \neq 3$ is his only condition)

3. Is the expression $a \cdot x > 5 \rightarrow x > \dfrac{5}{a}$ true for the following values of a? (Circle your choices): [a] 65, [b] 1.37, [c] 0, [d] (-18.54), [e] π, [f] 63071. In each case, if it is not true, why?

Probably this can be done in a better way; I need to look in books and perhaps also consult some colleagues.

The 9 prospective teachers who believed that "Danny knows", and 2 other prospective teachers, offered no "good next-tasks". One of them recommended carrying on with the curriculum, and 8 answered that "It makes no difference", "I don't know" "I'll find something interesting".

Some Observation. In this segment we see prospective teachers using Fischbein's theory as a tool for analysing students' mathematical reasoning and in their design of future instruction. The theory promoted prospective teachers' ability to address possible sources for students' solutions (see Even & Tirosh, 1995). That is, when addressing issues such as, 'equations are taught before inequalities, so they might influence students' reasoning'; or 'the resemblance between equations and inequalities might intuitively lead students to assume that the two entities are identical', prospective teachers correctly *predicted* sources of students' common errors when solving inequalities (e.g., Tsamir & Almog, 2001; Tsamir & Bazzini, 2004).

Moreover, the prospective teachers' familiarity with Fischbein's theory led them to address a correct solution in an insightful, open minded way. They were not blinded by the correctness of the specific solution, but became sensitive to subtleties regarding Danny's incomplete knowledge of inequalities. The theory also contributed to the prospective teachers' problem-posing skills and to their diagnostic task-sequencing when aiming to examine a student's mathematical reasoning (PCK).

Research Segment 3: Using Theories when Teaching Integrals (In Practice)

This segment describes two interactions featuring Betty (a prospective teacher who was working with Tony, her mentor), and Tim (an experienced high school teacher), and 12th graders during calculus lessons. Betty and Tim were familiar with the two theories.

Betty's Experience. Students were working in pairs on tasks dealing with maxima, minima and integrals, while Tony (Betty's mentor) and Betty moved around the class responding to students' requests for help. At a certain moment, Betty incidentally overheard two students', Dan and Daffy's, discussion of a task (see, Figure 4):

Dan told Daffy that they had finished all they had to do, and she voiced a reservation: "No... no... we still have the last item" (part 2, Figure 4). Dan reacted sharply: "What's the matter with you? It's exactly the same solution as in Item 1... The same value of 'a' will lead to the maximum of the area, and to the maximum of the volume, created from the rotation of that area". Betty suggested that Dan and Daffy to check by looking at the solutions in the book, but Dan responded scornfully, "There might be a mistake in the book..."

A straight line $y = ax$ $(a > 0)$ intersects the parabola $y = -x^2 + 4x$ in two points $(0; 0)$ and another point, P. Another straight line, perpendicular to the x axis, passes through P.

1.   Calculate – For which value of 'a' will the area enclosed between the perpendicular line, $y = ax$ and the x-axis be maximal?

2.   Calculate – For which value of 'a' will the volume created by the rotation of the previous area around the x-axis be maximal?

(The solutions to the two items, $a(1) = \frac{4}{3}$, $a(2) = \frac{8}{5}$, were printed in the textbook).

Figure 4. The integrals task.

In her report of that incident Betty said that when she heard Dan's statement:

...it took me a moment to pull myself together... I mean at first glance the intuitive, same solution seemed reasonable... to me too, I mean... then... I felt... It's in line with same-same... so I have... like to double check if my intuition wasn't misleading me... and it was... the solution in the book was different... so... I recalled that same areas-same volumes are NOT as connected as they seem so that it may be: same parameter to both is also an illusion…

She added with excitement that it was striking to her that:

I had a real life example that the intuitive rule same A-same B really influences high school students' solutions… ehh… I mean that it is not merely a theoretical thing encountered only in academic discussions at the university. There was this same A-same B situation REALLY occurring out of the blue…

Here we witness Dan's and maybe also Daffy's same areas / maximum–same value of 'a' solutions. We then see the didactic power that familiarity with the intuitive rules theory granted Betty; her appreciation of the usefulness of theoretical materials she had studied at the university, and her satisfaction with being able to identify students' unexpected same-same considerations in real time – in class.

During class discussion, students easily solved Item 1 on the board, and several students declared that they did not get to do Item 2. They commented,

Daffy: We do the same…

Eddy: I did not solve it, but it's so similar… it would be much more helpful if we did the stars [the difficult problems]… I tried Problem 21 but I got stuck…

Tony: I agree that it is pretty much like Item 1… so let's just see what is DIFFERENT in Item 2 [of the present task].

Della: The formula is different… here it is volume…

Eddy: But it's this very area rotating…

Dan: It's the same solution…

Tony: What we change is… [writes the formula for the volume on the board] I believe you can do it from here…

Daffy: There's nothing to do… it's already done…

Tony: Let's look at number 21.

Here Tony provided an algorithmic formula-based hint, while ignoring any intuitive consideration, and sent the students to finish up the problematic part on their own, because he regarded it as trivial. After the lesson, Betty tried to persuade Tony that Dan's solution was problematic, intuitive and worth discussing in class. Tony's reaction was that he sees NO PROBLEM during this lesson, and he stated that he prefers doing more calculation tasks, like the ones presented in the matriculation exam, rather than working on intuition. Tony's reactions may result from his lacking either the means or the intention to look into the matter. However, since Tony was not asked about the reasons for his didactical decisions, his teaching might have been influenced by his sense of responsibility for his students' success in the approaching matriculation exam.

Tim's Lesson. Tim planned to discuss in class areas, volumes with functions that include trigonometric expressions. He asked to find the area between f(x)=sin(x), g(x)=cos(x), x=0 and x=¼ , and the volume formulated when this area rotates around the x axis. Dan and Shai wrote on the board the formula for the volume:

Dan: $v = \pi \int_0^{\frac{\pi}{4}} [\cos x - \sin x]^2\, dx$

Shai: $v = \pi \int_0^{\frac{\pi}{4}} \cos^2(x)\,dx - \pi \int_0^{\frac{\pi}{4}} \sin^2(x)\,dx$

Tim reported that these solutions immediately reminded him of Fischbein's distributive-law algorithmic model. He asked the class whether both solutions were acceptable.

Anat: It's actually the same...

Betty: They should be... it's just different ways, like in the areas... different ways, but equal areas.

T: So, you expect the same result for the two volume formulas?

Voices: yes...

Tim decided to confront the students with the different numeric results that Dan and Shai would reach, to discuss with the students their tendencies to intuitively use the "distributive-law" or "linearity" model, and to present a simple graphic illustration of the difference between the two formulas. So, he asked the class to calculate the two solutions. The students found that Dan's volume is 0.89 while Shai's is 1.57.

Then, Tim discussed with the students their tendencies to use this algorithmic model across curriculum, and asked them to provide related examples.

Naomi: $\sin(\alpha + \beta) \neq \sin \alpha + \sin \beta$, $|a+b| \neq |a| + |b|$

Voices: but $[f(x) + g(x)]' = f'(x) + g'(x)$

Jo: $\pi \int_a^b [f(x) - g(x)]^2\, dx \neq \pi \int_a^b f^2(x)\,dx - \pi \int_a^b g^2(x)\,dx$

T: We intuitively view all these as similar. We must be careful! You should be able to analyze your tendencies to err, and know that some errors seem intuitively reasonable. Therefore, I want you also to have a visual image of the two volumes, $v1 = \pi \int_a^b [f(x) - g(x)]^2\, dx$ and

$v2 = \pi \int_a^b f^2(x)dx - \pi \int_a^b g^2(x)dx$. Let's draw and calculate the volumes for $f(x) = 5$ and $g(x) = 2$, between $a = 1$ and $b = 11$.

The students drew V_1 (a cylinder, $r = 3$, $h = 10$) and V_2 (a hollow figure between two cylinders, $R = 5$, $H = 10$, and $r = 2$, $h = 10$), calculated $V_1 = 90$ and $V_2 = 210$, and concluded –

Ronit: So… the volume created by two function, one above the other, is the large volume minus the smaller one $\pi \int_a^b f^2(x)dx - \pi \int_a^b g^2(x)dx$, and NOT

$$\pi \int_a^b [f(x) - g(x)]^2 dx$$

Some Observations. Betty used the intuitive rules theory for reflecting on, and correcting, her initial, erroneous *same-same* ideas. She exhibited alertness when reaching a *same A-same B* solution and re-examined her initial ideas (SMK). Betty was also able to use intuitive-rules based analyses of the students' solutions, identifying *same value of a for max area – same value of a for max volume* responses (PCK). Most significant is Betty's ability to react on students' intuitive error "on the spot", in class, while Tony, an expert, could not. That is, the theoretical lenses allowed inexperienced Betty to close the professional gap between teachers' knowledge as acquired in academic courses, and its implementation in teaching (e.g., Goffrey & Oonk, 2001; Lampert & Ball, 1998). Similarly, Tim exhibited an impressive theory-based ability to identify sources for students' errors and theory based tools in teaching. In conclusion, Tim and Betty appreciated the benefits they gained from the theoretical tool, recommended that mathematics teachers be familiar with the theories, and that they should "do something" when encountering intuitive responses in class (Tsamir, 2006).

SUMMING UP AND LOOKING AHEAD

This chapter touches on the issue of "using theories as tools in mathematics teacher education" by drawing on three research segments chosen from a number of comprehensive research studies I conducted during the last decade, to examine the impact of teachers' familiarity with theoretical models on their knowledge and teaching. In my studies I made some decisions regarding the questions: What theories to present in teacher education programmes? In what ways and at what stages (e.g., prospective teachers or practising teachers) should theories be presented? and How to assess the impact of teachers' familiarity with theories on their professionalism? Let us examine these questions.

Theories in the Teacher Education Programmes: How to Choose?

Theories are widely regarded as an important component in teacher education programmes (e.g., Elmore, 2002; Graeber, 1999; Hawley & Valli, 1999; Sowder,

2007) and there is a vast offering of theories that are relevant to mathematics teachers (e.g., Silver & Herbst, 2007). Clearly, not all of these can be efficiently presented in any single professional development setting. Thus, choices need to be made. However, at the moment, there is no systematic analysis of criteria for choosing theories to be presented to teachers. One way to approach this issue is by examining the goals of mathematics teaching and of teacher professional development (e.g., Ball & Cohen, 1999; Sowder, 2007), and evaluating how teachers' familiarity with specific theories may contribute to the achievement of some of these goals. This chapter suggests that discussing Fischbein's theory and the intuitive rules theory with secondary school prospective mathematics teachers or practising mathematics teachers may lead to "a sound understanding of mathematics of the level taught", a "deep pedagogical content knowledge" (goals mentioned by Sowder, 2007, p. 161; see also Shulman, 1986), and to better teaching.

Regarding mathematical knowledge (SMK), it seems that on several occasions the prospective teachers who were familiar with theories managed "to develop the capacity... to analyse and keep under control [their] intuitive conceptions" (1987, p. 206; see also Schoenfeld, 1992). This is a most demanding goal in mathematics performance. Many of the prospective teachers who knew the theories promoted their secondary school related SMK in a wide sense by using the theories as tools to spot where their possibly-intuitive solutions need constant checking. Beyond the mathematical and psychological insights, prospective teachers became aware of their need to work on their own secondary school mathematics, which no longer seemed beyond scrutiny. The literature reports that "secondary prospective teachers' knowledge of secondary school mathematics cannot be taken for granted," and states that "teachers at all levels need to study more mathematics" (Cooney & Wiegel, 2003, p. 804).

Moreover, participants' reinforced SMK seemed to empower their PCK as well. In addition to the acquisition of knowledge, the theories served these prospective teachers in tuning their "listening skills", in refining their alertness to possibly erroneous, intuition-based solutions. Consequently, familiarity with the intuitive rules theory contributed to the prospective teachers' knowledge and to the skills that are regarded essential for teaching (e.g., Cooney, 1999; Davis, 1997).

As highlighted before, after getting to know the theories, the prospective teachers' knowledge-based performance was more proficient, i.e., they exhibited richer abilities to predict students' mathematical reasoning, to analyse sources for their solutions and design related next-tasks (e.g., in Segment 2; see also Even & Tirosh, 1995). Betty, while making her first steps in class, used her theory-based knowledge to critically reflect on her own reasoning, to identify the intuitive error made in class, and to make related didactical decisions. Moreover, Betty seemed to have gained professional confidence that allowed her to decide that something had to be done, and even to challenge the experienced teacher for not taking relevant steps. It granted an inexperienced, "pre-novice" teacher, Betty, the advantages of practising teachers, freeing her mind to address students' difficulties, and encouraged her, even to assertively approach a mentor who did not meet her expectations. This professional confidence, founded on knowledge, is valuable. (e.g., Borko et al., 1992). All in all, it is clear how familiarity with the two theories can promote participants' SMK and PCK. So it seems reasonable to recommend explicit reference to these theoretical frameworks, beyond field experience.

One may still wonder whether this is the best choice of theories to be presented in teacher education programmes (see also Tsamir, 2007a, 2007b). My answer to this question is conditional. I believe that teachers' familiarity with these theories is important, and as shown, the benefits may be significant. But there are at least two limitations: time restrictions and student diversity. Time, in teacher education programmes, is quite limited and there are many topics to be included. Moreover, some of my studies have indicated that not all prospective teachers have similarly gained from exposure to these theories (e.g., Tsamir, 2007a). This reinforces the above question: How should theories be chosen? How many theories should we present? These questions deserve further investigation.

Theories in the Teacher Education Programmes: How to Present? At what Stages?

Questions accompanying the design of mathematics education programmes are, for instance, what should be included, at what stage (to prospective teachers and to practising teachers)? Should we present theories even at this early stage of prospective teachers' professional development? If the answer is yes, should the same theories be also presented to practising teachers?

Considering the advantages listed below we decided that in the teacher education programmes at Tel-Aviv University, both prospective and practising teachers should be offered Psychological Aspects of Mathematics Education (further discussion of these issues, see Tsamir, 2006, 2007a). Even the limited data presented in this chapter indicate that to a substantial number of prospective teachers the theories that were presented in this course served to promote their SMK and PCK, to gain professional, knowledge-based confidence as well as motivation to reinvestigate secondary school mathematics. Additional data suggested that studying these theoretical models indeed had these and other benefits of teachers. We also faced the question of how the presentation of theories would be optimally meaningful and effective.

A significant guideline, underlying the design of both the prospective teachers and the teacher professional development programme, was that in addition to studying the course Psychological Aspects of Mathematics Education both populations were required to implement these theories in more courses. The prospective teachers had to study - Didactics of secondary mathematics and High-school mathematics from an advanced perspective (mathematics at the centre and theory in the background) and Peer Teaching (teaching at the centre and mathematics and theory in the background); and in their Practice at School (interviewing students, observing lessons, and teaching some lessons, as well as reporting on these activities and writing theory-based analyses in *Workshops* at the university).

The practising teachers addressed the theories in an academic course: *Mathematics – Research and Instruction* (mathematics, research and instruction at the center and theory in the background); and in a *seminar* (conducting mini research, where research, mathematics and teaching are at the center and theory in the background). All in all, participants had a wide spectrum for getting familiar with the theories and with ways to implement them in teaching.

The programme we offer is in line with Borasi and Fonzi's (2002, in Sowder, 2007, p. 171) recommendations to the effect that programmes be "sustained and intensive... [and] offer a rich set of diverse experiences" . Indeed, our programmes give participants the opportunity to acquire and exercise the theoretical issues academically, and also to use them as tools in teaching. Clearly, there is still a need to investigate alternative theories and to assess their impact on prospective teachers and teachers' professional conduct.

How to Assess the Impact of Teachers' Familiarity with Theories on Their Professionalism?

One way to assess the impact of teachers' familiarity with theories on their professionalism is by examining the answer the usages of these theories may give the goals set for teachers' professional development. However, we should constantly bear in mind that the ultimate objective is "to prepare teachers of mathematics and to provide them, while they progress in their careers, with the professional learning opportunities they need *to lead their students to succeed in learning mathematics*" (author's emphasis, Sowder, 2007, p. 157). Thus, one good, though challenging, way to examine the quality of a teacher education programme is by investigating the mathematics performances of students whose teachers participated in this programme.

Silver and Herbst claim that "Given that theory has become much more evident in scholarship in our field in the past decade or so, the moment seems propitious for a serious examination of the role that theory plays and could play in the formulation of problems, in the design and methods employed, and in the interpretation of findings in education research" (Ibid., 2007, pp. 40–41). I would like to add that the time has come to investigate the impact of teachers' familiarity with specific theoretical models on their SMK, PCK, on their actual teaching, as well as on their students' knowledge and mathematical confidence.

The literature offers various research methodologies and it is obvious that none of them provides a perfect answer for researching complex settings of teacher education--teaching and learning. However, while "the complexity of the educational machinery precludes the possibility of identifying clear-cut cause-effect relationships. The difficulty with telling the impact does not imply however its non-existence" (Sfard, 2005, p. 407). It is the responsibility of the mathematics education community to continue with our efforts to address the challenges posed by significant questions, such as: How should theories be chosen for teacher education programmes? How many theories? To whom should we present them (prospective teachers versus. practising teachers)? and, How to assess the impact of teachers' familiarity with theories on their professionalism? and to provide research-based answers to our theory-teaching-teacher education questions.

REFERENCES

Adler, J. (2004, July). The professional development of mathematics teachers. Plenary lecture presented at the 10th International Congress on Mathematical Education. Copenhagen, Denmark. www.icme10.dk/pages/02plenary.htm - 7k.

Adler, J., Ball, D., Krainer, K., Lin, F-L., & Novotna, J. (2005). Reflections on an emerging field: Researching mathematics teacher education. *Educational Studies in Mathematics, 60*, 359–381.

Arzarello, F. (2004, July). Mathematical landscapes and their inhabitants: Perceptions, languages, theories. *Plenary lecture presented at the 10th International Congress on Mathematical Education.* Copenhagen, Denmark. www.icme10.dk/pages/02plenary.htm - 7k.

Ball, D. L., & Cohen, D. K. (1999). Developing practice, developing practitioners: Towards a practice-based theory of professional education. In L. Darling-Hammond & G. Sykes (Eds.), *Teaching as the learning profession: Handbook of policy and practice* (pp. 3–32). San Francisco, CA: Jossey-Bass.

Borko, H., Eisenhart, M., Brown, C.A., Underhill, R.G., Jones, D., & Agard, P.C. (1992). Learning to teach hard mathematics: Do novice teachers and their instructors give up too easily? *Journal for Research in Mathematics Education, 23*, 194–222.

Bosch, M., Arzarello, F., Lenfant, A., & Prediger, S. (2007, February). Different theoretical perspectives and approaches in research in mathematics education. Working Group for *The Fifth Conference of the European Society for Research in Mathematics Education*. Larnaca, Cyprus.

Brousseau, G. (1997). *Theory of didactical situations in mathematics.* Dordrecht, the Netherlands: Kluwer Academic Publishers.

Brown, S. I., & Walter, M. I. (Eds.). (1983). *The art of problem posing* (pp. 31–62). Philadelphia, PA: The Franklin Institute Press.

Brown, T., Hanley, U., Darby, S., & Calder, N. (2007). Teachers' conceptions of learning philosophies: Discussing context and contextualising discussion. *Journal of Mathematics Teacher Education, 10*, 183–200.

Carrillo, J., Bills, L., Santos, L., & Marchive, A. (2007, February). From a study of teaching practices to issues in teacher education. *The Fifth Conference of the European Society for Research in Mathematics Education*, Larnaca, Cyprus.

Carrillo, J., Even, R., Rowland, T., & Serrazina, L. (2005, February). From a study of teaching practices to issues in teacher education. *The Fourth Conference of the European Society for Research in Mathematics Education.* Sant Feliu de Guixols, Spain.

Cochran-Smith, M., & Zeichner, K. M. (2005). *Studying teacher education.* Mahwah, NJ: Lawrence Erlbaum Associates.

Comiti, C., & Ball, D. L. (1996). Preparing teachers to teach mathematics: A comparative perspective. In A. J. Bishop, K. Clements, K. Keitel, J. Kilpatrick, & C. Laborde (Eds.), *International handbook of mathematics education* (pp. 1123–1154). Dordrecht, the Netherlands: Kluwer Academic Pulishers.

Confrey, J., & Kazak, S., (2006). A thirty year reflection on constructivism in mathematics education in PME. In A. Gutiérrez & P. Boero (Eds.), *Handbook of research on the psychology of mathematics education: Past, present and future* (pp. 305–345). Rotterdam, the Netherlands: Sense Publishers.

Cooney, T. J. (1999). Conceptualizing teachers' ways of knowing. *Educational Studies in Mathematics, 38*, 163–187.

Cooney, T. J., & Wiegel, H. G. (2003). Examining the mathematics in mathematics teacher education. In A. Bishop, M. A. Clements, C. Keitel, J. Kilpatrick, F. K. S. Leung (Eds.), *Second international handbook of mathematics education* (pp. 795–828). Dordrecht, the Netherlands: Kluwer Academic Publishers.

Davis, B. (1997). Listening for differences: An evolving conception of mathematics teaching. *Journal for Research in Mathematics Education, 28*, 355–376.

Dreyfus, T., Artigue, M., Bartolini-Bussi, M., Gray, E., & Prediger, S. (2005, February). Different theoretical perspectives and approaches in research in mathematics education. *The Fourth Conference of the European Society for Research in Mathematics Education*. Sant Feliu de Guíxols, Spain.

Elmore, R. F. (2002). *Bridging the gap between standards and achievement: The imperative for professional development in education*, Washington, DC: Albert Shanker Institute.

Even, R., & Tirosh, D. (1995). Subject-matter knowledge and knowledge about students as sources of teacher presentations of the subject-matter. *Educational Studies in Mathematics, 29*, 1–20.

Fischbein, E. (1987). *Intuition in science and mathematics*. Dordrecht, the Netherlands: Reidel.

Fischbein, E. (1993). The interaction between the formal and the algorithmic and the intuitive components in a mathematical activity. In R. Biehler, R. W. Scholz, R. Straser, & B. Winkelmann (Eds.), *Didactics of mathematics as a scientific discipline* (pp. 231–345). Dordrecht, the Netherlands: Reidel.

Furinghetti, F. (2001, February). Theory and practice of teaching from pre-service to in-service teacher education. *The Second Conference of the European Society for Research in Mathematics Education*. Mariánské Lázne: The Czech Republic.

Goffrey, F., & Oonk, W. (2001). Digitizing real teaching practice for teacher education programs: The MILE approach. In F.L. Lin & T.J. Cooney (Eds.), *Making sense of mathematics teacher education* (pp. 111–145). Dordrecht, the Netherlands: Kluwer Academic Publishers.

Graeber, A.O. (1999). Forms of knowing mathematics: What preservice teachers should learn. *Educational Studies in Mathematics, 38*, 189–208.

Grevholm, B., Carrillo, J., Even, R., & Szendrei, J. (2003, February). From a study of teaching practices to issues in teacher education. *Third Conference of the European Society for Research in Mathematics Education*. Bellaria, Italy.

Hawley, W. D., & Valli, L. (1999). The essentials of effective professional development: A new consensus. In L. Darling-Hammond & G. Sykes (Eds.), *Teaching as the learning profession: Handbook of policy and practice* (pp. 127–150). San Francisco: Jossey-Bass.

Hershkowitz, R., Schwartz, B., & Dreyfus, T. (2001). Abstraction in context: Epistemic actions. *Journal for Research in Mathematics Education, 32*, 195–222.

Jaworski, B. (2006). Theory and practice in mathematics teaching development: Critical inquiry as a mode of learning in teaching. *Journal of Mathematics Teacher Education, 2*, 187–211.

Jaworski, B., & Gellert, U. (2003). Educating new mathematics teachers: Integrating theory and practice, and the roles of practicing teachers. In A. J. Bishop, M. A. Clements, C. Keitel, J. Kilpatrick, & F. K. S. Leung (Eds.), *Second international handbook of mathematics education* (pp. 829–875). Dordrech, the Netherlands: Kluwer Academic Publishers.

Klartag, R., & Tsamir, P. (2000). The impact of the intuitive rule more A-more B on students' comparisons of functions. *Paper presented at the 12th annual meeting of the Israeli Association of Research in Education*. Tel Aviv University: Tel Aviv.

Krainer, K., & Goffree, F. (1998, August). From a study of teacher practices to issues in teacher education. *The First Conference of the European Society for Research in Mathematics Education*. Osnabrueck-Haus Ohrbeck, Germany.

Lampert, M., & Ball, D. (1998). *Teaching, multimedia and mathematics: Investigations of real practice*. New York, NY: Teachers College Press.

Lerman, S., (2006). Socio-cultural research in PME. In A. Gutiérrez & P. Boero (Eds.), *Handbook of research on the psychology of mathematics education: Past, present and future* (pp. 305–345). Rotterdam, the Netherlands: Sense Publishers.

Lerman, S., & Tsatsaroni, A. (2004, July). *Surveying the field of mathematics education research*, Paper presented at Discussion Group 10 at the International Congress on Mathematics Education, Copenhagen, Denmark. Retrieved July 20, 2005 at
http://myweb.lsbu.ac.uk/~lermans/ESRCProjectHOMEPAGE.html.

Lin, F-L., & Cooney, T. J. (Eds.) (2001). *Making sense of mathematics teacher education*. Dordrecht, the Netherlands: Kluwer Academic Publishers.

Llinares, S., & Krainer, K. (2006). Mathematics (student) teachers and teacher educators as learners. In A. Gutiérrez & P. Boero (Eds.), *Handbook of research on the psychology of mathematics education: Past, present and future* (pp. 305–345). Rotterdam, the Netherlands: Sense Publishers.

Mason, J., & Spence, M. (1999). Beyond mere knowledge of mathematics: The importance of knowing-to-act in the moment. *Educational Studies in Mathematics, 38*, 51–66.

Mason, J., & Waywood, A. (1996). The role of theory in mathematics education and research. In A. J. Bishop, K. Clements, K. Keitel, J. Kilpatrick, & C. Laborde (Eds.), *International handbook of mathematics education* (pp. 1055–1089). Dordrecht, the Netherlands: Kluwer Academic Publishers.

Minor Degree in Mathematics Education (2007). University of Cyprus. www.ucy.ac.cy/facultiesE/facultiese.html.

Noddings, N. (1992). Professionalization and mathematics teaching. In D. A. Grouws (Ed.), *Handbook of research on mathematics teaching and learning* (pp. 197–208). New York, NY: Macmillan.

Peter-Koop, A., Jaworski, B., Krainer, K., & Serrazina, L. (2003, February). Inter-relating theory and practice. *The Third Conference of the European Society for Research in Mathematics Education*. Bellaria, Italy.

Rowland, T., Huckstep, P. and Thwaites, A. (2005). Elementary teachers' mathematics subject knowledge: The knowledge quartet and the case of Naomi. *Journal of Mathematics Teacher Education, 8*, 255–281.

Schoenfeld, A. H. (1987). A brief and biased history of problem solving. In F. R. Curcio (Ed.), *Teaching and learning: A problem-solving focus* (pp. 27–46). Reston, VA: National Council of Teachers of Mathematics.

Schoenfeld, A. H. (1992). Learning to think mathematically: problem solving, metacognition, and sense-making in mathematics. In D. Grouws (Ed.), *Handbook for research on mathematics* (pp. 334–370). New York, NY: Macmillan.

Schoenfeld, A. H. (2002). Research methods in mathematics education. In L. D. English (Ed.), *Handbook of research in mathematics education* (pp. 435–488). London: Lawrence Erlbaum Associates.

Sfard, A. (2005). What could be more practical than good research? *Educational Studies in Mathematics 58*, 393–413.

Shulman, L. S. (1986). Those who understand: knowledge growth in teaching. *Educational Researcher, 15*, 4–14.

Sierpinska, A. (1999/2003). Lectures on the theory of didactic situations: Lecture notes for graduate mathematics education students. Concordia University. West Montréal, Québec: Canada. alcor.concordia.ca/~sierp/ - 8k.

Sierpinska, A. (2001). Lectures on theory and intuition in mathematics: Lecture notes for graduate mathematics education students. Concordia University. West Montréal, Québec: Canada. alcor.concordia.ca/~sierp/ - 8k.

Sierpinska, A., Kilpatrick, J., Balacheff, N., Howson, A. G., Sfard, A., & Steinbring, H. (1993). What is research in mathematics education, and what are its results? *Journal for Research in Mathematics Education, 24*, 274—278

Silver, E. A., & Herbst, P. G. (2007). Theory in mathematics education scholarship. In F. K. Lester, Jr. (Ed.), *Second handbook of research on mathematics teaching and learning* (pp. 39–67). Charlotte, NC: Information Age Publications & National Council of Teachers of Mathematics.

Silver E. A., & Kilpatrick, J. (1994). *E pluribus unum*: Challenges of diversity in the future of mathematics education research *Journal for Research in Mathematics Education, 25*, 734–754.

Skemp, R. R. (1971). *The psychology of learning mathematics*. Harmondsworth, UK: Penguin.

Sowder, J. T. (2007). The mathematics education and development of teachers. In F. K. Lester, Jr. (Ed.), *Second handbook of research on mathematics teaching and learning* (pp. 157–223). Charlotte, NC: Information Age Publications & National Council of Teachers of Mathematics.

Special Issue. (2006). Inter-relating theory and practice in mathematics teacher education. *Journal of Mathematics Teacher Education, 2*, 109–211.

Stavy, R., & Tirosh, D. (1996a). Intuitive rules in science and mathematics: the case of 'more of A–more of B'. *International Journal of Science Education, 18*, 653–667.

Stavy, R., & Tirosh, D. (1996b). Intuitive rules in science and mathematics: the case of 'everything can be divided by two'. *International Journal of Science Education, 18*, 669–683.

Stavy, R., & Tirosh, D. (2000). *How students' (mis-)understand science and mathematics: Intuitive rules.* New York, NY: Teachers College Press.

Tall. D. (2005, July). A theory of mathematical growth through embodiment, symbolism and proof. Plenary Lecture for the *International Colloquium on Mathematical Learning from Early Childhood to Adulthood*, Belgium.

Tall, D., & Vinner, S. (1981). Concept image and concept definition in mathematics, with special reference to limits and continuity. *Educational Studies in Mathematics, 12*, 151–169.

Tirosh, D., & Stavy, R. (1999). Intuitive rules: A way to explain and predict students' reasoning. *Educational Studies in Mathematics, 38*, 51–66.

Tirosh, D., Stavy, R., & Tsamir, P. (2001). Using the intuitive rules theory as a basis for educating teachers. In F-L Lin & T. Cooney (Eds.), *Making sense of mathematics education*, Dordrecht, the Netherlands: Kluwer.

Tsamir, P. (1999). The transition from comparison of finite to the comparison of infinite sets: Teaching prospective teachers. *Educational Studies in Mathematics. 38*, 209–234.

Tsamir, P. (2002). The intuitive rule 'same A–same B': The case of triangles and quadrilaterals. *Focus on Learning Problems in Mathematics, 24*, 54–70.

Tsamir, P. (2006). Enhancing prospective teachers' knowledge of learners' "same A–same B" conceptions: The case of area and volume. *Journal of Mathematics Teacher Education, 8*, 469–497.

Tsamir, P. (2007a). When intuition beats logic: Prospective teachers' awareness of their same sides-same angles solutions. *Educational Studies in Mathematics, 65*, 255–279.

Tsamir, P. (2007b). How may the use of two theoretical approaches contribute to our understanding of students' errors? The case of areas, volumes and integration. *For the Leaning in Mathematics, 27*, 52–57.

Tsamir, P., & Almog, N. (2001). Students' strategies and difficulties: The case of algebraic inequalities. *International Journal of Mathematical Education in Science and Technology, 32*, 513–524.

Tsamir, P., & Bazzini, L. (2004). Consistencies and inconsistencies in students' solutions to algebraic "single-value" inequalities. *International Journal of Mathematics Education in Science and Technology, 35*, 793—812.

Tsamir, P., & Tirosh, D. (2006). PME 1 to 30 – summing up and looking ahead: A personal perspective on infinite sets. In J. Novotna, H. Moraova, M. Kratka, & N. Stehlikova (Eds.), *Proceedings of the 30th Conference of the International Group for the Psychology of Mathematics Education* (Vol. 1, p. 49). Charles University in Prague, Czech Republic:

Wood, T. (1999). Approaching teacher development: Practice into theory. In T. Wood, B. Jaworski, & A. J.. Dawson, (Eds.) (1999). *Mathematics teacher education: Critical international perspectives.* London, UK: Falmer Press.

Wood, T., Jaworski, B., & Dawson, A.J.. (Eds.)·(1999). *Mathematics teacher education: Critical international perspectives.* London, UK: Falmer Press.

Yackel, E., & Cobb, P. (1996). Sociomathematical norms, argumentation, and autonomy in mathematics. *Journal for Research in Mathematics Education, 22*, 390–408.

Pessia Tsamir
Tel Aviv University
Israel

BARBARA CLARKE

10. A FRAMEWORK OF GROWTH POINTS AS A POWERFUL TEACHER DEVELOPMENT TOOL[1]

This chapter outlines how frameworks of research based-growth points in Number, Measurement and Geometry were developed and used with grade K-2 practising teachers in the Early Numeracy Research Project (ENRP) in Victoria, Australia from 1999 to 2001. The growth points were accompanied by a closely-related one-to-one, task-based assessment interview, which was administered by teachers to their own students. The chapter will detail the key principles underpinning the development of the framework as well as the ways in which the framework was shared with teachers in professional development sessions. In several questionnaires, teachers were invited to identify those aspects of their teaching practice that had changed as a result of their involvement in the ENRP. The most common theme emerging was summarised as "growth points inform planning," indicating the value that teachers saw in these as a professional learning tool.

BACKGROUND

There is increasing evidence that the provision of knowledge based on students' thinking, particularly for teachers in the early years of schooling, is contributing to improved teaching practice and student outcomes (Carpenter & Lehrer, 1999; Franke, Kazemi & Battey, 2007). The use of research based learning frameworks and assessments based on children's mathematical thinking which informs teaching practice has contributed to significant improvements in student learning in a number of contexts in Australia and New Zealand (Bobis, Clarke B. A., Clarke D. M., Thomas, Wright, Young-Loveridge & Gould, 2005). This builds further on the approach of the Cognitively Guided Instruction (CGI) Project in the USA which provided

> strong evidence that knowledge of children's thinking is a powerful tool that enables teachers to transform this knowledge and use it to change instruction. These findings, when viewed in conjunction with those of other studies, provide a convincing argument that one major way to improve mathematics instruction and learning is to help teachers understand the mathematical

---

[1] This chapter is developed from a paper presented at annual meeting of the American Educational Research Association, San Diego, CA, April 2004.

D. Tirosh and T. Wood (eds.), Tools and Processes in Mathematics Teacher Education, 235–256.
© 2008 Sense Publishers. All rights reserved.

thought processes of their students. (Fennema, Carpenter, Franke, Levi, Jacobs & Empson, 1996, p. 432)

Baturo, Cooper, Dietzmann, Heirdsfield, Kidman, Shield, Warren, Nisbet, Klein and Putt (2004), in a project involving 8 primary schools and 37 classes in Queensland, Australia aimed at determining the elements of the learning environment that promoted enhanced student numeracy outcomes found that:

> Students' numeracy outcomes were enhanced when teachers' pedagogic knowledge incorporated a theoretical framework that enabled them to plan and implement units that focused on the development of structural knowledge. Such knowledge took into account appropriate sequences, connections, task, talk, and generic strategies, as well as how students comprehend, misconstrue and forget. (p. xviii)

This chapter will provide background and results from a project in which teachers were provided with a research-based framework of children's thinking, a linked assessment interview, and related professional development. Discussion will include the impact of this on teacher learning and insights into the development and use of such frameworks.

THE EARLY NUMERACY RESEARCH PROJECT

The Early Numeracy Research Project (ENRP) was a collaborative venture between Australian Catholic University, Monash University, the Victorian Department of Employment, Education and Training, the Catholic Education Office (Melbourne), and the Association of Independent Schools Victoria. The project began in January 1999 and was funded to early 2002 in 35 project ("Trial") schools and 35 control ("Reference") schools, in the first three years of school ("Prep", Grade 1, and Grade 2) from ages 5 to 8. (For more detail and background see Clarke D. M., Cheeseman, Gervasoni, Gronn, Horne, McDonough et al, 2002.)

The term "numeracy" has become used more frequently in the Australian context by politicians and school systems in recent years, but in the context of young children, for the purpose of this project, the terms numeracy and mathematics are used interchangeably.

There were three main components of the ENRP:
- a framework of growth points provided a means for understanding young children's mathematical thinking in general;
- an interview provided a tool for assessing this thinking for particular individuals and groups; and
- a professional development program that was geared towards developing further such thinking.

The ENRP Learning and Assessment Framework

The impetus for the Early Numeracy Research Project was a desire to improve mathematics learning and so it was necessary to quantify such improvement. It would not have been adequate to describe, for example, the effectiveness of the professional development in terms of teachers' professional growth, or the children's engagement, or even to produce some success stories. It was decided to create a framework of key "growth points" in numeracy learning. Students' movement through these growth points in trial schools could then be compared to that of students in the reference schools.

The project team first came across the term "growth points" in the work of O'Toole, Rubino, Parker, and Fitzpatrick (1998). The earliest use of this term within the Australian context (to our knowledge) was by Pengelly (1985). The project team studied available research on key "stages" or "levels" in young children's mathematics learning (e.g., Bobis, 1996; Boulton-Lewis, 1996; Clements, Swaminathan, Hannibal, & Sarama, 1999; Fuson, 1992; Lehrer & Chazan, 1998; McIntosh, Bana, & Farrell, 1995; Mulligan & Mitchelmore, 1995, 1996; Owens & Gould, 1999; Pearn & Merrifield, 1998; Thomas, 1996; Wilson & Osborne, 1992; Wright, 1998; Young-Loveridge, 1997), as well as frameworks developed by other authors and groups to describe learning.

The New South Wales Department of Education initiative Count Me In Too (CMIT, Bobis & Gould, 1999) that developed a learning framework for number (Wright, 1998) was a major influence on this project. It was soundly based on prior research and, in particular, on the stages in the construction of the number sequence (Steffe, Cobb, & von Glasersfeld, 1988; Steffe, von Glasersfeld, Richards, & Cobb, 1983) and it formed the basis of an individual interview designed to measure children's learning against the framework.

In developing the ENRP framework, as detailed in D. M. Clarke (2001, pp. 10–11), it was intended that the framework would

— reflect the findings of relevant research in mathematics education from Australia and overseas;
— emphasise important ideas and strategies in early mathematics understanding in a form and language readily understood and, in time, retained by teachers;
— reflect, where possible, the structure of mathematics;
— allow the description of the mathematical knowledge and understanding of individuals and groups;
— form the basis of planning and teaching;
— provide a basis for task construction for interviews, and the recording and coding process that would follow;
— allow the identification and description of improvement where it exists;
— enable a consideration of those students who may benefit from additional assistance;
— have sufficient "ceiling" to describe the knowledge and understanding of all children in the first three years of school; and
— build on the work of successful, similar projects.

These principles informed the process of developing and refining the framework to the form it eventually took. The decision was taken to focus upon the strands of Number (incorporating the domains of Counting, Place Value, Addition and Subtraction Strategies, and Multiplication and Division Strategies), Measurement (incorporating the domains of Length, Mass and Time), and Space (incorporating the domains of Properties of Shape, and Visualisation and Orientation) in both the framework and the interview.

In each mathematical domain, growth points were stated with brief descriptors in each case. There are typically five or six growth points in each domain. For example, the six growth points for the domain of Addition and subtraction strategies are shown in Figure 1. The difference between growth point 1 and 2 illustrates the notion. Consider the child who is asked to find the total of two collections of objects (with nine objects screened and another four objects). Many young children "count-all" to find the total ("1, 2, 3, …, 11, 12, 13"), even once they are aware that there are nine objects in one set and four in the other. Other children realise that by starting at 9 and counting on ("10, 11, 12, 13"), they can solve the problem in an easier way. Counting All and Counting On are therefore two important growth points in children's developing understanding of Addition.

1. *Count-all (two collections)*
    Counts all to find the total of two collections.
2. *Count-on*
    Counts on from one number to find the total of two collections.
3. *Count-back/count-down-to/count-up-from*
    Given a subtraction situation, chooses appropriately from strategies including count-back, count-down-to and count-up-from.
4. *Basic strategies (doubles, commutativity, adding 10, tens facts, other known facts)*
    Given an addition or subtraction problem, strategies such as doubles, commutativity, adding 10, tens facts, and other known facts are evident.
5. *Derived strategies (near doubles, adding 9, build to next ten, fact families, intuitive strategies)*
    Given an addition or subtraction problem, strategies such as near doubles, adding 9, build to next ten, fact families and intuitive strategies are evident.
6. *Extending and applying addition and subtraction using basic, derived and intuitive strategies*
    Given a range of tasks (including multi-digit numbers), can solve them mentally, using the appropriate strategies and a clear understanding of key concepts.

Figure 1. ENRP growth points for the domain of addition and subtraction strategies.

The growth points combine two areas: addition and subtraction. This reflects the close relationship between the two operations, and the fact that many children solve subtraction problems using addition. There are close parallels with the learning progressions for single-digit addition (count all, count on, thinking strategies for larger numbers) and single digit subtraction (take away, count up to/count down, and thinking strategies for larger strategies) described in Kilpatrick, Swafford and Findell (2001).

It is important to stress here one of the desired characteristics of our framework as stated earlier - it needed to be in a form and language readily understood and, in time, retained by teachers. Our aim was that teachers would, in time, carry the framework in their heads, using it as a kind of "lens" through which they could view interactions with children individually, in small group or whole class interactions, as well as during lesson planning.

In discussions with teachers, we came to describe growth points as key "stepping stones" along paths to mathematical understanding, collectively a kind of conceptual landscape (Fosnot & Dolk, 2001). However, we do not claim that all growth points are passed by every student along the way. For example, growth point 3, above involves "count-back", "count-down-to" and "count-up-from" in subtraction situations, as appropriate. But there appears to be a number of children who view a subtraction situation (say, 12-9) as "what do I need to add to 9 to give 12?" and do not appear to use one of those three strategies in such contexts.

The interpretation of these growth points reflects the description by Owens and Gould (1999) in the CMIT project: "the order is more or less the order in which strategies are likely to emerge and be used by children ... intuitive and incidental learning can influence these strategies in unexpected ways" (p. 4). As van den Heuvel-Panhuizen (2001) emphasised, "a learning-teaching trajectory should not be seen as a strictly linear, step-by step regime in which each step is necessarily and inexorably followed by the next" (p. 13), as it needs to do justice to individual learning processes, discontinuities in the learning process, and the fact that multiple skills can be learned simultaneously. She stressed that a trajectory needs to be seen as having a certain "bandwidth." While our growth points take the form of point-wise, quite succinct statements of increasingly sophisticated strategies we would argue that this matched their purpose and use.

In discussing "higher" level growth points in a given domain, the comments of Clements, Swaminathan, Hannibal, and Sarama (1999) in a geometrical context were also helpful: "the adjective higher should be understood as a higher level of abstraction and generality, without implying either inherent superiority or the abandonment of lower levels as a consequence of the development of higher levels of thinking" (p. 208). Similarly, Konold, Khalil, Higgins, and Russell (2001), proposed five perspectives children take in reasoning about data, and described them as follows:

> These categories form a hierarchy of sorts, where a higher level subsumes or encapsulates lower ones. Different contexts may cue different views of data even within the same student .... Thus we see these not as levels or perspectives to graduate from, but rather to master. (p. 1)

Also, the growth points should not be regarded as necessarily discrete. As with Wright's (1998) framework, the extent of the overlap is likely to vary widely across young children, and "it is insufficient to think that all children's early arithmetical knowledge develops along a common developmental path" (p. 702).

Willis (2000) cautioned on assuming that such frameworks robustly describe all learners, particularly those with culturally and contextually different early mathematical experiences.

The ENRP Task-Based Assessment Interview

Every teacher in the trial schools had the opportunity to conduct a one-to-one interview with every child in their class. A random sample of around 40 children in each reference school was also interviewed at the beginning and end of the school year (February/March and November respectively), over a 30- to 40-minute period. A range of procedures were developed to maximise consistency in the way in which the interview was administered across the 70 schools.

Although the full text of the ENRP interview involved around 60 tasks (with several sub-tasks in many cases), no child was posed all of these. The interview was of the form of a "choose your own adventure" story, in that the interviewer makes a decision after each task, as instructed in the interview schedule. Given success with the task, the interviewer continues with the next task in the given mathematical domain as far as the child could go with success. Given difficulty with the task, the interviewer either abandoned that section of the interview and moved on to the next domain or moved into a detour, designed to elaborate more clearly the difficulty a child might be having with a particular content area.

All tasks were piloted, refined and further trialled in order to gain a sense of their clarity and their capacity to reveal a wide range of levels of understanding in children. The form and wording of the tasks were influenced by the growth points for which they are intended to provide evidence, while at the same time the consideration of the data provided by a given task lead to a refining of the wording of a given growth point.

The interview provided information about those growth points achieved by a child in each of the nine domains. Figure 2 shows three questions from the interview, from the section on Addition and subtraction strategies. Words in italics are instructions to the interviewer; normal type are the words the interviewer used with the child. A major feature of the interview was the use of small, plastic teddy bears as manipulative materials. For clarity, some instructions to the interviewer have been removed here. For example, lack of success with question 19 (in both parts a and b) would lead the interviewer to skip question 20 and the remainder of the Addition and subtraction strategies section.

Question 18 provides information on whether the child is able to count-on or use a known fact, needs to count-all, or is unable to find the total by any means. The aim in the interview was to gather information on the most powerful strategies that a child accesses in a particular domain. However, depending upon the context and the complexity of the numbers in a given task, a child (or an adult) may use a less powerful strategy than they actually possess, as the simpler strategy may do the job adequately in that situation. Questions 18-20 illustrate this well. Question 19 is often solved by children modelling the eight biscuits with their fingers and then counting back. By the nature of the numbers involved in Question 20, neither modelling the 12 objects nor counting back 9 is easy. Children are therefore given the opportunity to use a more sophisticated strategy (if they possess it), such as count-down-to 9 (11, 10, 9) or count-up-from 9 (10, 11, 12).

---

18) Counting On
a) Please get four green teddies for me.
Place 9 green teddies on the table.
b) I have nine green teddies here (*show the child the nine teddies, and then screen the nine teddies with the ice-cream lid*).
That's nine teddies hiding here and four teddies here *(point to the groups)*.
c) Tell me how many teddies we have altogether …. Please explain how you worked it out.
d) *(If unsuccessful, remove the lid)*. Please tell me how many there are altogether.

19) Counting Back
For this question you need to listen to a story.
a) Imagine you have 8 little biscuits in your play lunch and you eat 3.
How many do you have left? … How did you work that out?
If incorrect answer, ask part (b):
b) Could you use your fingers to help you to work it out? *(it's fine to repeat the question, but no further prompts please)*.

20) Counting Down To / Counting Up From
I have 12 strawberries and I eat 9. How many are left? … Please explain.

Figure. 2. An excerpt from the addition and subtraction interview questions.

It is important to stress that the growth points are big mathematical ideas and that much learning takes place between them. As a result, a child may have learned several important ideas or skills necessary for moving towards the next growth point, but perhaps not of themselves sufficient to do so. Also, to achieve many of the growth points requires success on several tasks, not just one or some. This enables us to know that a child uses a more powerful strategy consistently and appropriately.

In addition to the use of the interview and the framework of growth points, a program of professional development within the ENRP occurred (formally) at three levels. Research data were also collected during these programs. The 220 or so teachers from trial schools met with the research team each year for five full days, spread across the year, with the focus on understanding and using the framework and interview, and on appropriate classroom strategies and activities for meeting identified needs of their students. On four or five occasions each year, the teachers met in regional cluster groups for two hours, usually after school. There was usually a time of sharing, during which teachers discussed recommended readings, or particular activities or approaches that they had tried since the previous meeting. This was followed by the content focus for the day, and further tasks were set that needed to be completed before the groups met again.

241

The third level of professional development experiences took place at the school and classroom level. The cluster coordinator visited each school at least three times per year, spending time in classrooms team teaching or observing, participating in planning meetings, jointly leading parent evenings, and acting as a "sounding board" for teachers, coordinators and principals. In addition, there were weekly or fortnightly meetings of the mathematics "professional learning team" within the school, to maintain continuity, communication, cohesion and purpose. For further information, see D. M. Clarke et al. (2002).

The only required component for implementation with a particular teacher's classroom was use of the assessment interview with all students at the beginning and the end of each school year. Some trialling of teaching activities was of course encouraged, and the "professional learning team" provided an opportunity for joint planning and professional discussion. In the Victorian context, teaching programs are a school based decision with curriculum guidelines provided by the state, and there are no prescribed or recommended texts.

FINDINGS

Major Sources of Data

In addition to the extensive data collected through the interviews with children described earlier, a range of data was collected from trial school teachers. The following sets of data are used in the analysis and discussion:
− teachers' entry questionnaires (March, 1999);
− teachers' exit questionnaires (November, 2001);
− highlights and surprises survey (May, 1999); and
− open response survey focusing on impact and changes (November, 2001).

The entry and exit questionnaire data are particularly relevant for this chapter because the major focus of the entry and exit questionnaires was to provide baseline and then comparison data on teachers' beliefs about what mathematics is, their personal confidence with the mathematical content and the teaching of mathematics, and their expectations of young children in their learning of mathematics. The open-question surveys about highlights and surprises from the interviews and changes in teaching asked the teachers to provide written reflections from their perspective. These data were analysed for common themes presented in the data.

While the focus here is on the impact of the growth points on teachers, it is important to establish the impact of the project on student mathematical learning. In the final year of the project, students in trial schools outperformed significantly ($p < .05$ level) children in reference schools, at every grade level and in every mathematical domain (Clarke, D. M. et al., 2002). As an example, a summary of the data for the domain titled Strategies for Addition and Subtraction can be found in Bobis et al. (2005). While there was considerable growth for children in the trial schools, there was also considerable variation within classes.

Growth Points as a Powerful Professional Development Tool

In this section, I will outline the different ways in which the growth points or key *"stepping stones"* served as a powerful tool in the professional learning of teachers. It is important to stress that the growth points were used and interpreted *in conjunction with the interview* and that the teachers were provided with focused professional development to support the implementation. So even though the focus of the chapter is largely on the impact of the growth points, within this project the growth points and interview can in some ways be viewed as a "package."

More Realistic Expectations

Following the completion of the first student interviews in March 1999, teachers were asked to write about *highlights* and *surprises* that had emerged from the interview process. The first set of interviews provided teachers with information about their individual children that had not been previously obtainable to this level of detail, and initially many were surprised by what their children knew. Several quotes capture the spirit of many teachers' comments, as they reflected on highlights and surprises that emerged.

> My greatest surprise was that most children performed significantly better than I anticipated. Their thinking skills and strategies were more sophisticated than I expected.

> [a highlight was] working with a gifted five year-old who actually worked out the answers quicker than I did. Reading 24 746 154 on the calculator. Amazing!

> I have one Grade 2 student in my P/1/2 class whom I know loves maths – number in particular. He worked out the answer for 134 and 689 in his head. This child was able to articulate all the strategies he used.

It should be noted however, that the raising of expectations was not "across the board." There were several areas where teachers were surprised with the difficulty that many children appeared to have on particular tasks, for example:
- Many children had difficulty with the task involving sharing 12 teddies between 4 teddy mats, and with the tasks relating to abstracting multiplication.
- Quite a few children were able to read and write two- and three-digit numbers, but were unable to order one-digit numbers from smallest to largest.
- Reading clocks was more difficult for children than many teachers expected, given its emphasis in their programs.
- Many children had a "prototypical view" of geometric shapes (e.g., a triangle always has a horizontal base and is either equilateral or isosceles).

On a humorous note, a favourite anecdote from the interviews was the following. Children had been asked to "draw a clock," for use as a basis of discussion of their understanding of how time and clocks work. The teacher takes up the story:

I asked the child "What are the numbers on the clock doing?" The child looked strangely at me and said "the numbers are doing nothing, they are waiting for the arrows to come around. Don't you know that? Are you stupid or something?"

This was within the first few months of the project. The power of the interview and the increasing power of the growth points are explored now using the data from later in the project.

Enhanced Teacher Knowledge and Changing Beliefs

The ENRP had a significant impact on teachers' beliefs and understandings, in relation to their teaching of mathematics. In the final professional development session in 2001, the 220 teachers present were asked to write about "how has your teaching changed (if it hasn't changed, feel free to say so)?" Their responses to this open question were then grouped in themes. Most teachers' responses involved two or three themes. Though the focus of the question was on how their *teaching* had changed, six of the top ten themes or categories related to aspects of teachers' knowledge and attitudes, suggesting that these aspects were fore-grounded in their thinking about their current teaching. This was a surprising result from the research team's perspective. The specific themes are listed here. In summary, the teachers were more likely to:

- use growth points to inform planning (63 responses – the top category). This relates to knowledge of how children learn mathematics and how mathematical understanding develops. Teachers here were reporting the use of the knowledge provided through the framework of growth points.
- use knowledge of individual understanding/ better assess needs (49). These responses indicated an application of the knowledge gained about particular students to address learning needs.
- challenge and extend children and have higher expectations (42). These responses illustrated the understanding of the range of abilities in their classes and the belief about the importance of extending children, and an increased capacity for doing so.
- have more confidence in teaching mathematics (28). These responses indicated a more positive approach to the teaching of mathematics.
- enjoy mathematics more, have fun and make mathematics more interesting (27). This speaks to the teachers' attitudes, often accompanied by improvements in the children's attitudes.
- have greater knowledge of how children learn (24). This was a direct appreciation of the impact of the project on knowledge of how children learn.

Teachers' specific responses reflected the importance placed on the knowledge and understandings that they had developed and on subsequent changes in their beliefs and practices. Three teachers' comments are given below:

I now have a much better knowledge of strands of Mathematics through our extensive PD. I have also a better understanding of how children learn, i.e., through the growth points, etc. The great array of ideas that we have been presented with during our PD sessions have really enriched my mathematics teaching. I am much less "worksheet" oriented. I am trying to employ more open-ended/problem solving tasks. I am constantly surprised now by my children's mathematical understandings.

I now have a far greater understanding of all domains of Numeracy. I always have worked using many games and "hands on" materials. My teaching is far more focused now. My teaching groups are constantly changing. I spend far more of my time on mental computation now. My expectations are far higher now. Data from ENRP in February has shown my children are far more capable. I feel I challenge children more. My planning is far more extensive.

I used to avoid maths when something had to be missed, now I can't find the time to do enough! I'm more confident and I enjoy it more. I'm more flexible and more responsive to the children. I have a better understanding of how children think and reason, due to the assessment. This has impacted on what/how I teach.

Developing knowledge of typical "learning trajectories" in mathematics
The ENRP Growth Points were designed to provide teachers with a framework to think about children's learning in mathematics and how it develops. From their responses to the questions relating to changes in their practice, this has clearly been the case, and the growth points have also provided teachers with a language to talk about learning as well as a guide for planning. The following quotes are illustrative of this point:

I now have a much better knowledge of mathematics and how children learn maths.

I have a greater understanding of the developmental stages in mathematical learning. Therefore I am catering for all children in more specific ways.

The growth points! Have been teaching in P-2 for nine years and didn't have a clear picture of growth points before this.

The growth points (stepping stones) have helped me see clearly the sequential steps I need to take the students through.

The growth points provided not only a way to discuss what the children already know but the direction to move. The notion of *trajectories of learning* or *learning landscapes* are helpful ones here:

Knowledge of mathematics must also be linked to knowledge of students' thinking, so that teachers have conceptions of typical trajectories of student learning and can use this knowledge to recognise landmarks of understanding in individuals. (Carpenter & Lehrer, 1999, p. 31)

Bobis and Gould (1999), reporting on the CMIT project, also found that the provision of a research-based learning framework enhanced teachers' knowledge

245

of how children learn mathematics. In a major project in New Zealand, the National Numeracy Project, the learning framework gave teachers "direction for responding effectively to children's learning needs" (Higgins, Parsons, & Hyland, 2003, p. 166).

Developing knowledge of individual children's mathematical understanding
In addition to increasing the general knowledge of children's mathematical understandings provided by the ENRP framework of growth points, the linking to the interview provided specific knowledge about individual children that was important to the teachers:

> It has given me great direction – teaching from the point of knowing and moving on to the next growth point.

> Understanding where children are currently working at and where they need to be going.

> I've become much better at building on what children know. I base my teaching on what they know.

Similar sentiments are evident in this quote from a teacher interview in the final year of the project:

> I think that the interview is crucial to finding out what the children can do and then taking it on from there. ... For the last three years that's what we've done and it gives a really clear picture of what the kids can do and you build on those skills.

Developing teacher's confidence in teaching mathematics
Table 1 shows the various themes that emerged from the responses to the open question "How do you feel about teaching mathematics?"p246, in both the entry and exit questionnaire. The number of teachers whose responses were categorised as being positive or confident in their teaching of mathematics increased from 47 to 103 and the number who volunteered that they were lacking in confidence decreased from 26 to 11. The teachers were not limited in their number of responses and so the number of responses is higher than the number of teachers in both the entry and exit questionnaires.

Table 1. Frequencies of themes in teachers' responses in entry and exit questionnaires (attitudes to teaching mathematics)

Themes	Entry Frequency (N = 195)	Exit Frequency (N = 220)
Confident/positive	47	103
Enjoy it	110	133
Okay	12	17
A challenge/keen to improve	13	21
Important educationally/sense of obligation to do it well	5	12
Lacking in confidence	26	11
Other	6	7

In addition to this question, there was a 0 to 10 scale on which teachers were asked to indicate how confident they felt in their teaching of mathematics. The item was as follows:

How confident do you feel in your *teaching* of mathematics?

0	1	2	3	4	5	6	7	8	9

10

No confidence   Highly
confident

For those teachers who responded to both the entry and exit questionnaires ($n = 103$), there was an increase in the mean from 6.94 to 7.93–a highly significant difference (t test, df = 102, $p < 0.001$).

It should be noted that there was considerable movement of teachers in and out of project schools over the three-year project, though no more so than typical for the state. Approximately 100 new teachers joined the project after the first year, for example. The data discussed in this section therefore were obtained from only those teachers who were involved for the full three years.

The following quotes on the changes on their teaching support this finding and focus clearly on the connection between the teachers' knowledge and their confidence:

The main thing that has changed is my confidence in my maths teaching, because I have more knowledge of how children learn maths, what they should know and some ideas of how to get them there. My lessons are more varied and fun now.

It has given me a greater understanding of why and how I teach maths, therefore increasing my confidence in my maths teaching.

Teachers in the ENRP gained the kinds of knowledge described above, and therefore developed a clearer picture of the typical trajectories of student learning, and could recognise landmarks of understanding in individuals. Such a picture

247

guided the decisions they made, in planning and in classroom interactions, as their knowledge of the understanding of individuals informed their practice. In August 2000, half way through the project, 74% of the ENRP teachers claimed to have the framework in their heads to some extent and the rest (26%) understood it but did not "have it in their heads." It is interesting that the teachers commonly used terms such as "direction" and "building further" suggesting that they had internalised a framework/ trajectory that is accessible and useful.

Clements and Sarama (2004), in the context of the *Building Blocks* project in the United States, used the term learning trajectories as "descriptions of children's thinking and learning in a specific mathematical domain, and a related, conjectured route through a set of instructional tasks designed to engender those mental processes or actions hypothesized to move children through a developmental progression" (p. 83). Their "trajectories" featured point-wise key stages or descriptions and similarly involved the mathematics of young children.

This has much in common with the way that growth points were conceived of and used in the ENRP, though in the case of the ENRP the instructional tasks were developed largely by the teachers based on the specific knowledge accessed through the interview and then on-going classroom interactions. Learning trajectories were developed for the *Building Blocks* curriculum, and Clements and Sarama (in press) have argued that the success of the curriculum in improving student learning can be attributed in large part to the "distinct contribution of research-based learning trajectories" (p. 36). They claim that:

> *Building Blocks* teachers were more likely than comparison, as well as control, teachers to monitor and be actively involved with activities, using formative assessment based on their knowledge of children's developmental progressions and a greater number of activities linked to children's developmental level, all indicating their use of the learning trajectories. (p. 32)

This supports the findings from the ENRP of the value of the increased knowledge of student mathematical thinking through the provision of a learning framework and related individual student assessment.

Growth Points in Other Mathematical Domains

In order to illustrate further the notion of growth points and some issues relating to their development, I will focus now on geometric and spatial development. In developing the framework and interview for this area, it was decided to focus on two domains: *Properties of Shape* and *Visualisation and Orientation*. The first of these had a reasonable research base but limited frameworks, while the second was not well defined in terms of young children's development. It was also necessary to develop related interview tasks that were able to be administered consistently across contexts. This was particularly problematic in relation to mapping and location questions, where children's experiences and representations are often idiosyncratic. Having said this, these areas were included in the professional development for teachers and within their teaching programs, though not within the assessment interview or framework of the project. Among the best-known research in geometric thinking is that of the van Hieles (see, e.g., van Hiele, 1986). They believed that secondary school geometry in The Netherlands emphasised deductive reasoning and proof, requiring a high level of thinking, and that this was not being developed in the primary years. They formulated a model of "five levels of thinking" and proposed instructional phases to promote movement from one level to the next (Fuys & Liebov, 1993). According to the van Hieles, given appropriate instruction, students moved from visual recognition of shapes by their appearance as a whole (level 1–"it's a triangle because it looks like one") to analysis and description of shapes in terms of their properties (level 2–"it's a triangle because it has three points").

Lehrer, Jenkins and Osana (1998) described the transition as "children first find salient the overall appearance of shapes ... and then come to recognise shapes as carriers of properties such as the number of sides of a figure or the measure of its angles" (p. 138).

In the early years of school, most emphasis is appropriately on the first two van Hiele levels. In considering the ENRP Growth Points for *Properties of Shape* (see Fig. 3), it is clear that only Growth Point 4 is somewhat close to van Hiele level 3. Growth Points 2 and 3 focus on properties. A distinguishing feature from Growth Point 1 is that a shape is defined by its properties, not by its appearance. It was a powerful notion for the teachers that "a shape is not defined by its shape."

0. Not apparent
   Not yet able to recognise and match simple shapes.
1. Holistic recognition of shape
   Can recognise resemblances and match some simple shapes, using standard "prototypes".
2. Classification of shapes, attending to visual features
   Can sort and compare shapes, using some geometrical language to describe features.
3. Identification of "classes of shapes" by some properties
   Uses properties of shapes to classify shapes into classes, using appropriate language.
4. Definition of shapes using properties
   States and understands conditions for defining key shapes.

Figure 3. ENRP growth points for the domain of properties of shape.

For *Visualisation and Orientation*, the limited research base available calls into question the validity of the framework that was developed, but it did provide teachers with a focus for their interpretation of children's spatial understanding and highlighted this as a key component of mathematical understanding.

Publications focusing on the growth points and interviews as well as results for children in specific mathematical domains include B. A. Clarke (2004), B. A.

Clarke, D. M. Clarke and Cheeseman (2006), and Sullivan, Cheeseman, B. A. Clarke, D. M. Clarke, Gervasoni, Gronn et al. (2000).

DEVELOPING AND USING GROWTH POINTS

The Nature and Form of a Framework of Growth Points

There is strong evidence that provision of a learning framework that focuses on research-based progression of increasing sophistication of young children's thinking is a powerful tool for teacher development. Earlier in this chapter the intentions of the ENRP framework were outlined and the revisiting of these will now provide a way of thinking about how such frameworks might be structured and used in the future:

– *reflect the findings of relevant research in mathematics education from Australia and overseas.* There is a strong research literature on young children's development in number and the framework had many common features with those of others. In the areas of measurement and geometry, while the growth points reflected the research at the time, these areas are less structured and developed. However, the continuing work of a range of researchers (e.g., Battista, 2007; Clements & Sarama, 2007) has the potential to inform a continuing revision process.

– *emphasise important ideas and strategies in early mathematics understanding in a form and language readily understood and, in time, retained by teachers.* Baroody, Cibulskis, Lai and Li (2004) emphasise the key role of "big ideas" in mathematics teaching and learning, in teachers supporting students to develop increasingly sophisticated strategies that have the potential to help them move to greater mathematical understanding and fluency. If the teacher is to be regarded as a curriculum maker rather than just someone who "delivers" teacher-proof materials (see D. M. Clarke, Volume 1), then the frameworks need to be manageable and accessible to the teacher. An example of how knowledge of the framework can guide the work of teachers is in geometry, where a teacher's aim may appropriately be moving children away from a holistic, prototypical view of shapes to a greater focus on properties (Clarke B. A, 2004).

– *reflect, where possible, the structure of mathematics.* One of the ongoing tensions in curriculum decisions is the balance between mathematical structure and children's development. Should the teacher be focusing on moving students through a developmental sequence according to what is known about children's cognitive development or moving them through increasingly complex ideas in a mathematical sense? And how can the "natural developmental sequence" be determined independent of the curriculum provided, and the range of experiences of children outside the classroom? For example, are the addition and subtraction growth points listed earlier in the chapter a reflection of increased cognitive development or increased mathematical complexity? The answer is almost certainly a bit of both as we are clearly aiming for increased mathematical sophistication in a developmentally appropriate sequence.

– *allow the description of the mathematical knowledge and understanding of individuals and groups.* There is little doubt that the use of the ENRP framework and interview enabled clear and helpful descriptions of both the knowledge and understanding of individuals and groups, and was possibly the most useful feature of the project. The challenge of how this might be accomplished in more complex mathematical domains such as rational number remains a researchable area. In the CGI project mentioned earlier in the chapter, the team faced a challenge in interpreting the research findings for teachers, beyond the early years of schooling.

– *form the basis of planning and teaching.* This assumes that teachers have a key role in planning and teaching decisions. It is clearly more difficult for those teachers who see their contexts as limiting their opportunities or where accountability measures are stifling of their professional decision making. In the Australian setting, particularly in the early years, the responsibility for enacting the curriculum resides with individual teachers and/or groups of teachers at a grade level or groups of grade levels, and the use of prescribed texts are rare. There is ample evidence in the earlier parts of this chapter that this aim of informing planning and teaching was clearly achieved for the ENRP. Clements and Surama (2004) commented on the fact that "the nascency and complex nature of learning trajectories has led to a variety of interpretations and applications" (p. 83). They claim that "although studying either psychological development progressions or instructional sequences separately can be valid research goals and studies of each can and should inform mathematics education, the power and uniqueness of the learning trajectories construct stems from the inextricable interconnection between these two aspects" (p. 83). Although the ENRP framework does not strictly include instructional sequences, the project as a whole and the work of individual teachers who were regarded by the project team as "curriculum makers," brought the two concepts together in effective ways.

– *provide a basis for task construction for interviews, and the recording and coding process that would follow.* The interview was vital in understanding the framework. It brought the framework to life. It made research knowledge accessible to teachers. A professional development footnote at this point is that in making decisions about the strategies used by children in solving tasks within the interview, the teachers were themselves becoming increasingly comfortable with the distinction between the various strategies and their various levels of sophistication and subsequently their understanding of the growth points. This is an important step in being able to facilitate the movement of their children to higher level thinking during classroom teaching. The coding process, involving taking the teacher's completed record sheet from the interview and assigning growth points to students, was largely the role of the project team, as it was considered important in the research context to guard against any concerns that teachers may have assigned growth points too generously to their students. In the final school term of the project, the coding process was shared with teachers, and they realised then that they had effectively internalised it along the way, as their familiarity with the interview and growth points had increased.

– *allow the identification and description of improvement where it exists.* Although teachers in the ENRP had important and useful evidence of improvement simply through the use of the interview, by providing summary data back to them in the form of growth point change (for their own students and for thousands of other students across the state), such information was of considerable encouragement, while at the same time helpful in knowing which areas required additional attention in the curriculum.

– *enable a consideration of those students who may benefit from additional assistance.* As part of the ENRP, Gervasoni conducted an extensive doctoral study which focused on identifying those students who may benefit from additional assistance in mathematics, in class, in a withdrawal situation, or both. She also trialled and continues to refine a structured program for the support of such students (Gervasoni, 2004). As part of her research, she has nominated particular student profiles (i.e., particular growth points achieved or more importantly not achieved within various domains), which are indicative of students who might need such support.

– *build on the work of successful, similar projects.* It is clear that there is not one unique way to present such frameworks. However the common features include a number of the points listed above and most importantly on providing a direction – a possible pathway for learning that is research based, accessible, manageable, observable, and reflective of what real children know and can do. In the same way that the ENRP built on the work of other scholars in developing the framework and interview, there are now many examples of our work informing similar projects in countries including Germany, New Zealand, Sweden, the USA, Canada and South Africa.

The Essential Combination of the Framework and the Interview

The requirement of teachers to participate in the assessment interviews meant that they were involved deeply in researching the understanding of their children, as individuals and as a group. This process proved very powerful in teachers' own professional development. They increased their knowledge of how children learn mathematics in general, they had a much clearer picture of their own children's understanding, and they had a repertoire of teaching approaches to enhance this understanding. The power of the combined interview and framework of growth points in underpinning decisions and action in the early year's mathematics classroom is exemplified by the following quote:

> The assessment interview has given focus to my teaching. Constantly at the back of my mind I have the growth points there and I have a clear idea of where I'm heading and can match activities to the needs of the children. But I also try to make it challenging enough to make them stretch.

The research team noted with considerable pleasure, particularly in the third year of the project, the increasing fluency of trial school teachers with mathematics education research terminology, and the willingness to engage in discussion of complex ideas over extended periods.

The Framework of Growth Points as a Lens for Teachers

When the ENRP learning and assessment framework was first developed, a major purpose for its creation was to enable a measure of the effectiveness of the professional development aspect of the project, by monitoring student movement through the growth points. However, the framework proved powerful in a variety of other ways. Teachers increasingly "owned" the framework, and used it to enhance their own knowledge of children's mathematical learning. Teachers' understanding of the framework was enhanced by their familiarity with the interview. As the framework became better known, teachers viewed student responses during the interview in the light of their understanding of the growth points. Most importantly, the growth points provided a kind of "lens" through which children's mathematical thinking could be viewed, in all individual, small group and whole class interactions. The framework was not however intended as a prescription for instruction. As Clements and Sarama (2004, p. 85) noted, "a priori learning trajectories [which is an appropriate description of the ENRP framework of growth points] are always hypothetical in that the actual learning and teaching, and the teacher's recognition of these, cannot be completely known in advance."

Concluding Comments

Sowder (2007) argued that developing an understanding of how student think about and learn mathematics can "be thought of as an interpretive lens that helps teachers think about their students, the mathematics they are learning, the tasks that are appropriate for the learning of that mathematics, and the questions that need to be asked to lead them to better understanding" (p. 164), and that professional development thus focused can have an impact on teachers' knowledge and practice. The provision of the research-based framework of growth points and the interview within the ENRP brought about important changes in teachers' knowledge and empowered them to use this knowledge to develop young children's mathematical thinking. The professional development environment was carefully built around the teachers' emerging understanding of the framework and interview, and provided considerable opportunities for dialogue and the support of colleagues.

Rather than a *recipe* for teaching, the notion of *rich ingredients* that are combined in a range of ways, using the professional judgement of teachers, was a powerful and successful approach. There is little doubt that the framework and growth points were key ingredients in equipping teachers to exercise their judgement as reflective professionals and produce increased student outcomes in the ENRP.

REFERENCES

Baroody, A., Cibulskis, M., Lai, M-L., & Li, X. (2004). Comments on the use of learning trajectories in curriculum development and research. *Mathematical Thinking and Learning, 6*(2), 227–260.

Battista, M. (2007). The development of geometric and spatial thinking. In F. K. Lester (Ed.), *Second handbook of research on mathematics teaching and learning* (pp. 843–908). Charlotte, NC: Information Age Publishing & National Council of Teachers of Mathematics.

Baturo, A., Cooper, T., Dietzmann, C., Heirdsfield, A., Kidman, G., Shield, P., Warren, E., Nisbet, S., Klein, M., & Putt, I. (2004). *Teachers enhancing numeracy.* Canberra: Commonwealth of Australia.

Bobis, J. (1996). Visualisation and the development of number sense with kindergarten children. In J. Mulligan & M. Mitchelmore (Eds.), *Children's number learning: A research monograph of MERGA/AAMT* (pp. 17–34). Adelaide: Australian Association of Mathematics Teachers.

Bobis, J., & Gould, P. (1999). The mathematical achievement of children in the count me in too program. In J. M. Truran & K. M. Truran (Eds.), *Making the difference. Proceedings of the 22nd annual conference of the Mathematics Research Group of Australasia* (pp. 84–90). Adelaide: MERGA.

Bobis, J., Clarke, B. A., Clarke, D. M., Thomas, G., Wright, R., Young-Loveridge, J., & Gould, P. (2005). Supporting teachers in the development of young children's mathematical thinking: Three large scale cases. *Mathematics Education Research Journal, 16*(3), 27–57.

Boulton-Lewis, G. (1996). Representations of place value knowledge and implications for teaching addition and subtraction. In J. Mulligan & M. Mitchelmore (Eds.), *Children's number learning: A research monograph of MERGA/AAMT* (pp. 75–88). Adelaide: Australian Association of Mathematics Teachers.

Carpenter, T., & Lehrer, R. (1999). Teaching and learning mathematics with understanding. In E. Fennema, & T. Romberg (Eds.), *Mathematics classrooms that promote understanding* (pp. 19–32). Mahwah, NJ: Lawrence Erlbaum Associates.

Clarke, B.A. (2004). A shape is not defined by its shape: Developing young children's geometric understanding. *Journal of Australian Research in Early Childhood Education, 11*(2), 110–127.

Clarke, B. A., Clarke, D.M., & Cheeseman, J. (2006). What mathematical knowledge do young children bring to school. *Mathematics Education Research Journal, 18*(1), 81–105.

Clarke, D. M. (2001). Understanding, assessing and developing young children's mathematical thinking: Research as powerful tool for professional growth. In J. Bobis, B. Perry, & M. Mitchelmore (Eds.), *Numeracy and beyond Proceedings of the 24th Annual Conference of the Mathematics Education Research Group of Australasia,* (Vol. 1, pp. 9–26). Sydney: MERGA.

Clarke, D. M., Cheeseman, J., Gervasoni, A., Gronn, D., Horne, M., McDonough, A., Montgomery, P. & Roche, A., Sullivan, P., Clarke, B. A., & Rowley, G. (2002). *Early numeracy research project Final report.* Melbourne, Australia: Mathematics Teaching and Learning Centre, Australian Catholic University. [extracts available at http://www.sofweb.vic.edu.au/eys/num/ENRP/]

Clements, D. H., & Sarama, J. (in press). Experimental evaluation of the effects of a research-based preschool mathematics curriculum. *American Educational Research Journal.*

Clements, D. H., & Sarama, J. (2007). Effects of a preschool mathematics curriculum: Summative research on the Building Blocks project. *Journal for Research in Mathematics Education, 38*(2), 136–163.

Clements, D. H., & Sarama, J. (2004). Learning trajectories in mathematics education. *Mathematical Thinking and Learning, 6*(2), 81–89.

Clements, D. H., Swaminathan, S., Hannibal, M. A. Z., & Sarama, J. (1999). Young children's conceptions of space. *Journal for Research in Mathematics Education, 30*(2), 192–212.

Fennema, E., Carpenter, T.P, Franke, M. L., Levi, L., Jacobs, V. R., & Empson, S. B. (1996). A longitudinal study of learning to use children's thinking in mathematics instruction. *Journal for Research in Mathematics Education, 27,* 403–434.

Fosnot, C. T., & Dolk, M. (2001). *Young mathematicians at work: Constructing number sense, addition and subtraction.* Portsmouth, NH: Heinemann.

Franke, M.L, Kazemi, E., & Battey, D. (2007). Mathematics teaching and classroom practice. In F. K. Lester (Ed.), *Second handbook of research on mathematics teaching and learning* (pp. 225–256) Charlotte, NC: Information Age Publishing & National Council of Teachers of Mathematics.

Fuson, K. (1992). Research on whole number addition and subtraction. In D. A. Grouws (Ed.). *Handbook of research on mathematics teaching and learning* (pp. 243–275). New York: Macmillan.

Fuys, D. J. & Liebov, A. K. (1993). Geometry and spatial sense. In R. J. Jensen (Ed.), *Research ideas for the classroom: Early childhood mathematics* (pp. 195–222). New York: Macmillan.

Gervasoni, A. (2004). The challenge of meeting the instructional needs of grade 1 and grade 2 children who are at risk in mathematics. In I. Putt, R. Faragher, & M. McLean (Eds.), *Mathematics education for the third millennium: Towards 2010. Proceedings of the 27th annual conference of the Mathematics Education Research Group of Australasia* (pp. 247–254). Townsville: MERGA

Higgins, J., Parsons, R., & Hyland, M. (2003). The Numeracy Development Project: Policy to practice. In J. Livingstone (Ed.), *New Zealand Annual Review of Education* (pp 157–174). Wellington: Victoria University of Wellington.

Kilpatrick, J., Swafford, J., & Findell, B. (2001). *Adding it up: How children learn mathematics.* Washington, DC: National Research Council.

Konold, C., Khalil, E., Higgins, T., & Russell, S. J. (2001, April). *Learning to see data as an aggregate.* Paper presented at the annual conference of the American Educational Research Association, Seattle, Washington.

Lehrer, R., & Chazan, D. (1998). *Designing learning environments for developing understanding of geometry and space.* Mahwah, NJ: Lawrence Erlbaum Associates.

Lehrer, R., Jenkins, M., & Osana, H. (1998). Longitudinal study of children's reasoning about space and geometry. In R. Lehrer, & D. Chazan (Eds.), *Designing learning environments for developing understanding of geometry and space* (pp. 137–168). Mahwah, NJ: Lawrence Erlbaum Associates.

McIntosh, A., Bana, J., & Farrell, B. (1995). *Mental computation in school mathematics: Preference, attitude and performance of students in years 3, 5, 7, and 9* (MASTEC Monograph Series No. 1). Perth: Mathematics, Science & Technology Education Centre, Edith Cowan University.

Mulligan, J., & Mitchelmore, M. (1995). Children's intuitive models of multiplication and division. In S. Flavel, I. Isaacs, D. Lee, R. Hurley, T. Roberts, A. Richards, R. Laird, & V. M. Ram (Eds.), *GALTHA* (Proceedings of the 18th Annual Conference of the Mathematics Education Research Group of Australasia, pp. 427–433). Darwin: MERGA.

Mulligan, J., & Mitchelmore, M. (1996). Children's representations of multiplication and division word problems. In J. Mulligan & M. Mitchelmore (Eds.), *Children's number learning: A research monograph of MERGA/AAMT* (pp. 163–184). Adelaide: AAMT.

O'Toole, T., Rubino, V., Parker, G., & Fitzpatrick, S. (1998). *Planning for students' mathematical thinking: Measurement R-8.* Adelaide: Catholic Education Office.

Owens, K., & Gould, P. (1999). *Framework for elementary school space mathematics* (discussion paper).

Pearn, C., & Merrifield, M. (1998, October). *Mathematics intervention.* Paper presented to the Early Numeracy Networks, Department of Education, Melbourne, Victoria.

Pengelly, H. (1985). *Mathematics making sense.* Adelaide: Department of Education.

Sowder, J. (2007). The mathematics education and development of teachers. In F. K. Lester (Ed,), *Second Handbook of research on mathematics teaching and learning* (pp. 157–223). Charlotte, NC: Information Age Publishing & National Council of Teachers of Mathematics.

Steffe, L. P., Cobb, P., & von Glasersfeld, E. (1988). *Construction of arithmetical meanings and strategies.* New York: Springer-Verlag.

Steffe, L.P., Von Glasersfeld, E., Richards, J., & Cobb, P. (1983). *Children's counting types: Philosophy, theory, and application.* New York: Praeger.

Sullivan, P., Cheeseman, J., Clarke, B. A., Clarke, D. M., Gervasoni, A., Gronn, D., Horne, M., McDonough, A., & Montgomery, P. (2000). Using learning growth points to help structure numeracy teaching. *Australian Primary Classroom, 5*(1), 4–8.

Thomas, N. (1996). Understanding the number system. In J. Mulligan & M. Mitchelmore (Eds.), *Children's number learning: A research monograph of MERGA/AAMT* (pp. 89–106). Adelaide: Australian Association of Mathematics Teachers.

Van Hiele, P. M. (1986). *Structure and insight.* Orlando, FL: Academic Press.

van den Heuvel-Panhuizen, M. (Ed.). (2001). *Children learn mathematics.* Utrecht, the Netherlands: Freudenthal Institute.

Willis, S. (2000). Strengthening numeracy: Reducing risk. In *Improving numeracy learning: What does research tell us?* (Conference Proceedings of the Improving Numeracy Learning: What Does Research Tell Us? Conference, pp. 31–33). Brisbane: ACER.

Wilson, P. S., & Osborne, A. (1992). Foundational ideas in teaching about measure. In T. R. Post (Ed.), *Teaching mathematics in grades K-8: Research-based methods* (pp. 89–122). Needham Heights, MA: Allyn & Bacon.

Wright, R. (1998). An overview of a research-based framework for assessing and teaching early number learning. In C. Kanes, M. Goos, & E. Warren (Eds.), *Teaching mathematics in new times* (Proceedings of the 21st annual conference of the Mathematics Education Research Group of Australasia, pp. 701–708). Brisbane: MERGA.

Young-Loveridge, J. (1997). From research tool to classroom assessment device: The development of Checkout/Rapua, a shopping game to assess numeracy at school entry. In F. Biddulph & K. Carr (Eds.), *People in mathematics education* (pp. 608–615). Rotorua, New Zealand: Mathematics Education Research Group of Australasia.

Barbara Clarke
Faculty of Education
Monash University
Australia

SUSAN B. EMPSON AND VICTORIA R. JACOBS

11. LEARNING TO LISTEN TO CHILDREN'S MATHEMATICS

Listening effectively and responding to children's mathematical thinking is surprisingly hard work. Research indicates that years, not months, are required to develop the personal resources needed to teach in ways that incorporate responsive listening. Drawing upon a synthesis of research, the authors offer a set of benchmarks that describe notable trends in the development of teachers' listening expertise in which children's mathematics becomes progressively more central. Directive listening refers to listening to a child's thinking in a way that seeks to determine whether it matches an expected response and actively tries to elicit that expected response even when it is inconsistent with the child's understandings. Observational listening refers to listening with an attempt to hear the child's thinking but with nascent formulations about what is heard and few active attempts to support or extend that thinking. Responsive listening refers to listening in which the teacher not only intends to hear the child's thinking but also actively works to elicit, make sense of, and respond to that thinking. The authors detail three ways in which mathematics teacher educators have organized learning experiences for teachers to develop responsive listening: (a) discussions of children's written work, (b) discussions of videotaped interactions with children, and (c) opportunities for teachers to interact with children and then to reflect on those experiences with other teachers.

"If we listen, they will hear their own answers"
(Lisa Schneier, as reported in Duckworth, 2001, p. xiii)

INTRODUCTION

Ask teachers whether they listen to their learners, and they will say that they do. Yet questions remain about how teachers make sense of what they hear and how they use what they hear in teaching. In typical classrooms in most countries, when teachers ask questions, they listen for whether the learner knows what has been explained or can do what has been shown; a surprisingly small percentage of teachers request further information (Black, Harrison, Lee, Marshall, & Wiliam, 2004; Kawanaka & Stigler, 1999). Many simply may not realize that children have their own mathematical ideas and strategies – which can differ from teachers' own thinking about mathematics – and so they do not expect to hear these ideas and strategies. Even when teachers *do* ask children to express their thinking, listening effectively is surprisingly hard work.

D. Tirosh and T. Wood (eds.), Tools and Processes in Mathematics Teacher Education, 257–281.

To illustrate some of the difficulties inherent in listening to children, we describe how a group of experienced U.S. teachers (teaching Grades 3–9) responded to a video of a seven year-old girl, Laura Rose, solving a division problem.[1] In the video, Laura Rose is working one-on-one with an interviewer, who poses this problem to her: *Janelle has 21 beads. She wants to make three braids in her hair and put the same number of beads in each braid. How many beads can go in each braid?* Laura Rose begins by putting up seven fingers. Her lips move while she thinks to herself and moves her fingers.

Laura Rose:	Well, I'd say 2, but there'd be 1 left – No, excuse me [furrowing brow]. There would be 6, but there would also be some left over.
Interviewer:	Okay, how many would be left over if she put 6 in each braid?
Laura Rose:	[Thinking] Oh. No. There would be 7 beads. No. Let me check that [puts her head in her hands to think].
Interviewer:	Okay.

Laura Rose thinks some more. Her hands are under the table. Finally, she looks at the interviewer, and continues her explanation resolutely:

Laura Rose:	Yeah, there *would* be 7.
Interviewer:	Tell me how you got 7.
Laura Rose:	Well, because I knew that 7 [putting up seven fingers] threes was 21, and then I took 2 from each [pairing up her fingers], and that would make 6, and then there'd be 3 *others*, and then you'd put 1 from that 3 into each one. And the 2 would be 6, so plus 1 more would be 7. [Smiles.]

After watching the episode, the teachers were bewildered about what Laura Rose had done. Several confessed later to thinking privately that the child did not understand the problem. After all, she had put up seven fingers at the beginning, which was the *answer*, and then proceeded to make confusing comments. Even after watching the episode again, many teachers still felt confused. While the teachers talked to one another in small groups, the mathematics teacher educator, one of the authors of the chapter, heard some teachers creating explanations that were inconsistent with what Laura Rose had done. For example, one group decided that Laura Rose had dealt 2 beads to each braid until she had 6 altogether per braid. Although a few groups understood Laura Rose's strategy, most did not. After showing the episode a third time, the mathematics teacher educator invited the teachers who felt most confident to provide an explanation of what Laura Rose had done. As they used manipulatives to show concretely what Laura Rose had only

---

[1] This episode can be found on the CD "Children's Strategies," which accompanies the book *Children's Mathematics: Cognitively Guided Instruction* (Carpenter et al., 1999).

indicated with her fingers, all around the room teachers began to exclaim, "Oh, *now* I get it."

Laura Rose's strategy explanation was not straightforward and she misspoke at the end of her explanation, using a count ("one") to refer to both a single bead and a group of 3 beads, which only added to the teachers' confusion. However, her strategy was both mathematically sound and consistent with what research has discovered about children's mathematical thinking. The way she discussed her strategy also provided evidence that she understood the mathematics. She used a number fact she knew, 7 groups of 3 make 21, to derive a relationship she did not know, 3 groups of what size make 21? Using a finger to stand for a group of three, she manipulated 7 groups of three into 3 groups of seven, through a process of trial and error. Specifically, she first put up seven fingers to represent 7 groups of three. Because only three braids were needed in the problem, this configuration of 7 groups did not solve the problem for Laura Rose. So she transformed the 7 groups (i.e., fingers) into 3 groups by pairing two fingers, and then another two fingers, and then another two fingers so that each pair of fingers represented a braid with 6 beads. After creating the three pairs, Laura Rose still had one extra finger representing 3 beads. She distributed these 3 beads, 1 bead to each of the three braids. Now she had three braids each with the 6 original beads and the 1 extra bead, so she could confidently answer, "Seven."

Why was making sense of Laura's Rose's strategy so difficult? For the most part, it seems these veteran teachers were unprepared to hear and see the things that Laura Rose did. They had not experienced children solving similar problems in this way, and they would not have used this strategy themselves. Several were quick to attribute their own confusion about the strategy to Laura Rose. Without encouragement to do otherwise, they would have concluded that Laura Rose needed a great deal of guidance when, in fact, she was making sense of the mathematics, understood her own reasoning, and used fairly sophisticated thinking for a 7-year-old.

In this chapter, we use *children's mathematics* to refer specifically to the mathematical thinking that children such as Laura Rose use to solve problems, create representations, and make arguments. This episode illustrates how difficult listening effectively to children's mathematics can be. Many teachers are unaware of the extent of the valid and noteworthy mathematical content of children's thinking and so have not considered how to teach in ways that acknowledge this content. Research suggests that the use of children's mathematics in teaching is a specialized skill and, for most teachers, requires a significant shift in how they conceptualize their role.

We posit that learning to listen is at the core of a teacher's ability to use knowledge of children's mathematics productively. We use *listening* in a broad sense to mean an orientation to eliciting and making sense of children's actions and comments. Listening in this way has been described as a "reaching activity" and as such is interactive and participatory (Davis, 1996, p. 44). Listening to children's mathematics is, therefore, far from a passive activity and has important implications for children's learning. Davis (1997) observed that "the quality of student articulations [in classrooms] seemed to be as closely related to teachers' modes of attending as to their teaching styles" (p. 356), and, thus, how a teacher listens can transform how children talk and what they learn.

In this chapter we discuss what is entailed in teachers' learning to listen to children's mathematics in teacher preparation programs and in professional development. Our intention is to provide a set of benchmarks for teachers' listening that mathematics teacher educators can use to support teachers while they are learning to listen closely and actively to children's mathematics. The benchmarks, based upon a synthesis of research, describe notable trends in the development of teachers' orientations to listening to learners. We want to emphasize that ultimately, listening consists of the use of an integrated set of competencies and resources that cannot be reduced to a list of discrete steps. Further, teachers' learning to listen interacts with their conceptions of their role. Teachers' learning to listen to children's mathematics reflects all of this complexity. We begin with a brief overview of what children's mathematics is and why listening to children's mathematics is important for teachers. Next, we provide an extended example of a teacher listening in a way that is closely attuned to a child's mathematical thinking. We then present our benchmarks, and conclude with a discussion of implications of this body of work for teacher education.

A note about terminology: for simplicity, we refer to both prospective and practising teachers as *teachers*. We also use *mathematics teacher education* to refer both to contexts such as university-based certification programs in which prospective teachers are learning and to contexts usually described as professional development, in which practising teachers are learning, perhaps in school-based groups or in district-organized meetings.

CHILDREN'S MATHEMATICS

Researchers have documented how the kinds of strategies, representations, and reasoning used by children often differ from those used by mathematicians and other adults (e.g., Carpenter, Fennema, Franke, Levi, & Empson, 1999; Carruthers & Worthington, 2006; Empson, Junk, Dominguez, & Turner, 2006; Fischbein, Deri, Nello, & Marino, 1985; Gravemejier & van Galen, 2003; Steffe, 1994). Thus, by saying *children's* mathematics, we imply the existence of a coherent and logical approach to reasoning that differs in important ways from that of mathematicians and other adults. For example, most adults would view and solve the following problems similarly because they involve the same numbers (3, 7, and 21) and number relationships.

– Janelle has 21 beads. She wants to put 3 beads in each braid. How many braids can Janelle make?
– Janelle has 21 beads. She wants to make 3 braids in her hair and put the same number of beads in each braid. How many beads can go in each braid?

Research suggests that, unlike adults, children like Laura Rose would view and solve these problems differently because the situations described in the problems are not alike. Young children initially solve the first problem by continually making groups of 3 beads until all 21 beads are exhausted. To find the answer, they count the number of groups (braids) created. In contrast, they generally solve the second problem by making 3 groups (braids), and then distributing beads to the braids until all 15 beads are exhausted. To find the answer, they count the number of beads on one braid (Carpenter et al., 1999). From her work we learn that Laura Rose knew that "seven threes was 21." This number fact may have been sufficient for her to immediately solve the first problem which explicitly indicated groups of 3 (beads). However, it was insufficient for Laura Rose to immediately solve the second problem. Not surprisingly, she did not use the commutativity principle because the reason x groups of y size would yield the same quantity as y groups of x size is not obvious to children at her age (Carpenter et al., 1999). Specifically, she did not see that 7 braids with 3 beads each was the same as 3 braids with 7 beads each, and she therefore modelled the situation in the second problem by mentally distributing the beads to three braids in a trial-and-error fashion.

Without debating whether there exists a single mathematics encompassed by modern mathematics or several, overlapping and related systems contextualized in different communities, we feel confident in singling out children's mathematics as distinct. A mathematician who visited a primary school and worked with young children discovered this mathematics for himself. "What surprised me most was that I learnt mathematics" he reported (Aharoni, 2003, p. 2), referring to a deep examination of elementary concepts, such as subtraction,[2] about which "it is rare that a mathematician cares to stop and think" (p. 3).

Why Is Listening to Children's Mathematics Important?

Research on young children's mathematics has shown that children use intuitive or informal knowledge to generate conceptually sound strategies for a variety of problems (Carpenter, Ansell, Franke, Fennema, & Weisbeck, 1993). Although this reasoning is not always completely accurate (Fischbein & Schnarch, 1997; Lehrer, Jenkins, & Osana, 1998), it is more powerful and productive than many teachers realize. Older children as well use a variety of strategies and models of their own invention (e.g., Confrey, 1991; Lesh & Harel, 2003).

This body of research has documented milestones in children's understanding, valid forms of alternative reasoning, and sequences of strategy development.[3]

---

[2] Aharoni (2003) recounted his learning that subtraction "has more than one meaning." Several subtraction stories involving apples can be written for 5 – 3, for example, including the traditional take-away model ("I had five apples and I ate three"), a comparison model ("Tom has 5 apples. Mary has 3 apples. How many more apples does Tom have than Mary?"), and a part-whole model ("I had 5 apples. Three of them were green. How many were red?"). These and other meanings for subtraction have been described and researched by mathematics education researchers (Carpenter, 1985; Carpenter et al., 1999), but the important point is that Aharoni experienced this mathematics as distinctive and significant.

[3] In-depth reviews of much of this research by mathematical topic can be found in Lester (2007).

These findings have played a critical role in framing the content for which teachers are to listen (e.g., Carpenter et al., 1999). The research base also includes a body of related research that investigated the types of errors and misconceptions produced by children and adolescents and ways this information can help teachers diagnose and remediate children's errors (Even & Tirosh, 2002). In general, however, instruction that focuses on listening to children's mathematics is characterized by attention to what children can do rather than what they cannot do, and the research base affords teachers frameworks for thinking about possible learning pathways. Listening to children's thinking during instruction appears to have multiple benefits including (a) improving children's understandings, (b) providing a means of formative assessment, (c) increasing teachers' mathematical knowledge, and (d) supporting teachers' engagement in generative learning.

Listening to improve children's understandings. In mathematics teaching, conceptual understanding is an elusive goal for many learners (Hiebert & Grouws, 2007). Compelling evidence indicates that when teachers listen to children's mathematical thinking as a routine feature of instruction, children's understanding of mathematics improves in measurable ways. For example, several studies have shown that learners whose teachers encourage them to solve problems or engage in inquiry using their own approaches and to communicate their thinking in some way demonstrate stronger conceptual understanding and are better problem solvers than learners in classrooms of teachers who do not (Boaler & Staples, in press; Carpenter, Fennema, Peterson, Chiang, & Loef, 1989; Saxe, Gearhart, & Seltzer, 1999; Villeseñor & Kepner, 1993). Similarly, in their review, Wilson and Berne (1999) found that professional development based on listening to children's thinking helped teachers create rich instructional environments that promoted mathematical inquiry and understanding, leading to documented improvement in student achievement.

Listening to provide formative assessment. Teachers who attend to children's mathematics are, by definition, engaged in ongoing assessment. By listening to a child's thinking, teachers can customize instruction by asking questions and posing new tasks on the basis of what they discover about the child's existing understandings. Thus, teachers are essentially able to fine tune their interactions with a learner in such a way that their assessment of the learner's thinking is tightly integrated with instruction (Davis, 1997; Franke, Carpenter, Levi, & Fennema, 2001; Kazemi & Stipek, 2001; Steinberg, Empson, & Carpenter, 2004). This kind of ongoing assessment of learners' understandings constitutes a type of *formative assessment* – which research has shown is one of the most effective interventions for improving instruction, producing learning gains that are roughly one-half standard deviation above the next most powerful intervention (Black & Wiliam, 1998).

Listening to increase teachers' mathematical knowledge. A perhaps unexpected benefit of listening to children's mathematics is that opportunities for teachers to improve their own mathematical knowledge also arise (Philipp et al., 2007; Silver, Clark, Ghousseini, Charalambos, & Sealy, in press).[4] For example, Philipp and colleagues found that, in connection with mathematics coursework, prospective teachers' knowledge of place value and rational number increased more for those with opportunities to study children's mathematical thinking than the comparison groups in which they did not study children's thinking.

To illustrate the potential mathematical content in children's thinking, we return to Laura Rose's strategy described at the beginning of the chapter and characterize her thinking in terms of the fundamental principles of arithmetic[5] (see Table 1).

Table 1. Laura Rose's strategy described in terms of the fundamental principles of arithmetic

Laura Rose's Description	Possible Equation	Fundamental Principles of Arithmetic
I knew that seven threes was 21.	$3 + 3 + 3 + 3 + 3 + 3 + 3 = 21$	Known fact
I took two from each.	$3 + 3 + 3 + 3 + 3 + 3 + 3 = (3 + 3) + (3 + 3) + (3 + 3) + 3$	Associative property of addition
That would make six, and then there'd be three others.	$(3 + 3) + (3 + 3) + (3 + 3) + 3 = 6 + 6 + 6 + 3$	Addition
You'd put one from that three into each one.	$6 + 6 + 6 + 3 = 6 + 6 + 6 + 1 + 1 + 1$ $6 + 6 + 6 + 1 + 1 + 1 = (6 + 1) + (6 + 1) + (6 + 1)$	Decomposition and commutative and associative properties of addition
The two would be six so plus one more would be seven.	$(6 + 1) + (6 + 1) + (6 + 1) = 7 + 7 + 7$	Addition

---

[4] Elementary school teachers are not the only ones who stand to benefit from listening more closely to their learners. The mathematician David Henderson wrote that he too learned mathematics from the learners in his geometry class. When he learned to "listen more effectively," he realized that more and more of the learners were "showing [him] something about geometry that [he] had not seen before" (Henderson, 1996, no page number).

[5] Thanks to Linda Levi of Teachers Development Group (Portland, Oregon, U.S.) for insight into children's algebraic reasoning. See also Carpenter, Levi, Franke, and Zeringue (2005).

We emphasize that Laura Rose did not use number sentences or formal terms to describe her mathematical reasoning. However, to solve the problem as she did, she must have some level of understanding of these principles, and the equations are one way of showing explicitly what was only tacit in her reasoning.

Listening to engage teachers in generative learning. Finally, we argue that learning to listen to children's mathematics is important because it is generative. By *generative learning*, we mean that teachers who listen effectively do not depend on a static knowledge base but instead can regularly *generate* new knowledge about children's mathematics as a result of their constant close attention to what children are saying and doing. By learning how to learn from the children in their classrooms, teachers can continue learning even after formal professional development support ends; thus children's mathematical thinking can provide a coherent and continuous source of professional development throughout teachers' careers (Franke et al., 2001). In the next section, we provide a vision for instruction in which teachers listen effectively to children's mathematics.

The Nature of Instruction in Which Teachers Listen to Children's Mathematics

To illustrate listening effectively to children's mathematics we provide an example of a teacher listening to a young child and highlight some critical features of the interaction. Instruction based upon effective listening is not of a single version and is inextricably linked to what a child says and does. We therefore describe one set of possible teaching moves and highlight their links to the child's thinking. We chose an example of a teacher working one-on-one with a child because it shows clearly the teacher's moves as she listened and responded to the child's thinking. Opportunities for similar types of interactions in whole-class settings arise as teachers ask questions, pose problems, support children's problem solving and inquiry, and lead discussions of children's solutions.

Example of an interaction. The teacher worked with a first grader, Darcy, to solve the problem: *Melanie has 4 pockets and in each pocket, she has 5 rocks. How many rocks does Melanie have?* Darcy was confused and offered, "I don't get it." The teacher initially repeated the problem and then tried to clarify the problem context, using pockets on her outfit.

Teacher: Okay. She has four pockets. I have two [pockets] here [pointing to her pockets] – 1, 2, 3, 4. In each pocket I have 5 rocks. So how many rocks am I carrying around?

Darcy: [Using a tone indicating that the teacher had asked a silly question] 5.

Teacher: [Pointing to a pocket]. That would be this pocket for 5.

Darcy: Oh!!

Darcy then chose to use base-ten blocks from a variety of manipulatives. She pulled out 5 cubes but was still confused. When the teacher asked her about the quantities in the problem ("Do you remember how many pockets she has?"), Darcy correctly answered but still insisted that she did not "get it." The teacher then changed the problem to be about Darcy and made explicit the idea that there were 5 rocks in *each* pocket.

Teacher: Well, why don't you stand up? [Darcy stands up] Okay, how many pockets do you have?

Darcy: [Counting the pockets on the front of her jeans] 1, 2 [looks for pockets in the back of her jeans, but there are none, so she sighs].

Teacher: You have two?

Darcy: Yeah.

Teacher: What if you had two in the back? We could pretend. [Darcy agrees.] So you have 5 in one pocket and 5 in another pocket and 5 in another pocket and 5 in another pocket.

Darcy: Ohhhh!

Teacher: That's a lot of rocks, huh?

Darcy: [Smiles and points to her front pockets] 5, 10 [looks to her pretend back pockets] 20.

Teacher: How did you get that?

Darcy: I counted by 5s.

Teacher: Show me again.

Darcy: [Points to each of her "four" pockets] 5, 10, and then 15, then 20.

At this point, the teacher initiated a series of extension problems beginning with Darcy's having 6 pockets and 10 rocks in each. Darcy started to count by 6s, but when the teacher reminded her that the problem was 6 pockets with 10 rocks in each pocket, she immediately responded, "60."

Teacher: How did you get that so quick?

Darcy: Because I know that 6 times 10 is 60.

Teacher: Ohh! Well, what's 7 times 10?

Darcy: 70.

Teacher: What's 2 times 10?

Darcy: 20.

Teacher: Oh, you know your 10s stuff really well. Sit down and let me see if I can give you a stumper. [Darcy giggles.] Okay, let's say Melanie had 4 pockets again, and she had 25 in each pocket.

Darcy asked for clarification of the quantities in the problem ("How many pockets are there?"), and then built the four 25s on a counting frame (10 rods with 10 beads on each rod) by efficiently moving two entire rows and a half row for each 25, obviating the need to ever count an individual bead. When she had finished, Darcy laughed and answered, "100." The teacher then asked how she knew 100 without counting, and Darcy explained, "I did all of them, and I knew that they were – every single bead. And I knew that there were 100 of them so 'One hundred.'"

Critical features of the interaction. In what ways did this teacher respond on the basis of listening to Darcy's mathematical thinking? We highlight four features of this interaction that are characteristic of interactions involving effective listening. First, the teacher supported Darcy's making sense of the problem by listening to and then addressing her confusion without telling her how to solve the problem. For example, in response to Darcy's expressed confusion, the teacher tried clarifying the problem context, identifying the quantities, and personalising the story. The teacher persisted until Darcy made sense of the problem, and she did so without ever taking over the thinking needed to solve the problem.

Second, after Darcy solved a problem, the teacher routinely asked her to articulate how she had arrived at her answer. She also attended to details in Darcy's actions and comments and then used these details to inform her responses. For example, because Darcy answered, "One hundred," by just looking at the counting frame on the last problem, the teacher asked how she got 100 *without counting* any of the beads. Similarly, when Darcy began counting by 6s (for the problem with 6 pockets and 10 rocks in each pocket), the teacher immediately recognized that this strategy was inconsistent with Darcy's way of making sense of this problem. She knew, and research has shown (e.g., Carpenter et al., 1999), that most children approach such problems by counting by the number in each group (10) rather than by the number of groups (6). The teacher did not tell Darcy how to solve the problem but instead simply reiterated the problem context to provide Darcy an opportunity to make sense of the mathematics. Thus, the teacher not only noticed important mathematical details but also responded on the basis of these details in ways that were consistent with Darcy's thinking and with the research base on children's mathematics.

Third, the teacher viewed this interaction as more than an opportunity to help Darcy solve a single multiplication problem successfully; this interaction was an opportunity for multiple cycles of listening followed by moves to extend Darcy's understandings. For example, instead of concluding the conversation after Darcy had successfully solved the original problem (4x5), the teacher built on Darcy's success and thinking by asking a series of related problems. These follow-up problems not only consolidated Darcy's understanding of this problem structure but also provided new challenges for Darcy (including a return to the original context of Melanie's pockets [instead of her own] and using larger numbers) and new information about Darcy's understandings for the teacher.

Fourth, rather than the initiation-response-evaluation [I-R-E] pattern that is the traditional interaction pattern between teachers and children (Mehan, 1979), the overall tone of Darcy's interaction with this teacher was conversational (back-and-forth turn taking). Darcy's mathematical thinking was consistently the impetus for the teacher's moves. Thus the teacher's questions and follow-up problems could not be predetermined ahead of time – and listening was key to the teachers' successful moves. Because these moves evolved in the midst of the teacher-child interaction, the teacher's role was to draw out, make explicit, and build on the details of Darcy's thinking.

LEARNING TO LISTEN TO CHILDREN'S MATHEMATICS EFFECTIVELY

Learning to listen to children's mathematics requires the development of an interrelated and situated set of skills for attending to children's mathematics in complex instructional environments. Studies of teachers who regularly listen and respond to their learners' mathematical ideas and explanations suggest that these skills are not usually acquired in teacher preparation programs (Ball, 1993; Davis, 1997; Fennema et al., 1996; Sowder, Philipp, Armstrong, & Schappelle, 1998; Wood, Cobb, & Yackel, 1991). However these skills are characterized – as knowledge, beliefs, practices, or, more recently, noticing expertise (Jacobs, Lamb, Philipp, Schappelle, & Burke, 2007; Sherin & van Es, 2003; see also Mason, volume 4) – research has shown that years, not months, are required to develop the competencies and resources needed to teach in ways that incorporate listening effectively to children's mathematics (Ambrose & Jacobs, 2006; Franke et al., 2001; Jacobs et al., 2007; Steinberg et al., 2004). Teachers' own reports corroborate these findings. For example, Therese Kolan, an experienced teacher, estimated that she had become "really comfortable" teaching in a manner that was responsive to children's mathematics only after more than three years of participation in Cognitively Guided Instruction (CGI)[6] professional development. She went on to explain:

> It wasn't an easy task. Because you're learning about all the different types of strategies children can use. You're also learning about all the different types of problems that there are. And so you're trying to put that altogether, and you're trying to make it usable for you. I remember feeling very overwhelmed, going, "Wait a minute. What *is* that child doing?" [...] Because it took a lot to be able to identify exactly what was going on. (Therese Kolan, interview on the videotape *Classrooms I*[7])

Kolan's story attests to the complexity of this learning, beginning with listening and observing to simply identify what children are doing. In this section, we draw on a synthesis of research on teaching to identify benchmarks in teachers' development of learning to listen effectively to children's mathematics. Although not yet empirically tested as a strict sequence of change, the benchmarks we propose are consistent with multiple studies reviewed as well as with our own experiences as mathematics educators conducting professional development. As a starting point for discussion and future research, we describe a pathway by which children's mathematics becomes progressively more central as teachers move from *directive* to *observational* to *responsive* listening.

---

[6] CGI is a research and professional development project focused on helping teachers learn to understand, value, and use children's mathematics (Carpenter, et al., 1999; Carpenter, Franke, & Levi, 2003).

[7] This quote can be found on *Classrooms I*, one of seven videotapes made for purposes of CGI professional development (Carpenter, Fennema, Franke, & Empson, 1995).

In identifying this pathway, we specifically build on Jacobs and Ambrose's (2008) work on characterising one-on-one teacher-student interactions, and we draw more generally from two types of studies: those that focused closely on the process of teachers' learning to use children's mathematics and those that focused on teachers' listening to children's mathematical thinking. In some of these studies, researchers explored teachers' use of children's mathematics in classroom instruction, whereas in others they focused on teachers' interacting with children in one-on-one contexts, such as in problem-solving interviews or in reaction to children's written work. Each of these teaching contexts provides valuable information because listening as well as many other teaching skills (e.g., questioning and designing follow-up tasks) are employed, regardless of the number of children engaged.

Directive Listening

Directive listening refers to listening to a child's thinking in a way that seeks to determine whether it matches an expected response and actively tries to elicit that expected response even when it is inconsistent with the child's understandings (Jacobs & Ambrose, 2008; see also Crespo, 2000; Davis, 1997; Wood, 1998). This kind of listening may involve excessive support and can be limiting by cutting off opportunities for learners to express their own understandings and by overgeneralising what learners understand. The research literature is replete with examples of directive listening, suggesting that it is pervasive in teachers' interactions with learners. For example, Nicol (1999) reported the reflective comments of a prospective teacher who initially rejected a child's representation of one third because he drew it as part of a rectangle instead of as part of a pie, as she had envisioned it, "I immediately doubted his accuracy because it did not concur with what I had in my mind" (p. 58). Wallach and Even (2005) described how a teacher overgeneralised when listening to two of her learners solve a problem about dividing 15 children into two groups so that one group had 4 children fewer than the other group. The teacher interpreted a child's ambiguous statement that "15 is odd, 4 is even, then it's impossible" to mean "When you have an odd number, and you take off an even [number], you will be left with an odd number, and you would not be able to divide it by 2" (p. 403). The researchers speculated that teachers' wishes to see their learners succeed may fuel the propensity to attribute more understanding to the learners than is warranted.

Observational Listening

As teachers begin to appreciate the potential power of children's mathematics, their listening appears to become temporarily passive, or observational, with respect to interacting with children (Jacobs & Ambrose, 2008; see also Crespo, 2000; McDounough, Clarke, D. M. & Clarke, B. A. 2002; Sherin & Han, 2004). *Observational listening* refers to listening with an attempt to hear the child's thinking but with nascent formulations about what is heard and few active attempts to support or extend that thinking.

In contrast to directive listening, teachers who engage in observational listening signal to children a genuine interest in their thinking, which helps children, in turn, see themselves as mathematical agents and develop a positive disposition toward mathematics (cf., Johnston, 2004). However, these teachers are generally unsure about their role in attending to children's mathematics. This uncertainty can lead to excessive wait time, and responses to children's explanations of their thinking tend to follow a set of generic questions (e.g., "How did you solve that?") accompanied by little or inconsistent probing of specific aspects of children's solutions, even when those solutions are unclear (Jacobs & Ambrose, 2008).

Because observing with limited interceding is a seemingly simple thing to do, one might underestimate the power of teachers' shift from directive to observational listening. First, observation can improve teachers' abilities to attend to the details in what a child is doing and saying (Kazemi & Franke, 2004). Attending to these details not only is more difficult than one might expect, as illustrated earlier by the teachers' difficulties in simply describing Laura Rose's strategy, but it is also a prerequisite skill for making inferences about children's understandings and responding on the basis of those understandings.

Second, observation can help teachers recognize that children can generate insights, representations, and strategies when given the opportunity. Many teachers become intrigued with the mathematics that children generate themselves. This curiosity can be a powerful hook for teachers who become motivated to learn more about children's mathematics and how to access it.

Third, case-study evidence suggests that the shift from directive to observational listening involves a dramatic shift in teachers' conception of their role, and during this shift teachers must grapple with confusion and uncertainty that can sometimes take surprising forms (Steinberg et al., 2004). For instance, we knew a small group of experienced teachers who were fascinated by children's mathematics, but they were still learning what it meant to actively support and extend children's thinking. When posing a problem that depended on counting legs for various numbers of lizards and beetles, they were unsure whether they could talk with the children, many of whom were English-language learners, about the number of legs on a beetle! We speculate that this type of uncertainty about the teacher's role could indicate that significant intellectual reorganization is underway (Duckworth, 1996), and thus an observational orientation to listening is a transitional, but quite possibly critical, period in teachers' learning to listen to children's mathematics.

Responsive Listening

When teachers begin to actively listen to children's mathematics, their role changes from observing to drawing out, making explicit, and building on the details of children's understandings (Jacobs & Ambrose, 2008; see also Ball & Cohen, 1999; Ball, Lubienski, & Mewborn, 2001; Fraivillig, Murphy, & Fuson, 1999; Mathematics Practice Classroom Study Group, 2007; Sherin 2002; Wood, 1998).

In this way, teachers can challenge children to advance their existing mathematical thinking by making connections among concepts, problems, or representations. *Responsive listening* refers to listening in which the teacher not only intends to listen carefully to the child's thinking but also actively works to support and extend that thinking, such as in the Darcy example presented earlier. In essence, children's mathematics becomes the core of interactions between teachers and learners.

In responsive listening, teachers' responses are intertwined with their listening. Thus, to engage in this type of listening, not only do teachers need genuine curiosity about children's ideas (Paley, 1986), but they also need expertise with a complex set of interrelated skills that allow them to attend to children's thinking, immediately make inferences about what children understand, immediately determine what response to provide, immediately execute that response and then begin the cycle again – many times, all in the midst of instruction.

Not surprisingly, given this complexity, learning to listen responsively takes several years (e.g., Schneier, 2001). However, when teachers do make the shift, it appears to constitute a fundamental and irreversible change in how they conceptualize their work. After teachers develop the acuity and ability to listen to children's mathematics, asking them not to notice it would be tantamount to asking a reader to refrain from forming words from clusters of letters.[8]

In contrast, when teachers are in the process of shifting from observational to responsive listening, their transition efforts may, at times, appear awkward, incomplete, or even directive (Jacobs & Ambrose, 2008; Knapp & Peterson, 1995; Wood, 1995). Because responsive listening cannot be planned ahead of time but instead must be constructed, on the spot, on the basis of what children are saying and doing, the development of this expertise involves a certain amount of trial and error. Jacobs and Ambrose (2008) documented three types of what they termed *exploratory* interactions, in which teachers in this transitional time worked toward listening responsively to children's mathematics. Specifically, teachers' exploration of children's thinking was (a) active but minimal, (b) active but then interrupted by the introduction of the teachers' thinking, or (c) active and extensive but awkward or poorly timed. With practice and support, teachers refine their listening skills to engage in responsive listening. Research has shown that teachers can also benefit from the support and encouragement of school leaders and a community of peers similarly engaged in explorations of children's mathematics (Davis, 1997; Franke et al., 2001; Jacobs et al., 2007; Sherin & Han, 2004). Finally, professional development can directly support the development of responsive listening. We provide some specific suggestions in the following section.

RECOMMENDATIONS FOR WORKING WITH TEACHERS

We claim that the act of listening for teaching requires a great deal of expertise, which culminates in the ability to listen responsively, that is, to listen in a way that

---

[8] Thanks to S. Greenstein (personal communication, 26 November 2007) for this comparison.

entails eliciting and making sense of the mathematics in children's actions and comments. In this section, we describe three types of professional development activities that have been used by mathematics teacher educators to help teachers learn to listen responsively: (a) discussions of children's written work, (b) discussions of videotaped interactions, and (c) opportunities for teachers to work with children and to reflect on those experiences with other teachers. The activities we describe serve dual purposes, which are in practice inseparable – to develop listening skills and to develop knowledge of children's mathematics. We do not suggest that a particular sequence is necessary. We do, however, think that taking into account the situated nature of teacher thinking is necessary (Hiebert, Gallimore, & Stigler, 2002), and thus all three learning activities preserve the complexity of teaching situations either by engaging teachers in practice or by using artefacts of practice.

Using Children's Written Work in Professional Development

Discussing children's written work is one of the most practical ways for teachers to learn to attend to children's mathematics, because written work is simple to collect, archive, and share with others. Mathematics teacher educators can use carefully selected samples of written work for particular purposes (Jacobs & Philipp, 2004), or ask participating teachers to collect learners' written work without time-consuming preparation or interruption of their classroom routines.

Written work is particularly useful in helping teachers become attuned to ascertaining the details of children's thinking – a foundational skill for responsive listening. For example, Kazemi and Franke (2004) organized a monthly work group of 10 teachers at an elementary school. Prior to each meeting, all the teachers were given the same problem to pose to the children in their classrooms, with the understanding that this problem could be adapted, as needed, by the teachers. When teachers shared their children's written work on the problem, the mathematics teacher educator then used this situation as an opportunity to press the teachers for details about what children had done and for evidence to justify their descriptions. Initially, teachers were simply unaware of the details of children's thinking. For example, one teacher presented the work of a child who had written "1 2 3 4 5," to solve the missing addend problem $7 + \Box = 11$. Collectively, the teachers generated several possible strategies involving this notation, but the child's teacher could neither confirm nor refute these strategies because he had not elicited that information from the child. Over time, as the group continued to discuss children's written work and become more aware of the type of detail needed to characterize children's strategies, the discussions became richer and better grounded in actual descriptions of children's strategies. This change in the group discussion reflected the fact that teachers learned to ask for and listen as children gave details and justifications for their work in the classroom. The teachers learned to listen to children's strategies and recognize when they needed to ask for more clarification. These researchers also found that the more able teachers became in listening to the details of children's mathematics in the classroom, the better they became at projecting possible pathways for children's learning.

Although written work is ideal for highlighting children's strategies and representations and the underlying mathematics, a major disadvantage is that teachers can neither question the child about his or her reasoning nor test their ideas for supporting or extending a child's thinking – both key elements of responsive listening. Because children's written records of their thinking often omit important strategy details as well as the justifications for what they have done, teachers, such as those described in the work group above (Kazemi & Franke, 2004), learn to recognize the limitations of using only written work to help them understand children's thinking.

Facilitating discussions of written work. Several practical considerations pertain to teachers' collecting and discussing written work from their own classrooms. Having all teachers pose the same (or a similar) problem or activity is helpful for purposes of comparison of children's strategies and learning to notice the specific details of what children have done. To allow teachers to see variety in children's mathematics, teacher educators should select problems or activities that invite several solutions or representations, can be adapted for multiple grade levels, and address meaningful mathematics. Teachers should also be encouraged to annotate a child's written work after their conversation with the child to clarify the reasoning involved.

Teachers are likely to arrive with several pieces of written work for each student; thus, a useful first step is to ask teachers to select a few samples to share. Criteria for selection can include typical work, sophisticated work, surprising work, and so on. A related, practical consideration is how to share small and hard-to-read written work with the group. Document cameras can be used to project the work, although small groups can effectively discuss written work by simply gathering around to view one another's samples.

The focus and structure of the discussions of written work are likely to evolve if the group meets regularly (Kazemi & Franke, 2004). Initially, as teachers are learning to make sense of rather than only evaluate children's thinking as correct or incorrect, the most successful discussions focus on helping teachers describe the details and logic of children's thinking. As teachers become proficient at observing and clarifying the details of children's thinking, discussions should shift to making inferences about what children understand and considering how to extend that understanding. For example, one way to organize discussions is to have teachers group the written-work samples they consider to be alike and then discuss the similarities and differences of the work samples within and between the groups. Teachers' early ways of categorising strategies often focus on differences in representations, such as tallies or drawing, signalling an emergent attention to detail. Later categorizations may focus on deeper dimensions, such as making use of the same mathematical principle. Still later, teachers use categorizations to discuss possible learning pathways; teachers can order strategy categories in terms of levels of sophistication and discuss how to help children move from one level to the next.

We also suggest that the mathematics embodied in the written work can itself serve as a productive focus. Teachers can be asked to solve the problem (or a similar problem) or to analyse the mathematical principles underlying the children's strategies (Jacobs & Philipp, 2004). When teachers discuss children's written work in conjunction with doing mathematics themselves, their motivation for grappling with challenging mathematical ideas often increases (Philipp et al., 2007).

Using Videotaped Interactions in Professional Development

Similar to discussing written work, viewing and discussing videotaped interactions between teachers and children help teachers learn to attend to the details of children's thinking and explore the underlying mathematical principles. In contrast to written work, however, video preserves details of teachers' *interactions* with children's mathematics and, as such, also affords opportunities for discussing teachers' listening skills as they are enacted. Processes involved in clarifying the details, interpreting the child's understanding, and deciding how to support or extend the child's thinking can be jointly constructed or imagined through discussion and deliberation. Eventually, these processes become integrated and appropriated for use by individual teachers as they listen to learners in their own classrooms. Most important, discussing video of teacher-child interactions ensures that teachers' actions are considered in response to children's thinking rather than in isolation.

Many types of video have been used by mathematics teacher educators to showcase children's mathematics and teachers' interactions with children's mathematics, and each has advantages and disadvantages. Decisions must be made about whether to use video depicting a teacher working with a single child, a small group, or a whole class. Decisions must also be made about whether to use video produced professionally or made by teachers. The use of each type of video has proven powerful, but creating or selecting video requires a great deal of advanced planning.

Video produced professionally. Several collections of video focused on children's mathematics have been professionally produced. Some U.S. examples include *CGI*,[9] *Developing Mathematical Ideas*,[10] *Integrating Mathematics and Pedagogy*,[11] *Thinking Mathematically: Integrating Arithmetic and Algebra in Elementary School*,[12] and *Math Time*.[13] There are several advantages to these professionally-

---

[9] See http://www.wcer.wisc.edu/ncisla/teachers/index.html.
[10] See http://www2.edc.org/CDT/dmi/dmicur.html.
[11] See http://vig.prenhall.com/catalog/academic/product/0,1144,0131198548,00.html.
[12] See Carpenter et al. (2003).

produced collections. First, the video has often been edited to provide clear examples of children's particular strategies. For example, video of children's counting strategies can help teachers unfamiliar with the many ways children use their fingers for counting. Second, video has often been organized to provide examples of frameworks for understanding children's mathematics. For example, a set of videos may provide multiple episodes to illustrate a clearly defined sequence of conceptual development, such as for base-ten understanding. Finally, professionally-produced video can provide a vision of teaching that the participants in the professional development have not yet achieved. Understanding children's mathematics and how it can be supported and extended is critical to responsive listening and these professionally-produced collections can serve as an important resource for mathematics educators who want to engage teachers with these ideas.

Video created by teachers. Some researchers have teachers videotape their own interactions with children, allowing teachers to receive feedback while directly working to improve their listening skills. What teacher-made videos may lack in production quality is made up for by their immediacy and relevance. These generally unedited videos include details that make them realistic to other teachers: a child who gets distracted, a phone ringing, or an interruption by another teacher. Hence teachers viewing these teacher-produced videos relate well to these authentic situations. In addition, the teacher in the video can serve as a resource by sharing information about the context in which the video was made and by providing missing details about the child's previous instruction and performance. On the other hand, discussing the teaching of a teacher in the room challenges the "politeness norm" (Ball & Cohen, 1999) by which teachers support but do not criticize each other. Thus to realize the benefits of teacher-produced video, mathematics educators need to help teachers develop what Lord (1994) calls "critical colleagueship" to allow teachers to critically examine teaching situations without having the teacher in the video view the discussion as a personal attack.

For example, Jacobs, Ambrose, Clement, and Brown (2006) reported on a group of elementary school teachers who worked together to view and discuss video created by themselves. The teachers each videotaped themselves working one-on-one with a child and then brought the videotape to a professional development session to be viewed and discussed by the group. To build trust within the group and to focus discussions productively, ground rules were set for video discussion (see also Sherin & Han, 2004). These teachers appreciated the opportunities to view and discuss interactions involving teachers who, like themselves, were working to grow in their ability to listen responsively. Jacobs and colleagues (2006) reported that the teachers revealed that "watching one another makes them feel better about their own efforts to change because, in contrast to published cases

---

[13] See http://edenrich.com/mathtime.html.

that often present polished exemplars, video clips produced by teachers typically depict teaching in the process of change" (p. 278).

Although there are technical considerations for teachers who want to produce video of their one-on-one or small-group work, this video production is generally quite feasible. In contrast, the technical problems of teachers videotaping themselves in whole-class settings can be significant. A single camera positioned on a tripod simply misses much of importance, and obtaining good sound (especially of children's voices) can be even more challenging. One option to enhance the quality of classroom video is to have the videos transcribed before discussing them (e.g., van Es & Sherin, 2008), but this step can be time consuming.

Working with Children in Professional Development

Interactions with an individual child or a small group of children provide opportunities for teachers to practice listening carefully and responding to children's thinking in real time. The major advantage to working directly with children is the authenticity of the experience – teachers experience all the complexities involved in understanding a specific child's or a group of children's thinking in the moment.

Teachers can interact directly with children in several ways. One-on-one problem solving interviews (e.g., Ginsburg, 1997) are a particularly beneficial activity for both prospective and practising teachers. Mathematics teacher educators can ask teachers, working in pairs with one child, to pose problems or investigations from a common set. This pairing enables teachers to help each other with listening, questioning, and note taking. Interacting with children can be overwhelming – particularly when children are not accustomed to explaining their reasoning – and it is helpful to remind teachers to focus on determining the details and ideas of children's thinking rather than the rightness or wrongness of those details and ideas. Furthermore, when pairs of teachers interview within a shared setting, the teacher educator, circulating among the pairs, has opportunities to scaffold interactions with children. For example, a teacher may not fully probe a child's reasoning or may be unsure what question to ask to clarify a child's unclear thinking; the teacher educator can provide support – in the moment – as a co-participant in the listening process.

The goal of one-on-one problem solving interviews will vary for teachers with different listening orientations. For teachers who are oriented to directive listening, an appropriate goal is to simply elicit a child's thinking taking care not to step in and show the child how to solve the problem. For teachers who are developing an observational listening orientation, an appropriate goal is to move beyond the use of generic questioning (e.g., How did you solve that?) to inquire about the specifics of what a child understands. For the responsive listener, an appropriate focus is on using questioning that is specific to the child's solution not only to understand but also to support or extend a child's thinking. This questioning can include pressing for justification or symbolization and posing further problems to build upon a mathematical idea as in the example of Darcy.

Many teachers find it a challenge to move beyond observational listening to responsive listening in which they are to actively support and extend a child's mathematical thinking. A typical approach for teachers in transition is to begin an interaction by attending to a child's thinking but to resort to imposing their own thinking, especially with a child who is struggling or having difficulty explaining his or her thinking (Jacobs & Ambrose, 2008). Teachers who understand intellectually the need to limit their own comments to let a child develop his or her own reasoning often report with bemusement how they intervened to direct a child down a particular path. It seems that interactions are driven by deeply ingrained routines rather than intentions. Working directly with children therefore gives teachers opportunities to develop new interactional routines that are focused on ensuring that listening to children's thinking is the focus in the interaction.

CONCLUSIONS

Our charge in this chapter was to write about how teachers learn to use knowledge of children's conceptions in teaching. From the large body of research on children's conceptions, we focused on what we called *children's mathematics* – the mathematical thinking that children use to solve problems, create representations, and make arguments. In asking ourselves what using knowledge of children's conceptions entailed, we decided that *listening* was a significant component that deserved to be singled out. We agree with Davis (1996) who argued that listening cannot be reduced to a set of techniques and that it is at the heart of teaching that engages learners in substantive thinking and reflection.

For some teachers, especially prospective teachers, *teaching* is synonymous with *telling*, although such a conception of teaching is too simplistic to capture what an effective teacher does. In fact, the research we have reviewed supports the assertion by Boles and colleagues that "teaching is listening and learning is talking" (Boles, Troen, & Kamii, 1997, p. 16). Effective teachers not only listen regularly and carefully, but they also use what they hear to decide, often on the spot, what to do next. Among the studies we cited, we found a great deal of variation in teachers' listening expertise. To this end, we identified three types of listening – directive, observational, and responsive – and outlined a developmental pathway in which children's mathematics becomes progressively more central in teachers' listening. We noted that the research base supporting our claims is limited but growing.

We conclude with a dilemma for mathematics teacher educators: learning to listen to children's mathematics is challenging to realize in the short term, but has enormous long-term benefits. This almost palpable tension can be difficult to negotiate with teachers and administrators, who, at least in the U.S., often have little institutional incentive to see beyond the current year and its pressing problems. Why does this tension exist? First, listening responsively in the classroom is hard work and can be accomplished only by a teacher possessing a complex set of interrelated competencies and resources that takes time – usually several years – to develop. As such, the development of this expertise must compete with the daily pressures of teaching in which teachers often choose to maintain lesson momentum (Kennedy, 2005) rather than to attend closely to an individual learner's unclear or unfamiliar way of reasoning.

Second, professional development focused on listening and responding to children's mathematics differs from much of the other professional development that teachers have experienced. Teachers often expect professional development to provide clear instructions about how to implement particular activities (e.g., Schweitzer, 1996). In contrast, when the focus is children's mathematics, teachers are given access to knowledge about children's mathematics and opportunities to adapt their own instruction to value and use children's mathematics. Teaching prescriptions are not provided and instead, teachers make deeply personal adaptations while working to rethink their roles, cultivate professional judgment, and design instruction that is appropriate for the specific learners in their classrooms. The expertise to make these adaptations takes time to develop, but once made, is lasting.

Finally, using children's mathematics in instruction does not have a single model of success. This flexibility is a short-term challenge but a long-term strength. Teachers can be initially unsure and, at times, frustrated, worrying about the "correctness" of their instructional moves. As teachers learn more about children's mathematics, this initial uncertainty transforms into an orientation in which teachers feel empowered to evaluate and improve their own interactions on the basis of what their learners are understanding. This profound transformation yields growth that is not only sustained but also generative (Franke et al., 2001). Teachers gain the ability to continue to learn substantially from interactions with learners in their classrooms. To fully realize the promise of instruction based on listening to children's mathematics, mathematics teacher educators need to recognize, but not be deterred by, the tension between these short-tem challenges and long-term benefits.

ACKNOWLEDGEMENTS

This research was supported in part by a grant from the National Science Foundation (ESI-0455785). The views expressed are those of the authors and do not necessarily reflect the views of the National Science Foundation.

REFERENCES

Aharoni, R. (2003). *What I learnt in primary school*. Text of invited address. Retrieved November 21, 2007, from http://www.math.technion.ac.il/%7Era/education.html
Ambrose, R. C., & Jacobs, V. R. (2006, April). *Investigating teachers' abilities to support and extend children's mathematical thinking*. Paper presented at the annual meeting of the American Educational Research Association, San Francisco, CA.
Ball, D. L. (1993). With an eye on the mathematical horizon: Dilemmas of teaching elementary school mathematics. *The Elementary School Journal, 93*, 373–397.

Ball, D. L., & Cohen, D. K. (1999). Developing practice, developing practitioners: Toward a practice-based theory of professional education. In L. Darling-Hammond & G. Sykes (Eds.), *Teaching as the learning profession* (pp. 3–32). San Francisco: Jossey-Bass.

Ball, D. L., Lubienski, S. T., & Mewborn, D. S. (2001). Research on teaching mathematics: The unsolved problem of teachers' mathematical knowledge. In V. Richardson (Ed.), *Handbook of research on teaching* (4th ed., pp. 433–456). Washington, DC: American Educational Research Association.

Black, P., Harrison, C., Lee, C., Marshall, B., & Wiliam, D. (2004). Working inside the black box: Assessment for learning in the classroom. *Phi Delta Kappan, 86*(1), 9–21.

Black, P., & Wiliam, D. (1998). Inside the black box: Raising standards through classroom assessment. *Phi Delta Kappan, 80*(2), 139–148.

Boaler, J. & Staples, M. (in press). Creating mathematical futures through an equitable teaching approach: The case of Railside School. *Teachers College Record.*

Boles, K., Troen, V., & Kamii, M. (1997, March). *From carriers of culture to agents of change: Teacher-initiated professional development in the learning/teaching collaborative inquiry seminars.* Paper presented at the annual meeting of the American Educational Research Association, Chicago, IL.

Carpenter, T. P. (1985). Learning to add and subtract: An exercise in problem solving. In E. A. Silver (Ed.), *Teaching and learning mathematical problem solving: Multiple research perspectives* (pp. 17–40). Hillsdale, NJ: Lawrence Erlbaum Associates.

Carpenter, T. P., Ansell, E., Franke, M. L., Fennema, E., & Weisbeck, L. (1993). Models of problem solving: A study of kindergarten children's problem-solving processes. *Journal for Research in Mathematics Education, 24,* 427–440.

Carpenter, T. P., Fennema, E., Franke, M. L. (Producers) & Empson, S. B. (Director). (1995). *Cognitively guided instruction* [set of 7 videotapes]. Madison, WI: Wisconsin Center for Education Research.

Carpenter, T. P., Fennema, E., Franke, M., Levi, L., & Empson, S. B. (1999). *Children's mathematics: Cognitively Guided Instruction.* Portsmouth, NH: Heinemann.

Carpenter, T. P., Fennema, E., Peterson, P., Chiang, C., & Loef, M. (1989). Using knowledge of children's mathematics thinking in classroom teaching: An experimental study. *American Educational Research Journal, 26,* 499–531.

Carpenter, T. P., Franke, M. L., & Levi, L. (2003). *Thinking mathematically: Integrating arithmetic and algebra in elementary school.* Portsmouth, NH: Heinemann.

Carpenter, T. P., Levi, L., Franke, M. L., & Zeringue, J. (2005). Algebra thinking in elementary school: Developing relational thinking. *ZDM: The International Journal on Mathematics Education, 37,* 53–59.

Carruthers, E., & Worthington, M. (2006). *Children's mathematics: Making marks, making meaning* (2nd ed.). London: Sage.

Crespo, S. (2000). Seeing more than right and wrong answers: Prospective teachers' interpretations of students' mathematical work. *Journal of Mathematics Teacher Education, 3,* 155–181.

Confrey, J. (1991). Learning to listen: A student's understanding of powers of ten. In E. von Glasersfeld (Ed.), *Radical constructivism in mathematics education* (pp. 111–138). Dordrecht, the Netherlands: Kluwer Academic Publishers.

Davis, B. (1996). *Teaching mathematics: Toward a sound alternative.* New York: Garland Publishing.

Davis, B. (1997). Listening for differences: An evolving conception of mathematics teaching. *Journal for Research in Mathematics Education, 28,* 355–376.

Duckworth, E. (1996). *"The having of wonderful ideas" and other essays on teaching and learning* (4th ed.). New York: Teachers College Press.

Duckworth, E. (2001). *"Tell me more." Listening to learners explain.* New York: Teachers College Press.

Empson, S. B., Junk, D., Dominguez, H., & Turner, E. E. (2006). Fractions as the coordination of multiplicatively related quantities: A cross-sectional study of children's thinking. *Educational Studies in Mathematics, 63,* 1–28.

Even, R., & Tirosh, D. (2002). Teacher knowledge and understanding of students' mathematical learning. In L. English (Ed.), *Handbook of international research in mathematics education* (pp. 219–240). Mahwah, NJ: Lawrence Erlbaum Associates.

Fennema, E., Carpenter, T. P., Franke, M. L., Levi, L., Jacobs, V. R., & Empson, S. B. (1996). Mathematics instruction and teachers' beliefs: A longitudinal study of using children's thinking. *Journal for Research in Mathematics Education, 27,* 403–434.

Fischbein, E., Deri, M., Nello, M. S., & Marino, M. S. (1985). The role of implicit models in solving verbal problems in multiplication and division. *Journal for Research in Mathematics Education, 16,* 3–17.

Fischbein, E., & Schnarch, D. (1997). The evolution with age of probabilistic intuitively based misconceptions. *Journal for Research in Mathematics Education, 28,* 96–105.

Fraivillig, J. L., Murphy, L. A., & Fuson, K. C. (1999). Advancing children's mathematical thinking in *Everyday Mathematics* classrooms. *Journal for Research in Mathematics Education, 30,* 148–170.

Franke, M. L., Carpenter, T. P., Levi, L., & Fennema, E. (2001). Capturing teachers' generative change: A follow-up study of professional development in mathematics. *American Educational Research Journal, 38,* 653–689.

Ginsburg, H. (1997). *Entering the child's mind: The clinical interview in psychological research and practice.* New York: Cambridge University Press.

Gravemeijer, K., & van Galen, F. (2003). Facts and algorithms as products of students' own mathematical activity. In J. Kilpatrick, W. G. Martin, & D. Schifter (Eds.), *A research companion to principles and standards for school mathematics* (pp. 114–122). Reston, VA: National Council of Teachers of Mathematics.

Henderson, D. (1996). *I learn mathematics from my students. Multiculturalism in action.* Retrieved November 12, 2007, from http://www.math.cornell.edu/~dwh/papers/I-learn/I-learn.html

Hiebert, J., Gallimore, R., & Stigler, J. W. (2002). A knowledge base for the teaching profession: What would it look like and how could we get one? *Educational Researcher, 31,* 3–15.

Hiebert, J., & Grouws, D. (2007). The effects of classroom mathematics teaching on students' learning. In F. K. Lester Jr. (Ed.), *Second handbook of research on teaching and learning mathematics* (pp. 371–404). Charlotte, NC: Information Age Publishing & National Council of Teachers of Mathematics.

Jacobs, V. R., & Ambrose, R. (2008). A framework for understanding one-on-one teacher-student conversations during mathematical problem solving. Manuscript submitted for publication.

Jacobs, V. R., Ambrose, R., Clement, L., & Brown, D. (2006). Using teacher-produced videotapes of student interviews as discussion catalysts. *Teaching Children Mathematics, 12,* 276–281.

Jacobs, V. R., Lamb, L. C., Philipp, R., Schappelle, B., & Burke, A. (2007, April). Professional noticing by elementary school teachers of mathematics. Paper presented at the annual meeting of the American Educational Research Association, Chicago, IL.

Jacobs, V. R., & Philipp, R. (2004). Helping prospective and practicing teachers focus on children's mathematical thinking in student-work examples. *Teaching Children Mathematics, 11,* 194–201.

Johnston, P. (2004). *Choice words: How our language affects children''s learning.* Portland, ME: Stenhouse.

Kawanaka, T., & Stigler, J. W. (1999). Teachers' use of questions in eighth-grade mathematics classrooms in Germany, Japan, and the United States. *Mathematical Thinking and Learning, 1*, 255–278.

Kazemi, E., & Franke, M. L. (2004). Teacher learning in mathematics: Using student work to promote collective inquiry. *Journal of Mathematics Teacher Education, 7*, 203–235.

Kazemi, E., & Stipek, D. (2001). Promoting conceptual thinking in four upper-elementary mathematics classrooms. *Elementary School Journal, 102*, 59–80.

Kennedy, M. (2005). *Inside teaching: How classroom life undermines reform.* Cambridge, MA: Harvard University Press.

Knapp, N., & Peterson, P. (1995). Teachers' interpretations of CGI after four years: Meanings and practices. *Journal for Research in Mathematics Education, 26*, 40–65.

Lehrer, R., Jenkins, M., & Osana, H. (1998). Longitudinal study of children's reasoning about space and geometry. In R. Lehrer & D. Chazan (Eds.), *Designing learning environments for developing understanding of geometry and space* (pp. 137–168). Mahwah, NJ: Lawrence Erlbaum Associates.

Lesh, R. & Harel, G. (2003). Problem solving, modeling, and local conceptual development. *Mathematical Thinking and Learning, 5*(2/3), 157–189.

Lester, F. K Jr. (Ed.). (2007). *Second handbook of research on mathematics teaching and learning.* Charlotte, NC: Information Age Publishing & National Council of Teachers of Mathematics.

Lord, B. (1994). Teachers' professional development: Critical colleagueship and the role of professional communities. In N. Cobb (Ed.), *The future of education: Perspectives on national standards in education* (pp. 175–204). New York: College Entrance Examination Board.

Mathematics Classroom Practice Study Group. (2007, April). *Eliciting student thinking in elementary school mathematics classrooms.* Paper presented at the annual meeting of the American Educational Research Association, Chicago.

McDounough, A., Clarke, B. A., & Clarke, D. M. (2002). Understanding, assessing, and developing children's mathematical thinking: The power of a one-to-one interview for preservice teachers in providing insights into appropriate pedagogical practices. *International Journal of Educational Research, 37*, 211–226.

Mehan, H. (1979). *Learning lessons.* Cambridge, MA: Harvard University Press.

Nicol, C. (1999). Learning to teach mathematics: Questioning, listening, and responding. *Educational Studies in Mathematics, 37*, 45–66.

Paley, V. G. (1986). On listening to what the children say. *Harvard Educational Review, 56*, 122–131.

Philipp, R. A., Ambrose, R., Lamb, L. L., Sowder, J.., Schappelle, B. P., Sowder, L., et al. (2007). Effects of early field experiences on the mathematical content knowledge and beliefs of prospective elementary school teachers: An experimental study. *Journal for Research in Mathematics Education, 38*, 438–476.

Saxe, G., Gearhart, M., & Seltzer, M. (1999). Relations between classroom practices and student learning in the domain of fractions. *Cognition and Instruction, 17*, 1–24.

Schneier, L. (2001). A schoolteacher's view. In E. Duckworth (Ed.), *"Tell me more." Listening to learners explain* (pp. 188–194). New York: Teachers College Press.

Schweitzer, K. (1996). The search for the perfect resource. In D. Schifter (Ed.), *What's happening in math class?* (Vol. 2, pp. 46–65). New York: Teachers College Press.

Sherin, M. G. (2002). When teaching becomes learning. *Cognition and Instruction, 20*, 119–150.

Sherin, M. G., & Han, S. Y. (2004). Teacher learning in the context of a video club. *Teaching and Teacher Education, 20*, 163–183.

Sherin, M. G., & van Es, E. A. (2003). A new lens on teaching: Learning to notice. *Mathematics Teaching in the Middle School, 9*, 92–95.

Silver, E. A., Clark, L., Ghousseini, H., Charalambos, C., & Sealy, J. (in press). Where is the mathematics? Examining teachers' mathematical learning opportunities in practice-based professional learning tasks. *Journal of Mathematics Teacher Education.*

Sowder, J.., Philipp, R. A., Armstrong, B. E., & Schappelle, B. P. (1998). *Middle-grade teachers' mathematical knowledge and its relationship to instruction.* Albany, NY: State University of New York Press.

Steffe, L. P. (1994). Children's multiplying schemes. In G. Harel & J. Confrey (Eds.), *The development of multiplicative reasoning in the learning of mathematics* (pp. 3–40). Albany, NY: State University of New York Press.

Steinberg, R., Empson, S. B., & Carpenter, T. P. (2004). Inquiry into children's mathematical thinking as a means to teacher change. *Journal of Mathematics Teacher Education, 7,* 237–267.

van Es, E. A., & Sherin, M. G. (2008). Mathematics teachers "learning to notice" in the context of a video club. *Teaching and Teacher Education, 24*(2), 244–276.

Villaseñor, A. J., & Kepner, H. S. J. (1993). Arithmetic from a problem-solving perspective: An urban implementation. *Journal for Research in Mathematics Education, 24,* 62–69.

Wallach, T., & Even, R. (2005). Hearing students: The complexity of understanding what they are saying, showing, and doing. *Journal of Mathematics Teacher Education, 8,* 393–417.

Wilson, S., & Berne, J. (1999). Teacher learning and the acquisition of professional knowledge: An examination of research on contemporary professional development. *Review of Research in Education, 24,* 173–209.

Wood, T. (1995). An emerging practice of teaching. In P. Cobb & H. Bauersfeld (Eds.), *The emergence of mathematical meanings: Interaction in classroom cultures* (pp. 203–227). Hillsdale, NJ: Lawrence Erlbaum Associates.

Wood, T. (1998). Funneling or focusing? Alternative patterns of communication in mathematics class. In H. Steinbring, M. G. Bartolini-Bussi, & A. Sierpinska (Eds.), *Language and communication in the mathematics classroom* (pp. 167–178). Reston, VA: National Council of Teachers of Mathematics.

Wood, T., Cobb, P., & Yackel, E. (1991). Change in teaching mathematics: A case study. *American Educational Research Journal, 28,* 587–616.

Susan B. Empson
Department of Curriculum and Instruction
The University of Texas at Austin
USA

Victoria R. Jacobs
School of Teacher Education
San Diego State University
USA

KOENO GRAVEMEIJER

12. RME THEORY AND MATHEMATICS
TEACHER EDUCATION

*The theme of this chapter concerns the question of how mathematics teacher
education can prepare prospective teachers for mathematics education that is in
line with the domain-specific instruction theory for realistic mathematics education
(RME) – which aims at helping students to construct or reinvent mathematics.
Before answering this question, a reinvention approach that may avoid the
problems that are inherent in more conventional approaches to mathematics
education is elucidated. Next, the RME approach is elaborated in terms of the
instructional design heuristics, guided reinvention, didactical phenomenology, and
emergent modelling. The main question of this chapter is addressed by
subsequently investigating (a) what it takes to enable this form of mathematics
education in the classroom, (b) how this translates to teacher competencies that
are required, and (c) how these competencies may be fostered in mathematics
teacher education.*

INTRODUCTION

The goal of this chapter is to investigate the implications of the domain-specific
instruction theory for realistic mathematics education – RME theory for short – for
mathematics teacher education. The general point of departure of RME
approaches is that students should be given the opportunity to reinvent
mathematics. According to Freudenthal, who was the founding father of what we
now call realistic mathematics education, mathematics has to be (re)invented. This
singular point about student (re)invention or construction forms the basis for this
chapter. I will therefore spend a part of the chapter justifying this position and try
to show the shortcomings of mathematics education that is based on a view of
learning as making connections between what you know and what you do not yet
know. I will, then, illuminate how RME addresses those issues. It needs to be
acknowledged that enacting an RME approach is quite different from theorising
about it and that the RME approach is very demanding for teachers. This is why I
also elaborate on the requirements that need to be fulfilled in order to bring about
instruction that is consistent with RME principles.

The chapter has the following structure. I start by discussing the common view
of learning as making connections between what one knows, and what one needs to
learn. I do so by asking the question, 'What makes mathematics so difficult?' Next
I argue that the alternative notion of learning as constructing or (re)inventing offers
a better chance of helping students learn mathematics. Then, I describe the RME
approach as an example of a domain-specific instruction theory that tries to give

D. Tirosh and T. Wood (eds.), Tools and Processes in Mathematics Teacher Education, 283–302.

directions for how to guide students in such a process. I do this by elaborating RME in terms of three instructional design heuristics: (1) guided reinvention, (2) didactical phenomenology, and (3) emergent modelling. Finally, I turn to the question, what does it take to effectuate the intended form of mathematics education in the classroom? In this respect, I discuss the need for a 'reinvention route', the willingness of students to (re)invent, and the competency of the teacher to guide the reinvention process. These three requirements will be translated into teacher competencies, which are used for a final discussion of how teacher education may provide for such competencies.

LEARNING AS MAKING CONNECTIONS

The difficulty of learning mathematics is often explained by referring to the gap between the student's personal knowledge and the abstract formal mathematical knowledge that is to be acquired. From a constructivist perspective, however, it may be argued that the problem is not simply in the gap that has to be bridged. The problem is that, for the student, there is nothing at the other side of the bridge. The gap-metaphor presupposes an objective body of knowledge that exists independently of some agent. According to constructivism, knowledge is constructed by someone, and cannot be separated from the constructing individual. Thus for those who have not yet constructed the more sophisticated mathematical knowledge that has to be learned, this more sophisticated mathematical knowledge, literally, does not exist.

Nevertheless, the gap-metaphor seems to be rather generally treated as plausible. This may be explained by the fact that we, as adult mathematics educators, *perceive* our own abstract mathematical knowledge as an independent body of knowledge. We experience mathematical objects such as 'tens', 'ones', and 'hundreds', for instance, or 'linear functions', to mention another example, as object-like entities that can be pointed to and spoken about. This experience relates not only to our individual mathematical sophistication, but also to our experience of being able to talk and reason about these 'objects' unproblematically while interacting with others. As a consequence, we may assume that we can talk and reason about these 'objects' with students as well. Likewise, teachers and textbook authors may take their own abstract mathematical knowledge for an external body of knowledge, which can be communicated to students. The difference between the abstract knowledge of the teachers and the experiential knowledge of the students, however, constitutes a serious source of miscommunication – as ample research shows.

Identifying a problem, however, is not the same as solving it. Constructivism in itself does not give an answer to how to teach mathematics. To elaborate this point, we may turn to Cobb's (1994) discussion of the notion of 'constructivist pedagogy'. He starts by observing that constructivism is often reduced to the mantra-like slogan that 'students construct their own knowledge'. A mantra that, he argues, is not only erroneously treated as a fact that is beyond justification, but also as a direct instructional recommendation. Concerning the latter, the common line of reasoning is that, since the students necessarily construct their own knowledge, the teacher's role is limited to that of facilitating students' investigations and explorations. Cobb (1994, p. 4), however, argues,

> On alternative reading, the constructivist maxim about learning can be taken to imply that students construct their ways of knowing in even the most authoritarian of instructional situations.

In other words, the assumption that students construct their own knowledge cannot be directly translated into an instructional recommendation. This does not mean that constructivism cannot play a role in developing an instructional approach for mathematics education, but the critical issue is not whether students are constructing, but *what* and *how* they are constructing. Thus, taking a constructivist perspective implies that one has to consider the question, what it is that we want the students to construct, and how we want them to construct it.

LEARNING AS CONSTRUCTING OR INVENTING

Many years ago, Freudenthal (1971, 1973) addressed the theme of what mathematics is, or what we want it to be for our students, from a different angle. He took his point of departure in the notion of 'mathematics as a human activity'. Being a mathematician himself, he characterizes mathematics as the activity of mathematicians that involves solving problems, looking for problems, and mathematizing subject matter. The latter may concern mathematizing mathematical matter, or mathematizing subject matter from reality, in which mathematizing stands for organizing subject matter from a mathematical point of view. In his view, the main activity of mathematicians is that of mathematizing. The final stage of this activity is formalizing by way of axiomatizing. The result of this activity, he goes on to say, is taken as a starting point in traditional mathematics instruction. He calls this an anti-didactical inversion, for the endpoint of the work of generations of mathematicians is taken as the starting point for the instruction of students. As an alternative, he advocates for giving students the opportunity to do what mathematicians do. Instead of presenting mathematics as a ready-made product, the primary goal of mathematics education should be to engage students in mathematics as an activity. Then, similar to the way in which the mathematical activity of mathematicians has resulted in mathematics as we know it, the activity of students should result in the construction of such mathematics. In this scenario, the students have to be supported in inventing mathematics. In this respect, Freudenthal (1973) speaks of *guided reinvention*. Guidance by teachers and textbooks is not only needed to ensure that the mathematics that the students invent corresponds with conventional mathematics, but also to substantially curtail the invention process. Students cannot simply reinvent the mathematics that took the brightest mathematicians eons to develop. Teachers need to help students along, while trying to make sure that the students experience their learning as a process of 'inventing' mathematics.

Over time, Freudenthal's ideas have been elaborated in the so-called domain-specific instruction theory for realistic mathematics education (RME), which I elucidate in the following paragraphs. I start with an example, which concerns the constitution and flexible use of a framework of number relations up to 20.

Flexible Arithmetic Up to 20 as an Example

In the above, we marked the significant difference between the abstract knowledge of teachers and the experiential knowledge of students. Following Freudenthal (1991), we might even speak of different realities. He defines reality as, 'what (...) common sense experiences as real' (Freudenthal, 1991, p. 17). He argues that what is common sense for a layman is different from what is common sense for a mathematician. A similar distinction applies to teachers and students. We may illustrate this with the following example.

At a certain age, young children do not understand the question: How much is 4+4? Even though they may at this stage very well understand that 4 apples and 4 apples make 8 apples. The explanation for this apparent paradox is that, for those children, a number do not yet have an independent meaning in and of itself. For these children, numbers are tied to countable objects, as in 'four apples', 'four marbles', or 'four ice creams'. 'Four' is more like an adjective than a noun for them. At a higher level, '4' will be associated with various number relations, such as: $4 = 2+2 = 3+1 = 5-1 = \frac{8}{2}$, and so on. At this higher level, numbers have become mathematical objects that derive their meaning from a network of number relations (Van Hiele, 1973). We might in fact speak of the construal of a new mathematical reality in which numbers are experienced as mathematical objects.

When elementary-school teachers talk about numbers, they may very well be speaking about mathematical objects, which are not part of the students' experiential realities. The result is that teachers and students in fact speak different languages – without being aware of it. Teachers talk about numbers as mathematical objects that exist within a network of numerical relations. They may, for instance, explain that '7+6 equals 13 because 7+3 = 10, 6 = 3+3, and 10+3 equals 13'. The students, however, who have not yet construed the necessary network of numerical relations and think of numbers as adjectives, cannot follow this line of reasoning. The result of this miscommunication will be that the students will have to revert to copying and memorizing.

According to Van Hiele (ibid), we may avoid this problem by helping students to construct a network of number relations, within which numbers have become mathematical objects. The goal will be that the students will come to have the experience of directly perceiving numerical relationships as they interpret and solve arithmetical problem situations. That is to say that they will be able to flexibly solve tasks such as '7+6' by using numerical relationships that will be readily available for them, such as '7+3 = 10, 6 = 3+3, and 10+3', or '6+6 = 12, 6+1 = 7, and 12+1 = 13', or '7+7 = 14, 6-1 = 7 and 14-1 = 13'. Although *we* may perceive these solutions, as applying strategies – such as 'filling up ten', and so on, this does not have to be the case for the students. The instructional intent is that the students will be guided by their familiarity with number relations, and do not have to think of strategies.

This analysis suggests that the first step in a reinvention approach would be to involve the students in activities of structuring quantities in a wide variety of situations, to make them aware of the number relations involved, and to help them construct number relations by generalizing over the various situations. The question that arises here is which relations should be focused upon? To find an answer to this question, one may start by looking at research on students' informal solution strategies. Research shows that students frequently develop strategies that make use of the doubles, and five and ten as points of reference (Gravemeijer, 1994). The spontaneous use of five and ten as reference points can be traced back to the creation of finger patterns (Van der Berg & Van Eerde, 1985; Treffers, 1991). Assuming that these patterns themselves may emerge as curtailments of counting on the fingers by one, instruction may start by working with finger patterns. Students may be asked, for instance, to show 'eight' in different ways, and the teacher may draw the attention to the number relations involved. Eight is shown as '5+3', or as '4+4', whereas it may also be construed as '10-2'. As a next step in a reinvention route, we may want students to use this knowledge to derive new number relations. As a means of support, students might use a so-called *arithmetic rack* (Treffers, 1991, see Figure 1), which is designed to support numerical reasoning in which five, ten, and doubles are used as points of reference.

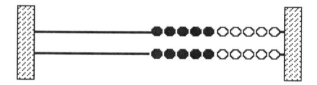

Figure 1. Arithmetic rack.

This device consists of two parallel rods each containing ten beads. The first five beads on the left of each rod are red, and the second five beads are white. Students use the rack by moving all beads to the right and then creating various configurations by sliding beads to the left. For example, if a student wants to show eight, he or she may move five beads on the top rod and three on the bottom, or he/she may move four beads on each rod. These ways of acting with the arithmetic rack may facilitate the use of the relations that come to the fore in finger patterns.

As a caveat, it should be noted that there is a danger of superficial learning in this set up. In fact, the only gain of the first example may be that, instead of being told that 4+4 equals 8, the students now 'come to see' that 4+4 equals 8. To avoid this, the instructional activities have to surpass the level of merely structuring sets of objects and reading of answers. Instead, we would want students be able to reason that 4+4=8, on the basis of some counting procedure, for instance. An important issue here is that the number patterns that the students construct come to signify curtailments of the procedure for quantifying sets of objects by counting individual objects. In this manner, visual patterns, such as finger patterns, come to embody the results of counting, to use Steffe, Cobb, and von Glasersfeld's (1988) terms. This implies that the students have to construe procedures for establishing sums or differences – such as counting on, and counting back – as extensions of the counting procedure that they use for quantifying sets of objects. The importance hereof is shown by research of Gray and Tall (1994), who observe that students, who have come to see the first and the latter as two unrelated procedures, do not use 'derived facts' strategies.

Similar risks are attached to the arithmetic rack. Here too, the intent is not that students will use the arithmetic rack configurations to read off number relations. Instead, students are expected to use the arithmetic rack as a means of scaffolding. To be able to use the arithmetic rack in this manner, students already have to have developed five-, ten-, and doubles-referenced number relations. To find the sum of 6 and 7, for instance, the students may then use their knowledge that 6=5+1 and 7=5+2 to visualize 6 and 7 on the rack as 5 red and 1 white on the top rod and 5 red and 2 white on the bottom rod, then to subsequently take the two fives together and reason, that 6+7 = 5+1+5+2 = 10+3 = 13. Or they may realize that 7=6+1, and 6+6=12, and relate this to of 6 on the top rod and 6 at the bottom and reason 7+6 = 12+1 = 13, while pointing to the rack.

As our example shows, the design of an instructional sequence that may give rise to a reinvention process is rather complicated. We would not expect teachers to design such instructional sequences themselves. This is a far more demanding task than what is usually taken on in lesson studies. Fortunately, however, that will not be necessary. Since the early 1970s, researchers/instructional designers at the Freudenthal Institute and elsewhere have worked on developing instructional sequences that would fit Freudenthal's conception of guided reinvention. An important aspect of this work was the explication of the rationales behind each of the instructional sequences. Such a rationale, or *local instruction theory*, consists of a theory about a possible learning process for a given topic, and the means of supporting that process. The theory is called local in that it is tailored to a given topic, such as addition of fractions, multiplication of decimals, or data analysis. Each local instruction theory offers a description of, and rationale for, the envisioned learning path as it relates to a set of instructional activities for a specific topic.

The local instruction theories developed at the Freudenthal Institute have been taken as a basis for the construal of a more general instructional theory. By generalizing over those local instruction theories, Treffers (1987) deduced, what he called, a framework for a domain-specific instruction theory for realistic mathematics education. Later, RME theory was recast in terms of three design heuristics: guided reinvention, didactical phenomenology, and emergent modelling (Gravemeijer, 1989), which I will discuss in the following section.

RME THEORY

Guided Reinvention as an Instructional Design Heuristic

Guided reinvention not only describes the overall approach of RME, but it can also be seen as an instructional design heuristic. Taken as a heuristic for design, the reinvention principle suggests the instructional designer to look at the history of mathematics to see how certain mathematical practices developed over time. The designer is advised to especially look for potential conceptual barriers, dead ends, and breakthroughs. These may be taken into account when designing a potential reinvention route. As a second guideline the reinvention principle suggests investigating whether students' informal interpretations and solutions might 'anticipate' more formal mathematical practices. If so, students' initially informal reasoning can be used as a starting point for the reinvention process. In summary, the designer may take both the history of mathematics and students' informal interpretations as sources of inspiration for delineating a tentative, potential route along which reinvention might evolve.

As a special point of attention we may note that reinvention has both an individual and a collective aspect, it is the interaction between students in particular that functions as a catalyst. The designer needs to develop instructional activities that are bound to give rise to a variety of student responses. What is aimed for is a variety in responses that to some extent mirrors the reinvention route. When some students come up with more advanced forms of reasoning than others, teachers can exploit these differences. They can try to frame the mathematical issue that underlies those differences as a topic for discussion. In orchestrating such a discussion, they can then foster the reinvention process. Without such differences, the teacher will not have a basis for organizing a productive classroom discussion, and will have to ask leading questions to solicit the preferred responses.

In relation to this, we may note that reinvention is intimately tied to the activity of mathematizing, more to vertical mathematization than to horizontal mathematization (which is more tied to mathematizing problem situations). In connection to this, we may distinguish between mathematical interest and pragmatic interest. One of the points of departure of RME is that contextual problems should not only be experientially real, the problems also have to be realistic. It has to be plausible for the students that someone wants to know the answer, thus the context has to offer a reason for wanting to know the answer. In this manner, students are to be motivated to solve contextual problems for pragmatic reasons. Vertical mathematizing, however, requires them to be interested in the mathematical aspects, for mathematics sake. This mathematical interest may not come naturally but has to be cultivated by the teacher by asking questions such as: What is the general principle here? Why does this work? Does it always work? Can we describe it in a more precise manner? We may assume that the teacher can foster the students' mathematical interest by making mathematical questions a topic of conversation, and showing a genuine interest in the students' mathematical reasoning.

Didactical Phenomenology as an Instructional Design Heuristic

The second RME design heuristic concerns the didactical phenomenological analysis, or *didactical phenomenology* for short (Freudenthal, 1983). Here the word 'phenomenological' refers to a phenomenology of mathematics. In this phenomenology, the focus is on how mathematical 'thought-things' (which may be concepts, procedures, or tools) organize – as Freudenthal (1983) puts it – certain phenomena. Knowing how certain phenomena are organized by the *thought thing* under consideration, one can envision how a task setting in which students are to mathematize those phenomena may create the need for them to develop the intended *thought thing*. In this manner, problem situations may be identified, which may be used as starting points for a reinvention process. Note that such starting-point-situations may also be used to explore the students' informal strategies. To find the phenomena that may constitute starting-point-situations, we may look at applications of the concept, procedure or tool under consideration. Assuming that mathematics has emerged as a result of solving practical problems, we may presume that the present-day applications encompass the phenomena, which originally had to be organized. Consequently the designer is advised to analyze present-day applications in order to find starting points for a reinvention route. Note, however, that as the students progress further in mathematics, applications may concern mathematics itself. Essential for valuable starting points is that they are experientially real for the students, that those concern situations, in which the students know how to act and reason sensibly.

Emergent, Modeling as an Instructional Design Heuristic

The third RME design heuristic is called *emergent modelling* (Gravemeijer, 1999). This design heuristic takes its point of departure in the activity of modelling. Modelling in this conception is an activity that students may employ when solving a contextual problem. Such a modelling activity might involve making drawings, diagrams, or tables, or it could involve developing informal notations or using conventional mathematical notations. The conjecture is that acting with the models will help the students to reinvent the more formal mathematics that is aimed for. Initially, the models come to the fore as context-specific models. The models refer to concrete or paradigmatic situations, which are experientially real for the students. Initial models should allow for informal strategies that correspond with situated solution strategies at the level of the situation of the contextual problem. Then, while the students gather more experience with similar problems, their attention may shift towards the mathematical relations and strategies. This helps them to further develop those mathematical relations, which enables them to use the model in a different manner: The model becomes more important as a base for reasoning about these mathematical relations than as a way of representing a contextual problem. In this manner, the model starts to become a means of support for more formal mathematics. Or more precisely: A *model of* informal mathematical activity develops into a *model for* more formal mathematical reasoning.

Underlying this transformation is a gradual shift in level of activity, from 'referential level' to a 'general level' (Gravemeijer, Cobb, Bowers, & Whitenack, 2000). At the referential level, the model derives its meaning for the students from its reference to activity in the task setting. With help of the teacher, the attention is shifted towards the mathematical relations involved. At the general level, the model starts to derive meaning from these mathematical relations, and starts to become a model for more formal mathematical reasoning. Finally the students may reach the level of more formal mathematical activity, when a new piece of mathematical reality is formed, and mathematical reasoning is no longer dependent on the support of a model. Note that although we may speak of a model that is first constituted as a *'model of'* that gradually changes into a *'model for'*, the students actually will be working with a series of sub-models, which may take the form of inscriptions or tools. From the perspective of the researcher/designer however, the series of sub-models constitute an overarching model. It is this overarching model that co-evolves with some new mathematical reality. The emergent, modelling design heuristic asks of the designer to explicate this new mathematical reality, i.e., the framework of mathematical relations and the mathematical objects that constitute this mathematical reality. This explication is not only important for instructional design, it can also inform teachers about what mathematical relations to focus on in classroom discussions.

An issue of concern is that even though the designer intends for the use of inscriptions or tools to be experienced as bottom-up by the students, this will not necessarily be the case. The teacher will therefore have to try to monitor, what new sub-models signify for the students. Here we may use the term 'imagery' to refer to the question of whether acting with the tools evokes an image of earlier activities, on the basis of which the students can make sense of the new sub-models.

In addition, measures may be taken to ensure that new (sub-) models come to the fore as a natural extension of earlier activities. The teacher may, for instance, introduce a new way of symbolising in an informal off-hand manner, and wait and see if the students will appropriate this way of notating. A decisive criterion here is whether the students adopt and adapt the new form of symbolising in a flexible manner. Another way may be to try to create the need for a new tool by problematizing the current state of affairs, and asking the students for their solutions. Then, after that the solutions offered by the students have been discussed, the teacher may present the next tool as the solution that was chosen by someone in the given context. Even if the students did not come up with the next tool, the preceding discussion would at least have provided a basis on which the students could conclude that the teacher's proposed solution was sensible under the given conditions.

RME Design Heuristics Clarified with a Local Instruction Theory for Flexible Arithmetic up to 20

We may briefly return to our example of flexible arithmetic up to 20, to further elucidate the aforementioned design heuristics. The reinvention principle suggests to not just teach some ready-made strategies, such as 'filling up ten', or 'using doubles'. Instead, the designers will ask themselves how flexible mental computation might emerge. The analysis of informal solution procedures showed that students may develop a framework of number relations that offers the building blocks for flexible mental computation (see also Greeno, 1991). In addition, we observed that 'counting on' and 'counting back' have their roots in counting as a means for establishing quantities.

For the didactical phenomenological analysis, we may refer to Freudenthal (1983), who observes that numbers organize the phenomenon of quantity, while addition organizes phenomena such as combining two sets – as in 5 cars and 3 cars or 5 marbles and 3 marbles. There are, however, he adds, other situations, where addition is not plainly recognizable as the union of two sets. Take for instance, John has 5 marbles, and Pete has 3 more. How many does Pete have? Here, the students must consider the imaginary set of Pete as split into two sets, and reason from there. He goes on to say that there are also spatial or temporal phenomena where one cannot speak of a union of two unstructured sets. With spatial or temporal phenomena such as adding 5 steps (of stairs) and 3 steps, 5 days and 3 days, or 5 kilometres and 3 kilometres, counting is used to organize magnitudes, in which sad the magnitude is articulated by the natural multiples of a unit. Continuous phenomena are made discrete by a one-to-one mapping of the successive intervals on a sequence of points that follow each other in space or time, in a process that in turn suggests a counting process. In line with this sequential character, the results of additions of magnitudes are obtained by counting on. In relation to this, Freudenthal (ibid, p. 99) points to the close relation between cardinal and ordinal numbers: '5+3 is defined cardinally, but from olden times it has been calculated ordinarily'. The result of 5+3 is obtained by starting with the mental 5, and counting on, 6, 7, 8. At the same time, it shows that counting strategies, such as counting on and counting back, rely on integrating the cardinal aspect of number (quantity) and the ordinal aspect of number (position/rank). Most addition and subtraction problems concern quantities, while the solution procedures consist of moving up and down the number sequence. From this we may conclude that it is important that the students connect the first and the latter.

For emergent modelling, we may focus on the role of the arithmetic rack, as it was elaborated in a research project in Nashville, Tennessee (Gravemeijer, Cobb, Bowers, & Whitenack, 2000). The arithmetic rack is designed with potential useful number relations in mind. In this manner, the students may use the rack as a means of scaffolding basic number relations, and as a basis for developing more elaborate frameworks of number relations. On a more practical level, the designer will first have to look for situations that can be modelled with the arithmetic rack. Here one may make use of instructional activities that are designed by Van den Brink

(1989), which involve the double-decker bus scenario. Initial tasks then concern different ways in which a given number of passengers could sit on the two decks of a double-decker bus. Follow-up activities involve situations in which some passengers get on and others get off the bus. Next the arithmetic rack can be introduced as a means of showing the number of passengers on each deck, and as means of keeping track of the number of people getting on or off the bus. In this way, the rack can initially function as a model of (the changes in) the number of passengers on the two decks. An important step in the modelling process will then be to ask the students to develop ways of notating their reasoning with the rack so that they can communicate it to others. Subsequent activities involve developing and negotiating symbolizations, the key criterion being that other children in the class could understand how the task had been solved. For example, the ways of reasoning with rack about 7+8 might be symbolized as shown in Figure 2.

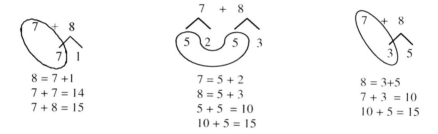

Figure 2. Ways of visualizing arithmetic rack solution strategies.

By then, drawings of the way of reasoning with the rack will be functioning as models for more formal mathematical reasoning. Finally the student may start using number sentences without any auxiliary drawings.

A Local Instruction Theory on Data Analysis as an Example

To clarify the emergent modelling design heuristic a bit further, I will briefly discuss another example of a local instruction theory that is taken from a teaching experiment on data analysis carried out by Cobb, Gravemeijer, McClain and Konold in a 7th-grade (12 year-olds) classroom in Nashville (see also Gravemeijer & Cobb, 2006). The general goal of this local instruction theory is that the students come to view data sets as distributions, of which one can discern characteristics that are relevant when resolving issues concerning the situation where the measurements have been taken. The starting points for the instructional activities are realistic problems that provide a reason for analysing data. Having a reason is essential in our view, for this rationale guides the very process of data analysis. In conventional statistics courses, statistical measures like mean, mode, median, spread, quartiles, (relative) frequency, regression, and correlation are taught as a set of independent definitions. These statistical measures, however, are characteristics of distributions. So, for these measures to have meaning, students have to have a notion of distributions as objects that can have certain characteristics. Likewise, conventional representations like histogram and box plot come to the fore as means to characterize distributions. We reasoned therefore, that instead of teaching statistical measures and representations as such, one should focus on helping students in developing the notion of distribution as an object.

The notion 'distribution' is closely tied to the graph with which we visualize a distribution. Distribution then can be thought of in terms of shape, density, and position. A way to think about such a graph is as a density function. This offers a way into a qualitative understanding of distribution. In such a conceptualization, the height of a point on the graph signifies the density of data points around that value. From a didactical phenomenological point of view, we may speak of the graph as a means for organizing density. Density in turn can be seen as means for organizing collections of data points in a space of possible data values. From the same phenomenological perspective, data points in a dot plot may be thought of as a way of getting a handle on a set of data. With such an analysis, we already have a rough outline of a series of sub models. In relation to this, we may describe the overarching model as 'a graphical representation of the shape of a distribution'.

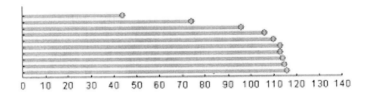

Figure 3. Value-bar graph.

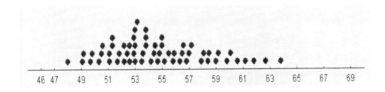

Figure 4. Dot plot.

The most common graph of a distribution is the graph of a density function we discussed earlier. However, the graph to start the sequence with would have to be a graph that would most closely match an intuitive visualization of a measure for the students. This in our view is a scale line. Especially measures of a linear type, like 'length', and 'time' are often represented by scale lines in primary school. These considerations let to the decision to start with a graph that consists of value bars, with each value bar signifying a single measure (Figure 3). Within a magnitude-value-bar graph, the distribution of the data values is visible in the way the endpoints of the value bars are distributed in regard to the axis. In relation to this, we can speak of *a graphical representation of the distribution* as a *model of* a set of measures. Next the students may come to see the dot plot as a more condensed form of a value-bar graph that leaves out the value bars and only keeps the end points (Figure 4). Within a dot plot, the density of the data points in a given region translates itself in the way the dots are stacked. Consequently, the height of the stacked dots at a given position can be interpreted as a measure for the density at that position. In this sense, the visual shape of the dot plot can be seen as a qualitative precursor to the graph of a density function. This aspect can be further developed by having the students' structure data into four equal groups, when resolving issues concerning the situations where the measurements have been taken. They may come to see the distance between two vertical bars that mark a quartile in a four-equal-groups display as indicating how much the data are 'bunched up'. Moreover, the median may start to function as an indicator of 'where the hill is' in a uni-modal distribution. Finally, the students are expected to begin to treat distributions as entities. In this regard, we may describe the four-equal groups displayed as *a graphical representation of the distribution* that starts to function as a *model of* a model for reasoning about distributions.

WHAT DOES IT TAKE TO ENACT RME?

RME Theory and Local Instruction Theories

After having depicted RME theory, I now move to the question, what are the implications of this theory for mathematics teacher education? I try to derive those implications from considering the question, what does it take to bring about instruction that is in tune with RME? I discern three requirements. As a first requirement, I argue that one has to have a sound idea about what the intended reinvention process may look like for a given topic. That is to say one has to have a plan for a possible reinvention route. A second requirement is that the students have to be willing to invent, which is less self-evident than it may sound. The third requirement concerns the capability of the teacher to support the intended reinvention process. I elaborate those three requirements in the following paragraphs.

The Need for a Planned Reinvention Route

In my view, designing reinvention processes is a very complicated task that surpasses the scope of what may be expected of teachers. I want to argue therefore that teachers should be offered a more general framework that enables them to design instructional activities on a day-to-day basis. Such a framework may be offered by a so-called local instruction theory, which consists of a theory about a possible learning process for a given topic, and the means of supporting that process. A valuable feature of RME theory is that it is (being) developed by way of generalizing over exemplary instructional sequences, or local instruction theories. A consequence of this is that RME theory comes with a set of local instruction theories, which are consistent with RME. Each local instruction theory offers a description of, and rationale for, the envisioned learning path as it relates to a set of instructional activities for a specific topic (such as 'addition and subtraction up to 20', 'area', 'fractions', and so forth). Those local instruction theories can function as frameworks of reference for teachers. Here we may refer to Simon's (1995) notion of a 'hypothetical learning trajectory'. Simon argues that a teacher who wants to build on the students' thinking and activity, and at the same time work towards given learning goals has to consider what mental activities the students might engage in as they participate in the instructional activities, he or she is considering. A decisive criterion of choice then would be how those mental activities relate to the chosen learning goal. In relation to this, Simon (ibid) speaks of designing a hypothetical learning trajectory. He emphasizes the hypothetical character of these learning trajectories; the teachers are to analyse the reactions of the students in light of the stipulated learning trajectory to find out in how far the actual learning trajectory corresponds with what was envisioned. Based on this information the teacher has to construe new or adapted instructional activities in connection with a revised learning trajectory.

Local instruction theories can function as frameworks of reference in this process. The relation between the local instruction theory and the hypothetical learning trajectories can be elucidated with a travel metaphor (Simon, 1995). In terms of a travel metaphor, the local instruction theory offers a 'travel plan', which the teacher has to transpose into an actual 'journey' with his or her students. The idea is that the teachers will use their insight in the local instruction theory to choose instructional activities, and to design hypothetical learning trajectories for their own students. Here the teachers will orient themselves to the actual thinking and reasoning of their students. Consequently, they may look for forms of assessment that are tailored to revealing student thinking and reasoning. In line with this idea a RME approach to assessment has been developed that aims at creating opportunities for students to show what they know and can do. Instead of, as is often the case with a test, showing what students are not (yet) able to. This kind of assessment is also called 'didactical assessment' (Van den Heuvel-Panhuizen & Becker, 2003) in that it tries to find footholds for instruction that may follow the test.

I close this section by noting, that the issue of how to document local instruction theories is not really resolved yet. The traditional form of textbooks and teacher guides will not be adequate. For, key in the kind of instruction that I discuss here is that it is responsive to the input of the students, and adaptable to the beliefs and concerns of the teachers. A possible solution may lay in an elaboration of the 'model-of/model-for' shift that can be taken as the backbone of an RME instructional sequence. As noted before, that model can take on different manifestations during the realization of an instructional sequence. Those sub-models can be described as a chain of signification (Whitson, 1997), which details not only the manifestations and progression of the model, but also the evolving taken-as-shared meaning and purposes of the classroom community. The local instruction theory then can be described as an anticipated chain of signification, by describing the anticipated tools that will be used and the imagery, mathematical activity and mathematical practices that correspond to them (Gravemeijer, 2004).

The Willingness of Students to (Re)Invent

In the above, I extensively discussed one of the basic prerequisites for reinvention, the plan for a reinvention route. Another prerequisite is that the students are willing to invent. This seems a rather trivial point. I have to take into account, however, that students are often familiar with a classroom culture in which the classroom social norms (Cobb & Yackel, 1996) are that the teacher has the right answers, that the students are expected to follow given procedures, and that correct answers are more important than one's own reasoning. In this type of classrooms teachers usually ask questions of which they already know the answer. Apart from being used to this situation, students have learned what to expect and what is expected from them. In relation to this, Brousseau (1988) speaks of an implicit 'didactical contract'. Significant, however, is that the students have learned this by experience, not because the teacher told them so. This may be illustrated by research of Elbers (1988), who asked students in kindergarten, 'What is heavier, red or blue?' The students gave different answers, but what was striking was that they gave answers at all. The explanation for this is that they already held very specific expectations for their role. For them, it was quite normal for the teacher to ask questions they could not answer. They had learned that they had to give an answer, any answer, to enable the teacher to proceed. Later on they might learn in retrospect why that question was asked.

In contrast to the traditional classroom culture, reinvention asks for an inquiry-oriented classroom culture. The classroom has to work as a learning community. To make this happen, the students have to adopt classroom social norms such as the obligation to explain and justify their solutions. They are expected to try and understand other students' reasoning, and to ask questions if they do not understand, and challenge arguments they do not agree with. In addition to those social norms, Cobb and Yackel (1996) discern socio-mathematical norms. Where the classroom social norms are, in a sense, content free – they could yield for any topic – socio-mathematical norms relate to what mathematics is. These socio-mathematical norms encompass, for instance, what counts as a mathematical problem, and what counts as a mathematical solution. Important also is, what counts as a more sophisticated solution, for this relates to vertical mathematizing. One has to have a norm for expecting what is mathematically more advanced to be able to advance in a reinvention process. In this respect, I may argue that socio-mathematical norms provide the basis for the intellectual autonomy of the students, as it enables them to decide for themselves on mathematical progress.

In addition to appropriating inquiry-based norms, students also have to be willing to invest effort in solving mathematical problems, discussing solutions, and discussing the underlying ideas. The students' willingness to participate in learning activities is the outcome of a reciprocal process that depends on both individual attributes and contextual features such as classroom climate and instructional support. Students may engage in learning activities for different reasons. The attitude of students in a mathematics classroom can be broadly divided in two categories, *ego orientation* and *task orientation* (Nicholls, Cobb, Wood, Yackel, & Patashnick, 1990). On the one hand, ego orientation implies that the student is very conscious of the way he or she might be perceived by others. Ego-oriented students are afraid to fail, or to look stupid in the eyes of their fellow students, or the teacher. As a consequence, they may choose to not even try to solve a given problem, in order to avoid embarrassment. Task orientation, on the other hand, implies that the student's concern is with the task itself, and on finding ways of solving that task. Research shows that task orientation and ego orientation can be influenced by teachers.

Cobb, Yackel and Wood (1989) report on a study on a socio-constructivist classroom, where task orientation was fostered. Part of their approach was to change the classroom culture from one of competition, where students would compare themselves with each other, and with the criteria set by the teacher, into a classroom culture, where students would measure success by comparing their results with their own results earlier. One may think of the latter perspective as one similar to that of an amateur painter or amateur musician. An amateur musician would not think of comparing him- or herself with others; there would always be many people performing better. Instead an amateur musician would be pleased if he or she would master a piece, which he/she could not play some time ago. A similar situation is possible in a mathematics classroom, where the goal for the students would be personal growth. Here, experiencing an 'Aha-Erlebnis', will function as an incentive. In such a classroom, students might even protest at being given 'the solution', for that would deprive them from the satisfaction of figuring out things for themselves. Such a process of figuring out may very well have the character of collaborative work, where the students see themselves as community that works towards shared understanding. In fact, the aforementioned research of Cobb et al. (1989) shows that a classroom culture that emphases the exchange of ideas, and the development of mathematical understanding as a collaborative endeavor, fosters the task orientation of the students. It may be noted, however, that teachers need to strike a balance between creating freedom for the students to figure things out by themselves and offering support. Research of Turner, Midgley, Meyer, Gheen, Anderman, Kang, and Patrick (2002) shows that too much freedom or challenge can have a negative effect on student's feeling of self-confidence, when the students may have too thin a knowledge base to build on.

Teacher Competencies for Guiding the Reinvention Process

The aforementioned requirements already imply a central role for the teacher. The role and competencies of the teacher constitute a third requirement for reinvention. One may structure those roles and competencies in three categories, one that concerns the planning and design of instructional activities and hypothetical learning trajectories, one that concerns the classroom culture, and one that concerns the orchestration of the collective reinvention process.

A central competency in the category *planning* is that of designing, evaluating, and revising instructional activities and hypothetical learning trajectories that both fit the current state of affairs in the classroom and a given local instruction theory. In connection with this the teacher has to be able to identify experientially real starting points, a competency that may be supported by the ability to design and use didactical assessment tasks. Another competency concerns the identification of mathematical objects and mathematical relations at which the instructional activities are aimed.

In the category *classroom culture*, of course, the competency to establish and maintain the intended classroom social norms and social-mathematical norms comes to the fore as a central competency. In addition to this I may mention the ability to cultivate mathematical interest, and to foster task orientation over ego orientation. An additional competency will be that of the ability to instill in the students an orientation towards a perspective of personal growth.

The first two categories are complemented by competency to orchestrate the *collective reinvention process*. The teacher has to be able to see his or her plans through, and to grasp and assess the students' thinking and reasoning. He or she has to be able to introduce a new way of symbolizing in an informal off-hand manner, or create the need for a new tool, and assess whether the new tool signifies earlier activities, and if the students adopt and adapt symbolizations or tools in a flexible manner. An additional competency concerns the ability to see what differences in mathematical understanding underlie the variation in student responses, to frame mathematical issues as topics for discussion on the basis of this insight, and to orchestrate productive whole-class discussions on those mathematical issues.

HOW TO FOSTER RME TEACHER COMPETENCIES IN TEACHER EDUCATION

The above list of teacher's roles and competencies sets the agenda for teacher education. It will be impossible to give a detailed account of how mathematics teacher education can help students in developing those competencies. A golden rule, however, will be to teach what you preach. That is to say that the prospective teacher has to be educated in a way that mirrors the way they are expected to teach by themselves. One of the main themes will be to enable the prospective teachers to work with local RME instructional theories. In particular, a course such as this may be designed to have the students experience classroom norms, and reflect on how those norms are established and maintained. They may also experience, and reflect upon, the role of imagery and history in the use of tools and inscriptions. And in a similar manner, task orientation, and personal growth may be addressed in a course that aims at hypothetical learning trajectories and local instruction theories. For now, I will limit myself to a brief elaboration of such a course.

Designing hypothetical learning trajectories on the basis of (externally developed) local instruction theories and resource materials differs significantly from following scripted textbook teacher guides. Mathematics teacher education therefore has to educate prospective teachers in working with local instruction theories. An overriding goal of such a preparation is to help them to develop an autonomous attitude, which allows them to take the liberty to interpret and adapt local instruction theories. More specifically, prospective teachers learn to construe, evaluate, and revise hypothetical learning trajectories on the basis of local instruction theories. In this respect it is fortunate that most local instruction theories are the product of design research (Gravemeijer & Cobb, 2006).

The methodological norm in design research is that the learning process of the researchers/designers justify what they claim to have learned. In relation to this, one speaks of trackability (Smaling, 1992). Research reports should offer outsiders the opportunity to retrace the learning process that the designer/researcher went through. Or as Freudenthal (1991, p. 16) put it (who speaks of 'developmental research' instead of 'design research'):

> Developmental research means: 'experiencing the cyclic process of development and research so consciously, and reporting on it so candidly that it justifies itself, and that this experience can be transmitted to others to become their own experience.

Ideally, prospective teachers should be given the opportunity to experience such learning processes by some form of reinvention. Solving sequence related problems, anticipating solutions of primary or secondary school students, analysing student work and teaching episodes and such could be the constituents of such a reinvention process – where analysing student work and teaching episodes may take the form of multimedia video case studies (Dolk, Hertog, & Gravemeijer, 2002). In addition, prospective teachers should be made familiar with the overall educational philosophy that underlies the local instruction theories that they may want to use. Otherwise, it will be difficult to come to grips with these instruction theories. This overall philosophy is an integral part of the justifications of local instruction theories. For, a local instruction theory is not just a theory of how to teach a given topic; it is a theory about how to teach that topic within the framework of a certain philosophy of mathematics education.

It may not be realistic to expect the prospective teachers to develop a detailed understanding of all local instruction theories he or she might need. Instead, prospective teachers might learn to make sense of new theories on their own accord. In relation to this it will be important that the prospective teacher comes to grips with key principles that hold for all local instruction theories within a given framework – which concern mathematics as an activity, guided reinvention, didactical phenomenology, and emergent modelling. This goal may be accomplished by having prospective teachers analyse, experiment with, and reflect on, some exemplary local instruction theories. In such activities, they might gain insight in the task of developing hypothetical learning trajectories. Moreover, the key principles of RME may emerge in reflective activities under the guidance of the mathematics teacher educator. Apart from this, it can be argued that prospective teachers should be made familiar with a whole set of local instruction theories that covers the curriculum. Insight in the key principles underlying these local instruction theories may help to come to grips with the essence of these local theories.

In conclusion we may note that if we want to create mathematics classrooms within which students construct their own knowledge, mathematics teacher education must play a central role. RME can be seen as an exemplary elaboration of such an approach to mathematics education. The work from RME has produced a wide variety of instructional activities, instructional sequences, and (local) instructional theories. These, however, are merely resources; in the end, it is the teacher who enacts realistic mathematics education in the classroom. And, we will have to acknowledge that this kind of teaching is extremely demanding, which in turn possess a challenge to mathematics teacher education, both for prospective and practising teachers.

REFERENCES

Brousseau, G. (1988). Le contrat didactique: Le milieu [The didactical contract: The environment]. *Recherche en didactique des mathématiques 9*(3), 33–115.

Cobb, P. (2004). Constructivism in mathematics and science education. *Educational Researcher, 23*, 4–14.

Cobb, P., Yackel, E., & Wood, T. (1989). Young children's emotional acts while doing mathematical problem solving. In D. B. McLeod & V.M. Adams (Eds.), *Affect and mathematical problem solving A new perspective* (pp. 117–148). New York, NY: Springer-Verlag.

Cobb, P., & Yackel, E. (1996). Constructivist, emergent, and sociocultural perspectives in the context of developmental research. *Educational Psychologist, 31*, 175–190.

Dolk, M., den Hertog, J., & Gravemeijer, K. (2002). Using multimedia cases for educating the primary school mathematics teacher educator: A design study. *International Journal of Educational Research, 37*(2), 161–178.

Elbers, E. (1988). *Social context and the child's construction of knowledge*. Unpublished doctoral dissertation, University of Utrecht, Utrecht.

Freudenthal, H. (1971). Geometry between the devil and the deep sea. *Educational Studies in Mathematics, 3*, 413–435.

Freudenthal, H. (1973). *Mathematics as an educational task*. Dordrecht, the Netherlands: Reidel.

Freudenthal, H. (1983). *Didactical phenomenology of mathematical structures*. Dordrecht, the Netherlands: Reidel.

Freudenthal, H. (1991). *Revisiting mathematics education*. Dordrecht, the Netherlands: Kluwer Academic Publishers.

Gravemeijer, K. P. E. (1994). *Developing realistic mathematics education*. Utrecht, the Netherlands: CD-ß Press.

Gravemeijer, K. (1998). Developmental research as a research method, In J. Kilpatrick & A. Sierpinska (Eds.), *Mathematics education as a research domain: A search for identity (An ICMI Study). New ICMI Studies Series, Volume 1, Book 2* (pp. 277–295). Dordrecht: Kluwer Academic Publishers.

Gravemeijer, K. (1999). How emergent models may foster the constitution of formal mathematics. *Mathematical Thinking and Learning, 1*(2), 155–177.

Gravemeijer, K. (2004). Learning trajectories and local instruction theories as means of support for teachers in reform mathematics education. *Mathematical Thinking and Learning, 6*(2), 105–128.

Gravemeijer, K., Cobb, P., Bowers, J., & Whitenack, J. (2000). Symbolizing, modelling, and instructional design. In P. Cobb, E. Yackel, & K. McClain (Eds.), *Communicating and symbolizing in mathematics: Perspectives on discourse, tools, and instructional design* (pp. 225–273). Mahwah, NJ: Lawrence Erlbaum Associates.

Gravemeijer, K. P. E., & Cobb, P. (2006). Design research from a learning design perspective. In J. Akker, K. Gravemeijer, S. McKenney, & N. Nieveen (Eds.), *Educational design research* (pp. 45–85). London: Routledge, Taylor Francis Group.

Greeno, J. G. (1991). Number sense as situated knowing in a conceptual domain. *Journal for Research in Mathematics Education, 22,* 170–218.

Gray, E.M., & Tall, D. O. (1994). Duality, ambiguity and flexibility: A proceptual view of simple arithmetic. *Journal for Research in Mathematics Education, 25,* 115–141.

Nicholls, J., Cobb, P., Wood, T., Yackel, E., & Patashnick, M. (1990). Dimensions of success in mathematics: Individual and classroom differences. *Journal for Research in Mathematics Education 21,* 109–122.

Simon, M. A. (1995). Reconstructing mathematics pedagogy from a constructivist perspective. *Journal for Research in Mathematics Education, 26,* 114–145.

Smaling, A. (1992). Varieties of methodological intersubjectivity – The relations with qualitative and quantitative research, and with objectivity. *Quality & Quantity, 26,* 169–180.

Steffe, L. P., Cobb, P., & von Glasersfeld, E. (1988). *Construction of arithmetical meanings and strategies.* New York, NY: Springer-Verlag.

Treffers, A. (1987). *Three dimensions. A model of goal and theory description in mathematics education: The Wiskobas Project.* Dordrecht, the Netherlands: Reidel.

Treffers, A. (1991). Het rekenrek 1&2. *Willem Bartjens, 8*(3), 151–153; *8*(4), 199–200.

Turner, J. C., Midgley, C., Meyer, D. K., Gheen, M., Anderman, E. M., Kang, Y., & Patrick, H. (2002). The classroom environment and students' reports of avoidance strategies in mathematics: A multimethod study. *Journal of Educational Psychology, 94*(1), 88–106.

Van Hiele, P. M. (1973). *Begrip en inzicht.* Purmerend: Muusses.

Van den Berg, W., & van Eerde, D. (1985). *Kwantiwijzer [Diagnostic set of instruments].* Rotterdam, the Netherlands: SVO/Erasmus University.

Van den Brink, F. J. (1989). *Realistisch rekenonderwijs aan jonge kinderen [Realistic mathematics education for young children].* Utrecht, the Netherlands: OW&OC.

Van den Heuvel-Panhuizen, M., & Becker, J. (2003). Towards a didactic model for assessment design in mathematics education. In A. J. Bishop, M. A. Clements, C. Keitel, J. Kilpatrick, & F. K. S. Leung (Eds.), *Second international handbook of mathematics education* (pp. 689–716). Dordrecht: Kluwer Academic Publishers.

Whitson, J. A. (1997). Cognition as a semiotic process: From situated mediation to critical reflective transcendence. In D. Kirshner & J. Whitson (Eds.), *Situated cognition. Social, semiotic, and psychological perspectives* (pp. 97–149). Mahwah, NJ: Lawrence Erlbaum Associates.

Koeno Gravemeijer
Eindhoven School of Education,
Technical University of Eindhoven
The Netherlands

GENERAL PERSPECTIVES AND
CRITICAL RESPONSE TO CHAPTERS

SHLOMO VINNER

13. SOME MISSING DIMENSIONS IN MATHEMATICS TEACHER EDUCATION

In this chapter I refer to the well known fact that teacher education programs prepare their students, mainly, to cover the current mathematics curriculum. No attempt is made to place mathematics as a tool to achieve educational goals. In this chapter, an attempt is made to suggest general educational values that the school system should recommend to its students, if it expects them to become educated adults. In this chapter I also explain how some characteristics of mathematics can be used in order to present these educational values and to promote them. Thus, since great part of school mathematics is procedural, the importance of procedures in society and in everyday life can be emphasized. Other characteristics of mathematics, as analytical thinking, reflection, rational thinking are discussed as well and their role in moral behaviour is explained. Finally, the question that bothers all adolescents, namely, what are they supposed to do with their life, is raised. In this chapter, I suggest that this question should be discussed in teacher training as well, since teachers as educators should be prepared to relate to all problems of their students, not only their mathematical problems.

The use of a common word as a key notion in a book title calls for reflection on the various meanings of this word and on the possible contexts in which it can appear. Dictionaries (e.g., Merriam-Webster) tell us that the principal meaning of "tool" is a physical instrument, but it can also be a means to an end. A means to an end can be understood in a metaphorical way. In other words, a tool does not have to be physical, it can also be abstract. And indeed, if you look at titles of different chapters of this volume you will find out that some of the chapters refer to physical tools (like machines, manipulatives, figures and video) while other chapters refer to abstract tools (like narratives, tasks, examples and theories). Generally speaking, any knowledge has the potential to be a tool. Human values of different kinds can also be a tool. They direct human behaviour. In teacher education it is important to raise the question what the desirable human behaviour is. If we consider mathematics teacher training in a narrow way, we are supposed to restrict our discussion to desirable mathematical behaviour. But if we consider teachers (of any discipline) also as educators then we are supposed to deal with the question in a general way, namely, as mentioned above: What desirable human behaviour should our society (with its schools as a tool) promote? This chapter is an attempt to answer this question from a mathematics educator's point of view. Namely, how

D. Tirosh and T. Wood (eds.), Tools and Processes in Mathematics Teacher Education, 305–320.
© *2008 Sense Publishers. All rights reserved.*

can we use the teaching of mathematics as a tool to promote general educational values in our students?

My claim is that some dimensions relating to the above direction are missing from teacher education practice. I am not going to establish this claim in the common academic way; namely, I am not going to refer the reader to curriculum of mathematics teacher education at well known institutions where mathematics teacher education takes place and to show that the dimensions I discuss here are not covered by the syllabuses of the courses of these institutions. Neither are they discussed in classes as extra curricular topics. Such a mission needs a full size paper which probably will be quite boring for the reader and moreover, so I believe, it is unnecessary. For mathematics educators involved in teacher education programs it is a common knowledge, perhaps, with very few exceptions. The missing dimensions which I discuss here are: 1) The goals of teaching mathematics; 2) The goals of education in general; 3) The ways in which the goals of teaching mathematics can be used in order to achieve the general goals of education; and 4) The meaning of the teacher's work.

GOALS FOR MATHEMATICS EDUCATION

It is extremely important for everybody who has a job to understand why they are involved in this job in addition to, usually, the main reason - making one's living. Making one's living is absolutely legitimate reason in our society, but in order to carry out the job in the best way, it is better if you understand the role of the job within the system in which you work. This is true about every job, but it is especially important for teaching. It is quite clear to those in the educational system who are in charge of teachers and teacher training. Therefore they made up a special rhetoric in order to attract people to the profession of teaching, to keep them in the profession, and to increase their motivation to improve, and to cope with the difficulties. Usually the rhetoric is beautiful but, as we all know about rhetoric, it might be misleading. Such situations are well known in politics where rhetoric about human values covers, sometimes, economical interests. Unfortunately, it is true also about education. "Come and study with us and you will have an opportunity to shape the face of the future generation," says a huge poster at the gate of a well known college of education. It is quite exciting. The claim that education is supposed to shape the face of the future generation is more than reasonable. Yet, will the curriculum and the teachers of this college address that invitation through their everyday practice? Of course, such an invitation is better than another invitation of another college (fortunately, not a teacher college) which says: "Come to us and we will make you rich and famous." By claiming that one rhetoric is better than the other one, I have already got myself into a value discussion where some people might disagree with my judgment. I assume that within the circle of educators my preference is quite acceptable because the first invitation does not appeal to selfish goals. Nevertheless, selfish goals are quite legitimate in our society, at least as long as they are not amoral.

So, let us get back to mathematics education and ask what its goals are, really. By posing the question this way, there is a hint that perhaps some goals which are declared to be the goals of mathematics education are not really the goals of mathematics education in practice. They might be just rhetoric. The common rhetoric of mathematics education emphasizes the importance of studying mathematics for the future of our children and for the future of our society. The rhetoric usually does not deal with the mathematical content. The community of mathematicians and the community of mathematics educators have never reached an agreement about the topics which should be taught to the entire student population. Thus, the rhetoric mentions other aspects of learning mathematics, such as how to think analytically, how to reason, how to solve problems and how to prove. The fact is that these goals have never been reached on any large scale. They can be considered as a vision. And, indeed, the National Council of Teachers of Mathematics [NCTM], (2000) admits that "*this vision of mathematics teaching and learning is not the reality in the majority of classrooms, schools, and districts. Today,*" adds the document, "*many students are not learning the mathematics they need*".

As I mentioned above, an agreement about the needs of mathematics students has never been reached. Therefore, let us ignore the curricular questions and focus on the vision. It would be interesting to do a historical research about mathematical education documents and the visions they try to promote. It seems to me that, besides the back to basics call and other similar calls, all the visions include, perhaps with different emphasis, almost the same goals mentioned above. These documents have served the mathematics education rhetoric at least half a century. Has not the time arrived to examine the rhetoric, to reflect on it and to analyze it? If there is a huge gap between the rhetoric and the practice why do we not give up the rhetoric? The answer, I think, is very simple – we need the rhetoric. Thus, the next question is why do we need it? Here, there are some possible answers. My suggestion is that we need the rhetoric because it makes our educational work meaningful. I will elaborate on this later on. In the meantime, let us discuss the practice.

The practice is that mathematics is considered by the majority of the students as a collection of procedures to be used in order to solve some typical questions given in some crucial exams (e.g., final course exams, psychometric exams, SAT, etc.). This reflects also the way mathematics is taught by many teachers in many classes. Again, we may ask why it is so, and my answer, again, may look trivial. It is so because it satisfies the need of the majority of people involved in the process. I mean the real need, not the declared need. In the rhetorical documents there is a difference between two issues: 1) What do we want, as educators, to accomplish by teaching mathematics; and, 2) Why it is advisable to a student to learn mathematics. This difference might be the result of the difference between educators' goals and students' goals. Our goal as educators might be to promote analytical thinking, moral values and appreciation of science and art. The students' goal in life might be to enhance their chance to become "rich and famous." Therefore, the curricular documents should present some arguments to convince

SHLOMO VINNER

the students to learn mathematics. They should tell the students why it is desirable for them to study mathematics. In other words, they should explain to the students how mathematics might help them in their careers.

> *We live in a mathematical world, whenever we decide on a purchase, choose insurance or health plan, or use a spreadsheet, we rely on mathematical understanding .... The level of mathematical thinking and problem solving needed in the workplace has increased dramatically ... Mathematical competence opens doors to productive future. A lack of mathematical competence closes those doors. (NCTM, 2000)*

This is not the place to elaborate in length how misleading are these claims. In short I will say only the following: – no doubt mathematical knowledge is crucial to produce and maintain the most important aspects of our present life. This does not imply that the majority of people should know mathematics. Farming is also crucial to at least one aspect of our life – the food aspect, and yet, in developed countries, about 2% of the population can supply the needs of the entire population. In addition to this argument, if you are not convinced, I recommend that you look around and examine the mathematical knowledge of some high ranking professionals that you know – physicians, lawyers, business administrators, and many others, not to mention politicians and mass communication/media people. Thus, if the above claims about the need to study mathematics are misleading, why do our students study mathematics in spite of it all? You might suggest that the students believe in these claims although these claims are misleading. I suggest that the students have very good reasons to study mathematics. It is not the necessity of mathematics in their future professional life or their everyday life. It is because of the selection role mathematics has in all stages of our educational system. Mathematical achievements are required if you want to study in a prestigious place (whether this is a junior high school, a senior high school or university). A prestigious school increases your chance for getting a good job. This might help the vision of richness and fame become real. Confrey formulated it clearly at a Psychology of Mathematics Education presentation in 1995. *"In the vast majority of countries around the world, mathematics acts as a draconian filter to the pursuit of further technical and quantitative studies."* To this I would like to add that quite often, at some institutions, mathematics is a requirement not only for technical and quantitative studies but also for several disciplines that do not use mathematics at all, like literature, history and art.

If this is true we have a convincing argument for why we should study mathematics. We also have at least a partial explanation for the fact that mathematics is considered, and very often also taught, as a collection of procedures. This is a form which provides reasonable success to the majority of students' on the crucial exams. So, let us elaborate a little about the gap between vision and practice. It is quite clear that the vision is in the official documents and not in the classrooms. The educational system has not found a way to translate the rhetoric to practice. On one hand, the teachers are supposed to be the mediators between the rhetoric and practice. *"Educational decisions made by teachers have*

308

important consequences for students and for society," claims the NCTM (2000). On the other hand, the teachers cannot make any decision which might distract them from their presumably only task – to prepare their students for the crucial exams. In other words, their ultimate goal is to cover the syllabus. These circumstances eliminate the option to develop analytical thinking, reflection and problem solving strategies. If you want to develop these, you should relate to students' ideas, mistakes, and misconceptions; you should give examples of failure in analytical thinking, you should analyze problem solving processes and you should discuss the principles of proof and justification. A teacher who has to cover an overloaded syllabus (and all curriculum are, unfortunately, overloaded) does not have time to do anything besides the syllabus. Thus we are left with the practice mentioned above, namely, that mathematics is taught and being studied to the majority of the students as a collection of procedures to be used in order to solve some typical questions given in some crucial exams.

A reasonable conclusion of this state of affairs is to give up mathematics as a compulsory subject in schools. However, even expressing this view is dangerous to any speaker who dares to express it in any educational forum. Even less extreme suggestions about mathematics as a compulsory topic to the entire population, such as decreasing the amount of mathematics in the curriculum for the majority of the population, face strong objections from influential mathematicians and academic administrators. They consider this tendency as an attempt to lower the academic level of the country involved. But is it really the case? I doubt it. I suggest that behind it, there is the belief of some professional mathematicians that people who are mathematically ignorant are not good enough for any intellectual job. In addition, giving up mathematics as a compulsory topic will be giving up the power and influence they have on our society, and, of course, it has also some serious economical consequences to mathematics departments at the universities, as well as to the mathematical community of school mathematics teachers. Also, giving up mathematics as a compulsory topic will imply giving up mathematics as a selection tool of the different stages of the academic system, and no doubt, mathematics is an extremely efficient selection tool. Not necessarily because it leaves out those who are not suitable for higher education (and there are many people who are not suitable for higher education, fortunately and unfortunately). It is because mathematical exams can be easily formed and easily marked. Just imagine how hard it will be to use history or literature as selection tools for higher education.

Here, I return to the role of higher education for the majority of students. Its main role is to help the graduates to get a white collar job. In many such jobs, the ability to carry out procedures is crucial. So in a way, success in mathematics, the way it is taught now to the majority of students, can predict their ability to carry out many jobs in the workplace. Are mathematics teacher educators supposed to discuss such issues with their students? I believe that we have to tell our teacher-students the truth about the system in which they operate. Eventually, the teachers are the key. It is important for them to understand their role and the limits of their abilities to achieve some educational goals. Of course, it would be nicer if we could tell our student-teachers that their work is meaningful and important. However, if this is not the case, the result will be a cynical reaction. To understand what you are doing and the limits of your ability is extremely important. And again, it is much better if you can improve the situation. But sometimes, there is nothing you can do about it. It is analogous, in a way, to cognitive psychotherapy: Life is not a picnic, as we, unfortunately, all know. However, it is important for us to understand why it cannot be a picnic and hence to accept it without becoming bitter or desperate. At this point it will be suitable to quote Reinhold Niebuhr's famous prayer: *O Lord, grant me the serenity to accept the things I cannot change; the courage to change the things I can; and the wisdom to know the difference.* Another question is whether the common practice of teaching mathematics has, in spite of all, any educational values. This question leads us to a discussion about values.

THE GOALS OF EDUCATION

The assimilation of educational values in our students is supposed to be the main goal of education–but which educational values? An academic attempt to answer this question will imply infinitely long discussions, will raise bitter controversies and will last forever. In order to avoid this, I would like to suggest a non-academic and simple approach. The goal of education, according to this approach, is an educated person. Since this looks circular I will add—an educated person is a *thoughtful* person. "Thoughtful" in English, is ambiguous. It means contemplative as well as considerate. (The Merriam-Webster collegiate dictionary, for instance, claims that "thoughtful" is "careful reasoned thinking" as well as "given to heedful anticipation of the needs and wants of others.") I will elaborate on it later on. At this stage I would like to address the above question whether the common practice of teaching mathematics has, in spite of all, any educational values.

Procedures

In our everyday life we have infinitely many (non-mathematical) procedures which we are supposed to follow and to carry out. Just think about operating your TV system, your DVD player, your cellular phone, your washer and dryer. Think also about driving and parking and about other social interactions in shops, public transportation, banks, hospitals and so on and so forth. Many of these procedures are results of an attempt to be considerate. Some others are result of an attempt to be efficient. Thus, perhaps unintentionally, we are involved with two educational values – being considerate and being efficient. If our students ask us why they have to carry out meaningless mathematical procedures that they will never use in their future life, the answer can be: just to draw their attention to the importance of carrying out procedures in everyday life and to train one's mind to carry out procedures. It is similar to the demand from music students to play scales which they will never play in concerts or for their own musical enjoyment. Some procedures in everyday life are made by society. Others are made by individuals for their private everyday practice. Think of your private procedures which you have made up for your own convenience or safety: where to put your keys when you get into your home so that you will not have to look for them again and again before leaving home, how to take a shower in order to save water, how to park in a parking lot in order not to disturb another driver, etc. There are some mathematical procedures in which the order of the steps is crucial. When computing: 2+3*5-4*2+7, you have to carry out the multiplication before doing the addition or subtraction. On the other hand, the order of carrying out the addition and subtraction is not important. In everyday life, when dressing, you have to put on your socks before putting on your shoes. However, you can put on your socks before you put on your underwear. Sometimes, you can even put on your shoes before putting on your underwear, although, it is not recommended because of various reasons. All these, can be discussed in class while presenting mathematical procedures to the students or while carrying out mathematical procedures. Drawing the students' attention to the importance of following procedures in everyday life is, of course, not a part of the mathematical syllabus. It is the teacher's responsibility as a value messenger. If I were a school teacher today, after each mathematical procedure that I would teach my students, I would ask them, as a homework assignment, to suggest a procedure for a common everyday activity. In class I would discuss with the students the purpose of this procedure, its validity and its effectiveness. Some teachers will consider this as a waste of time. My answer is that it should not take too much time, and in addition, carrying out meaningless procedures again and again, can also be considered as a waste of time. This is only one example which demonstrates how teaching mathematics can be used in order to achieve a general goal in education.

Analytical Thinking

A common claim about learning mathematics is that it develops analytical thinking. I am not speaking yet about meaningful learning. Many mathematical assignments can be carried out by an analytical procedure which is not necessarily meaningful. For instance, one can calculate the area of a rectangle by multiplying two numbers mentioned in a word problem without knowing the meaning of area. Similarly, he or she can differentiate a given function without knowing the meaning of the derivative. This was explained in length in Vinner (1997). If I have to summarize it here in few words I would say that the essence of analytical procedures used in order to solve some mathematical word problems is the following: 1) analyzing the given problem in order to determine its sort and structure; 2) Examining a pool of procedures for problem solving and selecting an appropriate procedure for the sort and the structure of the given problem; and, 3) carrying out the selected procedure.

Coming back to the above claim about the ultimate goal of education, the considerate behaviour, I would like to explain why analytical thinking is required for considerate behaviour. When asked whether I can elaborate a little on the notion of considerate behaviour I usually point at the rule: what you hate – do not do to other people. This was the answer given in an ancient Jewish text to somebody who asked one of the sages to summarize the entire Jewish moral theory in one sentence. Few years ago, I saw in a London underground station a poster saying: "To be considerate means not to carry your backpack on your shoulders." This is a small example of the above rule and it is quite typical. Each day, in case we have interaction with other people, we face dozens of situations with similar characteristics. If we have decided to be considerate, we should be aware of the factors involved in the situation, foresee whether an action of ours can disturb another person and avoid such an action. This requires analytical thinking. So, here is another point where an element of mathematical thinking can be related to values in everyday life.

Moreover, one of the elements of problem solving is control. Schoenfeld (1985, p. 15) characterizes control as "global decisions regarding the selection and implementation of resources and strategies." It includes "planning, monitoring and assessment, decision making, and conscious meta cognitive acts." All these are also elements of considerate behaviour. The teacher has an opportunity to discuss it as an extra-curricular activity in case he or she consider themselves as value messengers and in my opinion, all teachers should consider themselves as such. Note that mathematics teacher educators, very often, speak about analytical thinking and control. They certainly do it in mathematics education conferences. Some of them may speak about it even in their mathematics classes, in case they teach mathematics, or in their mathematics education classes. In teacher education we encourage our students to include it in their future mathematics teaching. However, to the best of my knowledge, very few of us and very few mathematics teachers, when speaking about control in mathematical problem solving, point at the fact that its components are also relevant to our everyday life.

Rational Thinking

An indispensable part of the rhetoric which recommends the teaching and learning of mathematics is that it develops the students' thinking. This is also what I hear when I ask my students in a mathematics education program where I teach, at the beginning of each academic year. However, when I asked them to elaborate on it or to demonstrate it by means of some examples, their decisive majority practices is the legal right to remain silent. Thus, developing the students' thinking has become a common rhetoric associated with mathematics teaching, but for the majority of mathematics teachers (and all my students are already mathematics teachers) it is not clear at all what it really means and how their actions in class can help their students to develop their thinking. At this point I start a class discussion. I try to draw my students' attention to the fact that there are many kinds of thinking: religious thinking, scientific thinking, intuitive thinking, dogmatic thinking, mystical thinking, analytical thinking and more. "Which kind of thinking do we want to develop in our students?" I ask. "Mathematical thinking" (the answer does not hang around too long). With the previous frustration and being afraid of some more frustrating answers, I do not ask the student, who gave the answer, to elaborate on it this time. "Well," I say, "isn't mathematical thinking a too narrow goal? How will it help our students in the rest of their lives outside the mathematics classes?" Silence again. "Well," I say after a while, it is unfair to expect you to read my thoughts. What I have in mind is rational thinking." At this point, twenty pairs of cold eyes are staring at me. "All right", I am trying a new direction. "What is the teacher's main activity?" "Teaching" (another answer which does not hang around too long). "This is correct, but can you be more specific?" "Making silence in the class." "Again," I say, "it is unfair to expect you to read my thoughts. The main activity of the teacher is explaining" The twenty pairs of cold eyes become hostile at this point. "Consider a certain event," I suggest, "like somebody becoming sick. Assume you want to explain it. Can you think about two explanations to it, a religious one and a scientific one and tell the difference between them?" "Yes. The religious explanation will use arguments of punishment and award, where as the scientific explanation will use medical arguments." Something starts to move in the class. "And which one do you prefer?" I ask and add immediately, "please, don't tell me, because if you prefer the religious explanation you have a problem as science teachers." "But we are not science teachers, we are mathematics teachers. Didn't you tell us that mathematics is not about the real world, it is about an abstract world which exists only in our mind?" "I am glad you remember this," I reply, "but didn't you tell me that one of the main reasons for teaching mathematics is that science desperately needs mathematics in order to develop its theories? Are you trying to tell me that you work so hard serving science without believing in it?" "Is this discussion related to mathematical thinking?" (a sceptic reaction which comes directly from the seats of the opposition). "Well," I conclude with my own question, "isn't it related to rational thinking? And isn't rational thinking related to mathematical thinking?"

So far with this illustration – I would like to return now to my original line of thought and to suggest that promoting rational thinking should be an additional (and perhaps the most important) goal of mathematics education. Mathematical thinking and scientific thinking are parts of rational thinking. However, rational thinking is broader. Rational thinking is the kind of thinking which is needed to maintain our society. By "our society" I mean the liberal democratic society with its values, its various institutions, its science, technology and medicine. Other kinds of societies may need, perhaps, other kinds of thinking.

It seems, at this point, that if I recommend rational thinking as the main goal of teaching mathematics I have to define it. Well, definitions in the mathematical sense of the word exist mainly in mathematics. [This is another lesson that we should teach our mathematics students; namely, when they are outside the domain of mathematics and they want to clarify some notions, then looking for definitions is not necessarily a useful activity.] This does not necessarily have to be a problem. There are many notions for which we do not have strict definitions and yet we use them in academic discussions. But rationality is enormously broad, ambiguous and vague notion which has become a research topic for several academic domains like philosophy, psychology, economics, game theory, etc., and it will be extremely hard to uniquely characterize such a notion without arousing objection from scholars of different disciplines or of different people. It is quite typical to the academic community that controversies about central concepts of scholarly research never end. On the other hand, it seems that for ordinary people, using everyday language, the concept of rationality is quite clear. In everyday situations, some people recommend to each other to behave rationally. When they do it, it is quite clear what they mean. It is true that very often we fail to behave rationally, but this happens not because we do not know what it means to be rational. It happens because we are driven by strong impulses that we fail to control. This state of affairs does not imply that we should give up rationality as an educational goal. On the contrary, education is about overcoming and controlling negative tendencies. The claim that human beings are irrational is irrelevant to education exactly as the claim that human beings are evil (or in the biblical formulation: *The desire of man's heart is evil from his youth* (Genesis 8, 21)). The end of education is to teach us how to control our evil desires. Moreover, even the claim that human beings are irrational is quite inaccurate. Some people use the collective work of Tversky and Kahneman to establish this claim. As a matter of fact, what they show is that under certain circumstances, when people are given some intellectual tasks they fail to reach the correct answer. It happens because they make all kinds of mistakes. It does not happen because they do not care about rationality. To be irrational, in my opinion, means that we know what should be a rational decision in a given situation and in spite of that, we decide not to follow it. Such examples are gambling, smoking, eating 'junk' food and so on and so forth. Therefore, I would rather claim that what Tversky and Kahneman show us is that people even try to be rational but they fail because they do not have suitable tools to deal with the problems posed to them. An indication to this claim is the title of Kahneman's Nobel Prize lecture (2002), *Maps of bounded rationality*. More about this issue can be found in Leron and Hazzan (2006) and in Stanovich (1999). Therefore, if this is the case about people's attempt and failure to be rational, why do we not teach them?

When discussing rationality, some researchers prefer to speak about rational behaviour rather than rational people. This is quite reasonable, because a person can behave rationally under certain circumstances and irrationally under different circumstances. Robert Auman, in his Nobel Prize lecture (2005) suggested the following definition for rational behaviour: *A person's behaviour is rational if, when given his information, his behaviour is in his best interest.* This definition was given within the framework of game theory, and we see that rationality is related here only to means and not to goals. It can be applied to moral as well as amoral goals. A criminal planning a perfect robbery, having all the necessary information about the place he is going to rob, is demonstrating a rational behaviour. Even if he is caught later on, because he was not aware of some alarms in the place of the crime, his behaviour can still be considered as rational. It is such because Auman's definition is related to the information the person has. What I am saying here only demonstrates what I claimed earlier that the moment a definition is suggested, it arouses infinite discussions which never reach a conclusion. In addition, Auman's approach is not suitable for us because we want to speak of rationality in the context of education. Therefore, I suggest to use a non technical approach to the notion of rationality, namely, to use it as it is used in colloquial language. I am aware of the possibility that even here it might be hard to obtain a consensus. I have no illusions about that, and if somebody does not agree – we can just agree to disagree.

One way to clarify the meaning of a notion in a colloquial language is to look it up in a dictionary. The Merriam-Webster dictionary suggests that to be rational is to be *reasonable. Rationality is the quality or state of being agreeable to reason. Rationality is applied to opinions, beliefs and practices.* About being reasonable, the dictionary adds that reasonable is *not extreme or excessive* and it is *moderate and fair.*

If we wish to bring a broader support for the dictionary suggestion, we can collect various excerpts from newspapers, magazines, everyday discourse, and political statements and examine the meaning of rationality in these contexts. If you do this, you find support for the Merriam-Webster claims about rationality. A third resource can be looking the notion up in an encyclopaedia, although generally, encyclopaedias do not deal with colloquial terms. And indeed, the *Encyclopaedia Britannica* (the 1974 edition) does not have "rationality" as an entry. It discusses "rationalism" in its scholarly style. However, "rationalism" is not the technical equivalence for "rationality" in the colloquial language. On the other hand, Wikipedia, the free encyclopaedia of the Internet has "rationality" as an entry. In addition to its explication for "rationality" it also elaborates about the use of the term "rational." It suggests that, *in a number of kinds of speech, "rational" may also denote a hodge-podge of generally positive attributes, including: reasonable, not foolish, sane and good* (Wikipedia, 2006). I hope that this reference can be used as an additional support to my claim about the meaning of rationality, at least, in colloquial English. I would like to add that the interpretation of rationally which I am suggesting includes also one characterization of rationalism *that regards reason as the chief source and test of knowledge* (Encyclopaedia Britannica, 1974; rationalism). On the one hand, I am not considering "rationality" as a rival to empiricism (which is true about "rationalism"). On the other hand, I claim that to be rational implies taking into account science, medicine and technology. A person behaves rationally if he or she takes into account all the scientific information which is relevant to their decision making. Thus, rationality is a relative notion. A rational behaviour in Newton's era is not necessarily rational in our era since science has changed enormously. Again, the interested reader can find more about the subject of rationality in Leron and Hazzan (2006) and Stanovich (1999) which I mentioned earlier.

At this point, I hope that I have clarified my interpretation to the notion of rationality and I want to assume that it is quite close to its interpretation among people who have at least a college degree in Western society (especially, our mathematics and science teachers). I expect them to distinguish between rational thinking and other kinds of thinking (dogmatic, mystical, divine, etc.). However, I take into consideration that the gap between my expectation and the practice might be huge and therefore, I suggest that rationality in the above sense should be discussed in prospective and practicing mathematics teacher education. What I want to avoid is a university requirement of another dry academic highly sophisticated course in philosophy, which deals with rationality in a technical way. Such a course will, probably, discuss rationalism as a philosophical movement rather than rationality in the above sense.

I feel that after the above discussion about rationality I can return to mathematics teaching and suggest for it an educational goal. As I claimed earlier, education is primarily about values. I suggested that an educated person is a thoughtful person where the emphasis is on being considerate. My claim was that in order to be considerate we should use rational thinking. Please, note that my only concern here is about being considerate; this is not because I am unaware of other potential values. It is because I am aware of potential controversies over additional values that I can suggest. Even about being considerate some people may claim that it is inappropriate as an educational goal. They believe that selfish behaviour is more useful for their interests (and note that it is quite coherent with Auman's definition of rational behaviour and with the view that the human being is homo economicus (economic man) and as such he or she is logically consistent but not necessarily moral). However, within the educational domain, I hope, nobody will dare to recommend selfish behaviour as an educational goal. Currently, values and rationality are not part of any mathematics curriculum; they are not part of any curriculum at all. My suggestion is that teachers will address them in their classes at suitable moments. For example, when dealing with fractions one can discuss sharing as a value. (Sharing is one of the principle educational values mentioned by Postman (1996) quoting from Robert Fulghum's book, *All I ever really needed to know I learned in Kindergarten*. Fulghum's list is the following: *sharing everything, playing fair, don't hit people, put things back where you found them, clean up your own mess, wash your hands before you eat, and flush* (Postman, 1996, p. 46).) What I am suggesting here requires a different state of mind from the teachers. It requires that while dealing with a mathematical issue, the teacher is expected to be aware of the possibility to add a reflective dimension to the lesson and integrate in it a discussion about values. It requires from the teacher some improvisation skills (of course, one can plan it or partly plan it, but improvisation is better). This is clearly in contradiction with the current conception of mathematics lessons which are supposed to be strictly task oriented, structured and planned to the last detail. Space restrictions prevent me from presenting more examples in which particular mathematical topics can be used in order to discuss educational values.

MEANINGFUL TEACHING AND LEARNING.

Both students and teachers should feel better if they realize that they are involved in meaningful activities. Acts of meaning is the title of one of Jerome Bruner's books (1990). For the sake of my discussion in this section I would like to elaborate a little about the notion of meaning. I will point at three contexts in which this notion is used. The first context, and perhaps the most common one, is the context where we speak about the meaning of notions. The reader who is interested in an academic discussion about this context of meaning can find it in

Ogden and Richards (1930). Here, I restrict myself just to the ordinary use of this notion. When we ask about the meaning of a notion we simply want to know what it means. For instance, the meaning of a *solution of an algebraic equation in one unknown* is a number that if we substitute it instead of all the occurrences of the unknown and we carry out al the algebraic operations between the numbers on both sides of the equation, the result obtained at the left side will be equal to the result obtained at the right side. This is quite complicated. It can be formulated in a slightly more friendly way, but essentially this is it. No wonder why so many teachers prefer to avoid dealing with the meaning of the notions involved in mathematical assignments and, instead, teach only the procedures required for solving the given assignments. It is easier to teach the procedure of solving a quadratic equation than to explain the meaning of a solution to any given equation in general. In spite of that, mathematics educators recommend to discuss also the meaning of the notions involved in the mathematical activities. They recommend explaining to the students the meaning of function, the meaning of the derivative and so on and so forth. They consider this as meaningful teaching and learning.

The second context in which meaning is used is the context of values. People say, for instance: 1) I have a meaningful job – helping weak students to overcome their difficulties in learning mathematics; 2) nursing is a meaningful profession, and 3) my salary as a teacher is not very high but my compensation is the feeling that I am involved in meaningful work. Relating this to mathematics, I would say that learning mathematics is meaningful if the students adopt rationality as a way of life and use other, more specific thinking skills (like careful carrying out of procedures, analytical thinking, reflection and control) in their everyday activities.

The third context in which meaning is used is absolutely missing from school practices. Probably, it is missing because it is related to over-all school practices. "What is the role of school?" People ask on various occasions. The question also rises very often in parent-school principal meetings. "The role of school is to prepare the children for their life," says the principal. It sounds good, but what does it really mean? Is teaching the child the Pythagorean Theorem and the geography of Africa is preparation for life? In the famous TV series by Ingmar Bergman, *Scenes from a Marriage*, the hero of the series, a psychology professor, in a quite depressive monologue, says to his wife: "I'll tell you something which is quite banal. We are psychologically illiterate. At school they taught us everything about our body and about agriculture in Africa. Also they taught us that the sum of the squares on the two sides of a right-angle triangle is equal to the square on the hypotenuse and all the rest. But they did not teach us anything about our souls. Here we are deeply illiterate, about ourselves and about others." And indeed, few minutes after this dramatic declaration of illiteracy, the professor gives the viewers an ample proof of his illiteracy. He brutally beats his wife. This event is, undoubtedly a result of the illiteracy declared by the professor. But what is the professor's recommendation to the school system? How is the school system supposed to cope with this terrible illiteracy? The professor, of course, does not recommend anything. He is a psychology professor and not an educator. Also, a Bergman movie is not an educational essay. But what have educators to say about

317

it? What can the school system do in order that our graduates will not be psychologically illiterate? It seems to me that main cause for this illiteracy is that we do not have satisfactory answers to questions like: What is this life? What should we expect from it? What are we supposed to do with it? What goals should we try to achieve? In short, questions which can fall under the frightening title: The meaning of life.

Now, the meaning of life is extremely vague and ambiguous notion. This is quite a good reason for philosophers to develop infinite discussions about it. Since my paper is not a philosophical paper, my intention is to simplify and not to complicate things. So, perhaps, my analysis will not be approved by professional philosophers, but I do not mind because it is directed to educators and not to philosophers. It is not clear why, when and how people formed new contexts for the notion of meaning, in addition to the original context, the context of words. The answer to this question can be given, perhaps, by philosophers of language or by linguists. For me it is irrelevant at this moment. The fact is that people speak about the meaning of life. What do they mean by it? For many people, the meaning of life is the answer to the question why do we live. I believe that the origin of this question is in religion or theology. Within these frameworks, the question does not call for biological explanations. It looks for goals. What do we live for? What is the purpose of our life? There are immediate religious answers for these questions, like we live in order to please God, we live in order to serve God, we live in order to do things which God expects us to do and so on. Immediately after these answers, a list with more specific details is presented. Within the religious context, the claim that life is a mission, that it has goals which are determined by an external factor (God), is a postulate.

However, it is not a postulate for a secular person. For a secular person the question why do we live is misleading because it pre-supposes that there is a reason why we live. On the other hand, secular people do set goals for their lives. "My goal in life is to be rich and famous," some people declare. Others do not declare but do everything in order to become rich and famous. Some will be satisfied with being only rich or only famous. "I want to have a family and a career," a 19 year-old girl says to me. "Family, I understand," I reply," but what do you mean by career? "I would like to be a boss of some kind," she explains. One can see here goals. They are quite vague at this stage and they can change. However, they are related to the future of young people; and is not the future of young people relevant to education? Does the school system relate to it at all? It relates to it when it comes to drugs and violence. As a matter of fact, drugs and violence are not issues of the future. They are crucial issues of the present. Of course, most of the people try to do everything in order to prevent their children from becoming criminals.

But prevention is not enough if you do not point at alternatives, if you do not point at appropriate goals for young people life. Is this related to the meaning of life? It is, if you accept that the meaning of life means goals for your life. However, the notion (the meaning of life) turns off the educational system, students and teachers. It turns them off, probably, because it is associated with philosophy, with religion and with conservative moral values. Also the notion of moral values turns people off. It is recommended not to use it. But how shall we speak about moral values without the notion of moral values? Is the expression "educational values" better? Somehow, people's tendency is to avoid value discussions in schools. Their assumption (implicit or explicit) is that the goal of schools is knowledge acquisition. Unfortunately, this goal is hardly achieved, not only in mathematics, as I already claimed. On the other hand, appropriate goals for the students' future are not discussed at all. We consider it as a great educational achievement if we succeed to prevent our children from becoming drug addicts and prevent our young daughters from becoming pregnant at the age of 14.

There is an additional significance to the meaning of life, I think. It is the profession or activities that give us a real satisfaction. "For me, helping sick people is the meaning of my life," says the nurse. "Being a musician is for me the meaning of my life," says a young music student. "My life will be meaningless if I won't become a medical doctor," declares a young student when being asked by the medical school committee why he wants to be a medical doctor. So, here again if the notion the meaning of life is replaced by another expression the situation will be quite clear. Now, football, gambling, car racing and so on are the center of many people's lives. Are these the meaning of their lives? For sure, they would not use this terminology. However, are not these worthy issues to be discussed in schools?

To summarize this section I would say that the school system should relate to the meaning of life with the interpretations that I suggested above. In order not to turn off students and teachers from dealing with it I suggest not to use this notion and to replace it by some more attractive expressions. I do not have suggestions at this point, probably, because I am not creative enough. This lack of creativity is, perhaps, due to the fact that, somehow, I like the notion, despite the fact that I consider it meaningless in the worst case or vague and ambiguous in the better case. This is quite typical in poetry, where meaningless or vague expressions leave deep impressions on some readers. This is the reason why I do not stop using the notion at this point and I even recommend for my readers a wonderful book whose title is The meaning of life" (Klemke, 1981). In that book one can find extremely meaningful texts about the issues I discussed earlier from religious and from secular points of view.

I am not suggesting that the above issues will become a topic at the school curriculum. Forming them in a learning unit will be a disaster. However, it is important to discuss them with the students in teacher education as additional dimensions. A teacher should feel that he or she can contribute to his or her students something more than just covering the course syllabus – something which is relevant to the student's future; something which the student will consider as meaningful. Being a teacher myself I would like to conclude this chapter with a personal comment. I consider teaching as one of the most meaningful professions in our liberal democratic society. It is fascinating, it is challenging, and it is extremely important to our society. I am not claiming it without ignoring the difficulties, the burnout and (in many countries) the low income. For teachers who consider themselves as educators, teaching becomes a central factor of the meaning of their life. It makes their life meaningful. Is this not one of the major desires of so many human beings?

REFERENCES

Auman, R. J. (2005). War and peace. A Nobel Prize lecture. Stockholm, December 8.

Bruner, J. (1990). *Acts of meaning*. Harvard, MA: Harvard University Press.

Confrey, J. (1995). Student voice in examining "splitting" as an approach to ratio, proportions and fractions, *Proceedings of the 19th Psychology of Mathematics Education Conference* (Vol. 1, pp. 3–29). Recife, Brazil.

Kahneman, D. (2002). Maps of bounded rationality: Perspective on intuitive judgments and choice. A Nobel Prize lecture. Stockholm, December 2.

Klemke, E. D. (1981). *The meaning of life*. Oxford: Oxford University Press.

Leron, U., & Hazzan, O. (2006). The rationality debate: Application of cognitive psychology to mathematics education. *Educational Studies in Mathematics, 62*(2), 105–126.

National Council of Teachers of Mathemtics (2000). *Principles and standards for school mathematics*, Reston, VA.

Ogden, C. K., & Richards, I. A. (1930). *The meaning of meaning*. New York, NY: Harcourt, Brace and Company.

Postman, N. (1996). *The end of education*. New York, NY: Vintage Books.

Schoenfeld, A. (1985). *Mathematical problem solving*. New York, NY: Academic Press.

Stanovich, K. E. (1999). Who is rational? Mahwah, NJ: Lawrence Erlbaum Associates.

Vinner, S. (1997). The pseudo-conceptual and the pseudo-analytical thought processes in mathematical learning. *Educational Studies in Mathematics, 34*, 97–129.

Shlomo Vinner
Ben Gurion University of the Negev
and
Hebrew University of Jerusalem
Israel

ALAN H. SCHOENFELD AND JEREMY KILPATRICK

TOWARD A THEORY OF PROFICIENCY IN TEACHING MATHEMATICS

This volume of the *International Handbook of Mathematics Teacher Education* is concerned with tools and processes in mathematics teacher education. It offers essays on well-designed and well-tested tools organized into three broad categories: cases as tools, tasks as tools, and research as tools.

Viewing the collection as a whole, one might ask the following: What principles should guide the selection and use of these individually interesting and powerful tools? Where do they fit in a "tool space" – the entire collection of tools that mathematics teacher educators might bring to bear in their work? To address these questions requires a wide-ranging view.

In keeping with the tool metaphor, we note that a toolkit for automobile maintenance looks different from a toolkit for, say, furniture making, and that even some of the tools present in both toolkits (e.g., screwdrivers) have a different purpose and use depending on the context. Thus we must ask, Cases in the service of what? Tasks in the service of what? Research in the service of what? The answer, of course, is improved teaching. But that response is too vague; one needs to say more. Along what dimensions might teaching be improved? Or better, what are the dimensions of proficient teaching? One needs first and foremost a theory of proficiency in teaching mathematics that could be used to guide the selection and use of tools for mathematics teacher education.

Before providing a prospective outline of such a theory, we note that theories of proficiency have been used in a number of ways in mathematics education. Understanding how those theories have been used can set the stage for a discussion of a theory of proficiency in mathematics teaching. Consider, for example, the dimensions of proficiency in mathematical problem solving offered by Schoenfeld (1985). Schoenfeld argued that, in order to understand the success or failure of a problem-solving attempt, one needs to know about the individual's:

- knowledge base
- problem-solving strategies
- metacognitive actions
- beliefs and practices

That set of categories represents a set of dimensions in a theory of problem-solving proficiency and thus provides a set of goals for instruction in problem solving. That is, if one sets out to help students become proficient problem solvers, one needs to attend to questions of what should be in their knowledge base, what problem-solving strategies they should learn, how they should develop the

D. Tirosh and T. Wood (eds.), Tools and Processes in Mathematics Teacher Education, 321–354.

appropriate metacognitive skills, and what mathematical beliefs and practices they might abstract from their experiences with mathematics.

Similarly, the authors of *Adding it Up* (Kilpatrick, Swafford, & Findell, 2001) offered a characterization of the dimensions of proficiency in school mathematics: conceptual understanding, procedural fluency, strategic competence, adaptive reasoning, and productive disposition. Those same dimensions, appropriately modified, were also used to characterize proficient teaching of mathematics. As with the problem-solving work, such conceptualizations provide a set of goals for mathematics instruction – and with the goals, one can examine curricula and pedagogical practices (i.e., tools) for their potential utility.

With these examples and purposes in mind, we offer in Table 1 a provisional framework consisting of a set of dimensions of proficiency for teaching mathematics. In the balance of this chapter, we elaborate on these dimensions and examine the various chapters in this volume with regard to how the tools they offer can contribute to the framework.

Table 1. A provisional framework for proficiency in teaching mathematics

---

Knowing school mathematics in depth and breadth
Knowing students as thinkers
Knowing students as learners
Crafting and managing learning environments
Developing classroom norms and supporting classroom discourse as part of "teaching for understanding"
Building relationships that support learning
Reflecting on one's practice

KNOWING SCHOOL MATHEMATICS IN DEPTH AND BREADTH

Proficient teachers' knowledge of school mathematics is both broad and deep. It is broad in that such teachers have multiple ways of conceptualizing the current grade-level content, can represent it in a variety of ways, understand the key aspects of each topic, and see connections to other topics at the same level. It is deep in that such teachers know the curricular origins and directions of the content – where the mathematics has been taught and where it leads to – and they understand how the mathematical ideas grow conceptually. This kind of knowledge allows proficient teachers to prioritize and organize content so that students are introduced to big ideas rather than getting lost in a welter of details, and it allows them to respond flexibly to questions raised by their students. This kind of content understanding has been called "knowledge of mathematics for teaching" by Deborah Ball and her colleagues (Ball, Thames, & Phelps, 2007; Hill, Rowan, & Ball, 2005) and, as discussed below, involves more than "just" knowing the mathematics in the curriculum.

Breadth

Consider what it means to understand the meaning of a fraction, the multiple ways in which fractions are represented, and ways of interpreting operations on fractions. Teachers must have a firm grasp of all of these if they are to help students navigate through the territory of problems involving fractions. Consider, for example, the simple definition of a unit fraction. Independent of its representation, the fraction $1/n$ represents the selection of one object or subunit when a *unit* (which might itself be a collection of discrete objects) has been one partitioned into n equal subunits. Half of a pie – a standard model for fractions – is thus visualized as one of the two pieces that result when a pie is sliced into two equal pieces, as in Figure 1.

Figure 1. "Half a pie."

A third of a chocolate bar is viewed as one of three (perhaps imaginary) slices in a bar, dividing it into three equal pieces (Figure 2).

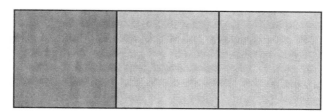

Figure 2. "A third of a chocolate bar."

The unit interval, divided into quarters or eighths, is also a standard reference (Figure 3).

0   1

Figure 3. The unit interval divided into 8 equal segments.

So far, so good – but the unit might also be an object that is unequally divided, such as in Figures 4 and 5.

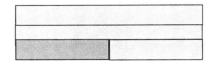

Figure 4. A rectangle divided into 4 unequal parts.

Figure 5. The unit interval divided into 5 unequal segments.

These unequal partitions cause many students difficulty, so teachers must know them. Moreover, the unit is less obvious in some cases, as when the task is to divide, say, one and a half pizzas fairly among n people, or when the distance to be covered is one-nth of one and a half miles. After unit fractions come nonunit fractions, including so-called improper fractions, and their equivalents.

Should all of these ideas seem straightforward, we assure the reader that for students, they are not. Further, teachers' rapid access to all of these representations is essential, including the knowledge of which ones are likely to be helpful for students in particular situations and which ones will help to reveal students' understandings and misunderstandings. For an example of an interview with a student that shows the kind of mathematical (and pedagogical) knowledge required and a discussion of the issues involved, see Ball and Peoples (2007) and Schoenfeld (2007).

The mathematics, even at this level, becomes more complicated when one is called upon to understand and explain operations on fractions. Consider the following problem:

Solve the following problem with a diagram:

a. Wanda really likes cake. She decides that a serving should be 3/5 of a cake. If she has 4 cakes, how many servings does she have?

b. Solve the problem by writing an arithmetic sentence.

c. How does your arithmetic sentence match the diagram?

    d.   After 6 portions are eaten, how much is left?

    e.   Why is the answer to the division problem 6 and 2/3 rather than 6 and 2/5?

(From SummerMath, *Making Meaning for Operations: Facilitators' Guide,* p. 69; cited in S. Cohen, 2004, p. 50.)

As Sophia Cohen (2004, pp. 48–79) shows, this kind of problem – especially Part (e), which requires one to see that 2/5 of a cake is 2/3 of a serving (which is 3/5 of a cake) – is a real challenge for many practicing teachers (see Figure 6). Is the remainder, the two unshaded pieces in the upper right, 2/3 or 2/5 of a portion?

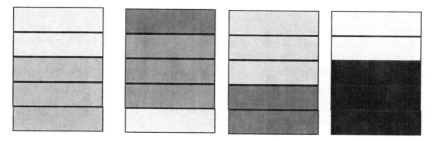

Figure 6. Four cakes divided into fifths, with 6 portions of 3/5 cake shaded in different colors.

A well-known problem that offers comparable challenges is discussed by Liping Ma (1999):

People seem to have different approaches to solving problems involving division with fractions. How do you solve this one?

$$1\frac{3}{4} \div \frac{1}{2} =$$

... Sometimes [teachers] try to come up with real-world situations or story problems to show the application of some particular piece of content. What would you say would be a good story or model for $1\frac{3}{4} \div \frac{1}{2} =$? (p. 55)

As Ma shows, only 9 of the 21 American teachers in her sample who attempted the computation did it successfully, and many of them had a hard time with it. Only one of the teachers in her sample was able to craft a story that corresponded to the division. In contrast, all 72 of the Chinese teachers in her sample performed the operation correctly – mostly justifying their work by saying "dividing by a number is the same as multiplying by its reciprocal" (p. 58) – and with many of them generating one or more nonstandard procedures for arriving at the answer. Sixty-five of the 72 Chinese teachers (90%) offered a correct story to model the calculation, and many of them offered multiple stories, corresponding to what Ma calls the *measurement model* ("how many ½-foot lengths are there in something that is 1 and ¾ feet long?"), the *partitive model* ("if half a length is 1 and ¾ feet, how long is the whole?") and the *product and factors model* ("If one side of a 1¾ square foot rectangle is ½ feet, how long is the other side?") (p. 72). Clearly, a teacher who knows such models can work more productively with students struggling with fraction division than a teacher whose knowledge is more limited.

Depth

The examples discussed thus far concern teachers' knowledge of the mathematics at the level being taught, but there are also issues of what knowledge students are likely to have when they enter a classroom and where they will be going mathematically in future years.

Not long ago Schoenfeld (in press) joined a workshop in which sixth-grade teachers were discussing the relationship between fractions and rates. Asked to create a problem that would assess student understanding of rates, one teacher posed the following:

> It takes John 50 seconds to run 400 meters. It takes Mary 60 seconds to run 500 meters. Who is faster?

The teacher's intention was for students to compute the two ratios. John runs at a rate of $400/50 = 8$ meters/second, and Mary at a rate of $500/60 = 8\ 1/3$ meters/second, so Mary is faster. The group spent some time discussing what would happen if students divided seconds by meters instead of the other way around. Although these calculations are nonstandard, the resulting values of 0.125 seconds/meter and 0.12 seconds/meter do make sense: They indicate that John takes slightly longer to run each meter than Mary does (i.e., Mary is faster). Such an understanding relates to the issue of breadth discussed above.

At that point, Schoenfeld suggested that it might be useful for the students to draw a graph representing John's and Mary's progress over time. The teachers were incredulous: What does graphing have to do with the topic at hand? He pointed out that over the next 2 years their students would be given problems in which Mary gives John a head start of so many meters and asked how long it would take her to catch up, and that the students would be asked to solve such problems analytically and graphically. Some of the teachers were unaware that the mathematics they were teaching would lead in that direction.[1]

In some countries, for example, Japan, teachers commonly "rotate" grade assignments, so that a teacher working at any particular grade is likely to have

---

[1] In the United States, the sixth grade is often a dividing line in mathematics (and in school more generally). Teachers of Grades K–6 are typically generalists who may or may not have studied much mathematics, in contrast to Grades 7–12 mathematics teachers, roughly half of whom have a college degree in mathematics.

taught both the preceding and the following grade (Fernandez & Yoshida, 2004). That practice provides the teachers with a sense of curricular and mathematical depth, which shapes the ways in which they orient their current instruction. Teachers are handicapped when they lack this kind of knowledge or, more generally, a deeper understanding of the core mathematical ideas that evolve as one proceeds through mathematics.

In short, mathematical knowledge of various types is necessary for proficient teaching. Professional development typically emphasizes depth over breadth, at least in the United States: Teachers are exposed to more advanced mathematics under the assumption that the more advanced one's mathematical knowledge, the better one can see how any particular piece of mathematics fits into the big picture. Studies such as those by Ma (1999) and S. Cohen (2004), cited above, and the work by Ball and colleagues (Ball et al., 2007; Hill et al., 2005), however, show that there are also benefits to be found in having a richly connected and broad knowledge base at the relevant grade level.

Finally, there is a form of knowledge known as "pedagogical content knowledge" or PCK. (Shulman, 1986). PCK includes knowledge of typical student understandings and misunderstandings, and of ways to deal with them. For example, every teacher of algebra will encounter students who compute $(a + b)^2$ as $a^2 + b^2$. Teachers will come to recognize the error as a frequent occurrence and will prepare for it, developing a set of responses for helping students see clearly what is wrong ("Why don't you try the values $a = 3$ and $b = 4$, and see if it works?"). They will also develop various ways to show the correct formula (including, possibly, using area models to show pictorially why there are two ab terms when $(a + b)^2$ is expanded).[2]

In sum, proficient teachers have mathematical knowledge of various types: broad and connected knowledge of the content at hand, deep knowledge of where the content comes from and where it might lead, an understanding of "big ideas" or major themes, knowledge of effective ways to introduce students to particular mathematical ideas, and ways to instill understanding or help to counter misunderstanding.

Mathematical knowledge in the broad sense we have described it is the backbone of mathematics teaching proficiency, so it is not surprising that many of the chapters in this volume discuss or provide tools for developing and enhancing teachers' knowledge of school mathematics. As Chapman argues, story telling is a way in which people encapsulate and trade knowledge; thus, it follows that narratives are a rich way of communicating and developing teachers' mathematical proficiency. The prospective teachers in Chapman's classes unpack their teaching stories as a means of challenging their "mathematics knowledge for teaching." She notes that narratives allow teachers to "deepen their understanding regarding the nature of mathematics and its teaching and learning."

---

[2] Note that the relationship between PCK and mathematics for teaching is not settled. One can see knowledge of mathematics for teaching, for example, as encompassing PCK or as separate from it, depending on one's epistemological views.

Like narratives, cases are typically about more than the mathematics, of course, but the mathematical issues in "The Ratio of Boys to Girls" case cited by Markovitz and Smith, as in the exemplars and problem situations they cite, make it clear how cases can highlight core mathematics content for discussion and teacher development.[3] Markovitz and Smith note that cases can provide

> prospective and practicing teachers with the opportunity to develop knowledge needed for teaching (e.g., knowledge of content, pedagogy and students as learners) as well as the capacity for knowing when and how to apply such knowledge, a capacity that depends on the ability to connect the specifics of real-time, deeply contextualized teaching moments with a broader set of ideas about mathematics, about teaching, and about learning.

They cite research demonstrating that the use of mathematical classroom situations, among other benefits, "enhanced teachers' mathematical content knowledge and pedagogical content knowledge."

Video cases, too, offer the potential to provoke rich mathematical discussions; Maher gives a number of examples of such cases. She observes, "Video recordings can capture how certain content is learned and how a teacher's knowledge of the subject for teaching influences the learning of that content during mathematics lessons." (The art in using these or any tools, of course, is to stimulate conversations that explore the mathematics that is potentially relevant.)

Lesson study, as described by Yoshida, may be one of the most comprehensive ways of addressing mathematical and pedagogical knowledge. A fundamental difference between the approach taken in Japan and in the United States is that in Japan, the assumption is that no matter how talented the beginning teacher, it will take years of development for that teacher to become truly proficient. Lesson study is a form of "on the job" professional development, built into the work week. In pursuing lesson design (What is the mathematics we consider central? How do we plan to have students approach it? What are students likely to do, and how will we react to it?), lesson study involves teachers in the full spectrum of knowledge issues we delineated above.

Tasks, examples, objects, and machines play a similar and sometimes more fine-grained role as mechanisms for focusing attention on what is mathematically important. For example, Sullivan and Watson describe the many roles and functions of the tasks used by Swan, pointing out how the tasks can generate talk about the mathematical ideas involved. Zazkis explicitly focuses on using examples as mechanisms: "(a) to improve and enhance teachers' personal understanding of mathematics, and (b) to examine and introduce to teachers the variety of students' possible understandings or misunderstandings of mathematics." These mechanisms address exactly the sort of knowledge for teaching that we have outlined above. Nührenbörger and Steinbring, and Bartolini Bussi and Maschietto

---

[3] The 1972 book by Bishop and Whitfield, published in England, contains situations very similar to the problem situations cited by Markovits and Smith.

demonstrate clearly the ways in which "hands on" objects can also become "minds on" objects when it comes to mathematical concepts.

Not surprisingly, each of the four theory chapters deals with the mathematical knowledge of teachers as well. Tsamir, for example, mentions research "promoting SMK [subject matter knowledge] and control when discussing polygons." Clarke discusses growth points (note that children's different conceptions of arithmetic operations are legitimate mathematics). Empson and Jacobs point out that listening to children's mathematics calls for unpacking some of the mathematics we as adults have come to think of as unproblematic. And Gravemeijer's "flexible arithmetic" provides an example of how a topic can be explored for breadth and connections.

Nonetheless, it is now time to pull back with regard to theory and practice and to take the long view. The chapters in this volume offer a range of theoretical and practical tools, but it is hard to see the proverbial forest for the trees: In the absence of a larger framework such as the theory of proficiency discussed here, it is difficult to situate any specific tool. It would seem that next steps along this content dimension of proficiency would be to elaborate and clarify the subdimensions of mathematical knowledge that are necessary for proficiency – depth, breadth, PCK, and so forth – and to push forward with a practical program to delineate the depth and breadth of the relevant knowledge for key topics in the curriculum.

KNOWING STUDENTS AS THINKERS

Over the past months, Schoenfeld has been involved in a series of meetings with middle school teachers whose purpose has been to explore student thinking. They chose the topic of word problems knowing that such tasks have been a chronic difficulty for middle school students. The ultimate goal of the project has been to help the lowest-performing students in the school district be able to cope with such problems. Teachers were given digital audiotape machines and invited to interview their students about problems they thought might be challenging for them. This section describes some of the events that transpired.

One group of teachers had chosen the following problem, which comes from a textbook used by the district:

A five-pound box of sugar costs $1.80 and contains 12 cups of sugar. Marella and Mark are making a batch of cookies. The recipe calls for 2 cups of sugar. Determine how much the sugar for the cookies costs.

A teacher had chosen a student (let us call her Amanda) to work with because Amanda had been performing significantly below grade level, and her work often seemed to indicate that she had made little sense of the problems at hand. Indeed, as the teacher pointed out, Amanda's written work was disjointed and somewhat confusing. A replica of the work is given in Figure 7. One can see how a teacher, confronted with 30 such papers to grade, could miss some of what the student was actually thinking and doing.

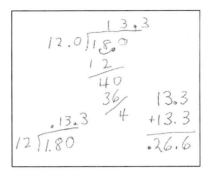

Figure 7. Student work on the sugar problem.

In an interview, Amanda's "thinking out loud" problem solving showed very clearly what she was thinking. She announced that she had to find the cost of one cup of sugar, and then double it; and the cost of that one cup would be $1.80 divided by 12. She then proceeded to get enmeshed in the division algorithm, as indicated in Figure 7. The teacher had a very strong and positive response to Amanda's work:

> I realized that Amanda had the problem nailed conceptually and that her difficulty was just with the algorithm. Because of this interview, I'm now convinced that she can do grade-level work. She's a perfect candidate for a computer-based remedial arithmetic program we have, and with that help, she'll do just fine.

The teacher went on to say, "I realized that I completely underestimated her understanding. I may have made similar goofs with other students. I have to interview every one of them to find out what they know!"

A second set of interviews concerned the following problem:

> A dragonfly, the fastest insect, can fly a distance of 50 feet in about 2 seconds. How long will it take for the dragonfly to fly 375 feet?

An elegant solution uses either rates (the dragonfly travels 25 feet/second and thus needs 375/25 seconds to travel 375 feet) or proportions (e.g., $\frac{50}{2} = \frac{375}{x}$) to arrive at the answer of 15 seconds. Both approaches employ multiplicative or proportional models of the motion described in the problem statement. Such approaches, at first, were what the teachers were looking for in the students' work. It turned out, however, not to be what some students found natural. One student (let us call him Ben), for example, said,

> It can fly 50 feet in about 2 seconds; 4 seconds would be 100 feet, so then 6 would be 200, 8 would be 300, and then 9 would be 350. But then there's 25 missing, so a half of it to get 375. So about 9½ seconds to get 375.

It is interesting to unpack what Ben did. He did not look for a unit rate. Instead, aiming at 375 feet – which is a lot larger than 50 feet – Ben began to use what appears at first to be a form of proportional or multiplicative reasoning. He reasoned correctly that if the dragonfly could cover 50 feet in 2 seconds, it could cover 100 feet in 4 seconds. He then lost track of the time units, incrementing the distance by 100 feet but the time by 2 seconds instead of 4 seconds. That gave him a distance of 200 feet in 6 seconds. Ben had inadvertently changed the dragonfly's rate of speed to 100 feet every 2 seconds. He followed through using that rate: 100 feet every 2 seconds (= 50 ft/sec = 25 ft/½sec) places the dragonfly at 300 feet in 8 seconds and 350 feet at 9 seconds; the last 25 feet are covered in a half second.

Once one realizes that Ben "lost the unit" in his second step, it becomes clear that he was using not a multiplicative model but rather an additive one. His "building block" in the additive model was a chunk of 100 feet that corresponded to 2 seconds; he added those building blocks until he came close to the desired distance and then had to cut the blocks into smaller pieces.

Another student, Carla, built a bar graph that showed the dragonfly's progress. She built up the graph 2 seconds at a time: The first vertical bar was 50 feet at 2 seconds; the next was 100 feet at 4 seconds, the next 150 feet at 6 seconds, and so on. The bar graph may look as though it captures a linear function and is an apparently obvious example of multiplicative reasoning. When one listens to the tape of what Carla said, however, it becomes clear that here, too, the student was actually using additive rather than multiplicative building blocks.

These observations gave rise to some interesting suggestions by the teachers for "meeting the students where they are." They wondered whether the students might be induced to think multiplicatively if they changed the numbers in the problem. For example, what would the students do if they gave this follow-up problem:

Suppose you start with the same information. How long will it take for the dragonfly to fly 5000 feet?

Or, how might students approach the first problem if it was changed to the following:

A dragonfly, the fastest insect, can fly a distance of 25 feet in about 1 second. How long will it take for the dragonfly to fly 375 feet?

Might those changes lead more directly to multiplicative reasoning? Those explorations are in progress as this chapter is being written. What is clear at this point is that increased sensitivity to what students are actually thinking provides additional information about how students are making sense of the mathematics at hand and how one might build on those understandings. In this case, informal interviews are a tool for improved learning and for professional development. As the more extended example in Ball and Peoples (2007) indicates, there are significant advantages to be gained from such interviews. More generally, all forms of informal assessment in mathematics are tools in the service of developing an understanding of what students know individually and collectively (see, e.g., Bright & Joyner, 1998; Wiliam, 2007). As suggested by the two examples discussed above, such interviews can lead both to more profitable interactions with individual students and to alternative ways of thinking about instruction.

It is not surprising that the cases section of the present volume offers potential tools for explorations of student thinking. As indicated by Chapman and as illustrated above, narrative can serve as a mechanism for engaging teachers with issues of student understanding. In Chapman's second example of a prospective secondary teacher's story of "good teaching," she points out that the student's rewritten story at the end of the semester "now contained features of an inquiry-based, student-oriented approach to teaching." Similarly, cases can be used to focus on issues of student thinking – although the particular cases discussed by Markovits and Smith, like the narratives used as illustrations by Chapman, allude to the cases' potential rather than deal with it directly. Maher's discussion of the Longitudinal Study of Student Learning at Rutgers University demonstrates how attention to students' "mathematical ideas and insights" as they proceed through school can allow researchers to trace changes in students' thinking and reasoning. Finally with regard to cases, it should be noted that lesson study is predicated on the examination of student understanding. Typical lessons are designed to provide students the opportunity to reveal their understandings, and to build on them. Thus, knowing students as thinkers is an inherent part of lesson study design. As Yoshida says, lesson study "puts students at the heart of the professional learning activity."

Tasks are neutral; their value as tools for illuminating student understanding resides in their use rather than in the tasks themselves. As Watson and Sullivan note, "Doing tasks does not guarantee learning." That is true whether, as in Section 2 of this volume, the tasks are individual mathematical tasks or collections thereof (Watson & Sullivan), examples (Zazkis), manipulatives (Nührenbörger & Steinbring), or machines (Bartolini Bussi & Machietto). Watson and Sullivan explicitly identify one purpose of task use as "to stimulate and inform teachers' theorising about students' learning"; their discussion of conceptual understanding is aimed at that kind of task use. Likewise, one of Zazkis's two major goals for her chapter is "to examine and introduce to teachers the variety of students' possible understandings or misunderstandings of mathematics," and she focuses on examples that "increase teachers' awareness of students' possible mathematical ideas." In contrast, neither Nührenbörger and Steinbring nor Bartolini Bussi and Machietto focus explicitly on the ways that the tools they describe can be used to help teachers develop a deeper understanding of student thinking.

Theory plays an interesting role with regard to student understanding. To make the obvious point, a teacher with a behaviorist perspective on learning would look for very different kinds of evidence regarding student performance and understanding than a teacher would who had a constructivist perspective. And a teacher with a sociocultural perspective might attend to different factors in thinking about shaping a student's learning than either of the others. Three less obvious but equally important points are the following:

1. Teachers have implicit theories regarding cognition that shape their attitudes toward student understanding whether or not they are aware of it.

2. Theoretical perspectives serve as constraints on what teachers consider relevant and appropriate, thus potentially limiting the teachers' actions in the classroom. (That is, like all tools, theoretical perspectives can have a negative or constraining impact as well as a positive one. Remember the old saying, "If you have a hammer in your hand, the whole world looks like a nail.")

3. What one professes to believe and how one actually acts may be two very different things. The difference was shown vividly by David Cohen (1990), who documented how a teacher's ostensibly "reform" practices and rhetoric were filtered through her traditional habits and understanding.

That said, it should be noted that each of the four chapters in the theory section provides positive examples of the impact of attending to theory. Tsamir's chapter does so if one considers the teachers in her courses as learners. Clarke's chapter illustrates how a theoretical description of student knowledge trajectories can lead to diagnostic teaching. "Learning to listen to children's mathematics" is not simply the title of Empson and Jacobs's contribution but also an exemplification of the power and value of attending carefully to what students say. And, as Gravemeier indicates, Realistic Mathematics Education (RME) provides a case study of how theory can be used to frame an approach to the development of instruction. A further discussion of the relevance, utility, and constraints and affordances of theories may be found in Cobb (2007).

KNOWING STUDENTS AS LEARNERS

Knowing students as learners overlaps substantially with the previous category, "knowing students as thinkers," but it includes many other things as well. It means being aware of one's theory of learning and how that plays out in terms of classroom activities and interactions with individual students.

Consider, for example, what happens when a student goes to front of the classroom and flounders or makes a mistake while working on a problem. There is a wide range of possible responses to such a situation, varying from (a) having the student sit down and calling on another student, to (b) leading the student through a correct solution, or to (c) using the situation as an opportunity to raise and explore the mathematical issues entailed in the problem statement and the student's work on it. What the teacher chooses to do is, in large measure, a function of the teachers' view of students as learners.

A response of Type (a) is typical of much direct instruction; indeed, it even has a name, the "IRE sequence," (for "Initiation-Response-Evaluation") coined by Bud Mehan (1979, 1984). A great deal of classroom discourse can be parsed into tripartite units in which
– The teacher *initiates* the interactive sequence, typically by requesting (a small amount of) information from a student;
– The student *responds*;

– The teacher *evaluates* the response as correct or incorrect, often calling on another student (if the response is incorrect), clarifying (if the response is correct or incomplete), and then moving on to the next IRE sequence.

The IRE classroom pattern must be seen as the surface manifestation of a set of beliefs and understandings about student learning: Knowledge comes in small pieces that can be "mastered" individually, it is built up by accretion, and it is bad for students to flounder or err because doing so can build up bad habits. (The notion of "errorless learning" was the holy grail of the behaviorists, and classroom practices grounded in behaviorism are still widespread.)

A response of Type (b) was discussed at some length by Aguirre and Speer (1999). It represents the action of a teacher in transition, not unlike Mrs. Oublier (D. Cohen, 1990). The teacher, Ms. Perry, while solicitous and respectful of her students and clearly desirous of crafting an open and collaborative classroom environment,

> believes that it is important for the students to experience a very straightforward, direct, and clear presentation of the material. It is important to share and discuss the methods that do not work but she believes that when a topic is being introduced it is important for students' incorrect solutions to be intercepted. This is to ensure that the wrong ideas are not floating around for the other students to hear, at a formative stage when the students are not very familiar with the correct methods. Since she believes that students learn by listening to explanations and problem solutions she feels that it is important for them to have the opportunity to hear correct ones the majority of the time. (Aguirre & Speer, 1999, p. 339)

Responses of Type (c) are manifest in some of the videotapes of Japanese classrooms collected as part of the Third International Mathematics and Science Study (TIMSS 1995; Stigler, Gonzales, Kawanaka, Knoll, & Serrano, 1999), reflecting an underlying belief that current student understandings are and should be the raw material from which lessons are crafted. That view, of course, is a core aspect of lesson study. It is also a core aspect of a number of well-known professional development programs, such as Cognitively Guided Instruction (CGI). Carpenter, Fennema, and Franke (1996) describe the approach underlying CGI as follows:

> We propose that an understanding of students' thinking can provide coherence to teachers' pedagogical content knowledge and their knowledge of subject matter, curriculum, and pedagogy. ... Our major thesis is that children enter school with a great deal of informal or intuitive knowledge of mathematics that can serve as the basis for developing much of the formal mathematics of the primary school curriculum. The development of abstract symbolic procedures is characterized as progressive abstractions of students' attempts to model action and relations depicted in problems. (p. 3)

It may be stating the obvious, but it is worth noting that the premises that underlie approaches of Types (a) and (c) are diametrically opposed: A Type (a) approach effectively ignores the knowledge with which a student enters a learning situation (or, if that knowledge is incorrect, treats it as something to be overcome), whereas a Type (c) approach uses such knowledge as a starting point for instruction. In short, one's theory of learning highly conditions one's actions in the classroom.

A significant challenge for professional development is that teachers' theories of learning, and their own understanding of the relationship between those theories and their actions, are often tacit. There are parallels here to the problem-solving literature. It is well established that people's beliefs regarding the nature of mathematics play a strong role in shaping their mathematical behavior even though they may be unaware that they hold such beliefs. For example, from their experience in mathematics classrooms, many students develop the understanding that the exercises they have been assigned can typically be solved in just a few minutes if they understand the material. As a result, they stop working on any problem that takes longer than that to solve – even though a more extended effort might yield a solution. Altering such beliefs is extremely difficult because they are built up over many years. Making them explicit can help, as can immersion in environments (e.g., problem-solving courses) where ongoing actions can lead to a revision of those core views. But the process is long and slow because one is seeking to modify understandings and behaviors that are deeply rooted.

Cases can be used in various ways to develop and challenge teachers' theories of learning. Chapman points out that stories provide opportunities for prospective teachers, among other things, "to construct or refine personal theories of learning and teaching."

Almost all tools can be used in radically different ways, depending on the purpose one has in mind. That is certainly true for tasks as tools. Consider, for example, a simple task such as filling in a three-by-three magic square. This task can be a piece of busy work; it can be an "ice breaker" in a class because it is easy to solve; it can be an introduction to mathematical problem-solving strategies such as working forward and working backward; and it can be a first step into the development of a mathematical culture, where students are encouraged to abstract and generalize their work and to reflect on the process (see, e.g., Arcavi, Kessel, Meira, & Smith, 1998). Thus, any discussion of tasks as tools may or may not address issues of how students learn and how they reveal their knowledge. Of the chapters in this volume addressing the uses of tasks as tools, the most explicit consideration of task use for purposes of unearthing student knowledge is that of Zazkis, who focuses on examples that "increase teachers' awareness of underlying mathematical ideas … and increase teachers' awareness of students' possible mathematical ideas." She goes on to observe that "the obvious role of examples, as tools in mathematics teacher education, is to extend teachers' personal and potential example spaces." The constructs of example spaces and schemas can prove useful when mathematics teachers consider student learning.

Our discussion of "knowing students as learners" focuses largely on theory; thus it is not surprising that all of Section 3, which focuses on research, is directly germane. Although the authors employ somewhat different language and characterize somewhat different approaches to their work with teachers, all of them address the issue of "listening to children's mathematics," as Empson and Jacobs put it. And that attention is as it should be: The more that teachers are attuned to their students' understanding, the more they can create learning environments that are responsive to them. Tsamir's chapter shows how aspects of Fischbein's work can be used to help teachers reflect on their own ideas about mathematics and thus those of their students. Clarke's first sentence states the case clearly: "There is increasing evidence that the provision of knowledge based on students' thinking, particularly for teachers in the early years of schooling, is contributing to improved teaching practice and student outcomes." Indeed, the three main components of the Early Numeracy Research Project described by Clarke show how the notion of teacher knowledge of student thinking undergirds the project's approach to professional development.

Realistic Mathematics Education (RME) deserves special notice in this regard in that it may represent the broadest and most ambitious attempt to develop a research and development program grounded in a particular theoretical approach to student thinking and learning. As Gravemeijer notes, the challenges are immense, but the kind of "systems approach" taken by RME provides a coherent way of looking at the various pieces of the mathematics education puzzle. When materials design and teacher preparation are grounded in the same philosophical basis (the reinvention approach), there is increased potential for synergy and coherence.

CRAFTING AND MANAGING LEARNING ENVIRONMENTS

When the authors were students there was one dominant model of the classroom across the United States and in most nations of Europe and the Americas. The teacher was clearly in charge; the students either sat at desks or, in the elementary grades, perhaps in some other configuration organized by the teacher (e.g., a circle for "story time"). Like an orchestra conductor, the teacher organized and sequenced activities, telling students precisely what to do and when. Activities typically included lecturing, with students taking notes; question-and-answer exchanges designed to reinforce content; having students do seatwork, typically with prepared worksheets or on a sequence of problems assigned from the text; and having students present work at the board, with corrections by the teacher. In that context, the job of "crafting and managing the learning environment" meant training the students to listen respectfully and follow directions. A well run classroom was one in which students had learned and implemented smoothly all the classroom routines (e.g., how to pass homework forward so the teacher could collect it quickly).

The skill of creating a classroom environment in which students attend respectfully to the teacher and are "on task" a very large percentage of the time is known as *classroom management*. A search of the scholarly literature on the Web for the phrase "classroom management" yields almost 40,000 hits; a search of the entire Web yields almost 1,700,000. One of the sponsored (i.e., paid commercial) links gives the flavor of the enterprise:

> **Classroom Management**
>
> Are Students Driving You Nuts?
>
> Get Control — Classroom Management
>
> ClassroomManagement101.com

Click on the link and you find the following:

> Dear Fellow Teacher,
>
> Did you know that in the UK and the US more than 50% of those who train to be a teacher leave the profession after only three years? ...
>
> Just spend five minutes walking down the corridor of any school you choose. It hits you like a ten ton pile of bricks. Pupil behavior deteriorating fast, and teachers left to pick up the pieces.
>
> Does this ring any bells?
>
> As hard as you try you just can't get them quiet? ...
>
> Poor pupil behavior which you just can't control? ...
>
> You have a noisy classroom that you just can't quieten? ...
>
> Students laugh and giggle because you have lost their respect? ...
>
> **Take Back Control NOW!**

In a nutshell, this description lays out the challenge of organizing and conducting a traditional classroom. How productive such environments might be is increasingly open to question. Over the past two decades or so, the field's notion of "productive learning environments" has changed substantially. One breakthrough piece was Collins, Brown, and Newman's (1989) essay on cognitive apprenticeship, which highlighted the fact that schooling in a discipline had the potential to serve as an introduction to disciplinary ways of thinking. Motivated by some of Lave's (1988) observations of apprenticeship environments in Liberia, and abstracting over Scardamalia and Bereiter's (1984) work in writing, Schoenfeld's work in mathematical problem solving, and Palincsar and Brown's (1984) work in reading, Collins et al. identified an enriched sense of instructional goals. These

337

included goals for learning (not merely domain knowledge but also heuristic strategies, control strategies, and learning strategies), teaching methods (pedagogical strategies including modeling, coaching, scaffolding, compelling students to articulate their understandings, inducing reflection, and engaging in exploration), aspects of task and topic sequencing (global before local skills, increasing complexity, and increasing diversity), and the sociology of the learning environment (focusing on situated learning, including authentic practices; creating classroom communities of practice; and exploiting intrinsic motivation and classroom cooperation).

Those principles have flowered in a range of well-known learning environments. There is, for example, the extraordinarily fine-grained and lucid description of multiple goals for the mathematics classroom in Lampert (2001). One sees an emphasis on learning *communities* (e.g., Brown & Campione, 1996; Scardamalia, 2002). Increasingly, there are conferences and volumes with titles such as *Powerful Environments for Promoting Deep Conceptual and Strategic Learning* (Verschaffel, De Corte, Kanselaar, & Valcke, 2005). In a chapter that abstracted some of the properties of such environments, Schoenfeld (2005) made the following claim:

> Despite differences in grade level (the instructional programs range from elementary school through graduate school) and subject matter (topics examined in these courses range over the life sciences, history, literature, and mathematics), there are strong commonalities in assumptions and practices across those environments [Schoenfeld's problem-solving courses, Brown & Campione's "Fostering a Community of Learners," and Scardamalia & Bereiter's Knowledge Forum]. They are:
>
> – Disciplines offer distinctive and powerful forms of sense-making.
> – Such sense-making includes knowledge, values, ways of seeing, and habits of mind.
> – These come to life for individuals via membership in rich, thriving intellectual communities.
>
> The learning environments discussed in this paper are successful because they are self-consciously designed to foster interactions that support all of the above. (pp. 29–30)

This set of assumptions (see also Engle & Conant, 2002) shapes the balance of the present chapter. We assume that the creation of productive learning environments includes a great deal more than "classroom management." Rather, it involves the creation of intellectual communities in which students engage in legitimate intellectual activity. This perspective is clearly on the ascendance, as reflected in the chapter "Mathematics Teaching and Classroom Practice" (Franke, Khazemi, & Battey, 2007) in the *Second Handbook of Research on Mathematics Teaching and Learning*. As Franke et al. stress, the current conception of mathematics classrooms as complex learning communities demands attention to issues such as the personal relationships engendered in them and the discourse patterns one finds in them – more specifically for mathematics classrooms, the social, mathematical, and sociomathematical norms (Cobb & Yackel, 1996; Yackel & Cobb, 1996) constructed and enforced in such communities. An understanding of the richness of desired mathematics learning environments is either tacit or explicit in all of the chapters in the present volume. Here we make global comments regarding the three main sections. More detailed comments pertaining to issues of discourse, norms, and interpersonal relationships are pursued later in the chapter.

To varying degrees of explicitness, the four chapters in Section 1 on cases address the notion of the character, if not the creation, of rich learning environments. Clearly, all the tools in that section can. Narrative is a powerful tool for describing one's intentions and how they played out (or failed to). Specific cases, whether written or video-based, can highlight the same by helping to raise questions about what was intended, how well the attempts played out, and why. Lesson study is predicated on the notion of a particular set of rich mathematical practices; hence involvement in it helps to develop deeper understanding in and fluency in those practices. Seen from a greater distance, any instance of lesson study is, like the other practices described in this section, a case in and of itself, which can be used for reflection on essential issues.

As should be clear by now, tasks live within a social context: In two different environments the same task can play out very differently. Hence what is central is not simply the mathematical nature of a task but also the affordances it offers for the kind of engagement that will be productive for a classroom community. Along those lines, the notion of "group-worthy" tasks – tasks that support collaborative engagement with powerful mathematical ideas – deserves special mention (see, e.g., Horn, 2007).

Finally, the role of theory in the enterprise of understanding classroom environments (and what they can be) is absolutely central. There is a dialectic relationship between what one understands and what one thinks is possible. Over the past decades, mathematics educators' understanding of thinking and knowing, how teaching works, and how learning environments work has gotten broader and deeper. The connection between theory and practice – understanding what one is doing and why – is essential. Each of the theory chapters contributes in its own way to that necessary dialectic.

DEVELOPING CLASSROOM NORMS AND SUPPORTING CLASSROOM DISCOURSE AS PART OF "TEACHING FOR UNDERSTANDING"

One of the best-known episodes of teaching in the literature is the January 19, 1990, third-grade mathematics lesson taught by Deborah Ball. (See Schoenfeld, 2008, for a collection of analyses of that class session.) In the lesson a student, Sean (known as Shea in some transcriptions), conjectures that the number 6 is both even and odd. His reasoning is the following, in essence: Since 6 is made up of a number of *twos*, 6 is thus even; but six is also made up of a number of *threes* (an odd number), and 6 is thus odd as well. Sean is sorting the issue out as he speaks and is not altogether clear. Neither the class nor the teacher has fully grasped what Sean is suggesting when another student, Mei (also known as Lin), says she thinks she understands. Ball asks Sean to stay at the board ("Could you stay there? People have some questions for you.") as Mei explains. The following dialogue (Ball, 1990) ensues:

> Mei: I think what he is saying is that it's almost, see, I think what he's saying is that you have three groups of two. And three is an odd number so six can be an odd number *and* a even number.

> Ball: Do other people agree with that? *Is* that what you're saying, Sean?

> Sean: Yeah.

> Ball: Okay, do other people agree with him? *(pause)* Mei, you *dis*agree with that?

> Mei: Yeah, I disagree with that because it's not according to like ... here, can I show it on the board?

> Ball: Um hm.

> Mei: *(She comes up to the board.)* It's not according to like ...

> Ball: Student 1, can you watch what Mei's doing?

> Mei: ... how many groups it is. Let's say that I have *(pauses)* Let's see. If you call six an odd number, why don't *(pause)* let's see *(pause)* let's say ten. One, two ... *(draws circles on board)* and here are ten circles. And then you would split them, let's say I wanted to split, spit them, split them by twos. ... One, two, ... one, two, three, four, five ... *(she draws)*

$$\text{o o}|\text{o o}|\text{o o}|\text{o o}|\text{o o}$$

> then why do you not call *ten* a, like – a ...

> Sean: ... I disagree with myself ...

> Mei: ... odd number and an even number, or why don't you call *other*, like numbers an odd number or – and an even number?

> Sean: I didn't think of it that way. Thank you for bringing it up, *so* – I say it's – ten can be an odd and an even.

Mei: Yeah, but what about ...

Liz: Ohh!!!

Mei: What about *other* numbers?! Like, if you keep on going on like that and you say that other numbers are odd and even, maybe we'll end it up with *all* numbers are odd and even. Then it won't make sense that all numbers should be odd and even, because if all numbers were odd *and* even, we wouldn't be even having this *discussion!*

Sean: It wouldn't be all odd and even like – I'm just skipping over to the even – I'm just using the even ones, like I'm just using the even ones, I could could be like um – ex – except like, except two. But everything else you could just, you could split so it could be an odd and an even number. All the, all the rest of the even numbers.

Student: Even a hundred?

Mei: Then here. It – let's say, for instance, three *(draws one circle, draws a second circle)*, two *(draws a third circle)*. You can split it, split it in half. And do you – and then you can also. ... That would be two groups so do you call three an even number too?

Sean: I'm not calling three an even number, because one a h – um, like one and a half on each side isn't a number. One and a half isn't a number. It's a number plus a little more.

Ball: Let's um, get some other people's reactions here. Um, Sean, do you want to turn around so that you can hear other people's ideas? Student 3, you've had your hand up for awhile.

There are many remarkable things about this exchange, not the least of which is Mei's *reductio ad absurdum* – a rather sophisticated form of argument for a third grader! We wish, however, to focus on this classroom as a discourse community and the work that Ball has done to create and maintain it. Earlier in the lesson, Sean had *conjectured* that six is both an even and an odd number; when he did so, another student asked if he could *prove* it. ("Prove it to us that it can be odd. Prove it to us.") In this exchange Mei, after clarifying Sean's statement (with his concurrence), goes on to *disagree* with him. All of these italicized terms are technical terms in this classroom, and they have entailments. When a student labels a statement as a conjecture, the student is signaling its importance and also indicating that he or she is expected to provide a rationale for its correctness – a proof. In more general terms, students in this classroom understand that any mathematical claim must be backed up with warrants – for example, when a student said he thought that zero was an even number, Sean said, "I disagree with

341

you because, um, if it was an even number, how – what two things could make it?" Here as in the dialogue quoted above, *disagree* is a discourse signal with entailments. It plays a social role, in that "I disagree" is more polite than "You're wrong!" – which is a much more typical third-grade utterance. But disagreeing also places a mathematical demand on the person who disagrees: There has to be a reason for doing so, and the resolution of any disagreement will be mathematical. In the case of the claim that zero is an even number, the challenge is on the form of an appeal to the definition: An even number is a number that is twice a number. Two threes "make" six, so six is even according to the definition, and Sean asks what two numbers could make zero. Similarly, Mei follows up her statement of disagreement with a clever argument that if six is odd, then every number is odd – so what's the point?

The point of this discussion is that the class has done a great deal more than learn the use of a technical vocabulary. Their interactions are governed by a set of sociomathematical norms (Cobb & Yackel, 1996; Yackel & Cobb, 1996) that are both respectful as a form of social interaction *and* mathematically productive. See Ball, Lewis, and Thames (2008) for a discussion of the various kinds of mathematical work the teacher does in a lesson such as this; see Horn (2008) for an analysis of this kind of discourse structure, which she labels "accountable argumentation."

The teacher's work in establishing and maintaining the nature of a discourse community cannot be underestimated. The lesson from which we have quoted took place in January, a substantial way through the school year. By that time productive discourse patterns had been established, and at first glance Ball's role as a teacher may not seem to be very great. A close look at her interventions, however, shows that she is carefully orchestrating the class's contributions and making sure that the discussions remain productive and respectful. In some parts of the lesson she provides metalevel commentary about the state of the class's discussion, and in other parts of the lesson she facilitates their entry into fertile new territory. Building such norms is decidedly nontrivial.

There are interesting parallels between the forms of sense-making in Ball's third-grade class and in Schoenfeld's college-level problem-solving classes. Here is a description of the opening weeks of Schoenfeld's (1994) course:

[Typically my college students] have little idea, much less confidence, that they can serve as arbiters of mathematical correctness, either individually or collectively. Indeed, for most students, arguments (or purported solutions) are merely proposed by themselves. Those arguments are then judged by experts, who determine their correctness. Authority and the means of implementing it are external to the students. Students *propose;* experts judge and *certify.*

One explicit goal of my problem solving courses is to deflect inappropriate teacher authority. I hope to make it plain to the students that the mathematics speaks through all who have learned to employ it properly, and not just through the authority figure in front of the classroom. More explicitly, a goal of instruction is that the class becomes a community of mathematical judgment which, to the best of its ability, employs appropriate mathematical standards to judge the claims made before it.

In the course discussed here, the explicit deflection of teacher authority began the second day of class when a student volunteered to present a problem solution at the board. As often happens, the student focused his attention on me rather than on the class when he wrote his argument on the board; when he finished he waited for my approval or critique. Rather than provide it, however, I responded as follows:

"Don't look to me for approval, because I'm not going to provide it. I'm sure the class knows more than enough to say whether what's on the board is right. So (turning to class) what do you folks think?"

In this particular case the student had made a claim which another student believed to be false. Rather than adjudicate, I pushed the discussion further: How could we know which student was correct? The discussion continued for some time, until we found a point of agreement for the whole class. The discussion proceeded from there. When the class was done (and satisfied) I summed up.

This problem discussion illustrated a number of important points for the students, points consistently emphasized in the weeks to come. First, I rarely *certified* results, but turned points of controversy back to the class for resolution. Second, the class was to accept little on faith. This is, "we proved it in Math 127" was not considered adequate reason to accept a statement's validity. Instead, the statement must be grounded in mathematics solidly understood by this class. Third, my role in class discussion would often be that of Doubting Thomas. That is, I often asked "Is that true? How do we know? Can you give me an example? A counterexample? A proof?", both when the students' suggestions were correct and when they were incorrect. (A fourth role was to ensure that the discussions are respectful – that it's the mathematics at stake in the conversations, not the students!)

This pattern was repeated consistently and deliberately, with effect. Late in the second week of class, a student who had just written a problem solution on the board started to turn to me for approval, and then stopped in mid-stream. She looked at me with mock resignation and said "I know, I know." She then turned to the class and said "O.K., do you guys buy it or not?" [After some discussion, they did.] (pp. 62–63)

One finds parallel discussions in Magdalene Lampert's (2001) exegesis of her teaching. In a chapter entitled "Teaching to Establish a Classroom Culture," Lampert describes how the physical organization of a classroom makes a difference – for example, seats in a row convey one message, and tables grouped

343

with four students around them convey a different one. She discusses some of the main themes introduced the first day of class, including rules of discourse and "revising your thinking." She explained that

having a hand raised meant to me that a person "had an idea." I also made it clear that those who had not raised a hand and were not speaking had a job to do beyond simply listening. They were to reflect on what they heard in such a way as to "see if you agree or disagree, or if you have something to add."...

The elements of this form [the classroom interactions she has just discussed] that would repeat themselves throughout the year included:

- Soliciting more than one contribution;
- Responding to each contribution in a way that communicated my understanding (not necessarily approval) of what the student was saying; and
- Asking the students to revoice the contributions of other students. (p. 61)

Lampert explains how, in the first week, she sets the ground rules for class discussions:

In the context of these lessons, I taught my students three new activities and named them as such for public identification:

- Finding and articulating the "conditions" or assumptions in problem situations that must be taken into account in making a judgment about whether a solution strategy is appropriate;
- Producing "conjectures" about elements of the problem situation including the solution, which could then be subject to reasoned argument; and
- Revising conjectures based on mathematical evidence and the identification of conditions. (p. 66)

Abstracting over a number of examples of classroom practices, including CGI (Carpenter et al., 1996; Carpenter, Fennema, Franke, Levi, & Empson, 1999), Franke et al. (2007) summarize their stance toward "teaching for understanding" as follows:

Maintaining our dual focus on what teachers do and how that is experienced by students; keeping equity central; drawing on a current, coherent conception of teaching and learning; and attending to the limits and strengths of the reform studies leads us to a particular focus for our review of classroom practice. Research suggests the value of listening to students' mathematical ideas and building on them, that attending to the details of student thinking and the mathematics (particularly the mathematical task) supports student learning, and creating opportunities for a range of ideas to be a part of the classroom discourse matters for students and teachers alike. Lampert's conception of teaching parallels these ideas and suggests that knowing the development of students' mathematical thinking, understanding the mathematical tasks, and orchestrating conversation around the particulars of student thinking and mathematics are all a part of teaching for understanding. (p. 230)

We concur, and turn to the question of how the tools and processes discussed in this volume can serve these purposes. Not surprisingly, there is a good fit at a general level: All of the chapters are concerned with teaching for understanding in some way. The direct relevance and application of the ideas varies. The case for cases (Section 1) is strong: Cases provides grist for exemplification of key ideas and for reflection. That is true whether the exemplification is by means of narrative, written or video case studies, or live or videotaped lesson study.

As described in Section 2, tasks are almost neutral with regard to norms and discourse: One can imagine a set of discourse practices that made rich use of the tasks, examples, manipulatives, and machines described in Section 2, but one can also imagine rather didactic uses of them. The challenge is to craft learning environments in which the patterns and processes of communal sense-making take advantage of the potential affordances of those tasks.

Any particular theory, depending on its nature, can be directly or tangentially germane to the issue of classroom discourse and norms. Fischbein's theory, for example, focuses on aspects of mathematical understanding; one can imagine teachers reading or being lectured to about this or any other theory, or one can imagine a set of tasks that engaged the teachers actively in constructing their understandings of them. The words *dialogue, discourse,* and *norms* do not appear in the chapters by Clarke and by Empson and Jacobs. In contrast, one finds the following statement in Gravemeijer's discussion of RME:

> In contrast to the traditional classroom culture, reinvention asks for an inquiry-oriented classroom culture. The classroom has to work as a learning community. To make this happen, the students have to adopt classroom social norms such as the obligation to explain and justify their solutions. They have to be expected to try and understand other students' reasoning, and to ask questions if they do not understand, and challenge arguments they do not agree with.

BUILDING RELATIONSHIPS THAT SUPPORT LEARNING

There has been an interesting change over time in the amount and character of the attention that (at least in the United States) has been devoted to building strong teacher-student relationships. The stereotype is that primary school education is, for the most part, devoted to the "whole child." Although content considerations are important, a tremendous amount of the primary school teacher's energy is devoted to helping students develop as people and as learners and to learn to function productively as members of the classroom community. Much of the primary teacher's work consists of getting to know the children as individuals, helping them to understand themselves and build their relationships with others. Such relationships are, in fundamental ways, the bases on which the classroom community is founded and foundations upon which the individuals in it get the work of growing and learning done.

The middle grades are typically a time of transition. The intact primary classroom, in which one or possibly two teachers spend the whole day with the same group of students, may give way (at least in the United States) to a transitional form in which the class may spend half its time with a "language arts" teacher and then move to a "math and science" teacher and possibly to other teachers for subjects such as physical education, art, and music. This arrangement gives way to the classic secondary school "bell schedule," in which students take five or six different courses and move from room to room. With this migration also comes a change in teacher responsibilities: High school teachers are content experts, and their responsibility shifts away from the "whole child" toward disciplinary instruction. Although some attempts are made to connect with the children and, on occasion, their families, student-teacher relationships typically become more distant as the students advance through secondary school.

Many things are happening, simultaneously, during the middle and high school years. As children mature, there are issues of identity formation, group affiliation, and more. It is precisely during these personally momentous times that the links between teachers and students weaken: Students move from interacting primarily with one or two teachers whose primary focus is the "whole child" to interacting with perhaps half a dozen teachers whose primary focus in on subject matter content. In the United States, a middle school or high school mathematics teacher typically teaches five sections of mathematics; thus he or she will have responsibility for the mathematics learning of 150 students or so. The amount of time available for building relationships with individual students drops significantly. In general, alienation, oppositional behavior, and dropout rates increase.

Collegiate experiences vary, of course (as do those in elementary and secondary school; we do not intend to imply homogeneity but rather that within-grade-band variation is much less than across-grade-band variation). By and large, however, students are increasingly independent. Save for the bonds that happen to develop between individual student and teacher, or for students who live in institutional housing, with adults in designated roles such as "house parents," the responsibilities of the faculty for their students and the cultivation of relationships between them are largely at individual discretion. The overarching assumption is that the students, now autonomous, are migrating toward their personal career choices, and that the faculty members are sharing their (discipline-related) wisdom with them along the way.

Interestingly, these relationships tend to change when students enter more advanced degree programs, for example, for teaching degrees or for doctorates. Both kinds of work are so arduous and so personally challenging that, at times, the students – although older and presumably more mature than secondary or college students – need a greater degree of personal support. (Having a student-teaching lesson fall apart, dealing with a disruptive class, or realizing that one is having major trouble with one's dissertation, all call for a level of personal knowledge, understanding, and support that far exceeds the typical demands placed on secondary or college teachers.)

Franke et al. (2007) address such issues directly, in their conception of mathematics teaching and classroom practice. In a section of their chapter entitled "A Conception of Teaching," they state that:

> Teaching is relational. Teachers, students, and subject matter can only be understood in relation to one another. The teacher works to orchestrate the content, representations of the content, and the people in the classroom in relation to one another. Students' ways of being, their forms of participation, and their learning emerge out of these mutually constitutive relationships. Teaching is also multidimensional. Within research on classroom practice, several images of this multidimensionality emerge, images that overlap with one another but that are often emphasized in one line of work. Teaching is creating an environment for learning mathematics, orchestrating participation so that students relate to representations of subject matter and to one another in particular ways. (p. 227)

Such teaching, Franke et al. (2007) note, draws on ideas of identity and culture. The idea is that students bring various mathematically productive cultural forms into the classroom and that teaching can draw upon those forms – see, for example, Moll's "funds of knowledge" (Moll & Gonzalez, 2004). Building relationships with the students grounded in their identities ("culturally relevant teaching"; see, e.g., Gallego, Cole, & the Laboratory of Comparative Human Cognition, 2001; Ladson-Billings, 1995; Mercado, 2001) is a potentially powerful way of connecting students and content. "And a growing body of research shows how African American, Latino, and Native American students draw on their cultural and community knowledge to help them succeed in mathematics" (Franke et al., p. 247).

For the most part, the chapters in the current volume do not directly address such issues. That omission is not surprising given that the notion of teaching mathematics as a fundamentally relational act is relatively new. Each of the three sections has potential affordances for enhancing relational practices in teaching. The use of cases is obvious: Whether by means of narrative, written, or video cases, the issues discussed here can be raised and reflected upon. Tasks can play a catalytic role, both in terms of structure and content. Earlier in this chapter, we discussed group-worthy tasks (Horn, 2007). Such tasks provide structures for student interaction and problem ownership, as well as different student-teacher relationships. Similarly, problems that deal in various ways with mathematizing aspects of students' lives (see, e.g., Gutstein & Peterson, 2005) provide more than "motivation": They can provide a different view of mathematics, a means by which students can collaborate in meaningful ways over content that is personally meaningful, and an opportunity for deeper personal relationships between students and teachers. Theory is a necessary tool. The very notion of teaching as a relational act is a theoretical statement. Theorizing in this arena, summarized by Franke et al. (2007), has expanded significantly over the past decade, but the work is just beginning. There is much more to be done in theoretical terms and in developing the tools to make use of the theoretical ideas.

REFLECTING ON ONE'S PRACTICE

Reflection is the ultimate key to one's professional growth as a teacher. On a local level, the question is essentially how the day's or the week's classes went, and what one might do about that. On a more global level, the question is about not just what one does, but why.

Attaining proficiency in teaching mathematics, like attaining mathematical proficiency, is a lifelong, iterative process. Confronted with a problem of teaching practice, the teacher of mathematics needs to think reflectively about the problem if he or she is to resolve it. Once it is habitual, reflection can become the principal mechanism for improving one's teaching practice.

John Dewey (1904/1965) was among the first to consider the role of reflection in education. He saw teacher education as providing an unparalleled opportunity for prospective teachers to reflect on problems of practice (Mewborn, 1999), but he also saw such reflection as needing to continue throughout one's teaching career. Dewey (1933) defined *reflective thinking* as "active, persistent, and careful consideration of any belief or supposed form of knowledge in the light of the grounds that support it and the further conclusion to which it tends" (p. 9). By thinking reflectively, a teacher can "transform a situation in which there is experienced obscurity, doubt, conflict, disturbance of some sort, into a situation that is clear, coherent, settled, harmonious" (pp. 100–101). As Mewborn (1996) notes, "In an educational context … reflecting on teaching practice can assist teachers in making intelligent choices about future teaching actions" (p. 14; see also Mewborn, 1999, 2004). Like Pólya's (1945/2004) "looking back" phase of problem solving, reflection on one's teaching practice is a bootstrap for improving one's proficiency.

As a fundamentally important habit of mind, reflection can be fostered by teacher preparation and professional development. It is, for example, an explicit part of the design of the 2-year teacher preparation program in which Schoenfeld is involved, at the University of California, Berkeley. We introduce the idea through an anecdote and then discuss the underlying principles.

When Schoenfeld first began teaching at Berkeley in the mid-1980s, he volunteered to offer a problem-solving course for students in the teacher preparation program. The course had a number of components. First, there was hands-on problem solving, using problems like those in Schoenfeld's (1985) regular mathematics problem-solving courses. Second, the class reflected on the mathematics they had done and the lessons about thinking and problem solving to be learned from that mathematics. Third, halfway through the course, the student teachers were asked to design a series of lessons that approached a topic that they were supposed to teach "from a problem-solving point of view." The student teachers were to be explicit about the intended goals, why they structured the lessons the way they did, and what they expected their students to learn from them.

Fourth, the student teachers taught the lessons, gathered data on students' performance, and reported on what happened. Fifth, they reflected on what happened and reported what they would do differently the next time.

A few years after one student had earned her teaching credential, Schoenfeld ran into her on the street. After some catching up, he said "Okay, you're independent now. I can't do anything to you, so you have nothing to fear. Tell me the truth: Did anything you learned in the course do you any good?" Her response was,

> Not for the first few years. I was too busy surviving. But as I settled in as a teacher and didn't have to worry so much about simple issues of survival, I found myself thinking more and more about the issues raised in the problem-solving course. Now I use them quite a bit to reflect on my teaching, and they're having a real impact on what I do.

That conversation played a significant role in the reshaping of Berkeley's program, which was revised in the early 1990s. The idea behind the 2-year post-baccalaureate program had been to provide a fair amount of knowledge and "how to," much of it along the lines of the earlier sections of this chapter. Not all of that could be done, for even 2 years is hardly enough time. Thus, for example, the program tended to select students with very solid mathematical backgrounds and reinforce their understanding through the problem-solving course. But the faculty realized that in the chaos of the first few years of teaching, much of what the students had learned in their coursework would be abstract "book knowledge" that they would not have the opportunity to put into practice while they were struggling to master the art of teaching. Thus, the question was how to develop the habits of mind that supported reflection.

That development was addressed in a number of ways. Methods seminars included routine debriefings and reflective memos. Students joined faculty research groups, where the inspection of practice was a routine activity. Course projects often involved reflection of the type described above: If you did something, can you say upon reflection about how you would do it differently, and why? In addition, the program (which offers a credential and a master's degree) culminates with a master's paper. There is great latitude in the selection of the paper topic, but the default is an expansion of the kind of project described above: The student thinks about a fundamental aspect of practice, designs a piece of instruction and a measure of student performance, tries the instruction and gathers relevant data, reflects on them, and then describes possible changes on the basis of that reflection. The hope is that, as in the case of the student quoted above, such reflection will become habitual and contribute to the teachers' ongoing professional growth.[4]

As with all of the categories of the framework we propose, the three sections of this volume offer potential affordances for stimulating and supporting teacher reflection. Cases (Section 1) are natural stimuli for that purpose, though they need to be accompanied by appropriate opportunities to reflect. Narratives can raise

---

[4] A framework and tools for engaging systematically in such reflective activities can be found in Artzt, Armour-Thomas, and Curcio (2008).

issues for reflection – about both one's practices and the reasons for them – and they can be used to promote reflective thinking through activities such as writing and rewriting one's teaching stories. Chapman notes that "narrative provides a reflective way of knowing, which is widely accepted as central goal in teacher education." As Markovits and Smith point out, quoting Merseth (1999, pp. xi–xii), "Cases in mathematics education share a common feature of providing realistic contexts for helping teachers 'develop skills of analysis and problem-solving, gain broad repertoires of pedagogical technique, *capitalize on the power of reflection* [italics added], and experience a positive learning community.'" The case activities they describe "are intended to invite exploration of and critical reflection on a teacher's own practice."

Likewise, Maher addresses the issue explicitly:

> Using videos as a tool to evaluate and improve one's practice, teachers can plan and implement lessons, study the videos of the lessons, and analyze students' developing understanding as they take into account their role as facilitators in the process. Teachers can also reflect on the extent and quality of their probing of student understanding. ... By studying their lessons, teachers can become more aware of their classroom behavior. They can reflect on the moves they make and then consider and discuss with others whether or not certain moves are effective.

Finally, reflection is a design feature of lesson study. The very nature of the practice is to propose a course of instructional action in theoretically grounded ways, to try it out, and to reconsider the approach and its underpinnings on the basis of carefully conducted observations of the lessons. Yoshida observes that "collaborative interactions with other teachers help the teachers to reflect on their own subject content and pedagogical knowledge."

The affordances for reflection of any task depend very much on the character of the task and the context within which it is used. After identifying four purposes for teachers' engagement with tasks, Watson and Sullivan note that teacher learning "may be mathematical, pedagogic, or a mixture of both depending on how task goals, discussion and reflection are structured in the teaching session," and they go on to say

> Teachers in educative settings often want tasks or task-types that can be used in their own classrooms with minimal transformation, while teacher educators might seek to offer tasks which influence teachers' learning. Here we combine these aims by concentrating on how teachers can be educated about classroom tasks through *reflective engagement* [italics added] with such activities.

Zazkis begins her chapter with the idea that carefully chosen examples can "persuade teachers to reconsider 'basic assumptions' used in teaching and learning of mathematics, or to become explicitly aware of these assumptions." The theme of reflection is less overtly manifest in the chapters by Nührenbörger and Steinbring, and Bartolini Bussi and Maschietto, but it is easy to imagine how the tasks they describe can be embedded in contexts that support reflections by students and teachers alike.

And last but not least, theory. Not surprisingly, reflection permeates the theory section of this volume. Tsamir devotes substantial space to descriptions of teachers' reflective notes. Clarke's concluding paragraph focuses precisely on the issue of reflection:

> Rather than a *recipe* for teaching, the notion of *rich ingredients* that are combined in a range of ways, using the professional judgement of teachers, was a powerful and successful approach. There is little doubt that the framework and growth points were two key ingredients in equipping teachers to exercise their judgement as reflective professionals and produce increased student outcomes in the ENRP [Early Numeracy Research Project].

In the section of Empson and Jacobs's chapter that deals with recommendations for working with teachers, they

> describe three learning activities mathematics teacher educators have used to help teachers develop responsive listening: (a) discussions of children's written work, (b) discussions of videotaped interactions with children, and (c) opportunities for teachers to interact with children (in real time) and then to reflect on those experiences with other teachers.

Finally, we note that the discussion of reflection in Gravemeijer's paper operates explicitly at two levels, as it should in all discussion of teaching. At the student level, Gravemeijer notes that a major goal of instruction is to have learners construct their own knowledge and that stimulating reflection is an important mechanism for fostering such knowledge construction. But that claim holds for teachers as well.

As we conclude, it is useful to recall the admonition from the editors of *How People Learn*:

> The principles of learning and their implications for designing learning environments apply equally to child and adult learning. They provide a lens though which current practice can be viewed with respect to K-12 teaching and with respect to the preparation of teachers. (Bransford, Brown, & Cocking, 2000, p. 27)

The habits of mind, including reflection, that we hope to instill in young learners will serve teachers equally well; and the kinds of respectful, supportive, interactive, mathematically rich and reflective learning environments we hope to provide young students will also serve as productive learning environments for teachers.

FINAL REMARK

In this chapter, we have offered what we consider to be the first steps toward a theory of proficiency in teaching mathematics. Undoubtedly, refinement and elaboration are called for; this effort is merely a first approximation. Even so, we hope that the framework described here will be useful. As noted in the introduction, a theory of proficiency provides an orientation to a domain. It says what is important – what skills people need to develop if they are to become proficient. With those goals in mind, mathematics teacher educators can make effective use of the rich collection of tools offered in this volume.

REFERENCES

Aguirre, J., & Speer, N. (1999). Examining the relationship between beliefs and goals in teacher practice. *Journal of Mathematical Behavior, 18*(3), 327–356.

Arcavi, A., Kessel, C., Meira, L., & Smith, J. (1998). Teaching mathematical problem solving: An analysis of an emergent classroom community. In A. H. Schoenfeld, J. Kaput, & E. Dubinsky (Eds.), *Research in collegiate mathematics education, III* (pp. 1–70). Washington, DC: Conference Board of the Mathematical Sciences.

Artzt, A., Armour-Thomas, E., & Curcio, C. (2008). *Becoming a reflective mathematics teacher: A guide for observations and self-assessment* (2nd ed.). Mahwah, NJ: Erlbaum.

Ball, D. L. (1990). *Transcript of January 19, 1990, class*. Unpublished manuscript, University of Michigan.

Ball, D. L., Lewis, J. M., & Thames, M. H. (2008). Making mathematics work in school. In A. H. Schoenfeld (Ed.), *A study of teaching: Multiple lenses, multiple views* (Journal for Research in Mathematics Education Monograph No. 14, pp. 13–44). Reston, VA: National Council of Teachers of Mathematics.

Ball, D. L., & Peoples, B. (2007). Assessing a student's mathematical knowledge by way of interview. In A. H. Schoenfeld (Ed.), *Assessing mathematical proficiency* (pp. 213–267). Cambridge: Cambridge University Press.

Ball, D. L., Thames, M., & Phelps, G. (2007). *Content knowledge for teaching: What makes it special?* Unpublished manuscript, University of Michigan.

Bishop, A. J., & Whitfield, R. C. (1972). *Situations in teaching*. London: McGraw-Hill.

Bransford, J., Brown, A., & Cocking, R. (Eds.). (2000). *How people learn*. Washington, DC: National Academy Press.

Bright, G. W., & Joyner, J. M. (1998). *Classroom assessment in mathematics: Views from a National Science Foundation conference*. Lanham, MD: University Press of America.

Brown, A., & Campione, J. (1996). Psychological theory and the design of innovative learning environments: On procedures, principles, and systems. In L. Schauble & R. Glaser (Eds.), *Innovations in learning: New environments for education* (pp. 289–325). Mahwah, NJ: Erlbaum.

Carpenter, T. P., Fennema, E., & Franke, M. L. (1996). Cognitively Guided Instruction: A knowledge base for reform in primary mathematics instruction. *Elementary School Journal, 97*(1), 1–20.

Carpenter, T. P., Fennema, E., Franke, M. L., Levi, L. W., & Empson, S. B. (1999). *Children's mathematics: Cognitively Guided Instruction*. Portsmouth, NH: Heinemann.

Cobb, P. (2007). Putting philosophy to work: Coping with multiple theoretical perspectives. In F. Lester (Ed.), *Second handbook of research on mathematics teaching and learning* (pp. 3–38). Charlotte, NC: Information Age Publishing.

Cobb, P., & Yackel, E. (1996). Constructivist, emergent, and sociocultural perspectives in the context of developmental research. *Educational Psychologist, 31*(3–4), 175–190.

Cohen, D. (1990). A revolution in one classroom: The case of Mrs. Oublier. *Educational Evaluation and Policy Analysis, 12*(3), 311–329.

Cohen, S. (2004). *Teachers' professional development and the elementary mathematics classroom: Bringing understandings to light*. Mahwah, NJ: Erlbaum.

Collins, A., Brown, J. S., & Newman, S. E. (1989). Cognitive apprenticeship: Teaching the crafts of reading, writing, and mathematics. In L. B. Resnick (Ed.), *Knowing, learning, and instruction: Essays in honor of Robert Glaser* (pp. 453–494). Hillsdale, NJ: Erlbaum.

Dewey, J. (1933). *How we think: A restatement of the relation of reflective thinking to the educative process*. Boston: Heath.

Dewey, J. (1965). The relation of theory to practice in education. In M. L. Borrowman (Ed.), *Teacher education in America: A documentary history* (pp. 140–171). New York: Teachers College Press. (Original work published 1904)

Engle, R. A. & Conant, F. C. (2002). Guiding principles for fostering productive disciplinary engagement: Explaining an emergent argument in a community of learners classroom. *Cognition and Instruction, 20(4)*, 399–483.

Fernandez, C., & Yoshida, M. (2004). *Lesson study: A Japanese approach to improving mathematics teaching and learning*. Mahwah, NJ: Erlbaum.

Franke, M., Khazemi, E., & Battey, D. (2007). Mathematics teaching and classroom practice. In F. Lester (Ed.), *Second handbook of research on mathematics teaching and learning* (pp. 225–256). Charlotte, NC: Information Age Publishing.

Gallego, M.A, Cole, M., & the Laboratory of Comparative Human Cognition. (2001). Classroom cultures and cultures in the classroom. In V. Richardson (Ed.), *Handbook of research on teaching* (pp. 951–997). Washington, DC: American Educational Research Association.

Gutstein, E., & Peterson, R. (2005) *Rethinking mathematics: Teaching social justice by the numbers*. Milwaukee: Rethinking Schools.

Hill, H., Rowan, B., & Ball, D. L. (2005). Effects of teachers' mathematical knowledge for teaching on student achievement. *American Educational Research Journal, 42*(2), 371–406.

Horn, I. (2007). Fast kids, slow kids, lazy kids: Framing the mismatch problem in mathematics teachers' conversations. *Journal of the Learning Sciences, 16*(1), 37–79.

Horn, I. (2008). Accountable argumentation as a participation structure to support learning through disagreement. In A. H. Schoenfeld (Ed.), *A study of teaching: Multiple lenses, multiple views* (Journal for Research in Mathematics Education Monograph No. 14, pp. 97–126). Reston, VA: National Council of Teachers of Mathematics.

Kilpatrick, J., Swafford, J., & Findell, B. (Eds.). (2001). *Adding it up: Helping children learn mathematics*. Washington, DC: National Academy Press.

Ladson-Billings, G. (1995). Toward a theory of culturally relevant pedagogy. *American Educational Research Journal, 32*(3), 465–491.

Lampert, M. (2001). *Teaching problems and the problem of teaching*. New Haven, CT: Yale University Press.

Lave, J. (1988). *Cognition in practice: Mind, mathematics and culture in everyday life*. Cambridge: Cambridge University Press.

Ma, L. (1999). *Knowing and teaching elementary mathematics*. Mahwah, NJ: Erlbaum.

Mehan, H. (1979). *Learning lessons: Social organization in the classroom*. Cambridge, MA: Harvard University Press.

Mehan, H. (1985). The structure of classroom discourse. In T.A. van Dijk (Ed.), *Handbook of discourse analysis* (pp. 119–131). London: Academic Press.

Mercado, C. (2001). The learner: "Race," "ethnicity," and linguistic difference. In V. Richardson (Ed.), *Handbook of research on teaching* (pp. 668–694). Washington, DC: American Educational Research Association.

Merseth, K. K. (1999). A rationale for case-based pedagogy in teacher education. In M. A. Lundeberg, B .B. Levin, & H. Harrington (Eds.). (1999). *Who learns what from cases and how? The research base for teaching and learning with cases* (pp. ix–xv). Mahwah, NJ: Erlbaum.

Mewborn, D. A. S. (1996). Learning to teach elementary school mathematics. *Dissertation Abstracts International, 56*, 3041A. (University Microfilms No. AAI9540450)

Mewborn, D. S. (1999). Reflective thinking in preservice elementary mathematics teachers. *Journal for Research in Mathematics Education 30*, 316–341.

Mewborn, D. S. (2004). Learning to teach elementary mathematics: Ecological elements of a field experience. *Journal of Mathematics Teacher Education, 3*, 1386–1416.

Moll, L., & Gonzalez, N. (2004). Engaging life: A funds-of-knowledge approach to multicultural education. In J. A. Banks & C. A. M. Banks (Eds.), *Handbook of research on multicultural education* (2nd ed., pp. 699–715). San Francisco: Jossey-Bass.

Palincsar, A. S., & Brown, A. L. (1984). Reciprocal teaching of comprehension-fostering and comprehension-monitoring activities. *Cognition and Instruction, 2*(2), 117–175.

Pólya, G. (2004). *How to solve it* (2nd ed.). Princeton, NJ: Princeton University Press. (Original work published 1945)

Scardamalia, M. (2002). Collective cognitive responsibility for the advancement of knowledge. In B. Smith (Ed.), *Liberal education in a knowledge society* (pp. 67–98). Chicago: Open Court.

Scardamalia, M., & Bereiter, C. (1984). Development of strategies in text processing. In H. Mandl, N. Stein, & T. Trabasso (Eds.). *Learning and comprehension of text* (pp. 379–406). Hillsdale, NJ: Erlbaum.

Schoenfeld, A. H. (1985). *Mathematical problem solving.* Orlando, FL: Academic Press.

Schoenfeld, A. H. (1994). Reflections on doing and teaching mathematics. In A. Schoenfeld (Ed.), *Mathematical thinking and problem solving* (pp. 53—70). Hillsdale, NJ: Erlbaum.

Schoenfeld, A. H. (2005). On learning environments that foster subject-matter competence. In L. Verschaffel, E. De Corte, G. Kanselaar, & M. Valcke (Eds), *Powerful environments for promoting deep conceptual and strategic learning* (pp. 29–44). Leuven, Belgium: Studia Paedagogica.

Schoenfeld, A. H. (2007). Reflections on an assessment interview: What a close look at student understanding can reveal. In A. H. Schoenfeld (Ed.), *Assessing mathematical proficiency* (pp. 269–277). Cambridge: Cambridge University Press.

Schoenfeld, A. H. (Ed.). (2008). *A study of teaching: Multiple lenses, multiple views* (Journal for Research in Mathematics Education Monograph No. 14). Reston, VA: National Council of Teachers of Mathematics.

Schoenfeld, A. H. (in press). Working with schools: The story of a mathematics education collaboration. *American Mathematical Monthly.*

Shulman, L. (1986). Those who understand: Knowledge growth in teaching. *Educational Researcher, 15*(2), 4–14.

Stigler, J. W., Gonzales, P. Kawanaka, T., Knoll, S., & Serrano, A. (1999). *The TIMSS 1995 Videotape Classroom Study: Methods and findings from an exploratory research project on eighth-grade mathematics instruction in Germany, Japan, and the United States* (NCES 1999-074). Washington, DC: National Center for Education Statistics.

Verschaffel, E. De Corte, G. Kanselaar, & M. Valcke (Eds.) (2005). *Powerful environments for promoting deep conceptual and strategic learning.* Leuven, Belgium: Studia Paedagogica.

Wiliam, D. (2007). Keeping learning on track: Classroom assessment and the regulation of learning. In F. Lester (Ed.), *Second handbook of research on mathematics teaching and learning* (pp. 1053–1098). Charlotte, NC: Information Age Publishing.

Yackel, E., & Cobb, P. (1996). Sociomathematical norms, argumentation, and autonomy in mathematics. *Journal for Research in Mathematics Education, 27*(4), 458–477.

Alan H. Schoenfeld
Graduate School of Education,
University of California, Berkeley
USA

Jeremy Kilpatrick
Department of Mathematics and Science Education
University of Georgia
USA

Printed in the United States
R3510000001B/R35100PG204999BVX1B/2}/P